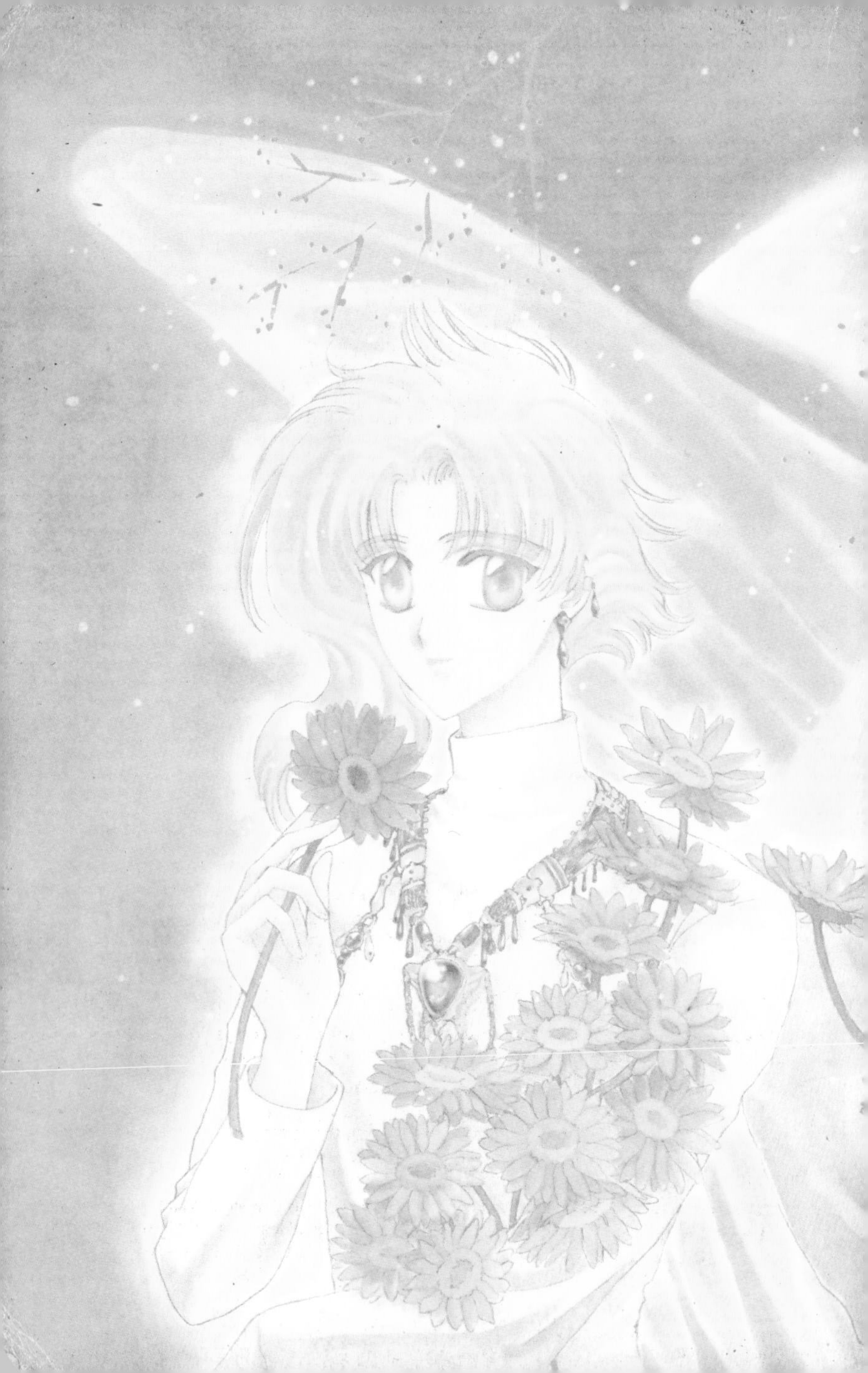

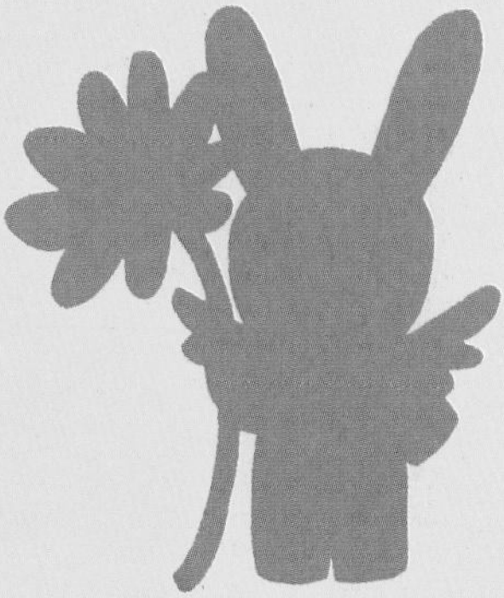

contents

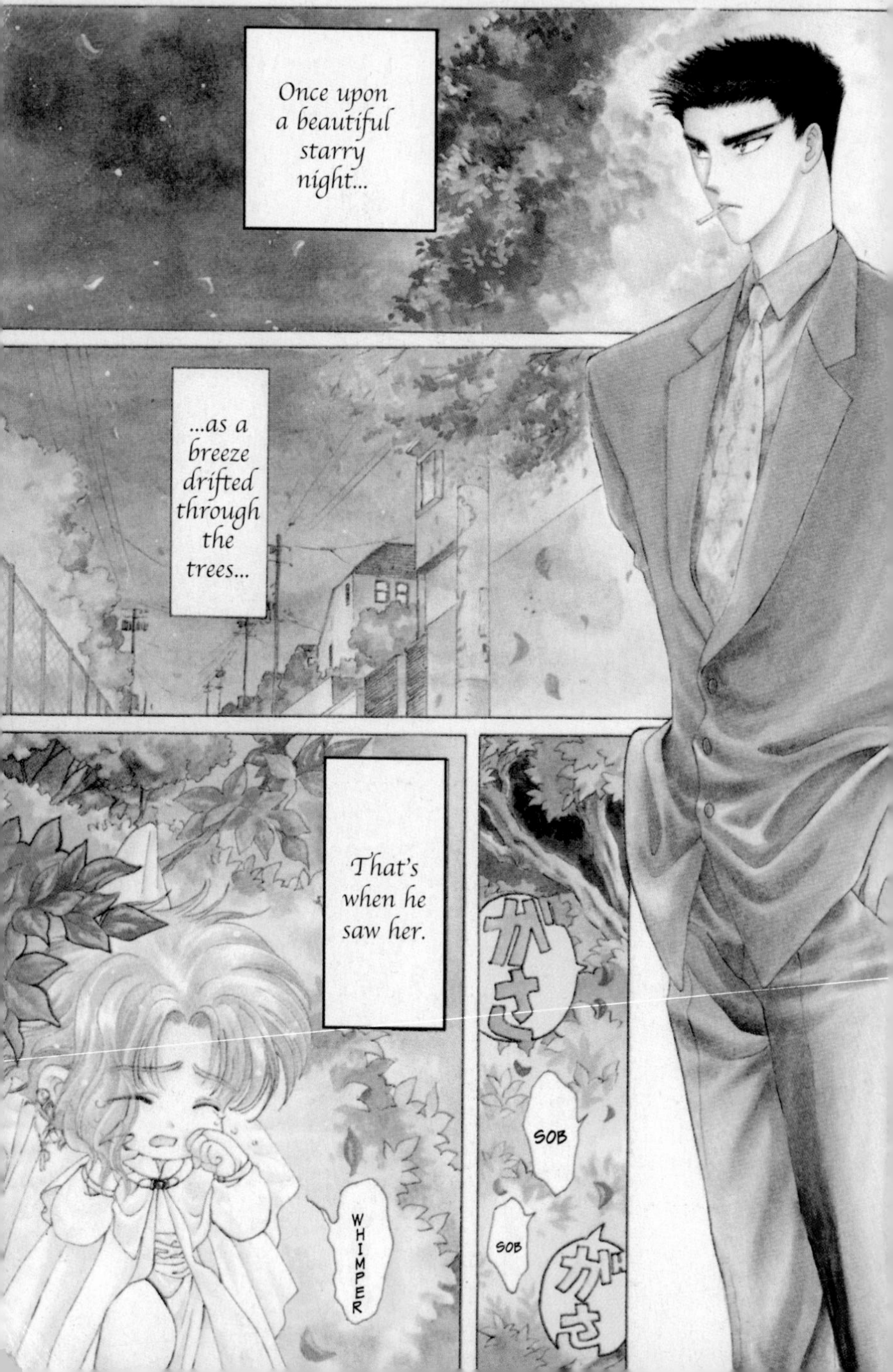
Once upon a beautiful starry night...
...as a breeze drifted through the trees...
SOB
SOB
That's when he saw her.
WHIMPER

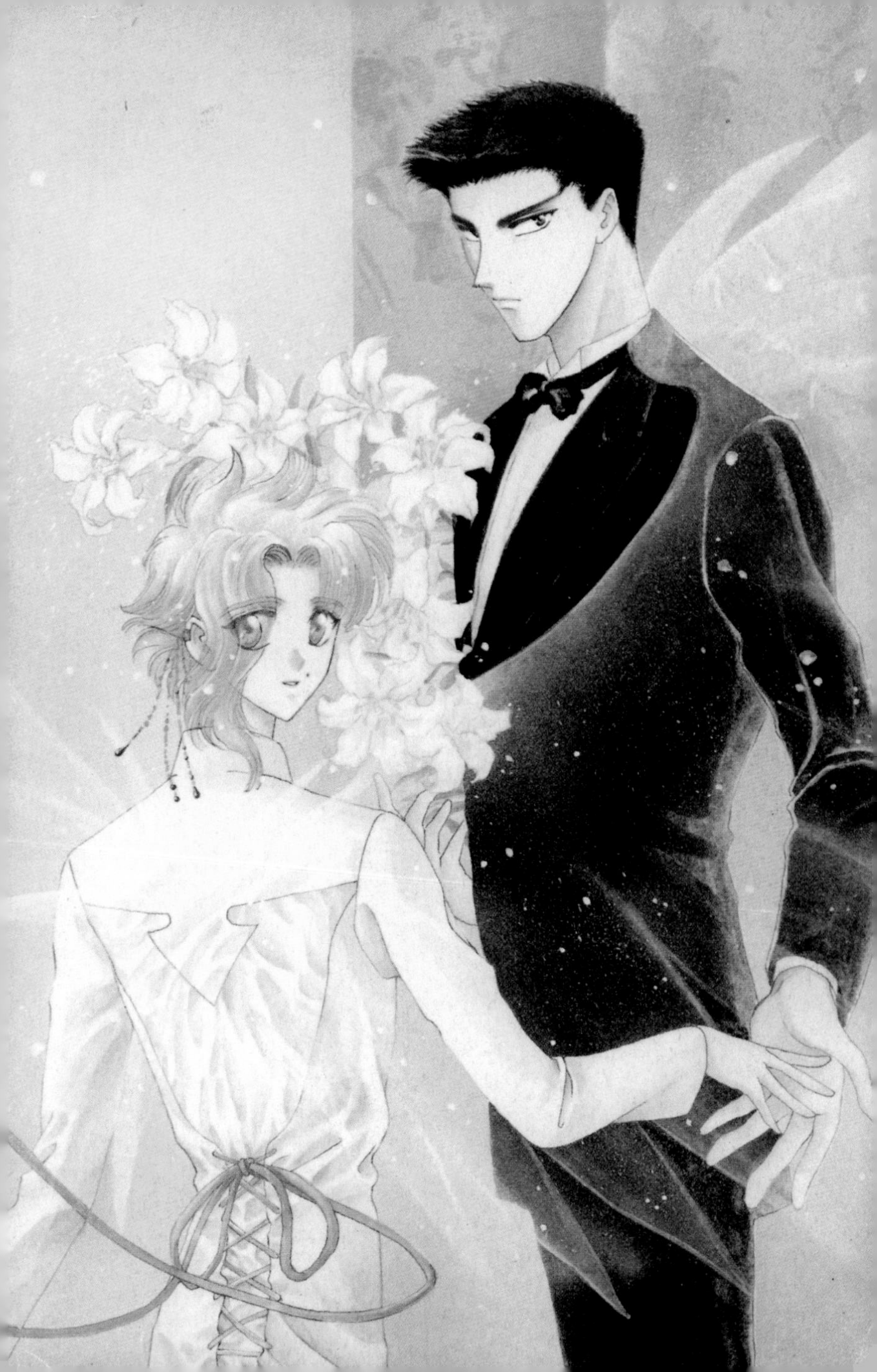

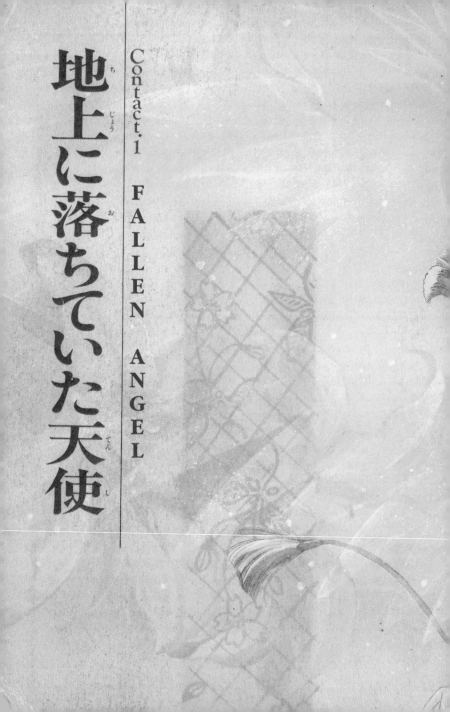

地上に落ちていた天使

Contact.1　FALLEN ANGEL

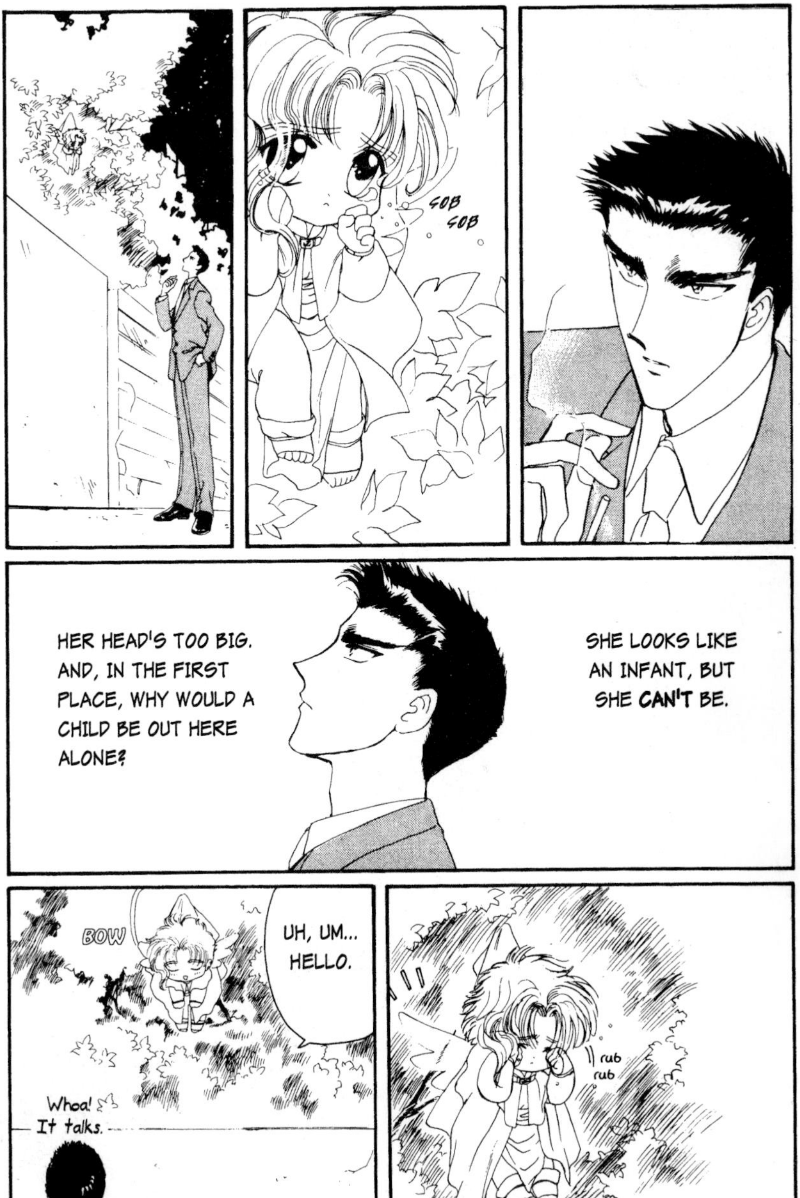
SOB
SOB
SHE LOOKS LIKE AN INFANT, BUT SHE **CAN'T** BE.
HER HEAD'S TOO BIG. AND, IN THE FIRST PLACE, WHY WOULD A CHILD BE OUT HERE ALONE?
rub
rub
UH, UM... HELLO.
BOW
Whoa! It talks.

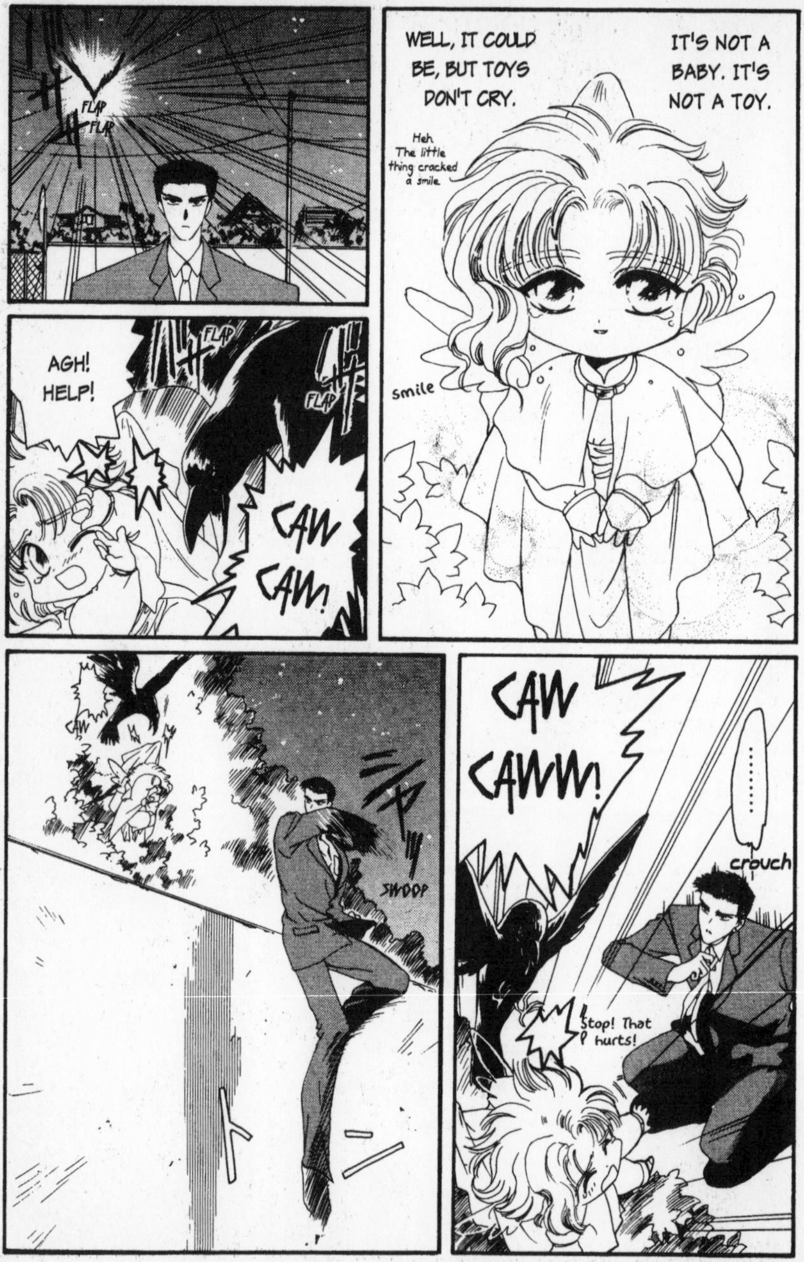
IT'S NOT A BABY. IT'S NOT A TOY.
WELL, IT COULD BE, BUT TOYS DON'T CRY.
Heh The little thing cracked a smile
smile
FLAP FLAP
FLAP
FLAP
AGH! HELP!
CAW CAW!
CAW CAWW!
......
crouch
Stop! That hurts!
CAW
SWOOP

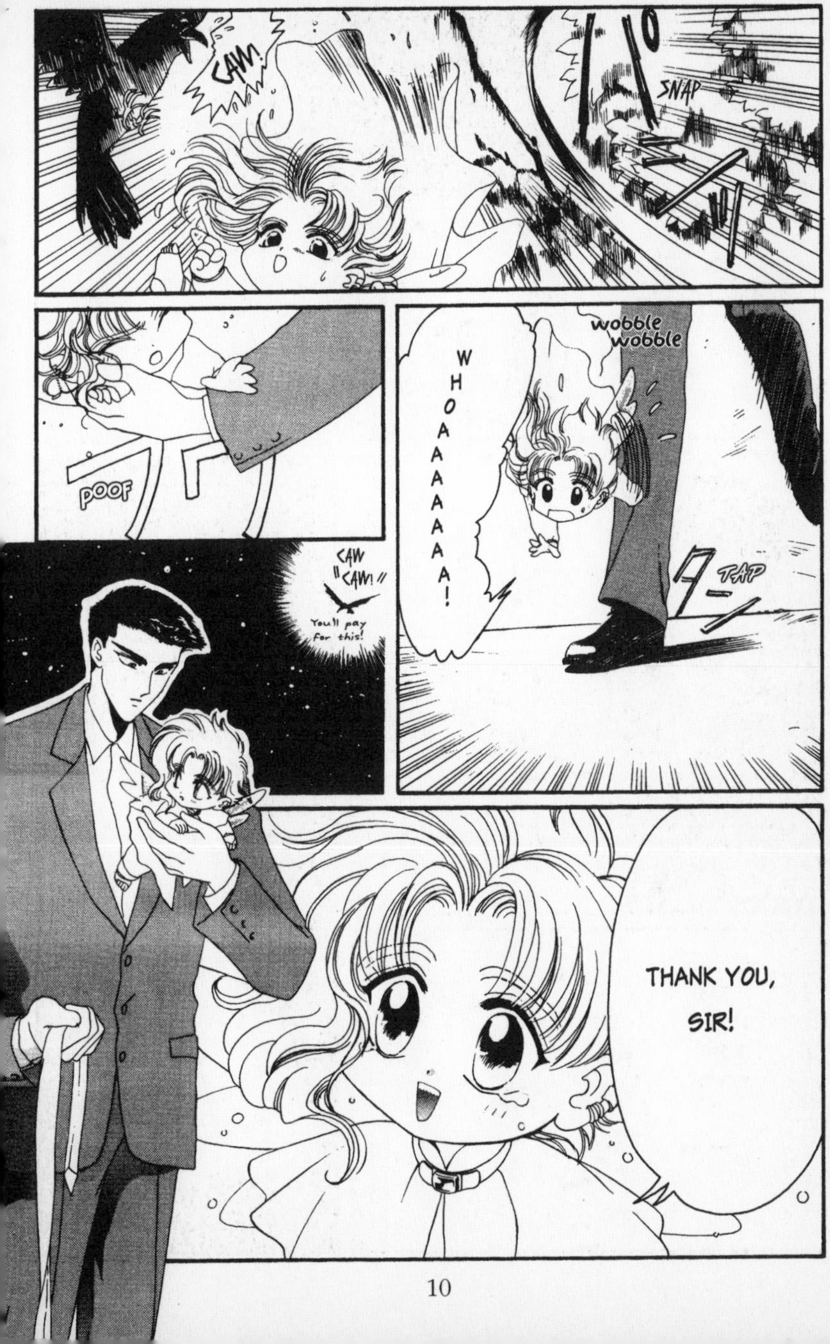
SNAP
CAW!
wobble wobble
WHOAAAAAAAA!
TAP
POOF
CAW "CAW!"
You'll pay for this!
THANK YOU, SIR!

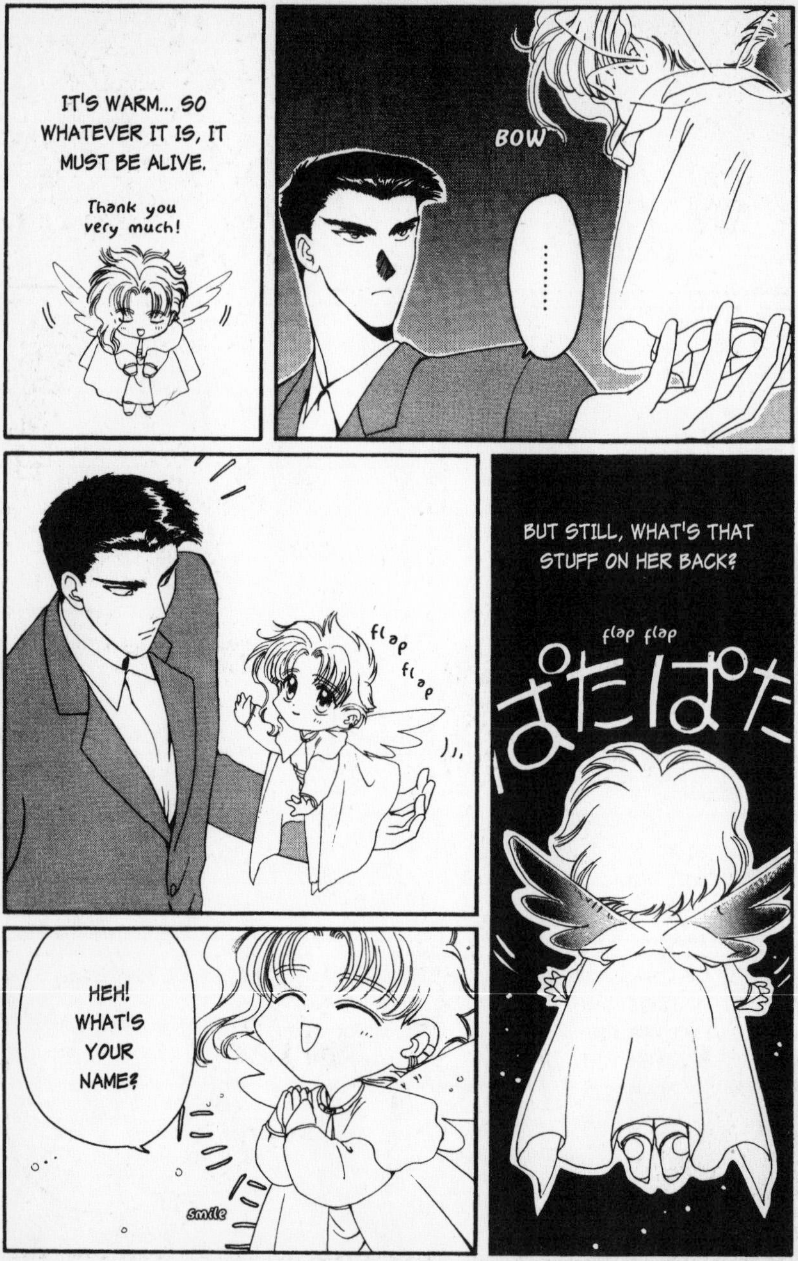
BOW
……
IT'S WARM... SO WHATEVER IT IS, IT MUST BE ALIVE.
Thank you very much!
BUT STILL, WHAT'S THAT STUFF ON HER BACK?
flap flap
ぱたぱた
flap flap
HEH! WHAT'S YOUR NAME?
smile

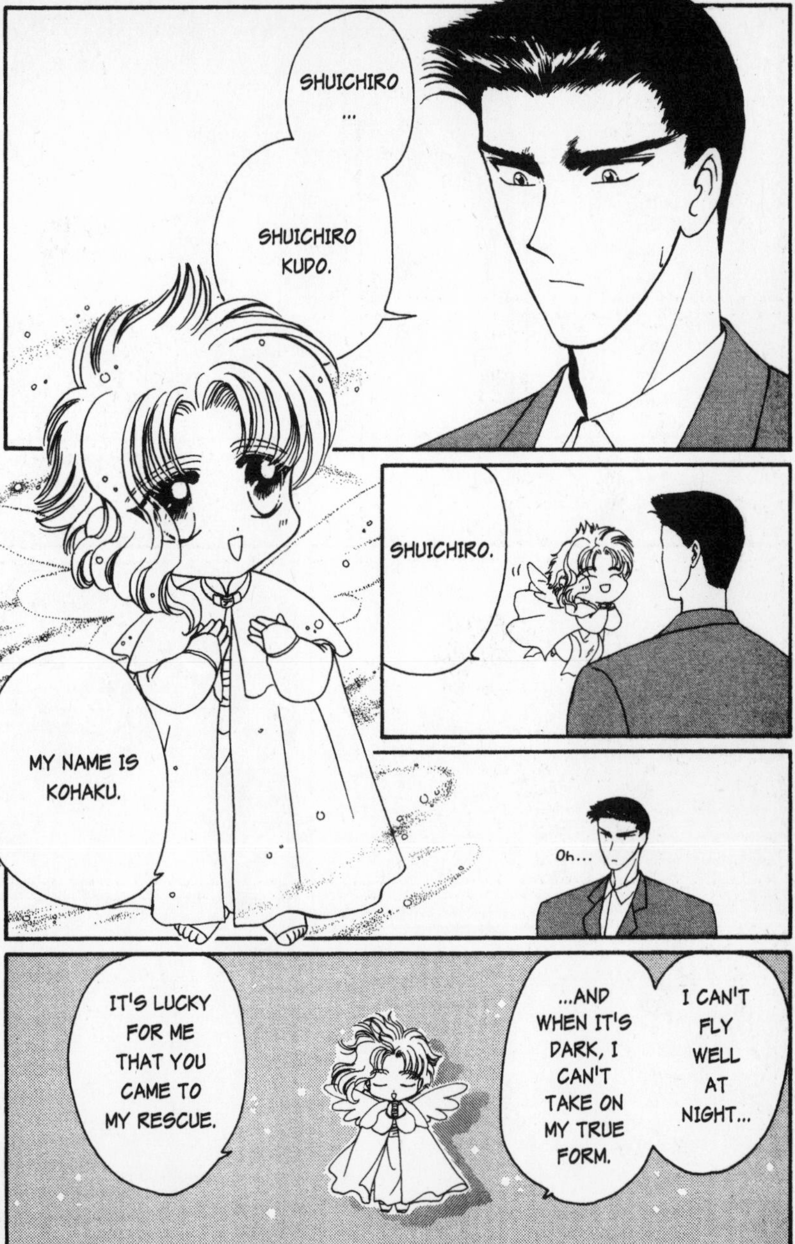
SHUICHIRO ...
SHUICHIRO KUDO.
SHUICHIRO.
Oh...
MY NAME IS KOHAKU.
I CAN'T FLY WELL AT NIGHT...
...AND WHEN IT'S DARK, I CAN'T TAKE ON MY TRUE FORM.
IT'S LUCKY FOR ME THAT YOU CAME TO MY RESCUE.

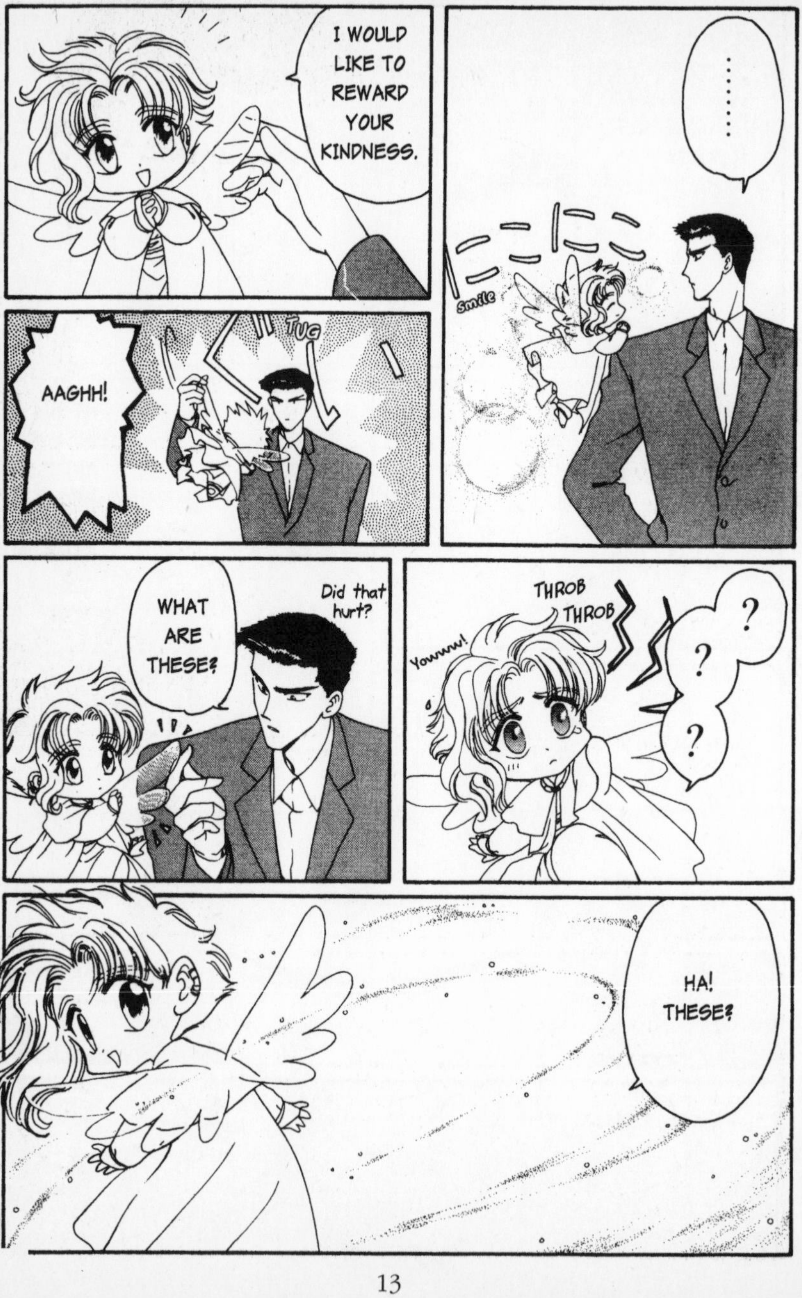
……
Smile
I WOULD LIKE TO REWARD YOUR KINDNESS.
AAGHH!
TUG
THROB THROB
Yowww!
? ? ?
Did that hurt?
WHAT ARE THESE?
HA! THESE?

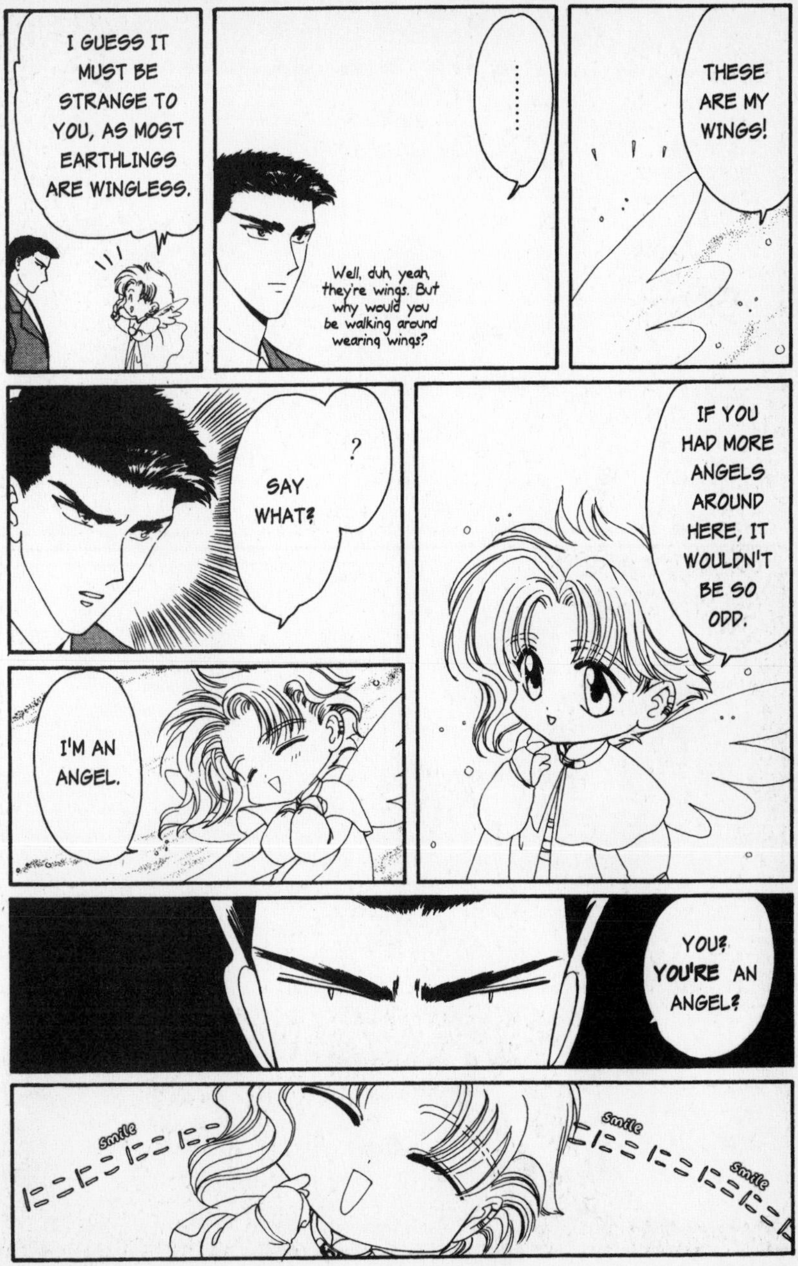

THESE ARE MY WINGS!
......
Well, duh, yeah, they're wings. But why would you be walking around wearing wings?
I GUESS IT MUST BE STRANGE TO YOU, AS MOST EARTHLINGS ARE WINGLESS.
IF YOU HAD MORE ANGELS AROUND HERE, IT WOULDN'T BE SO ODD.
?
SAY WHAT?
I'M AN ANGEL.
YOU? YOU'RE AN ANGEL?
Smile
Smile
Smile

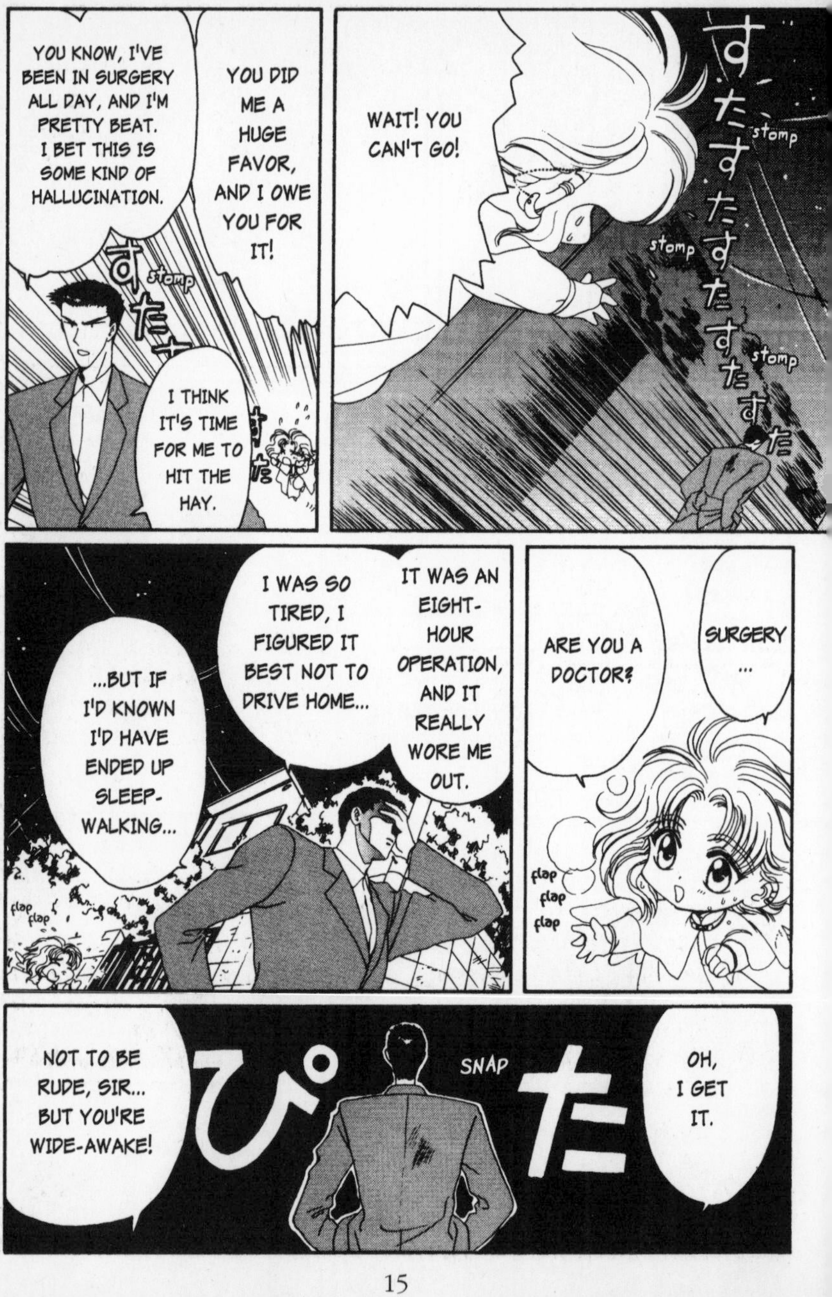
WAIT! YOU CAN'T GO!
すたすたすたすたすた
stomp
stomp
stomp
YOU DID ME A HUGE FAVOR, AND I OWE YOU FOR IT!
YOU KNOW, I'VE BEEN IN SURGERY ALL DAY, AND I'M PRETTY BEAT. I BET THIS IS SOME KIND OF HALLUCINATION.
すた
stomp
I THINK IT'S TIME FOR ME TO HIT THE HAY.
SURGERY ...
ARE YOU A DOCTOR?
flap flap flap
IT WAS AN EIGHT-HOUR OPERATION, AND IT REALLY WORE ME OUT.
I WAS SO TIRED, I FIGURED IT BEST NOT TO DRIVE HOME...
...BUT IF I'D KNOWN I'D HAVE ENDED UP SLEEP-WALKING...
flap flap
OH, I GET IT.
ぴた
SNAP
NOT TO BE RUDE, SIR... BUT YOU'RE WIDE-AWAKE!

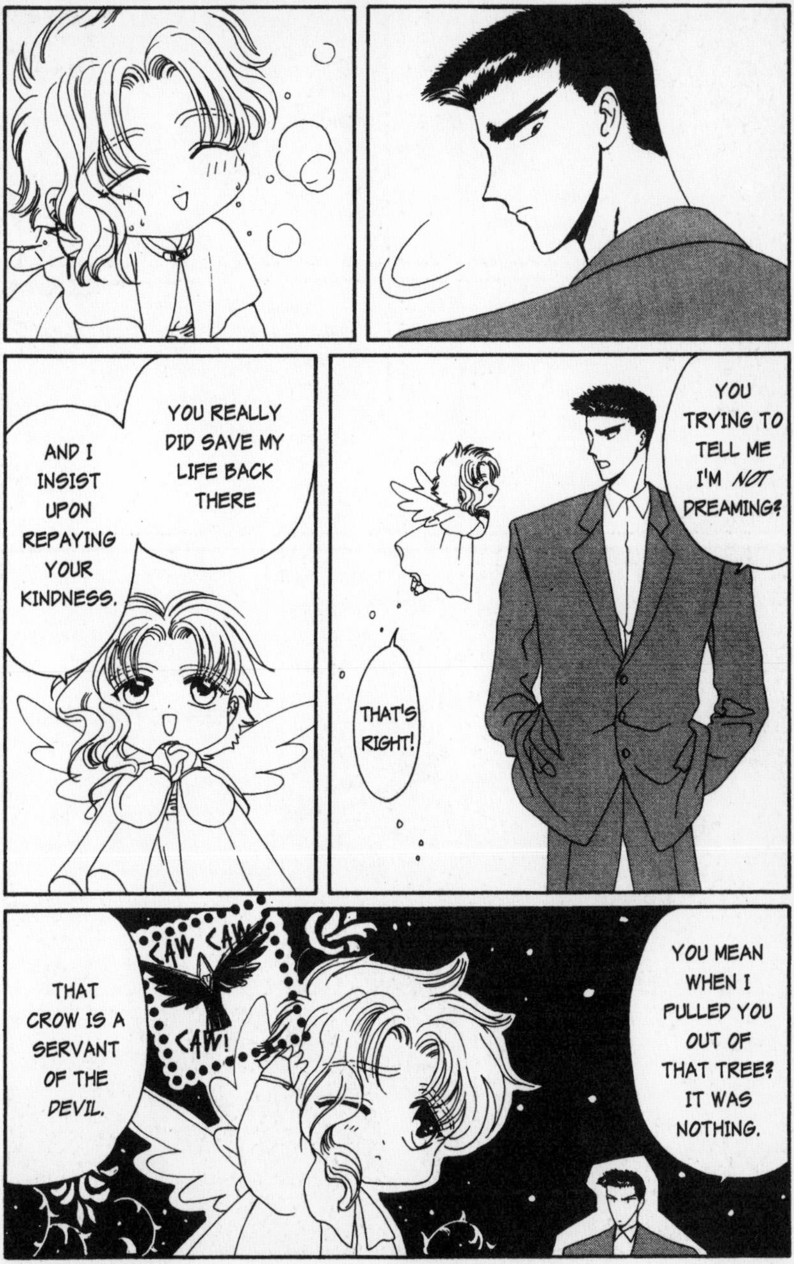
YOU TRYING TO TELL ME I'M *NOT* DREAMING?
THAT'S RIGHT!
YOU REALLY DID SAVE MY LIFE BACK THERE
AND I INSIST UPON REPAYING YOUR KINDNESS.
YOU MEAN WHEN I PULLED YOU OUT OF THAT TREE? IT WAS NOTHING.
CAW CAW
CAW!
THAT CROW IS A SERVANT OF THE *DEVIL*.

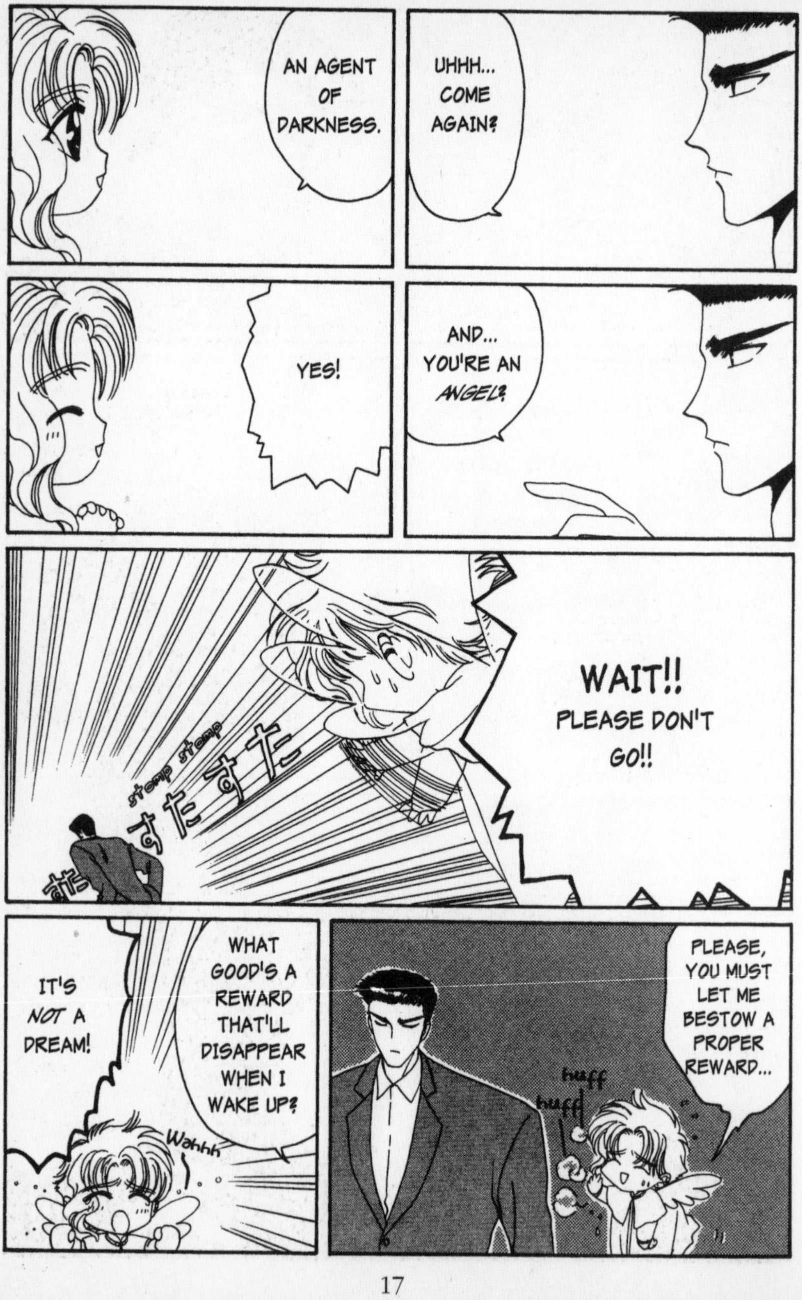
UHHH... COME AGAIN?
AN AGENT OF DARKNESS.
AND... YOU'RE AN *ANGEL*?
YES!
WAIT!! PLEASE DON'T GO!!
stomp stomp
PLEASE, YOU MUST LET ME BESTOW A PROPER REWARD...
huff huff
WHAT GOOD'S A REWARD THAT'LL DISAPPEAR WHEN I WAKE UP?
IT'S *NOT* A DREAM!
Wahhh

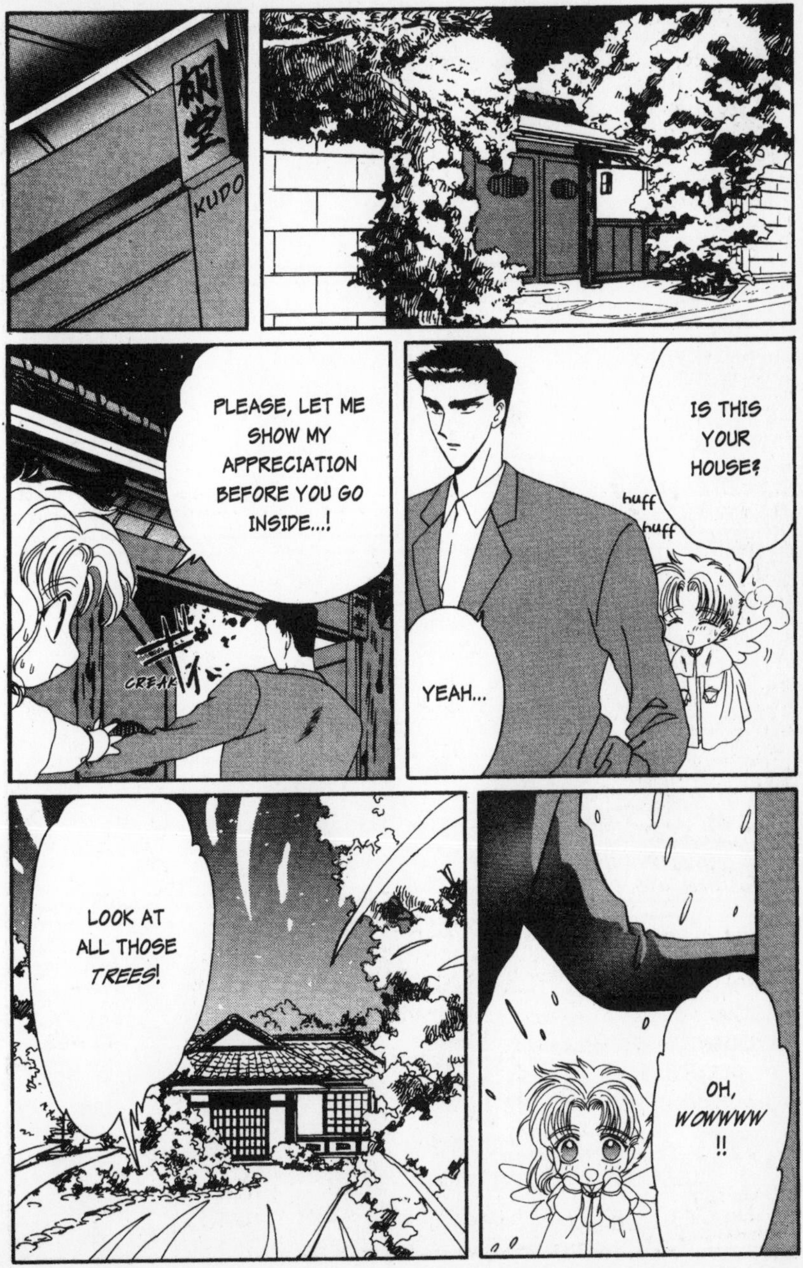
KUDO
IS THIS YOUR HOUSE?
huff huff
YEAH...
PLEASE, LET ME SHOW MY APPRECIATION BEFORE YOU GO INSIDE...!
CREAK
OH, WOWWWW !!
LOOK AT ALL THOSE TREES!

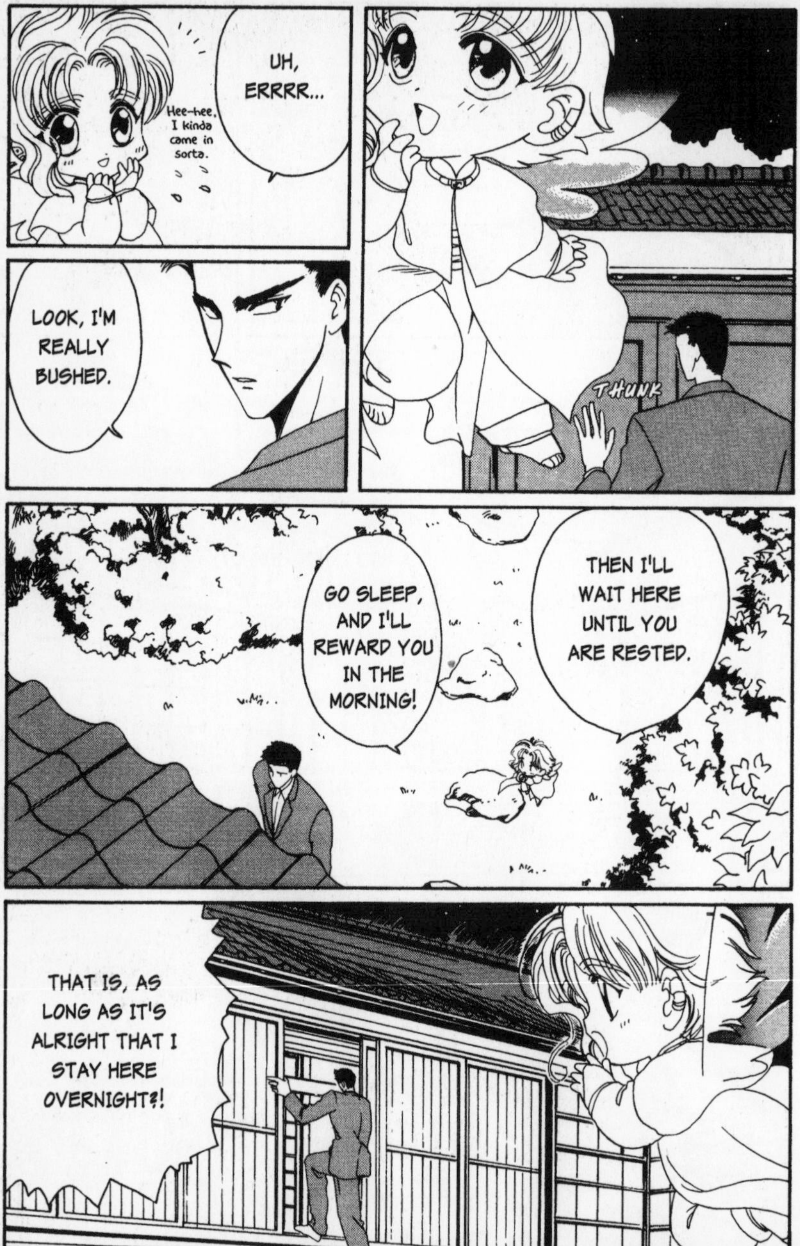
THUNK
UH, ERRRR...
Hee-hee, I kinda came in sorta.
LOOK, I'M REALLY BUSHED.
THEN I'LL WAIT HERE UNTIL YOU ARE RESTED.
GO SLEEP, AND I'LL REWARD YOU IN THE MORNING!
THAT IS, AS LONG AS IT'S ALRIGHT THAT I STAY HERE OVERNIGHT?!

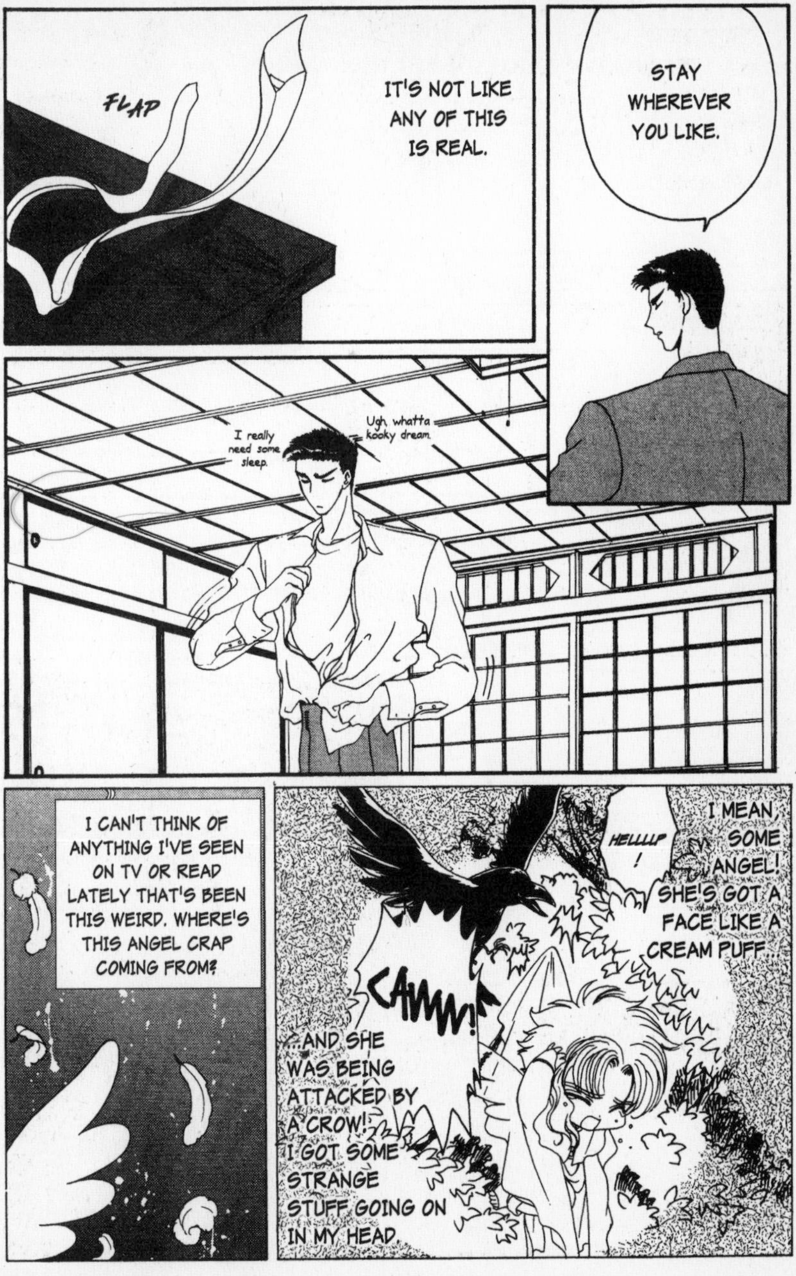
STAY WHEREVER YOU LIKE.
FLAP
IT'S NOT LIKE ANY OF THIS IS REAL.
Ugh, whatta kooky dream.
I really need some sleep.
I MEAN, SOME ANGEL! SHE'S GOT A FACE LIKE A CREAM PUFF...
HELLLLP!
CAWW!
...AND SHE WAS BEING ATTACKED BY A CROW! I GOT SOME STRANGE STUFF GOING ON IN MY HEAD.
I CAN'T THINK OF ANYTHING I'VE SEEN ON TV OR READ LATELY THAT'S BEEN THIS WEIRD. WHERE'S THIS ANGEL CRAP COMING FROM?

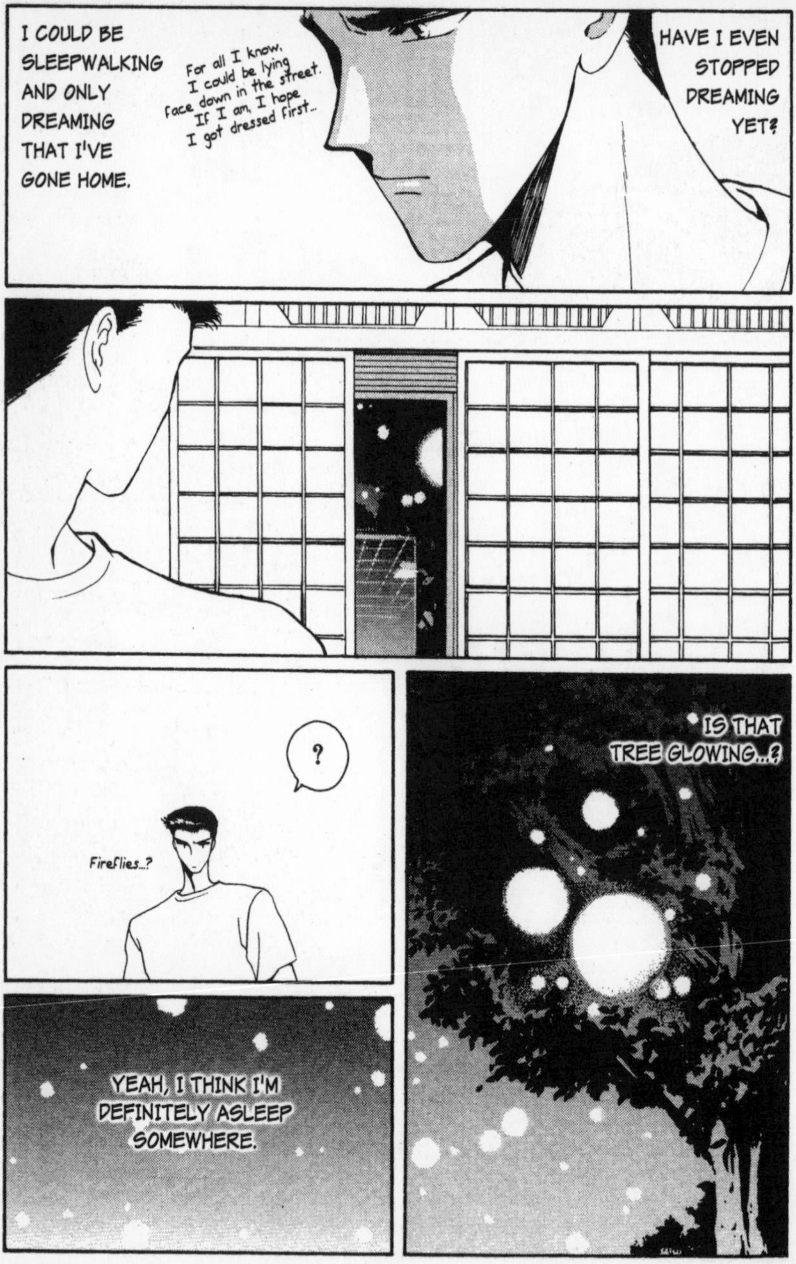
HAVE I EVEN STOPPED DREAMING YET?
For all I know, I could be lying face down in the street. If I am, I hope I got dressed first...
I COULD BE SLEEPWALKING AND ONLY DREAMING THAT I'VE GONE HOME.
IS THAT TREE GLOWING...?
?
Fireflies...?
YEAH, I THINK I'M DEFINITELY ASLEEP SOMEWHERE.

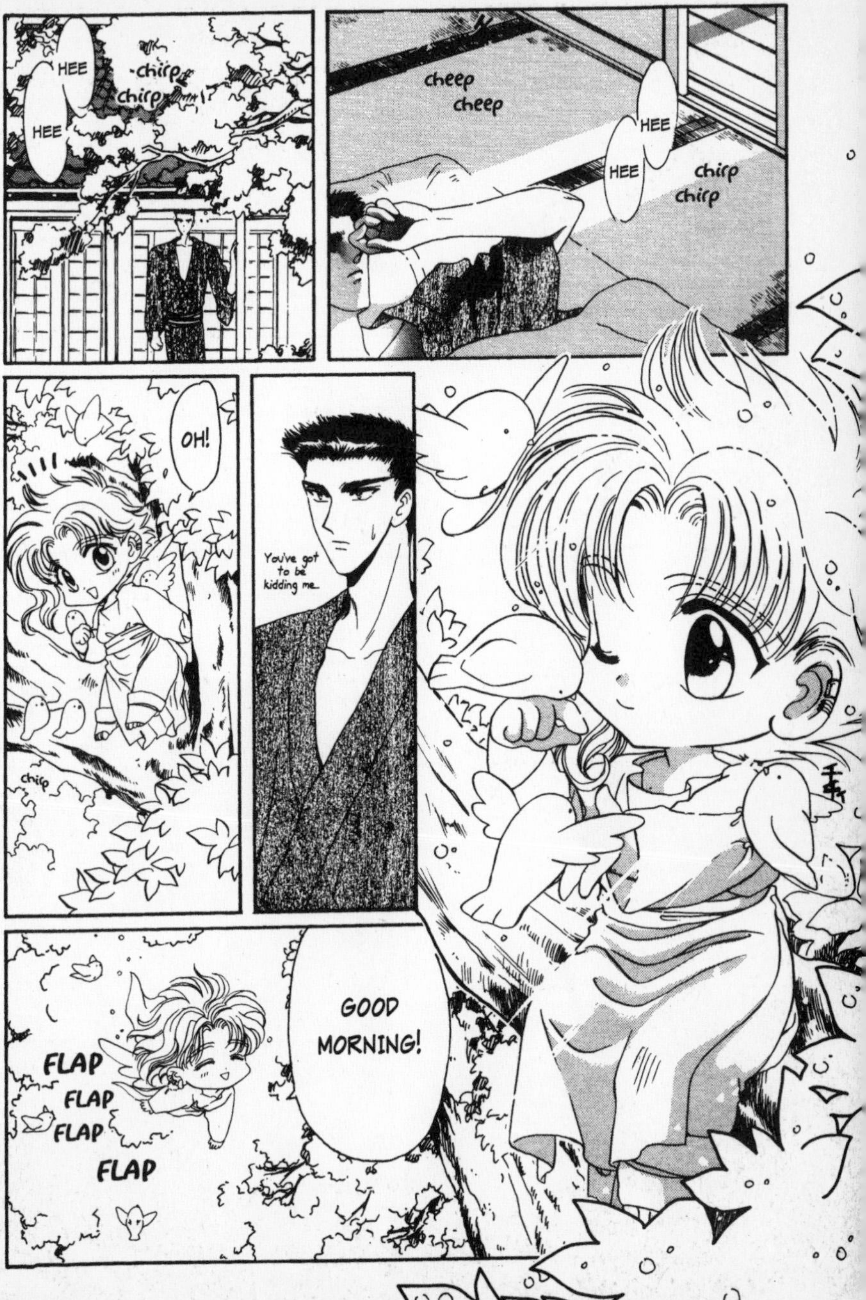
cheep
cheep
HEE
HEE
chirp
chirp
HEE
HEE
chirp
chirp
You've got to be kidding me
OH!
chirp
GOOD MORNING!
FLAP
FLAP
FLAP
FLAP

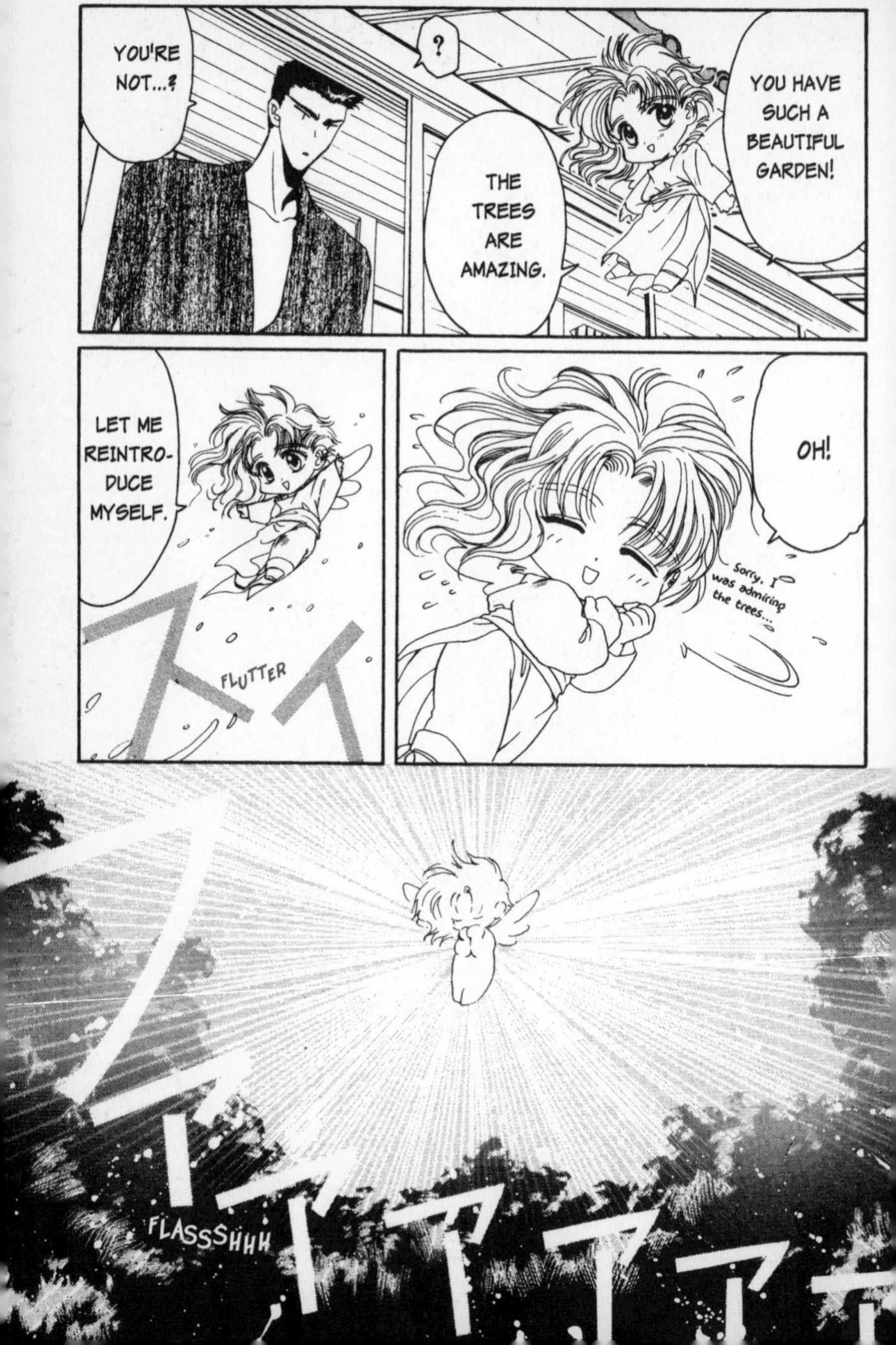
YOU HAVE SUCH A BEAUTIFUL GARDEN!
THE TREES ARE AMAZING.
?
YOU'RE NOT...?
OH!
Sorry. I was admiring the trees...
LET ME REINTRO-DUCE MYSELF.
FLUTTER
FLASSSHHH

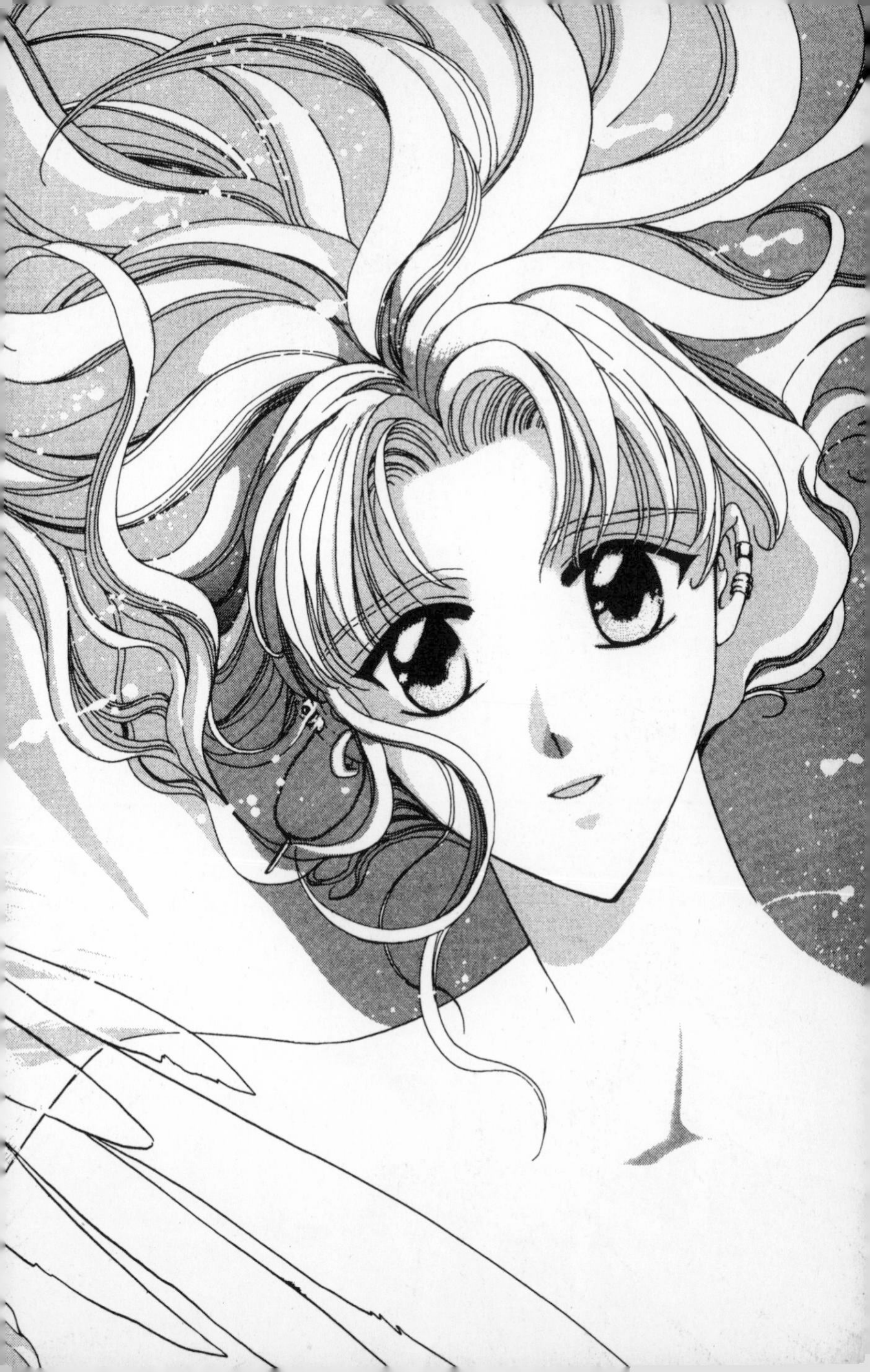

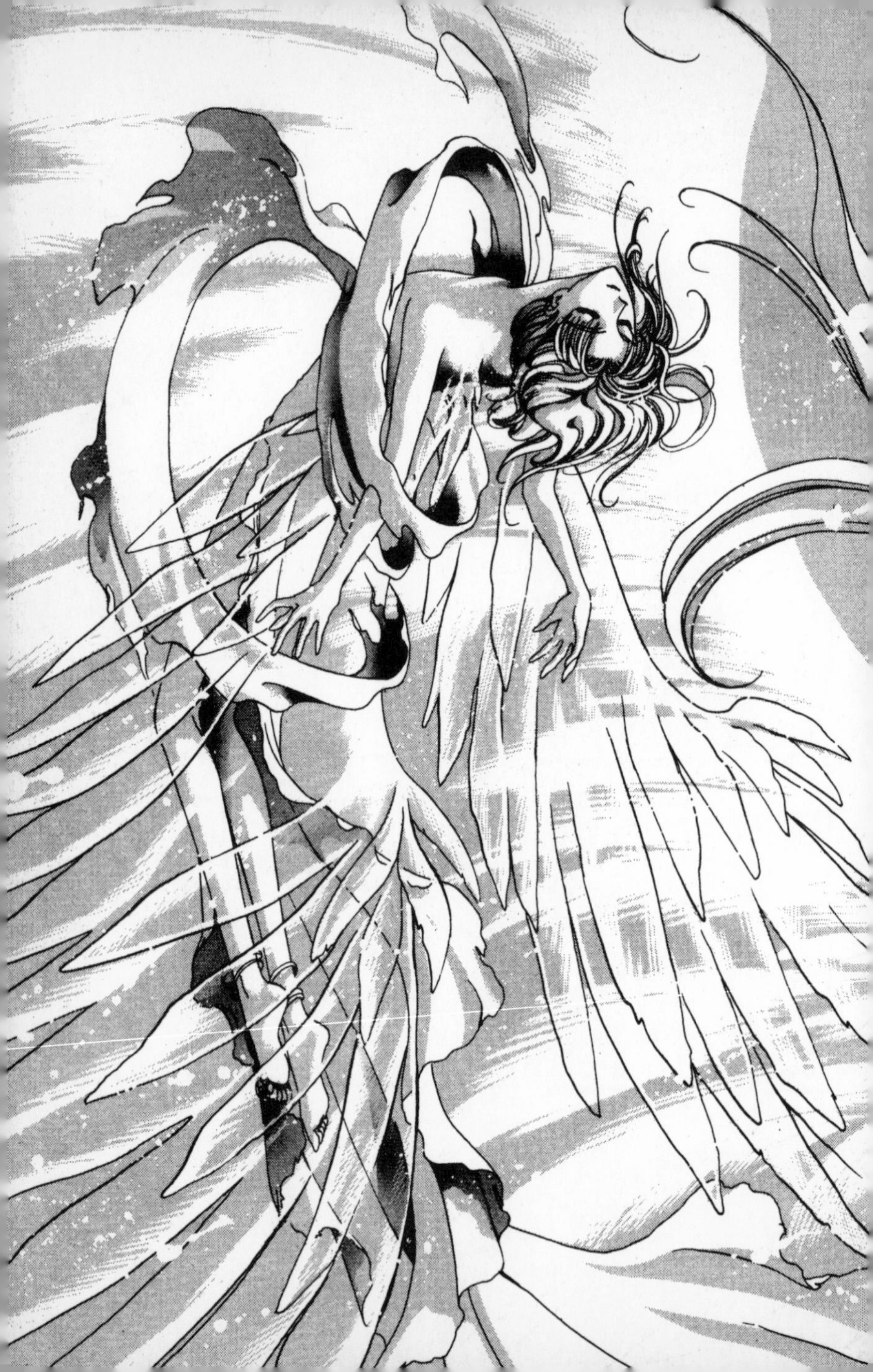

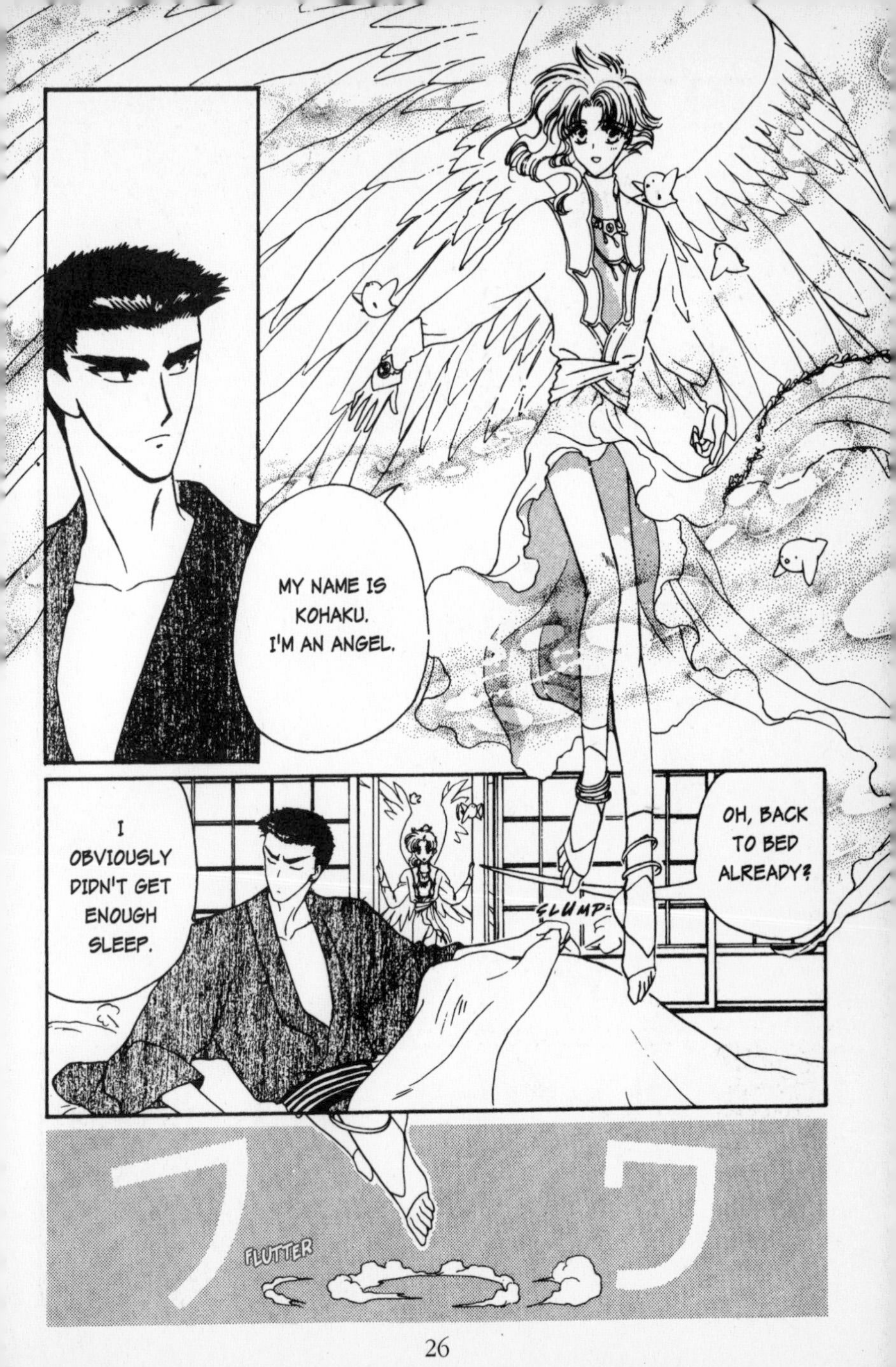
MY NAME IS KOHAKU. I'M AN ANGEL.
OH, BACK TO BED ALREADY?
SLUMP
I OBVIOUSLY DIDN'T GET ENOUGH SLEEP.
フワ
FLUTTER

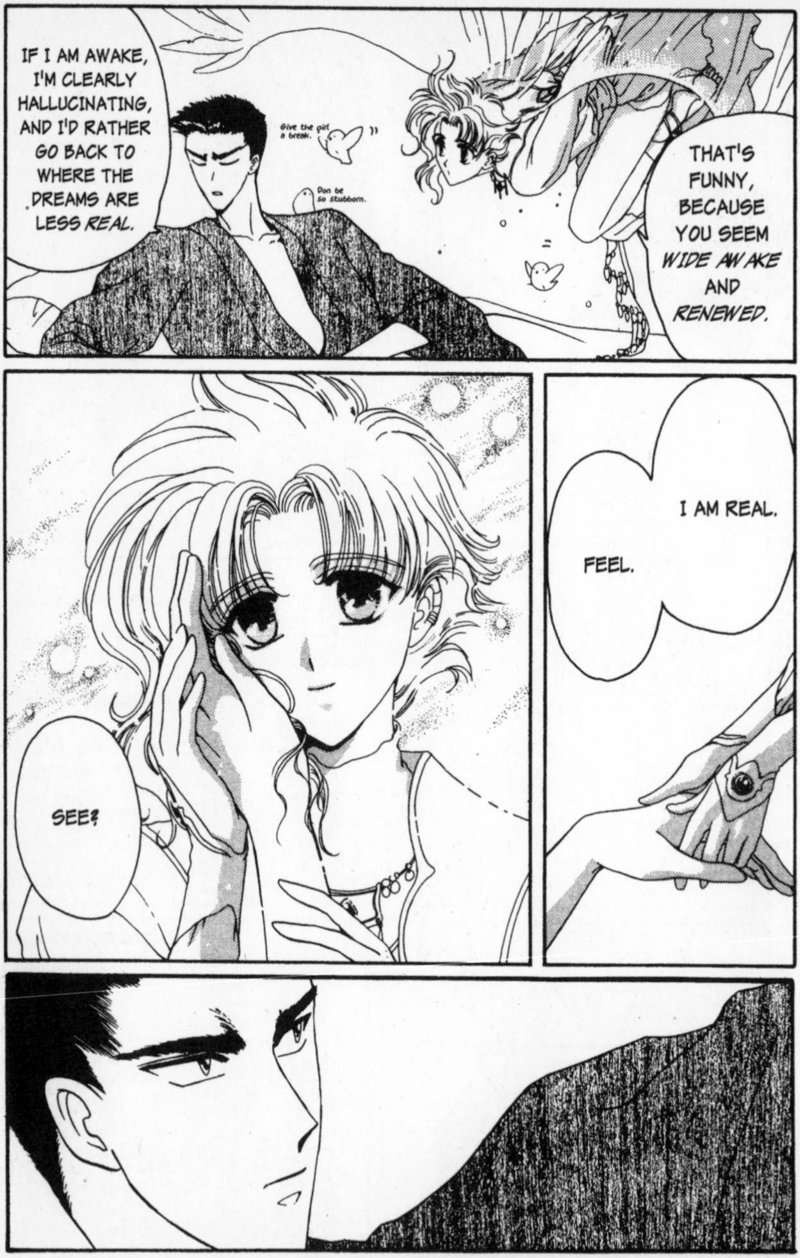
IF I AM AWAKE, I'M CLEARLY HALLUCINATING, AND I'D RATHER GO BACK TO WHERE THE DREAMS ARE LESS *REAL*.
THAT'S FUNNY, BECAUSE YOU SEEM *WIDE AWAKE* AND *RENEWED*.
Give the girl a break.
Don't be so stubborn.
I AM REAL.
FEEL.
SEE?

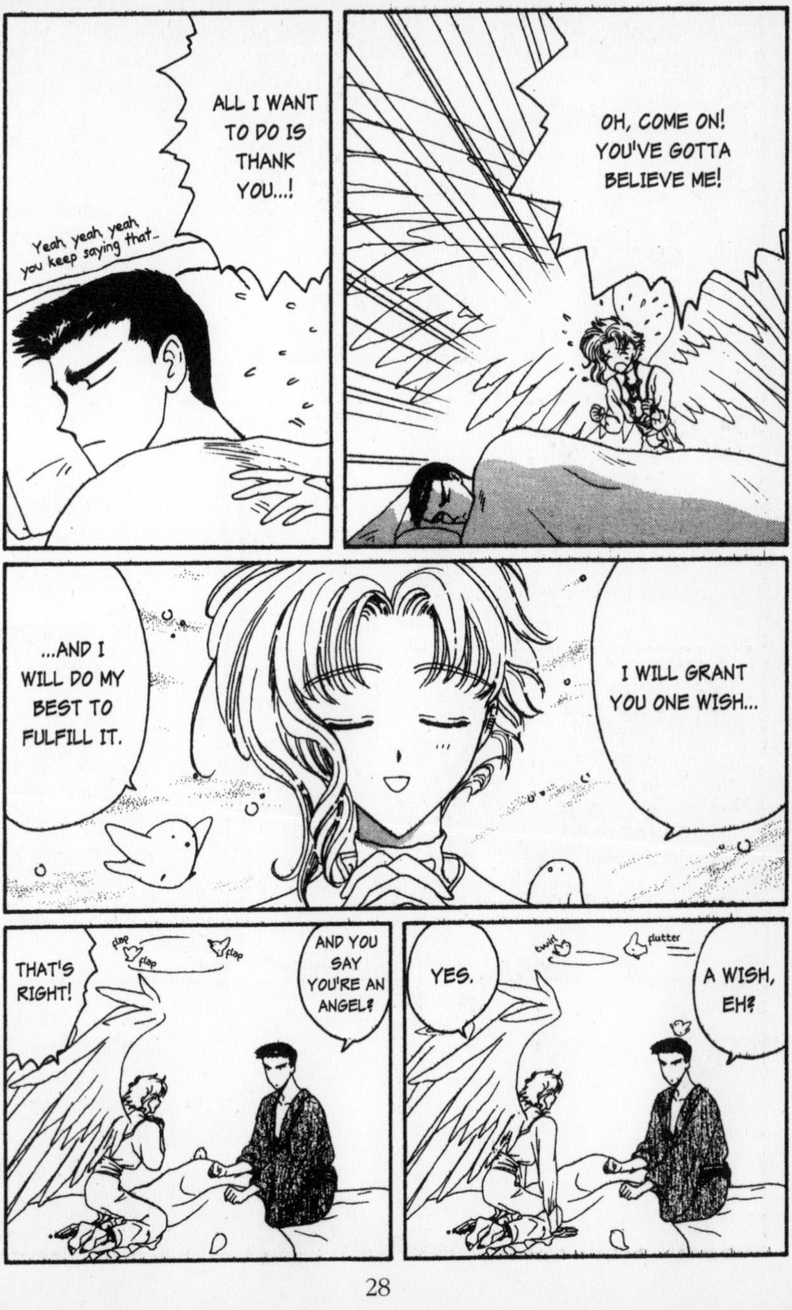
OH, COME ON! YOU'VE GOTTA BELIEVE ME!
ALL I WANT TO DO IS THANK YOU...!
Yeah, yeah, you keep saying that...
I WILL GRANT YOU ONE WISH...
...AND I WILL DO MY BEST TO FULFILL IT.
A WISH, EH?
flutter
twirl
YES.
AND YOU SAY YOU'RE AN ANGEL?
flap
flap
flap
THAT'S RIGHT!

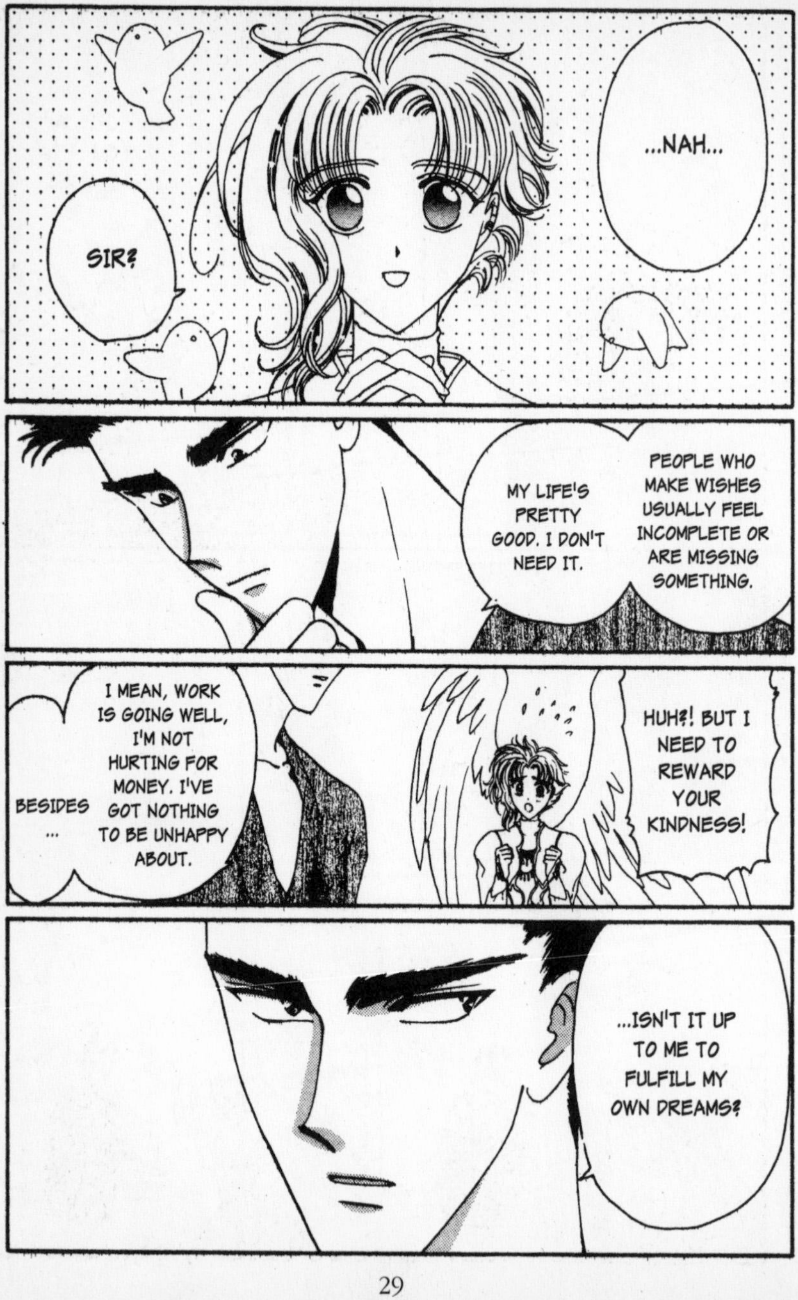
...NAH...
SIR?
PEOPLE WHO MAKE WISHES USUALLY FEEL INCOMPLETE OR ARE MISSING SOMETHING.
MY LIFE'S PRETTY GOOD. I DON'T NEED IT.
HUH?! BUT I NEED TO REWARD YOUR KINDNESS!
I MEAN, WORK IS GOING WELL, I'M NOT HURTING FOR MONEY. I'VE GOT NOTHING TO BE UNHAPPY ABOUT.
BESIDES ...
...ISN'T IT UP TO ME TO FULFILL MY OWN DREAMS?

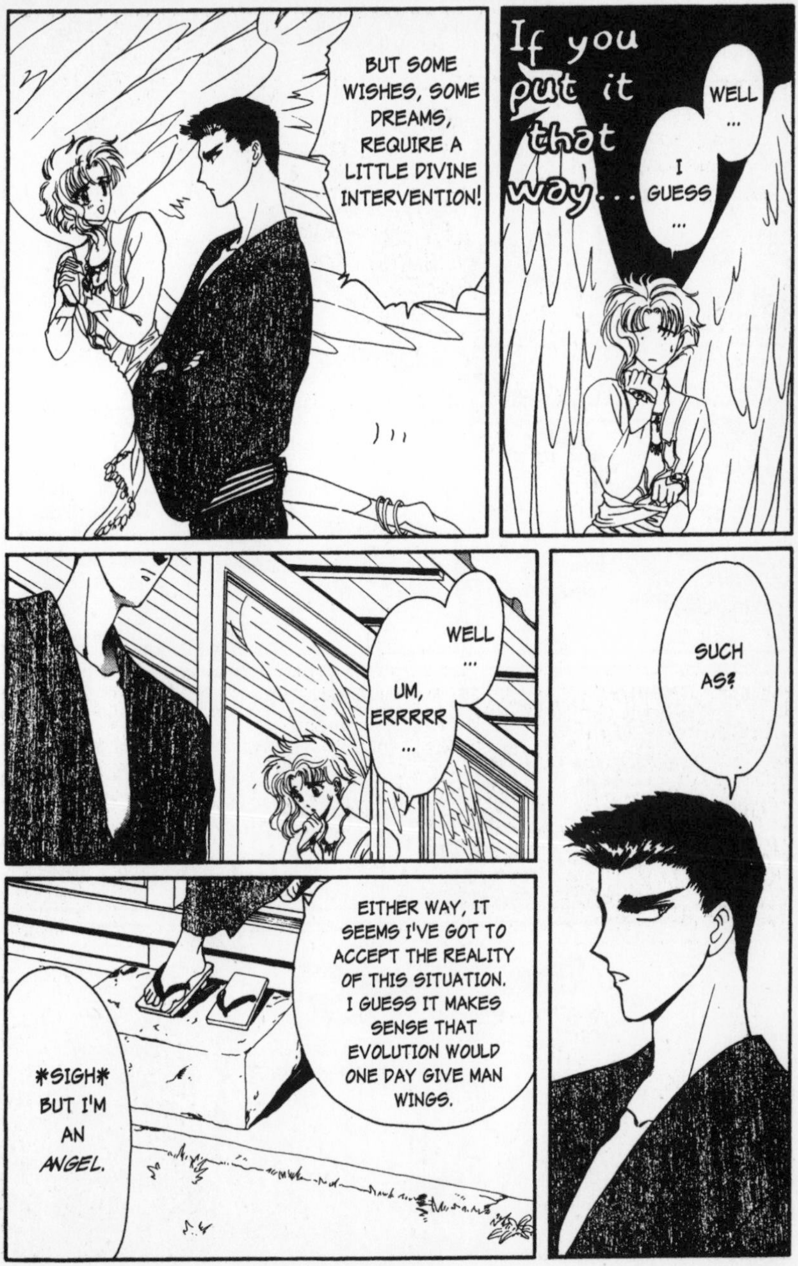
If you put it that way...
WELL ... I GUESS ...
BUT SOME WISHES, SOME DREAMS, REQUIRE A LITTLE DIVINE INTERVENTION!
SUCH AS?
WELL ... UM, ERRRRR ...
EITHER WAY, IT SEEMS I'VE GOT TO ACCEPT THE REALITY OF THIS SITUATION. I GUESS IT MAKES SENSE THAT EVOLUTION WOULD ONE DAY GIVE MAN WINGS.
SIGH BUT I'M AN ANGEL.

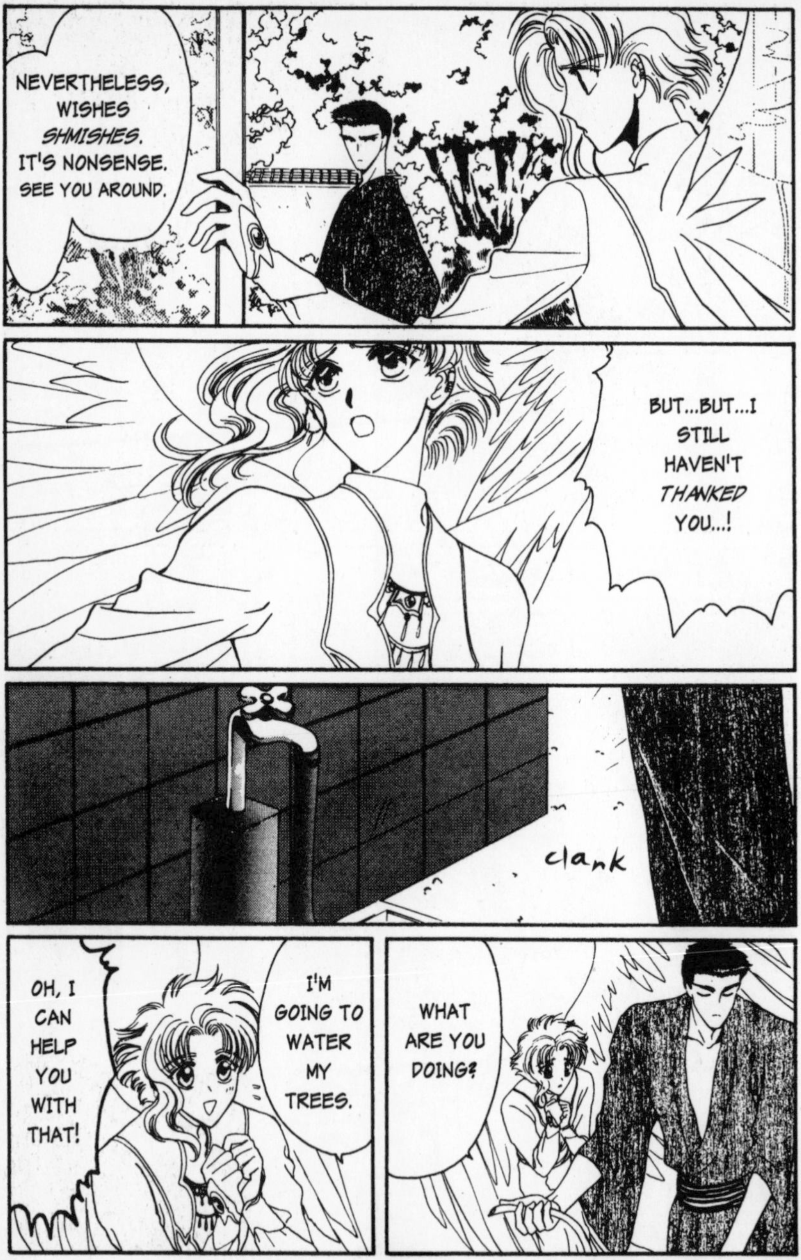
NEVERTHELESS, WISHES SHMISHES. IT'S NONSENSE. SEE YOU AROUND.
BUT...BUT...I STILL HAVEN'T THANKED YOU...!
clank
WHAT ARE YOU DOING?
I'M GOING TO WATER MY TREES.
OH, I CAN HELP YOU WITH THAT!

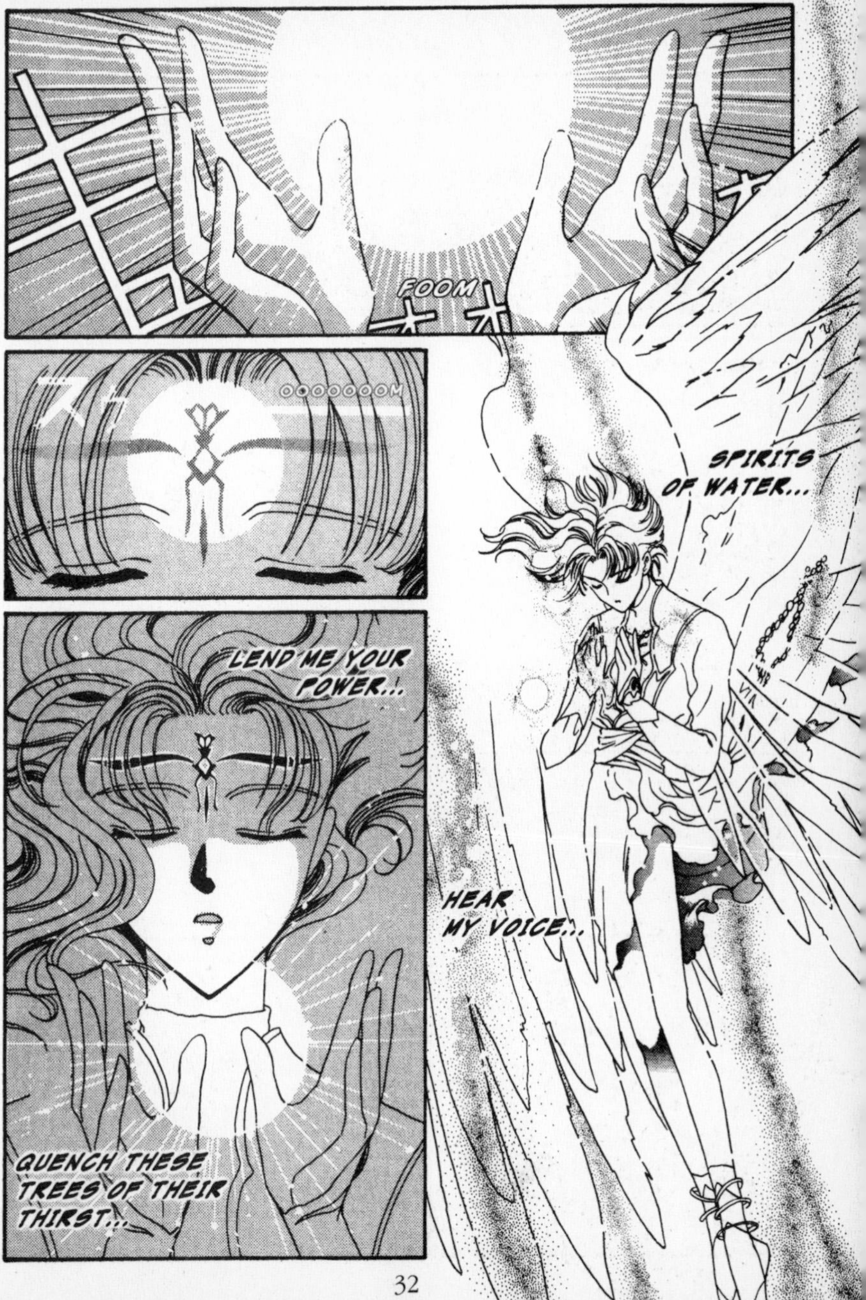
FOOM
SPIRITS OF WATER...
HEAR MY VOICE...
OOOOOOOM
LEND ME YOUR POWER...
QUENCH THESE TREES OF THEIR THIRST...

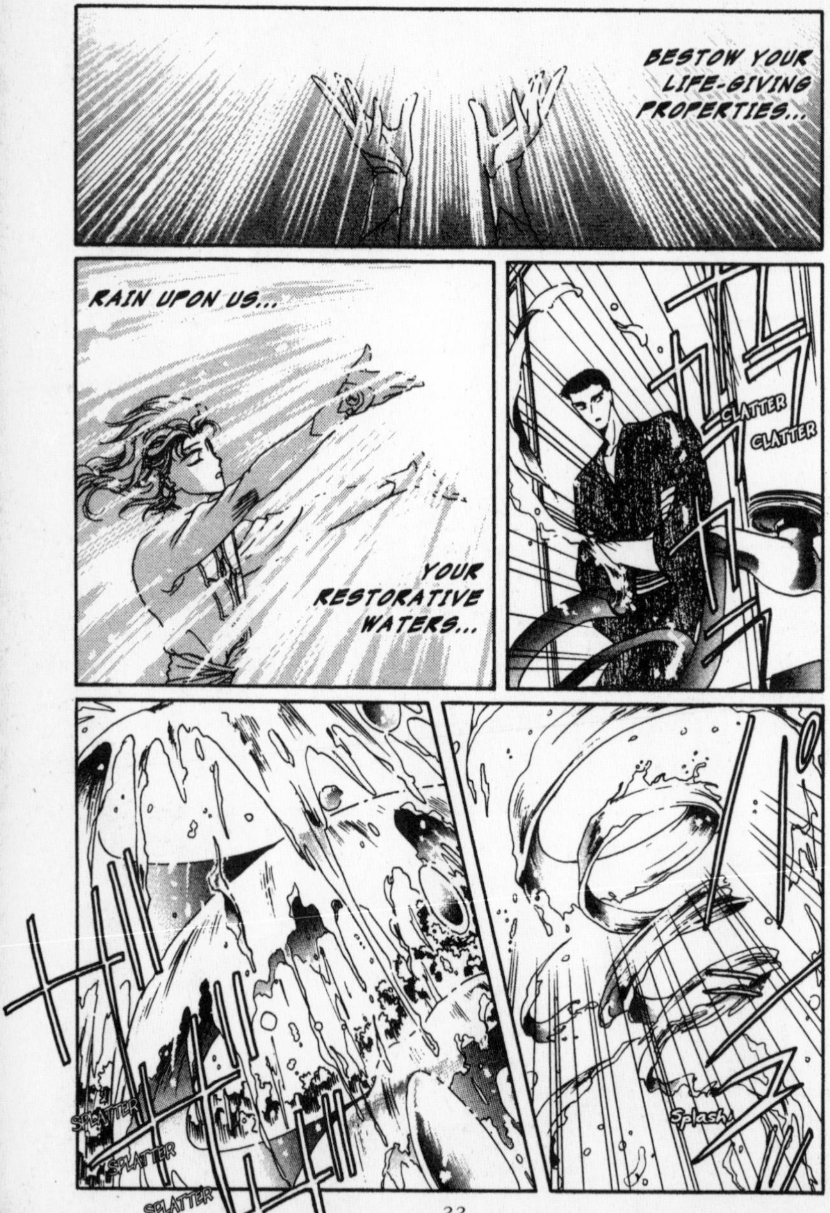
BESTOW YOUR LIFE-GIVING PROPERTIES...
CLATTER
CLATTER
RAIN UPON US...
YOUR RESTORATIVE WATERS...
Splash
SPLATTER
SPLATTER
SPLATTER

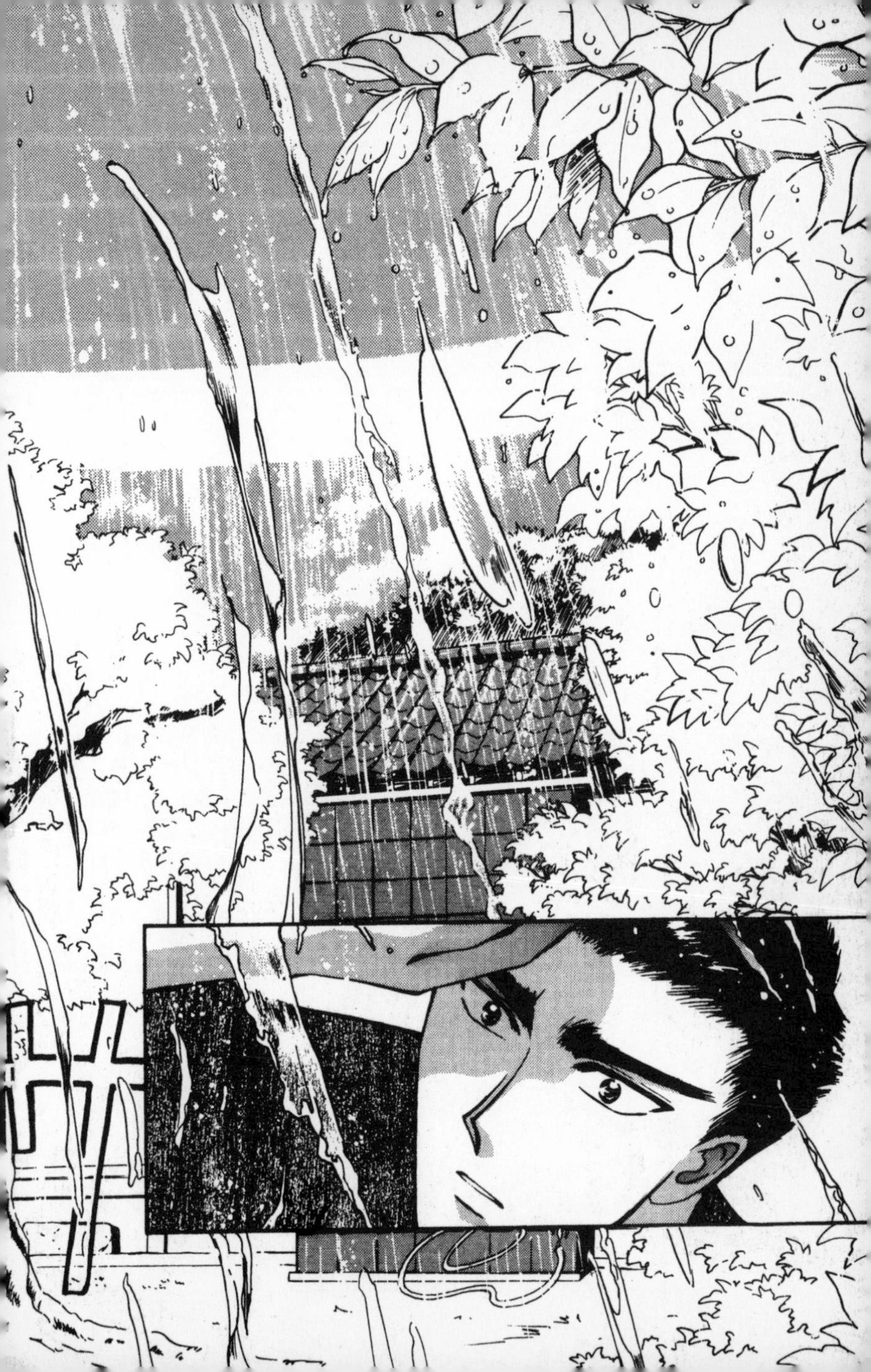

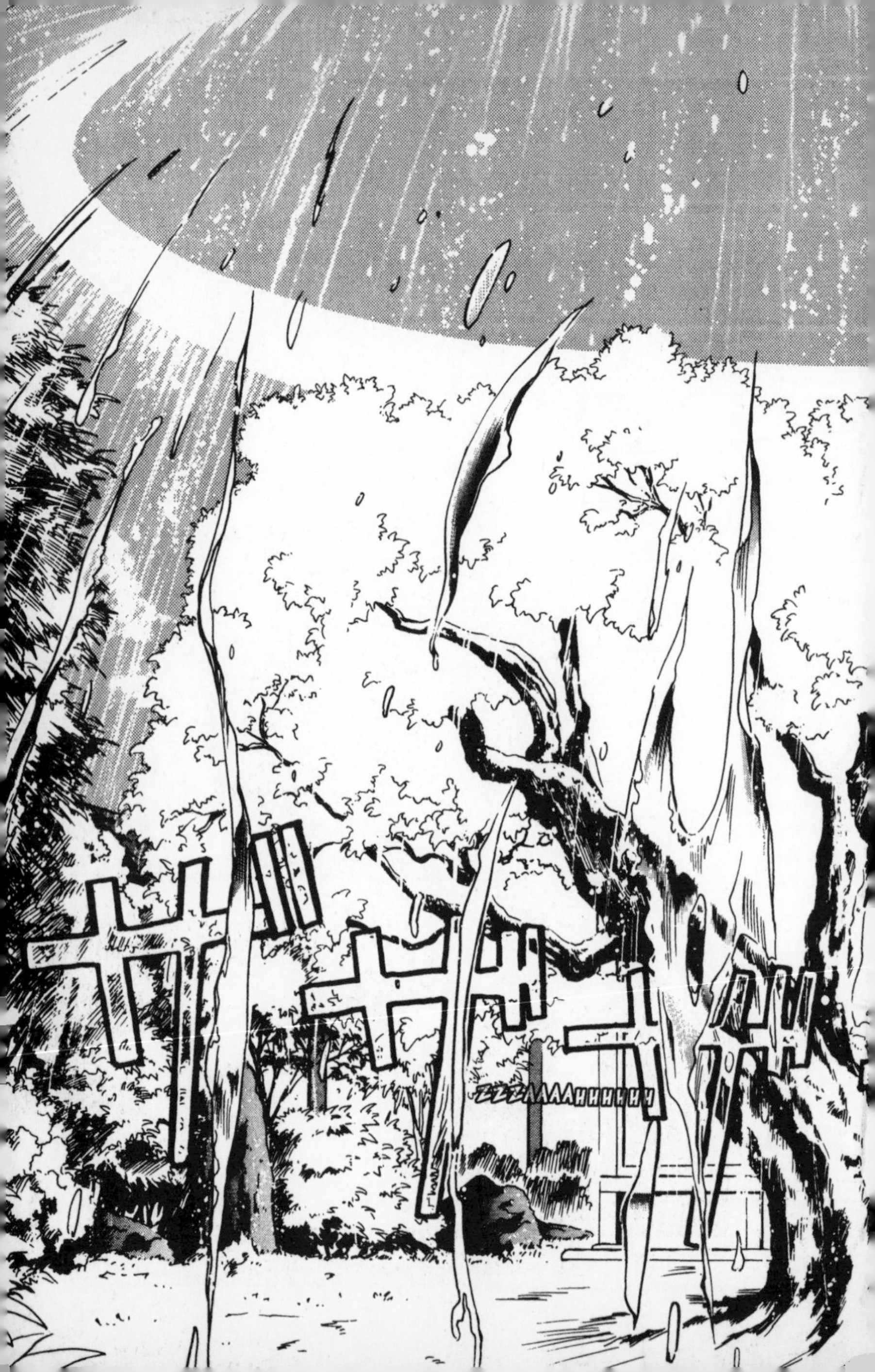
ZZZAAAAHHHHHH

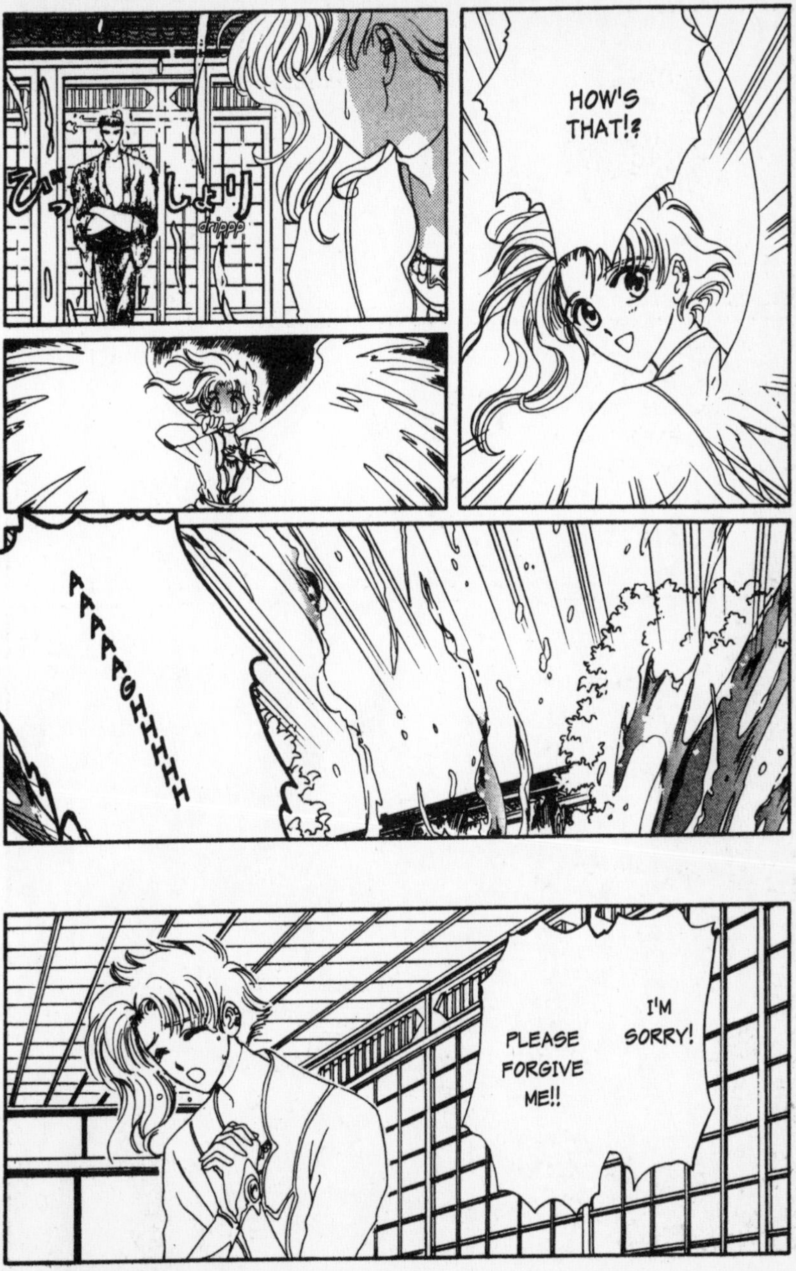
HOW'S THAT!?
びっしょり
drippp
AAAAAGHHHHH
I'M SORRY!
PLEASE FORGIVE ME!!

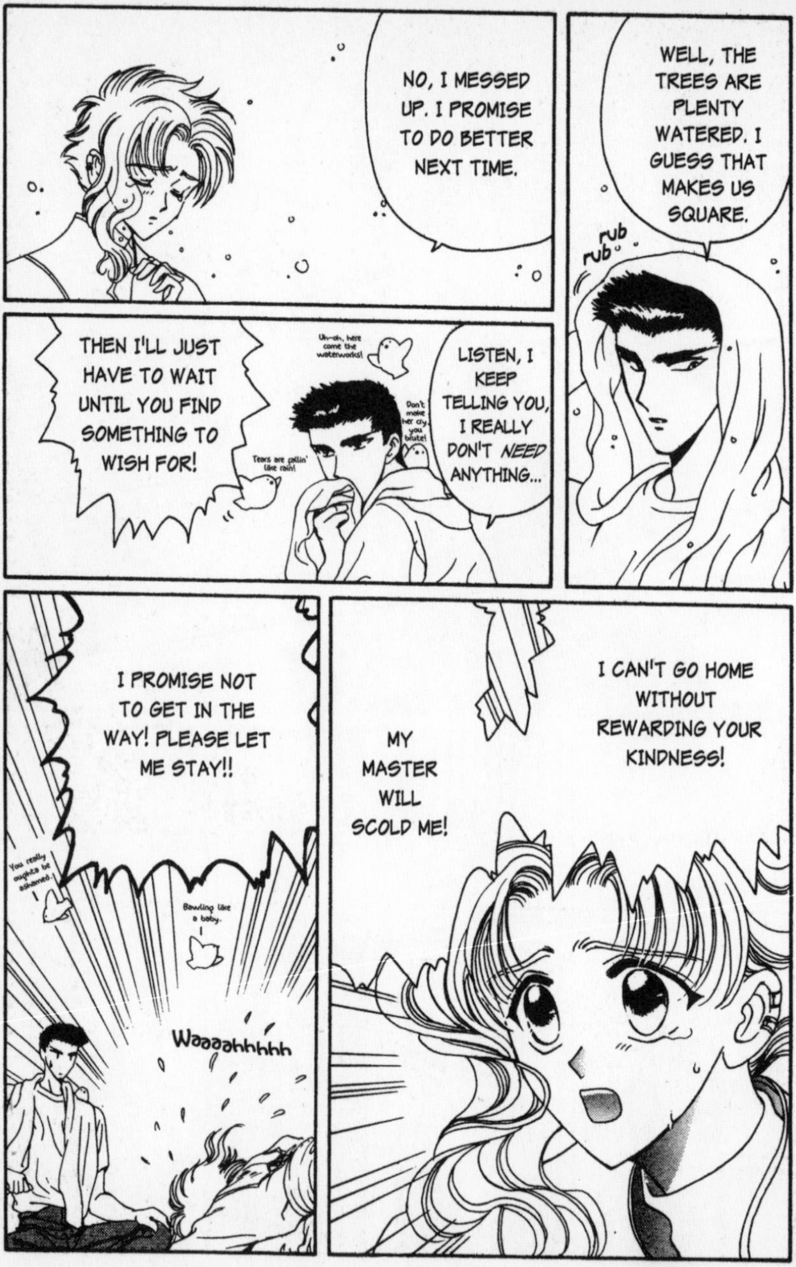
WELL, THE TREES ARE PLENTY WATERED. I GUESS THAT MAKES US SQUARE.
rub rub
NO, I MESSED UP. I PROMISE TO DO BETTER NEXT TIME.
LISTEN, I KEEP TELLING YOU, I REALLY DON'T NEED ANYTHING...
Uh-oh, here come the waterworks!
Don't make her cry, you brute!
Tears are fallin' like rain!
THEN I'LL JUST HAVE TO WAIT UNTIL YOU FIND SOMETHING TO WISH FOR!
I CAN'T GO HOME WITHOUT REWARDING YOUR KINDNESS!
MY MASTER WILL SCOLD ME!
I PROMISE NOT TO GET IN THE WAY! PLEASE LET ME STAY!!
Bawling like a baby.
You really oughta be ashamed.
Waaaahhhhh

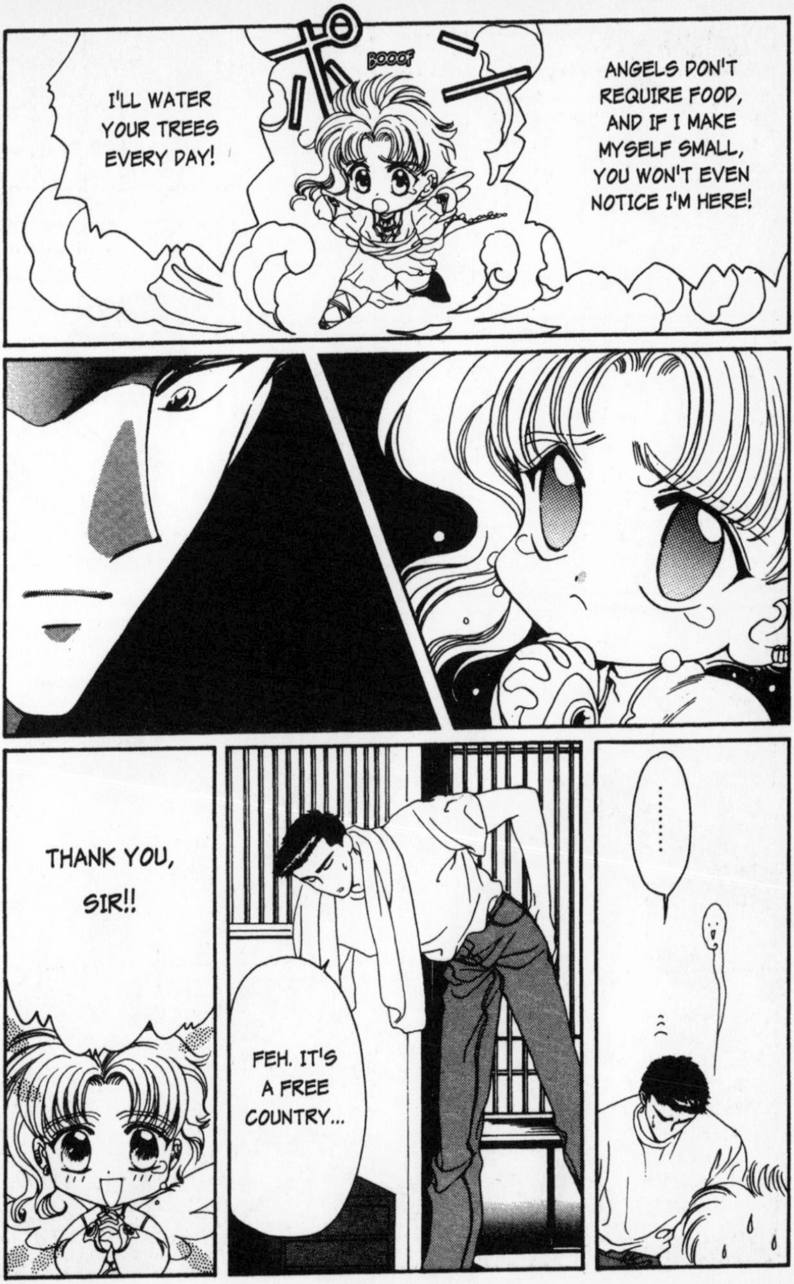
ANGELS DON'T REQUIRE FOOD, AND IF I MAKE MYSELF SMALL, YOU WON'T EVEN NOTICE I'M HERE!
BOOOF
I'LL WATER YOUR TREES EVERY DAY!
......
FEH. IT'S A FREE COUNTRY...
THANK YOU, SIR!!

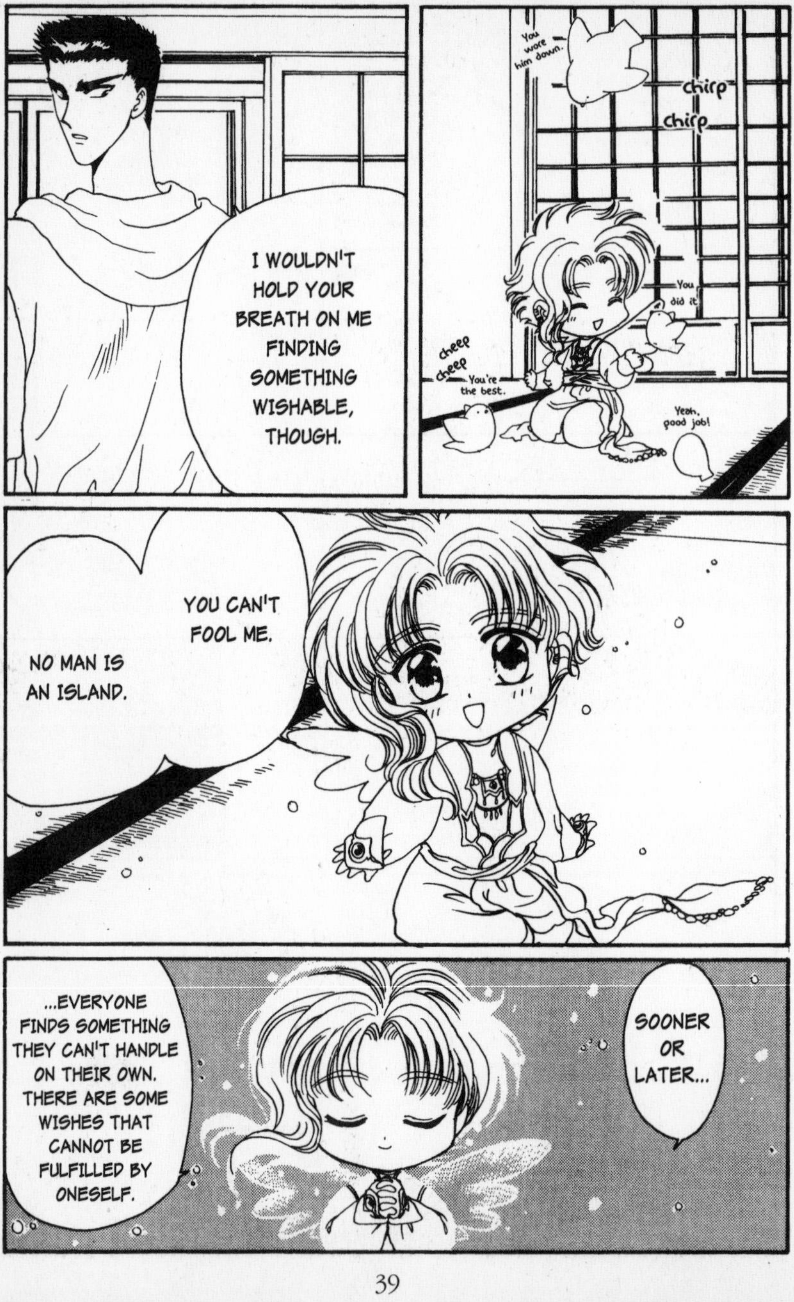
You wore him down.
Chirp
Chirp
You did it
Cheep cheep
You're the best.
Yeah, good job!
I WOULDN'T HOLD YOUR BREATH ON ME FINDING SOMETHING WISHABLE, THOUGH.
YOU CAN'T FOOL ME.
NO MAN IS AN ISLAND.
SOONER OR LATER...
...EVERYONE FINDS SOMETHING THEY CAN'T HANDLE ON THEIR OWN. THERE ARE SOME WISHES THAT CANNOT BE FULFILLED BY ONESELF.

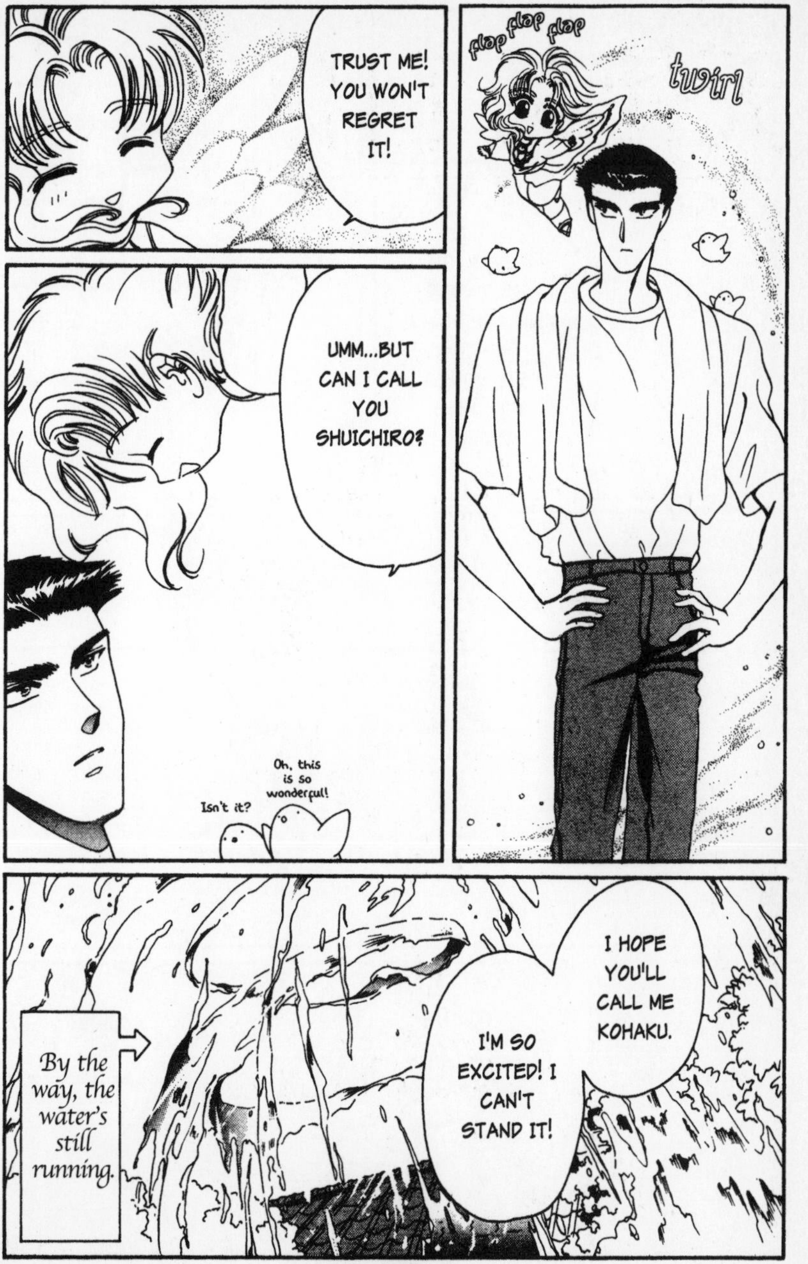
flap flap flap
twirl
TRUST ME! YOU WON'T REGRET IT!
UMM...BUT CAN I CALL YOU SHUICHIRO?
Oh, this is so wonderful!
Isn't it?
I HOPE YOU'LL CALL ME KOHAKU.
I'M SO EXCITED! I CAN'T STAND IT!
By the way, the water's still running.

END

Contact.2

天使の1日

AN ANGEL'S DAY

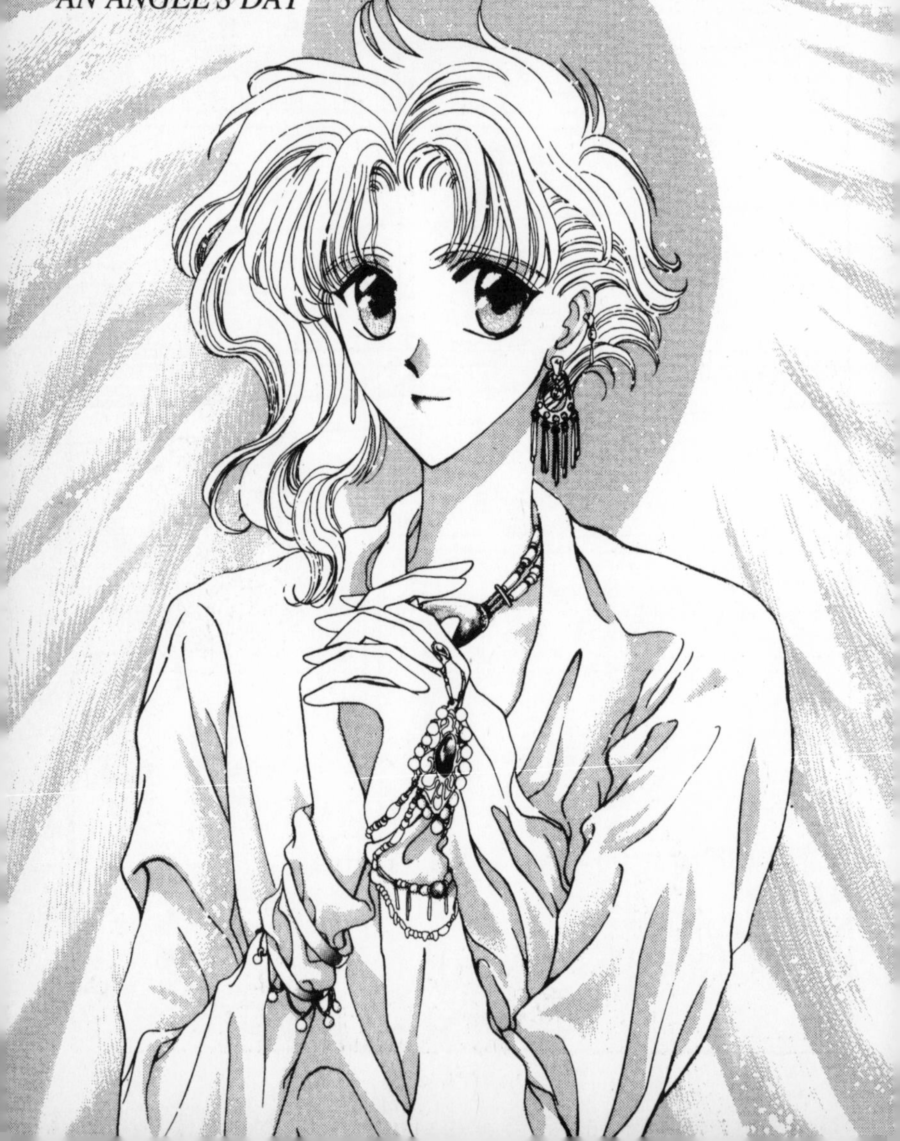

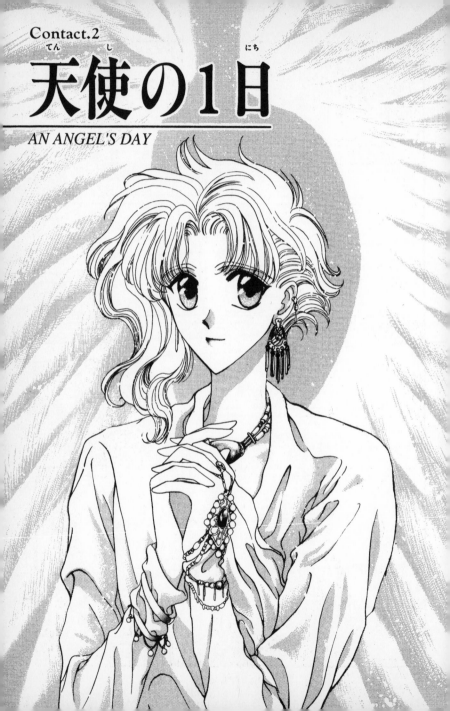

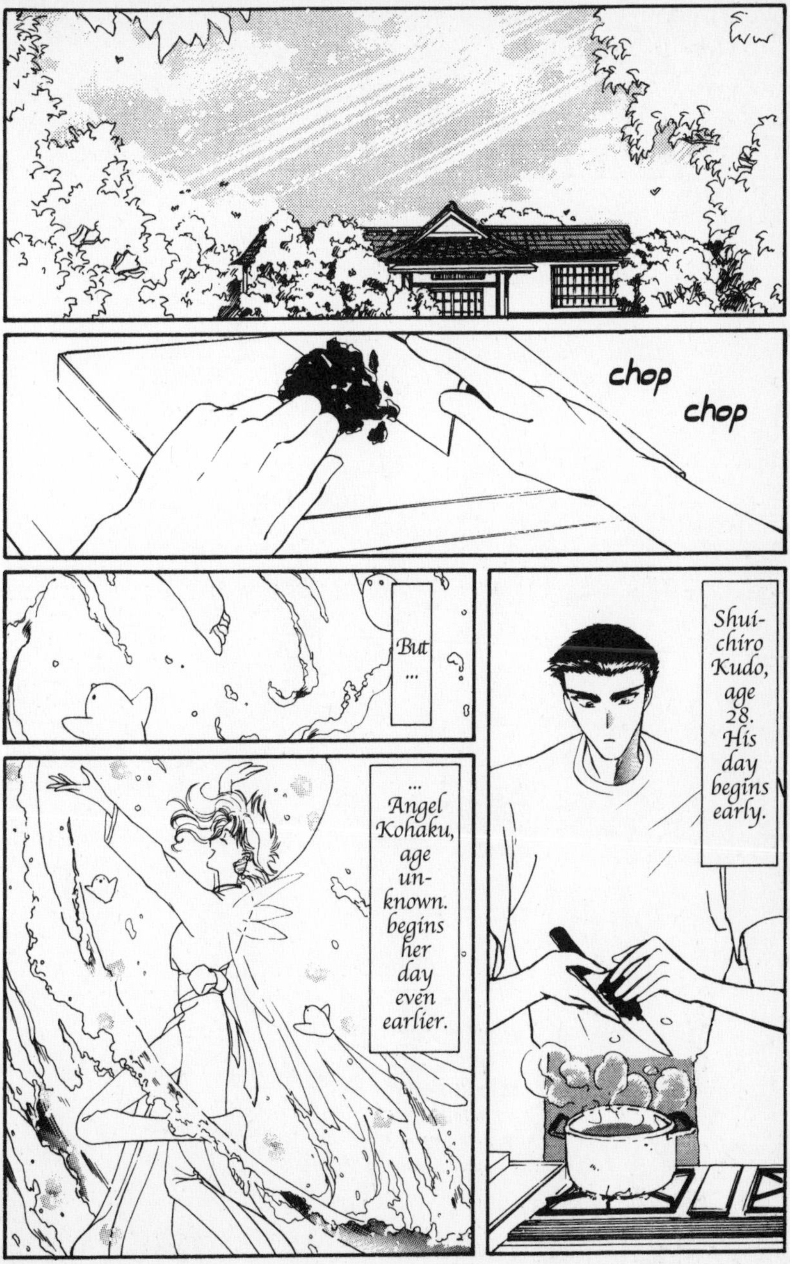
chop chop
Shuichiro Kudo, age 28. His day begins early.
But ...
... Angel Kohaku, age unknown. begins her day even earlier.

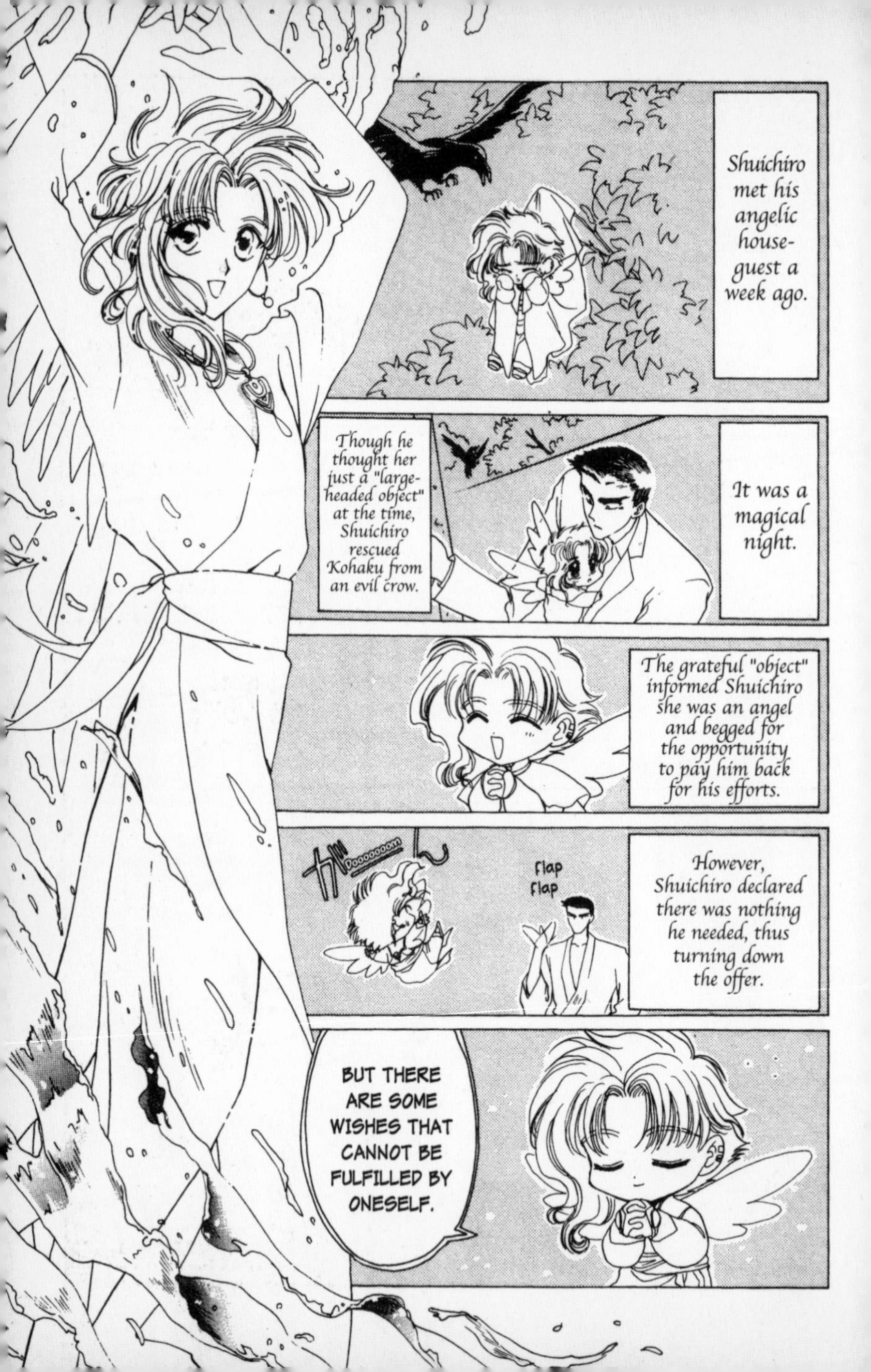
Shuichiro met his angelic house-guest a week ago.
It was a magical night.
Though he thought her just a "large-headed object" at the time, Shuichiro rescued Kohaku from an evil crow.
The grateful "object" informed Shuichiro she was an angel and begged for the opportunity to pay him back for his efforts.
However, Shuichiro declared there was nothing he needed, thus turning down the offer.
Flap flap
ガ
Doooooooom
BUT THERE ARE SOME WISHES THAT CANNOT BE FULFILLED BY ONESELF.

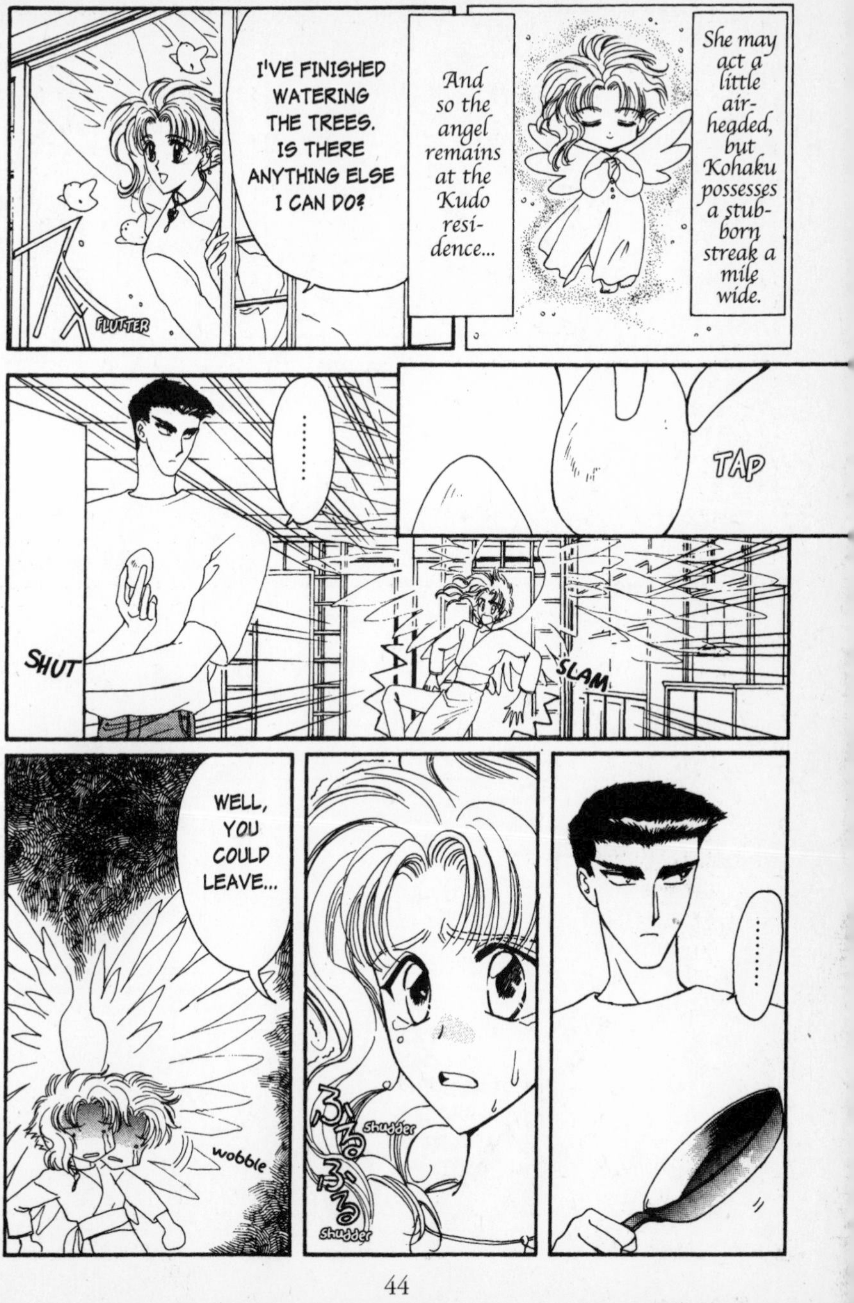
And so the angel remains at the Kudo residence...
She may act a little air-headed, but Kohaku possesses a stubborn streak a mile wide.
I'VE FINISHED WATERING THE TREES. IS THERE ANYTHING ELSE I CAN DO?
FLUTTER
TAP
SLAM
......
SHUT
......
Shudder
Shudder
WELL, YOU COULD LEAVE...
wobble

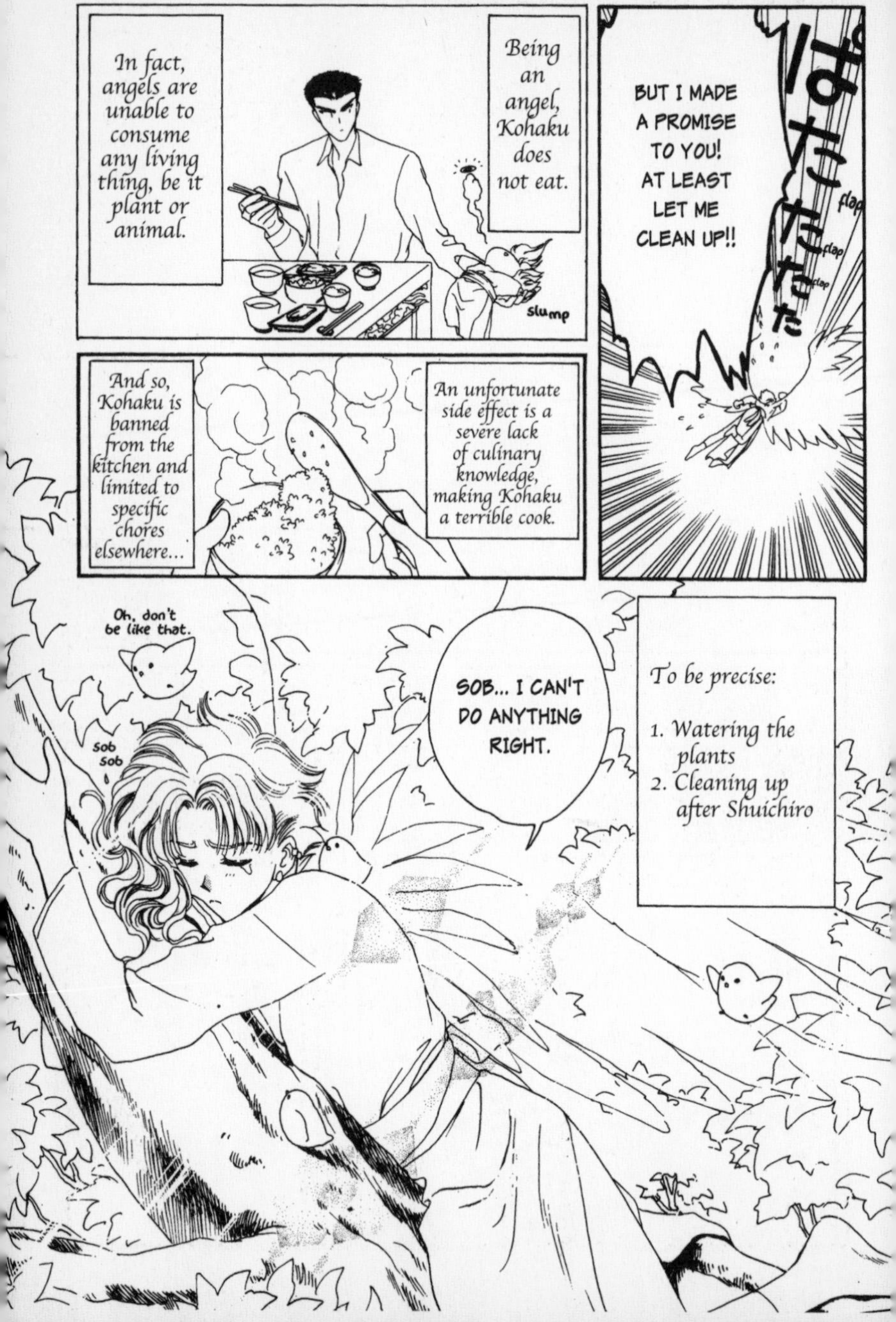
ぱたたたた
flap
flap
clap
BUT I MADE A PROMISE TO YOU! AT LEAST LET ME CLEAN UP!!
Being an angel, Kohaku does not eat.
In fact, angels are unable to consume any living thing, be it plant or animal.
slump
An unfortunate side effect is a severe lack of culinary knowledge, making Kohaku a terrible cook.
And so, Kohaku is banned from the kitchen and limited to specific chores elsewhere...
To be precise:
1. Watering the plants
2. Cleaning up after Shuichiro
SOB... I CAN'T DO ANYTHING RIGHT.
Oh, don't be like that.
Sob sob

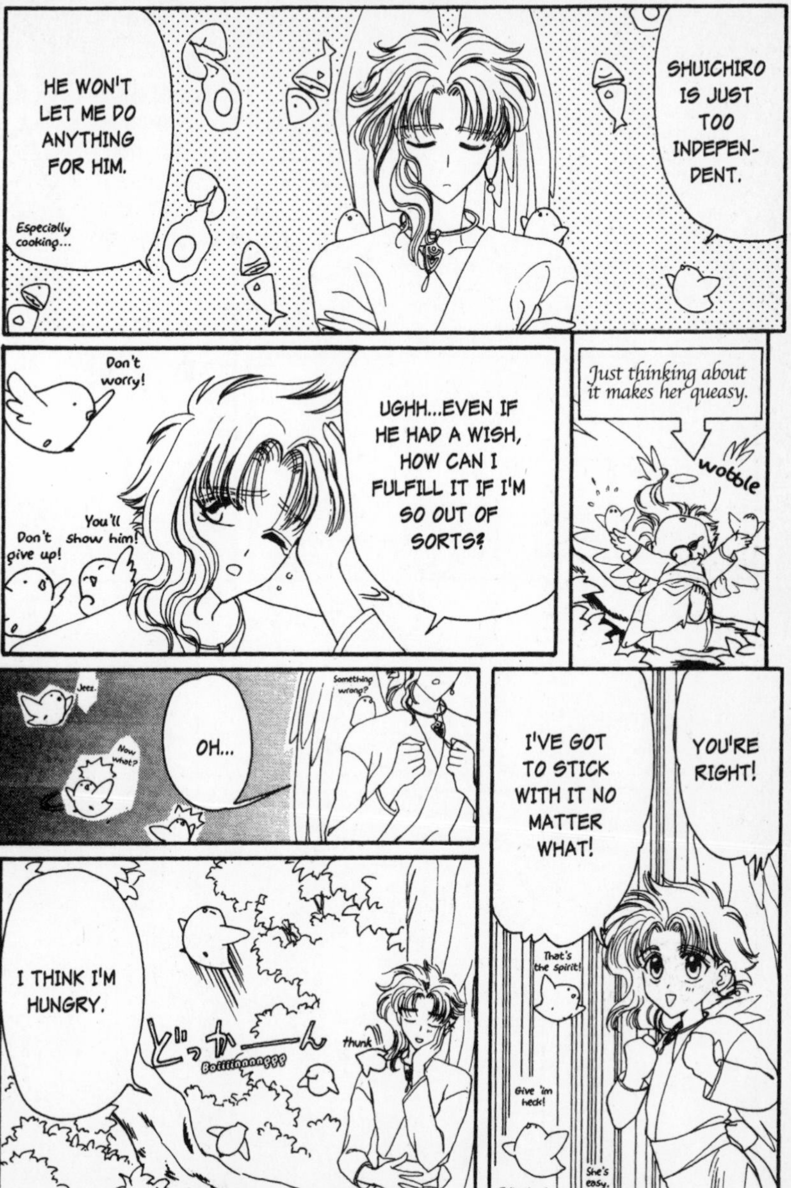
SHUICHIRO IS JUST TOO INDEPEN-DENT.
HE WON'T LET ME DO ANYTHING FOR HIM.
Especially cooking...
Just thinking about it makes her queasy.
wobble
UGHH...EVEN IF HE HAD A WISH, HOW CAN I FULFILL IT IF I'M SO OUT OF SORTS?
Don't worry!
You'll show him!
Don't give up!
YOU'RE RIGHT!
I'VE GOT TO STICK WITH IT NO MATTER WHAT!
That's the spirit!
Give 'im heck!
She's easy, isn't she?
Talk about a birdbrain.
Something wrong?
OH...
Jeez.
Now what?
I THINK I'M HUNGRY.
どっかーーん
Boiiiinnnnggg
thunk

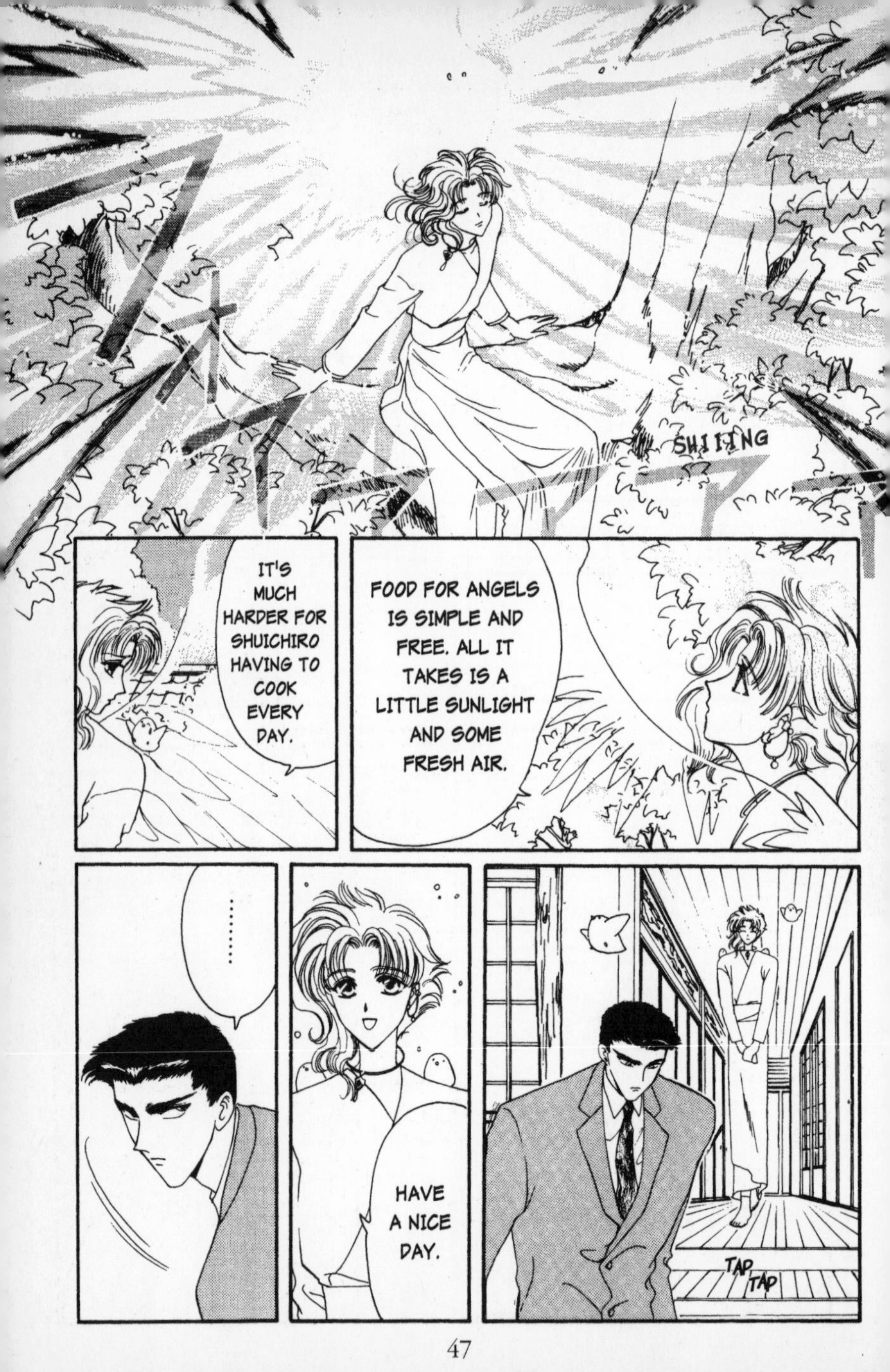
SHIIING
FOOD FOR ANGELS IS SIMPLE AND FREE. ALL IT TAKES IS A LITTLE SUNLIGHT AND SOME FRESH AIR.
IT'S MUCH HARDER FOR SHUICHIRO HAVING TO COOK EVERY DAY.
TAP TAP
HAVE A NICE DAY.
....

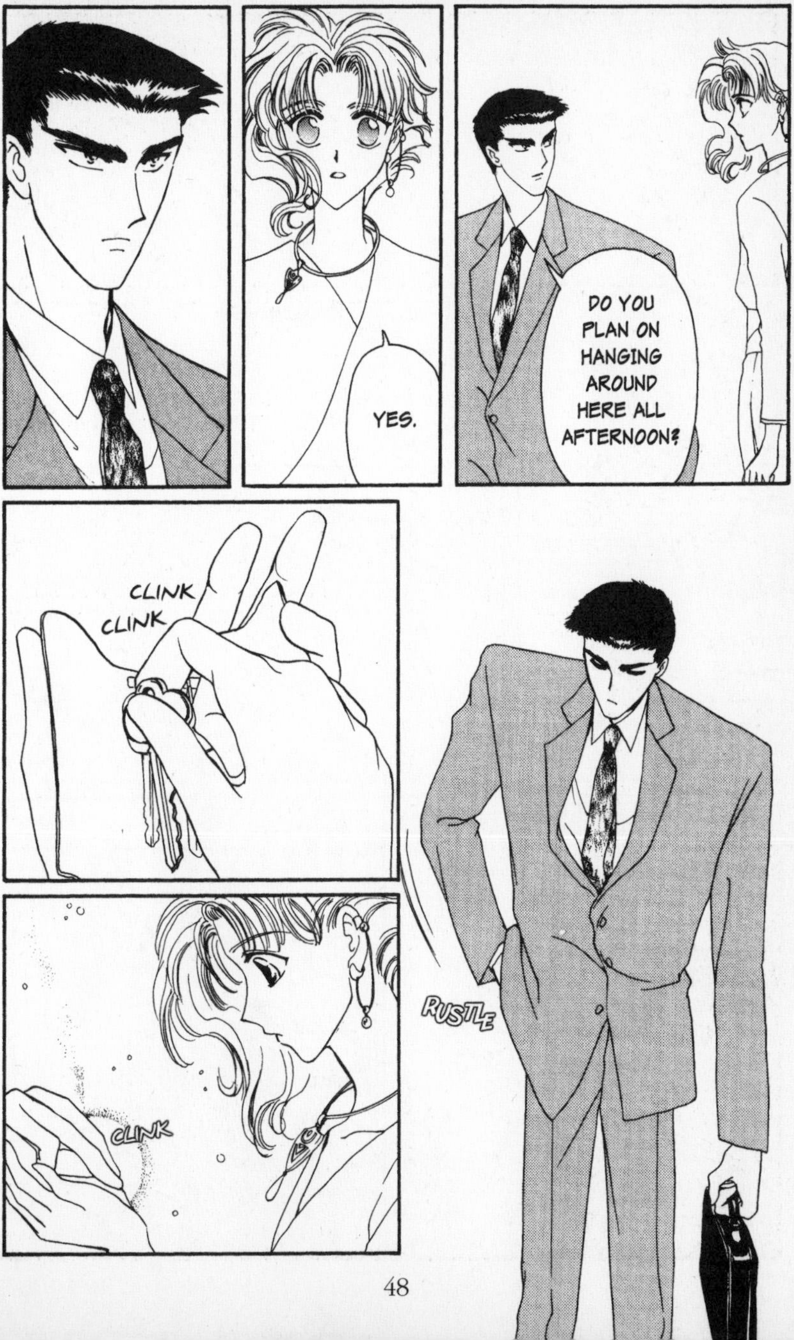
DO YOU PLAN ON HANGING AROUND HERE ALL AFTERNOON?
YES.
RUSTLE
CLINK CLINK
CLINK

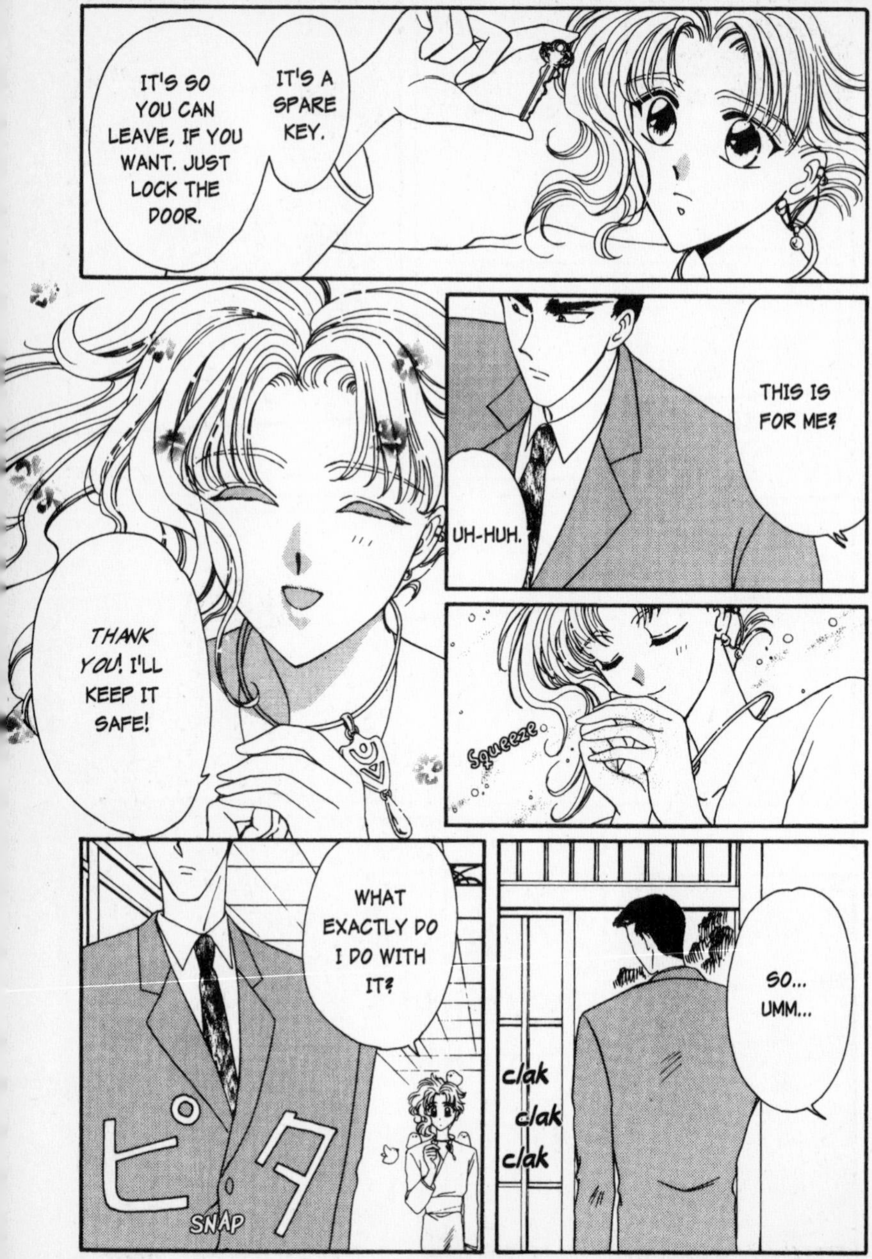
IT'S A SPARE KEY.
IT'S SO YOU CAN LEAVE, IF YOU WANT. JUST LOCK THE DOOR.
THIS IS FOR ME?
UH-HUH.
Squeeze
THANK YOU! I'LL KEEP IT SAFE!
SO... UMM...
clak clak clak
WHAT EXACTLY DO I DO WITH IT?
ピタ
SNAP

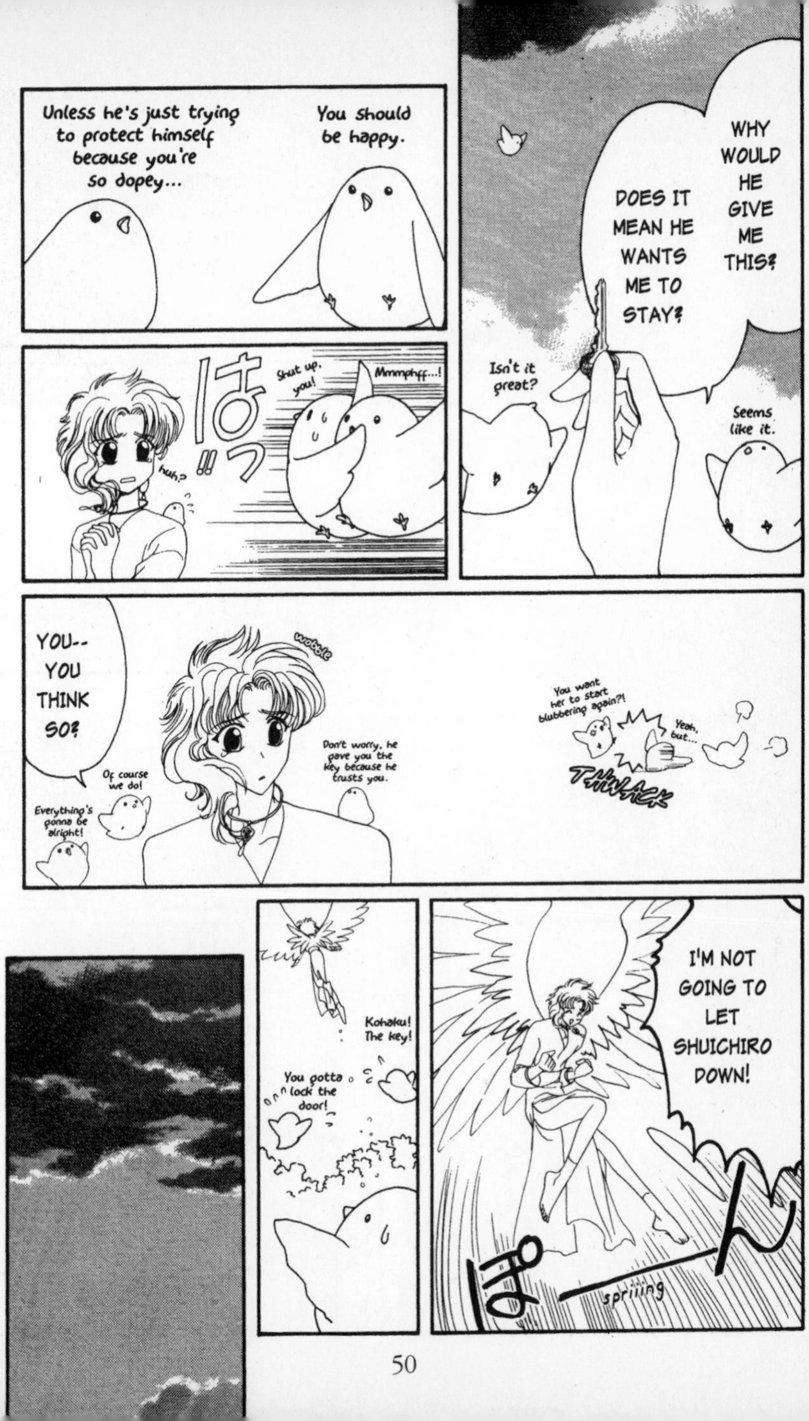
WHY WOULD HE GIVE ME THIS?
DOES IT MEAN HE WANTS ME TO STAY?
Isn't it great?
Seems like it.
You should be happy.
Unless he's just trying to protect himself because you're so dopey...
はっ!!
Mmmphff...!
Shut up, you!
huh?
You want her to start blubbering again?!
Yeah, but...
THWACK
Don't worry, he gave you the key because he trusts you.
wobble
YOU-- YOU THINK SO?
Of course we do!
Everything's gonna be alright!
I'M NOT GOING TO LET SHUICHIRO DOWN!
ぽーん
spriiing
Kohaku! The key!
You gotta lock the door!

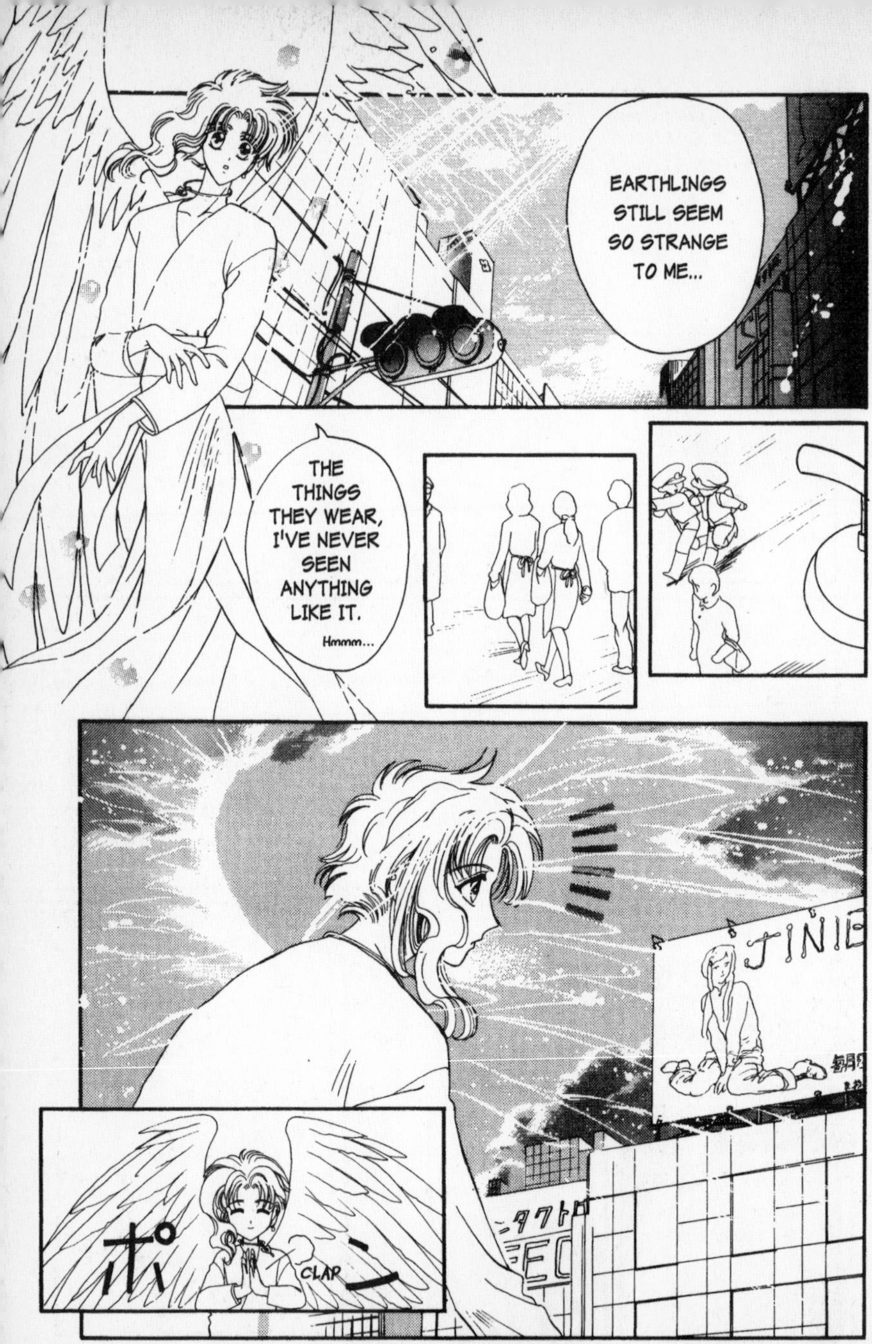
EARTHLINGS STILL SEEM SO STRANGE TO ME...
THE THINGS THEY WEAR, I'VE NEVER SEEN ANYTHING LIKE IT.
Hmmm...
ポ
CLAP

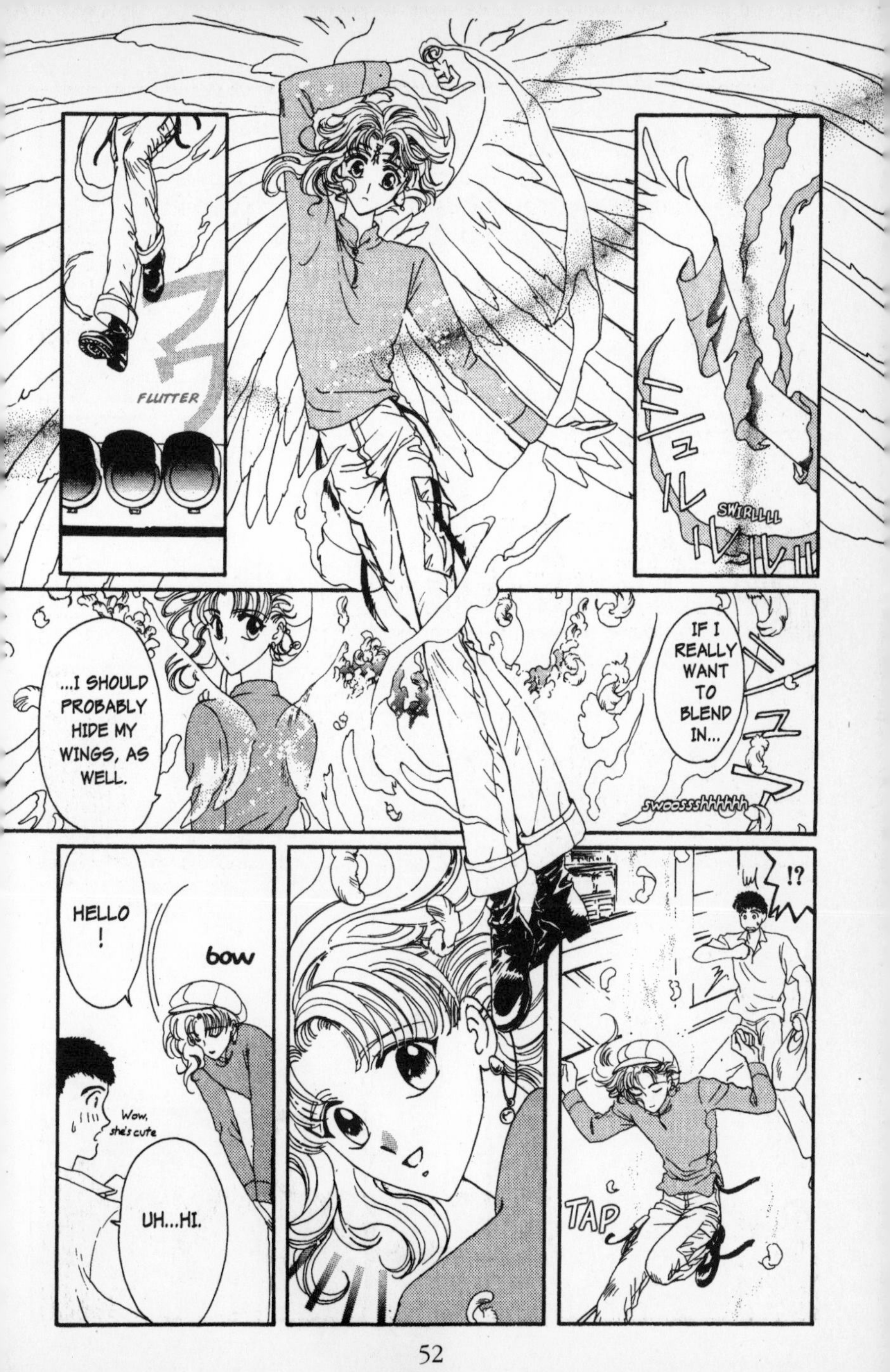
SWIRLLLL
FLUTTER
IF I REALLY WANT TO BLEND IN...
swoossshhhhhh
...I SHOULD PROBABLY HIDE MY WINGS, AS WELL.
!?
TAP
HELLO!
bow
Wow, she's cute
UH...HI.

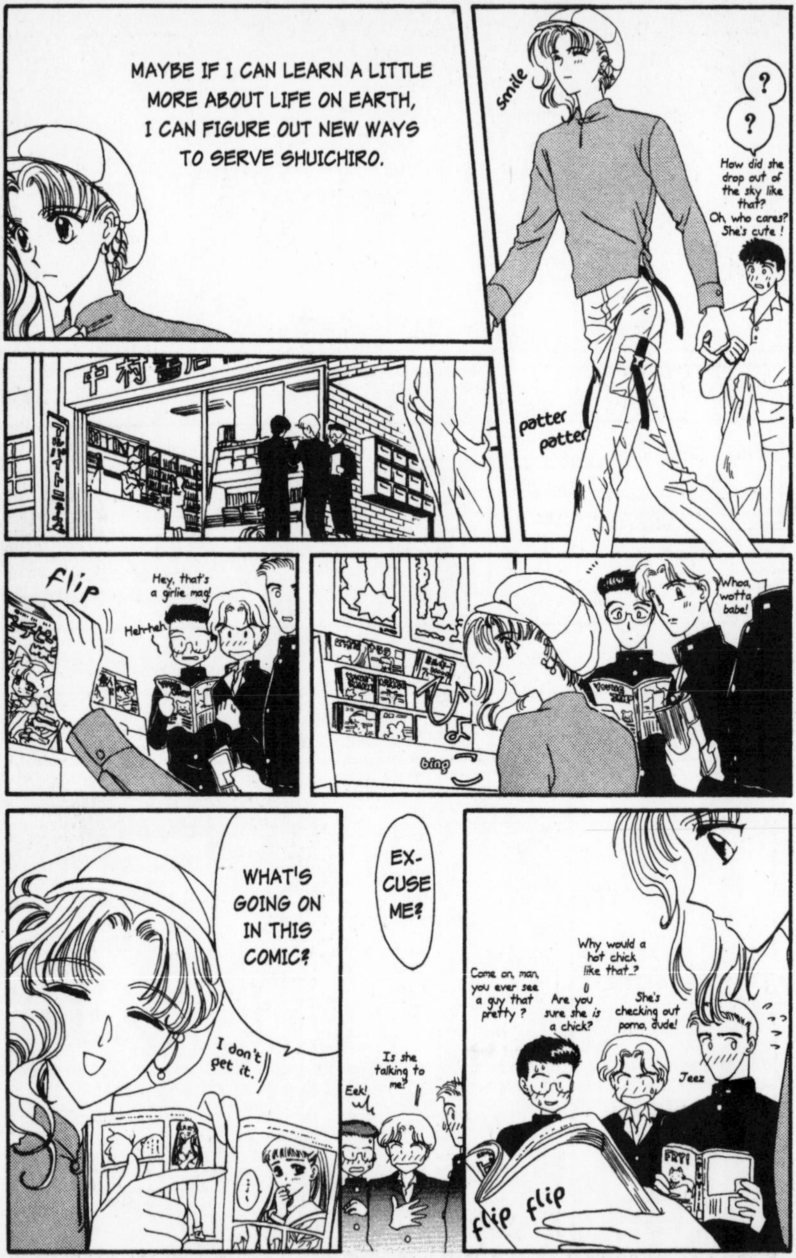
Smile
?
?
How did she drop out of the sky like that? Oh, who cares? She's cute!
patter patter
MAYBE IF I CAN LEARN A LITTLE MORE ABOUT LIFE ON EARTH, I CAN FIGURE OUT NEW WAYS TO SERVE SHUICHIRO.
Whoa, wotta babe!
bing
flip
Hey, that's a girlie mag!
Heh-heh
Why would a hot chick like that..?
She's checking out porno, dude!
Are you sure she is a chick?
Come on, man, you ever see a guy that pretty?
Jeez
flip flip
EX-CUSE ME?
Is she talking to me?
Eek!
WHAT'S GOING ON IN THIS COMIC?
I don't get it.

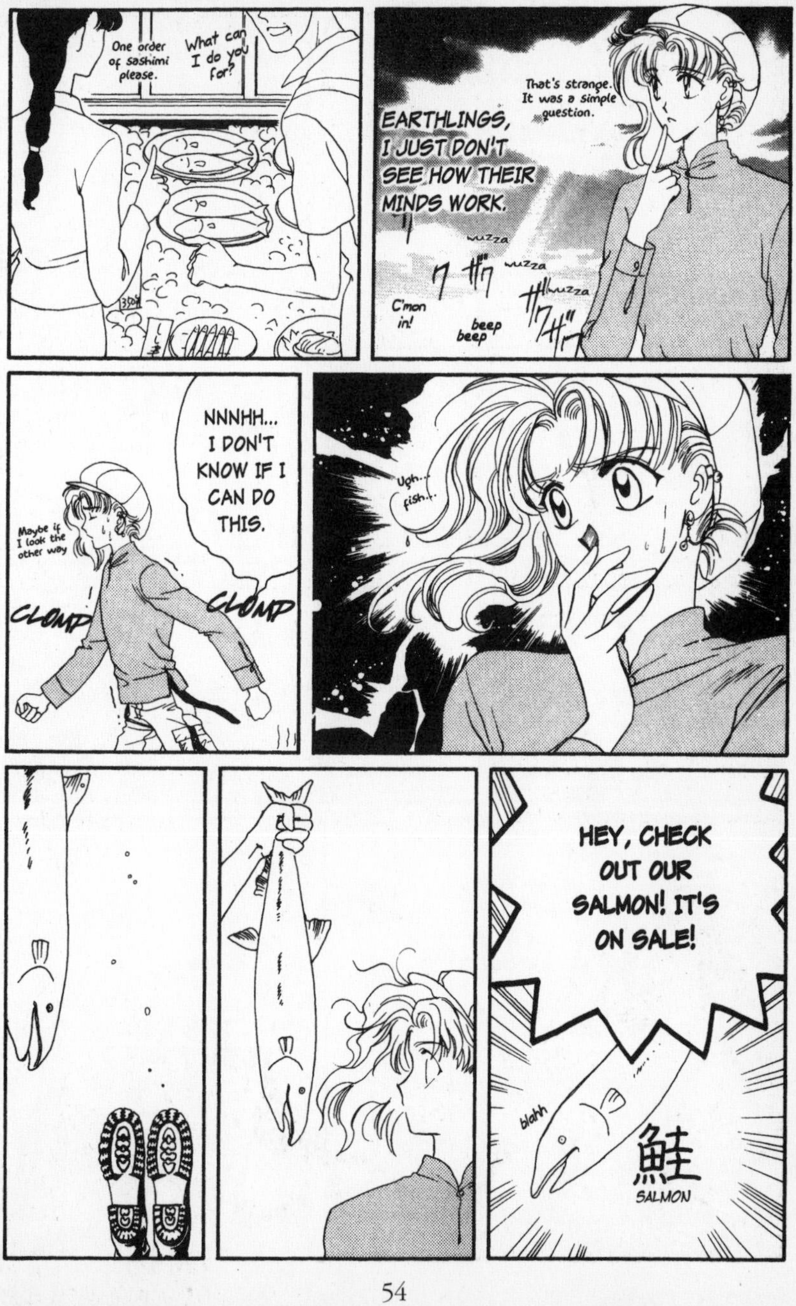
That's strange. It was a simple question.
EARTHLINGS, I JUST DON'T SEE HOW THEIR MINDS WORK.
wuzza
wuzza
wuzza
beep beep
C'mon in!
What can I do you for?
One order of sashimi please.
Ugh... fish...
NNNHH... I DON'T KNOW IF I CAN DO THIS.
Maybe if I look the other way
CLOMP
CLOMP
HEY, CHECK OUT OUR SALMON! IT'S ON SALE!
blahh
鮭
SALMON

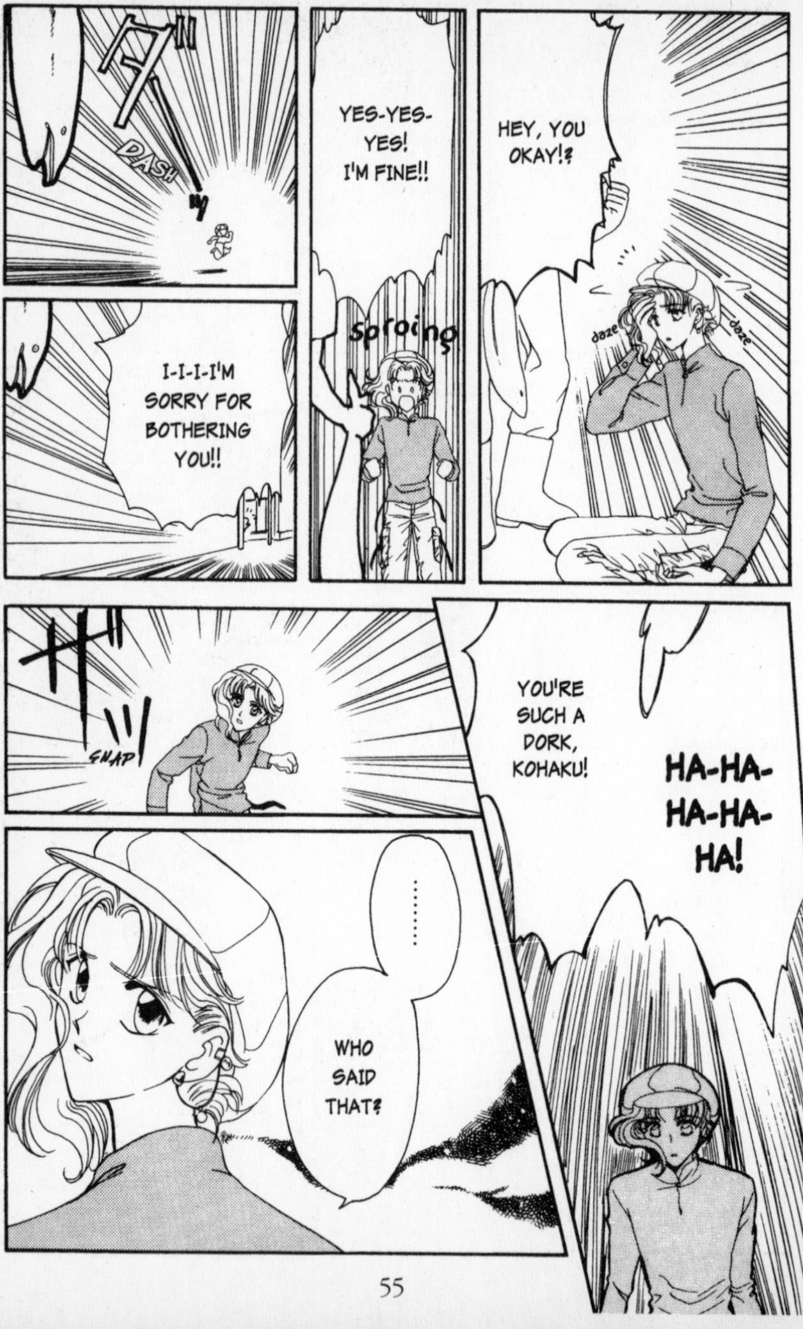
HEY, YOU OKAY!?
daze
daze
YES-YES-YES! I'M FINE!!
Sproing
DASH
I-I-I-I'M SORRY FOR BOTHERING YOU!!
YOU'RE SUCH A DORK, KOHAKU!
HA-HA-HA-HA-HA!
SNAP
......
WHO SAID THAT?

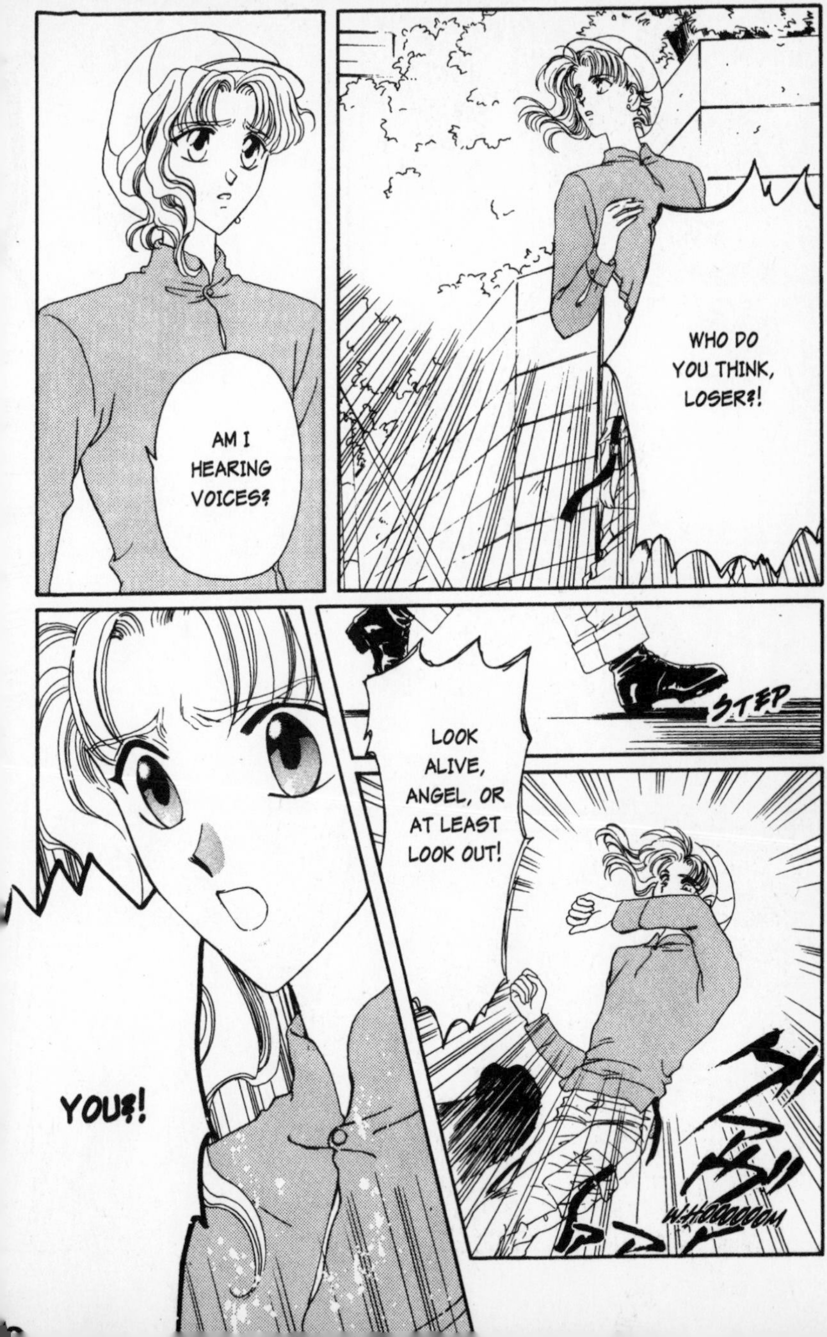
AM I HEARING VOICES?
WHO DO YOU THINK, LOSER?!
YOU?!
STEP
LOOK ALIVE, ANGEL, OR AT LEAST LOOK OUT!
WHOOOOOOM

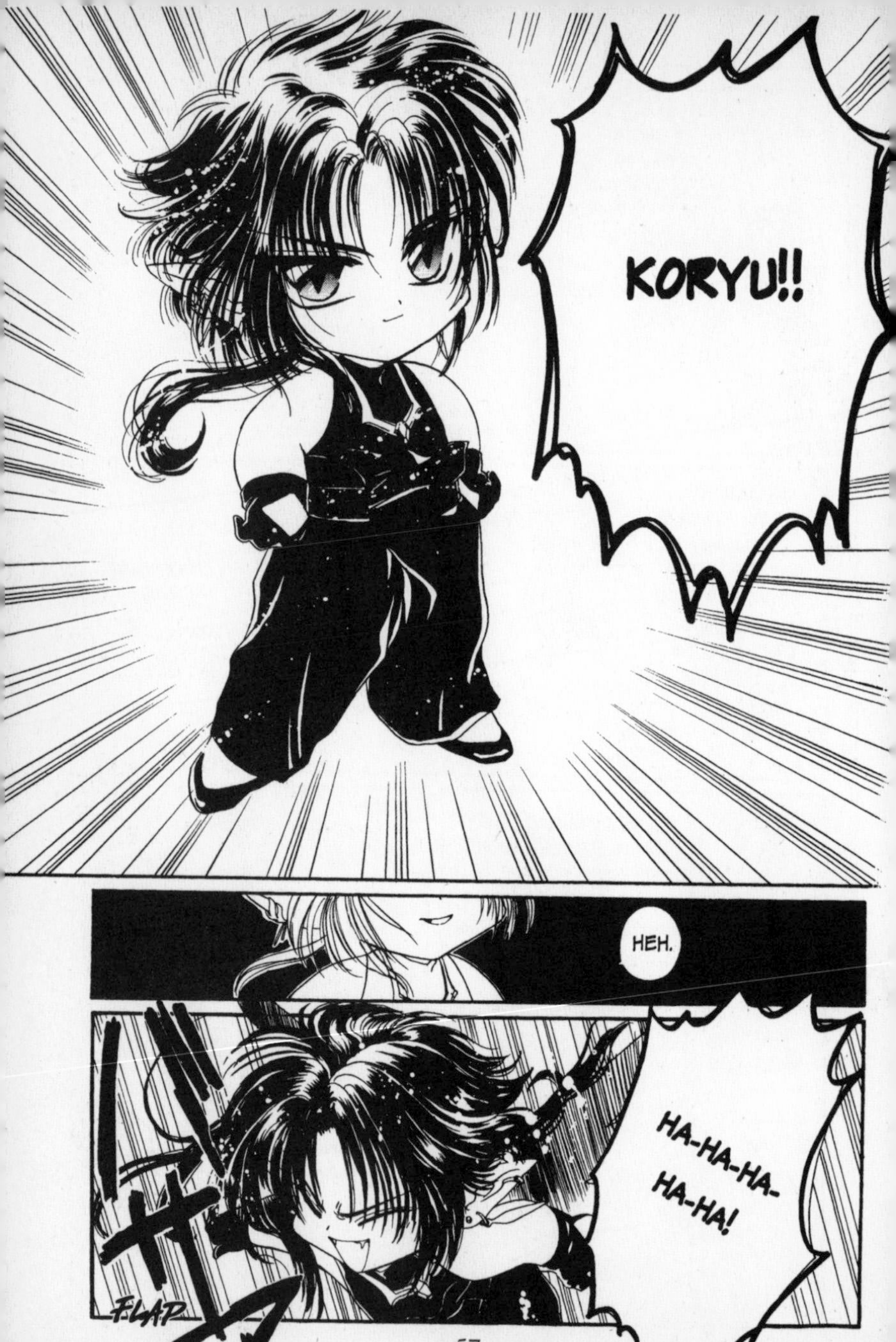
KORYU!!
HEH.
HA-HA-HA-HA-HA-HA!
FLAP

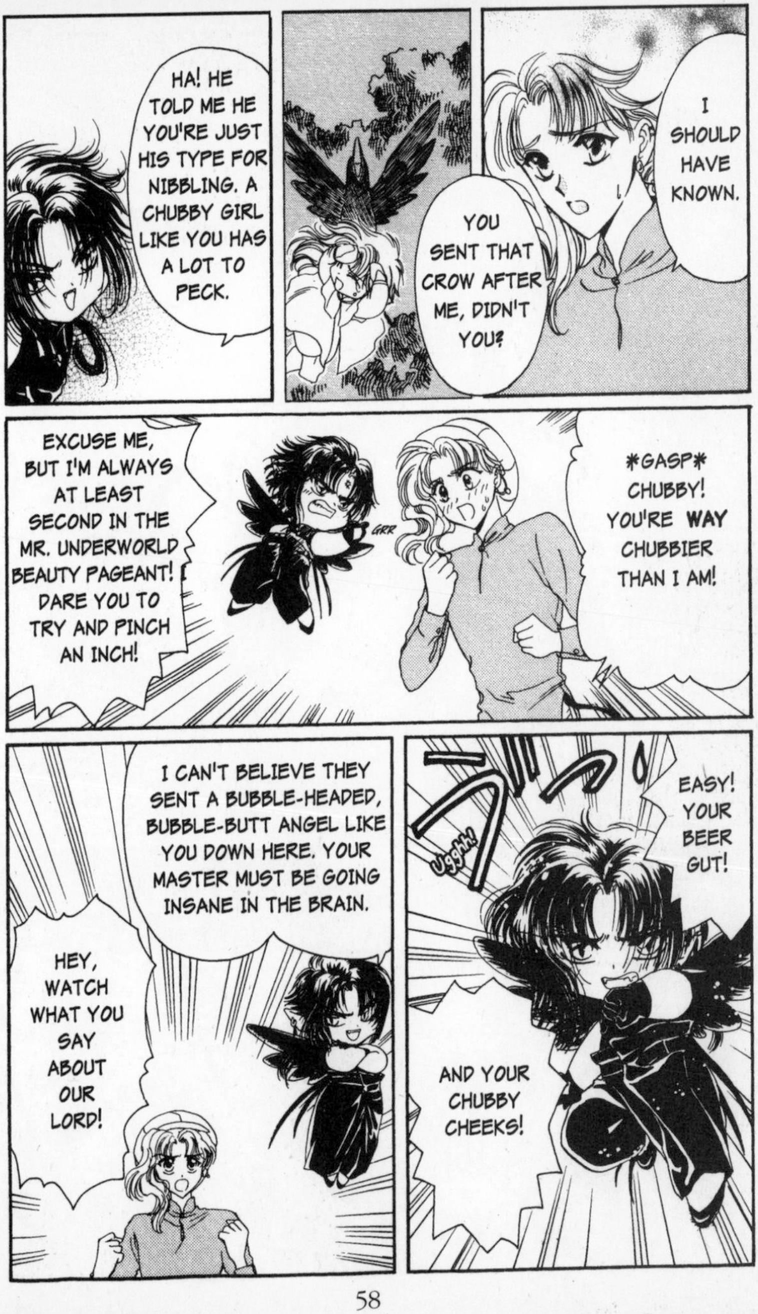
I SHOULD HAVE KNOWN.
YOU SENT THAT CROW AFTER ME, DIDN'T YOU?
HA! HE TOLD ME HE YOU'RE JUST HIS TYPE FOR NIBBLING. A CHUBBY GIRL LIKE YOU HAS A LOT TO PECK.
GASP CHUBBY! YOU'RE WAY CHUBBIER THAN I AM!
GRR
EXCUSE ME, BUT I'M ALWAYS AT LEAST SECOND IN THE MR. UNDERWORLD BEAUTY PAGEANT! DARE YOU TO TRY AND PINCH AN INCH!
EASY! YOUR BEER GUT!
UGGHH!
AND YOUR CHUBBY CHEEKS!
I CAN'T BELIEVE THEY SENT A BUBBLE-HEADED, BUBBLE-BUTT ANGEL LIKE YOU DOWN HERE. YOUR MASTER MUST BE GOING INSANE IN THE BRAIN.
HEY, WATCH WHAT YOU SAY ABOUT OUR LORD!

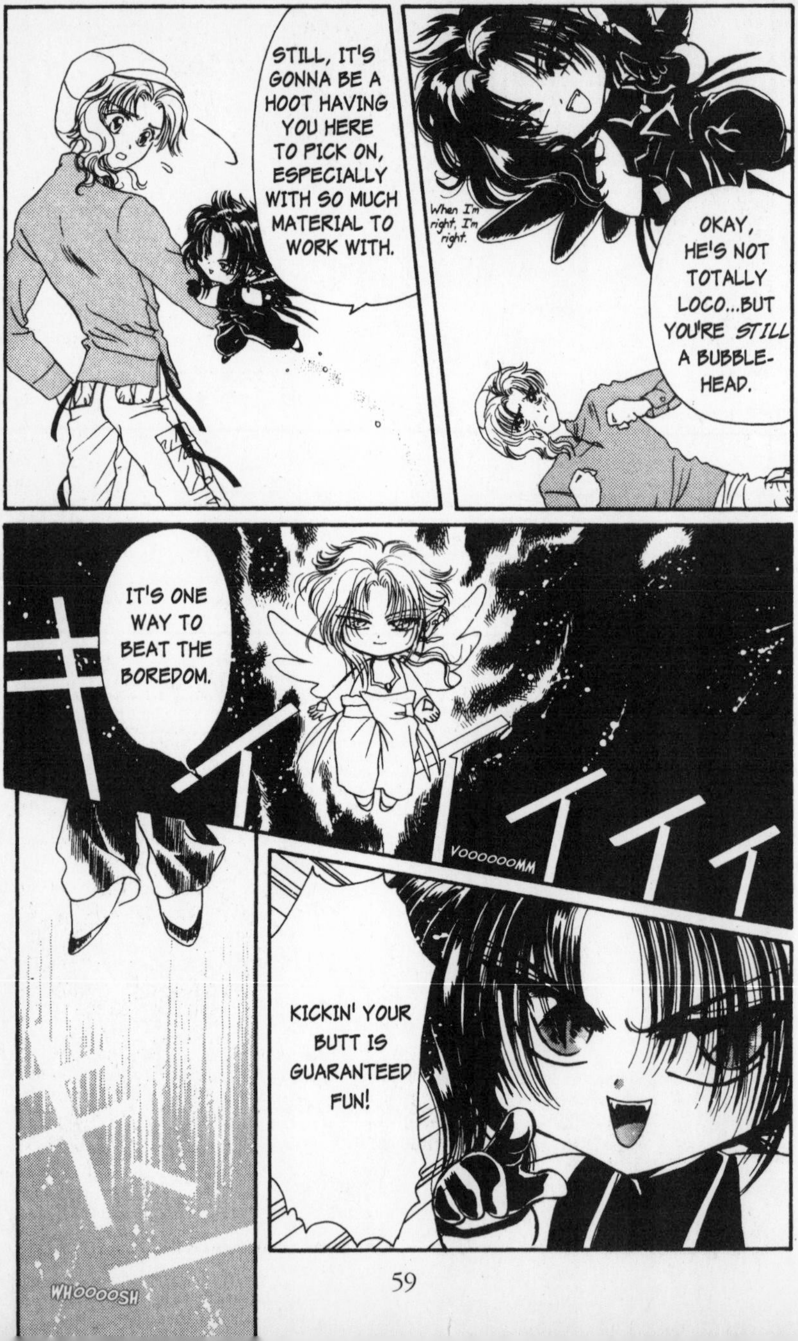
When I'm right, I'm right.
OKAY, HE'S NOT TOTALLY LOCO...BUT YOU'RE *STILL* A BUBBLE-HEAD.
STILL, IT'S GONNA BE A HOOT HAVING YOU HERE TO PICK ON, ESPECIALLY WITH SO MUCH MATERIAL TO WORK WITH.
IT'S ONE WAY TO BEAT THE BOREDOM.
VOOOOOOMM
KICKIN' YOUR BUTT IS GUARANTEED FUN!
WHOOOOSH

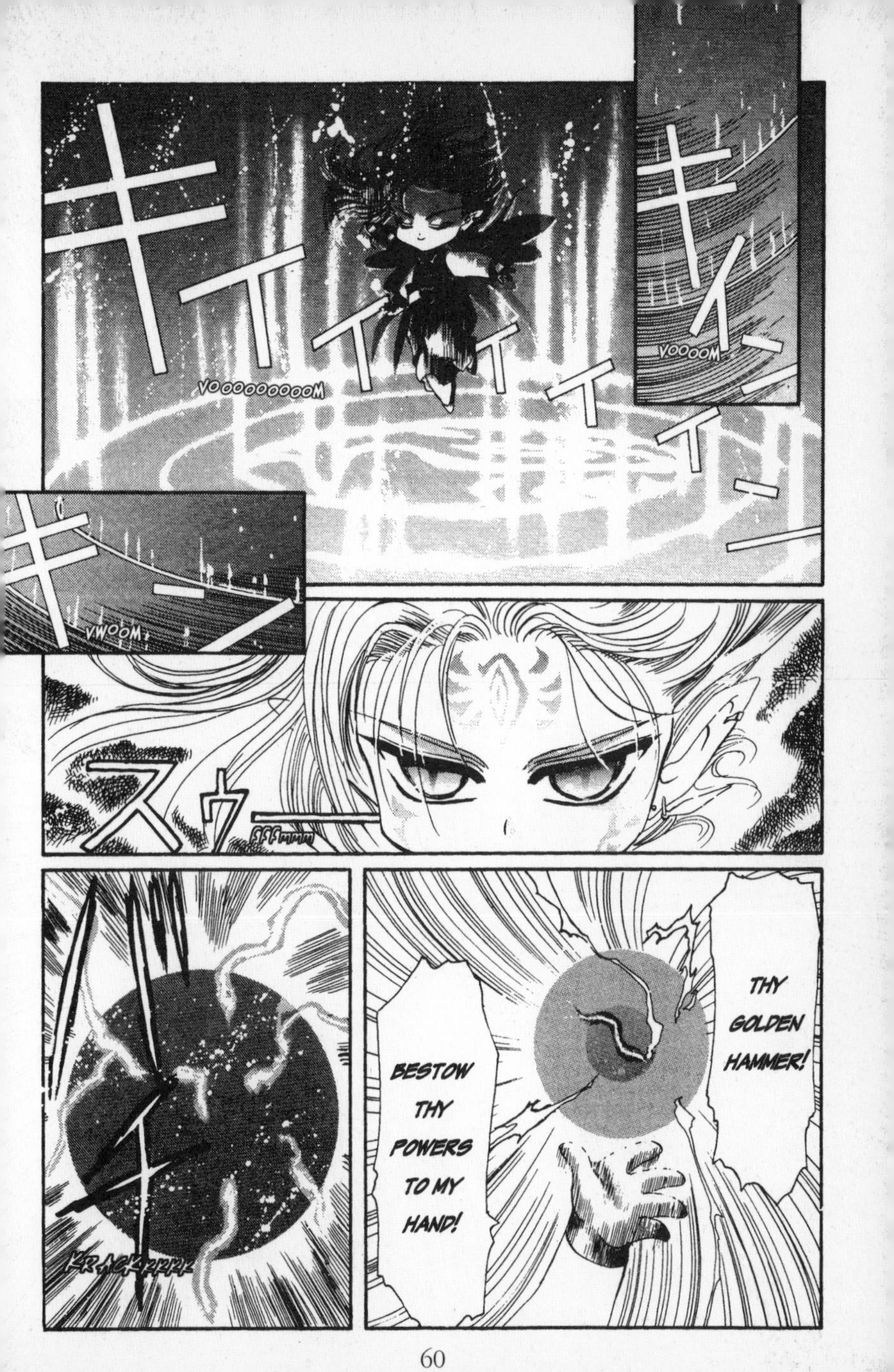
VOOOM
VOOOOOOOOOM
VWOOM
FFFmmm
THY GOLDEN HAMMER!
BESTOW THY POWERS TO MY HAND!
KRACKRRRK

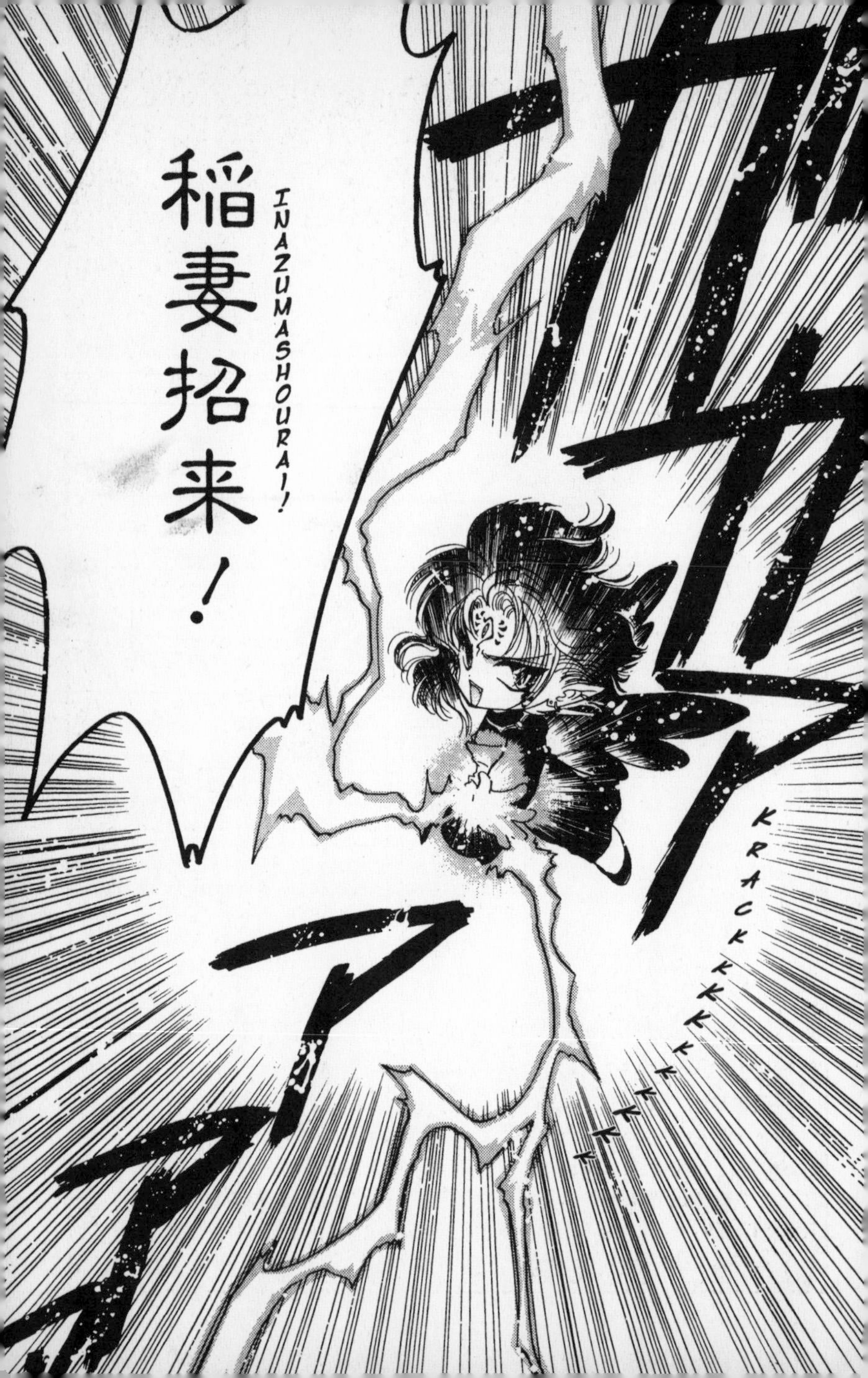
稲妻招来!
INAZUMASHOURAI!
KRACKKKKKKKKKK

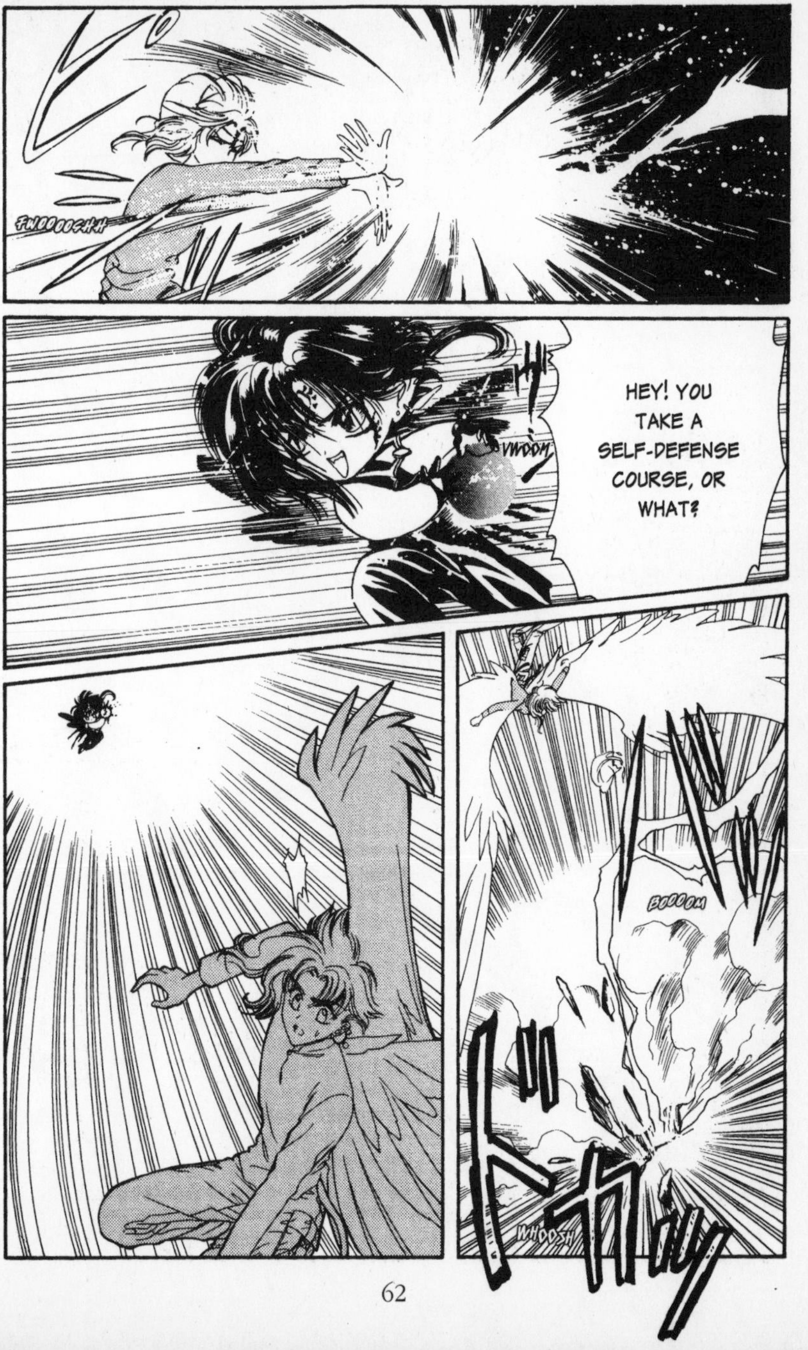
FWOOOOSHH
VWOOM
HEY! YOU TAKE A SELF-DEFENSE COURSE, OR WHAT?
BOOOOM
ドカッ
WHOOSH

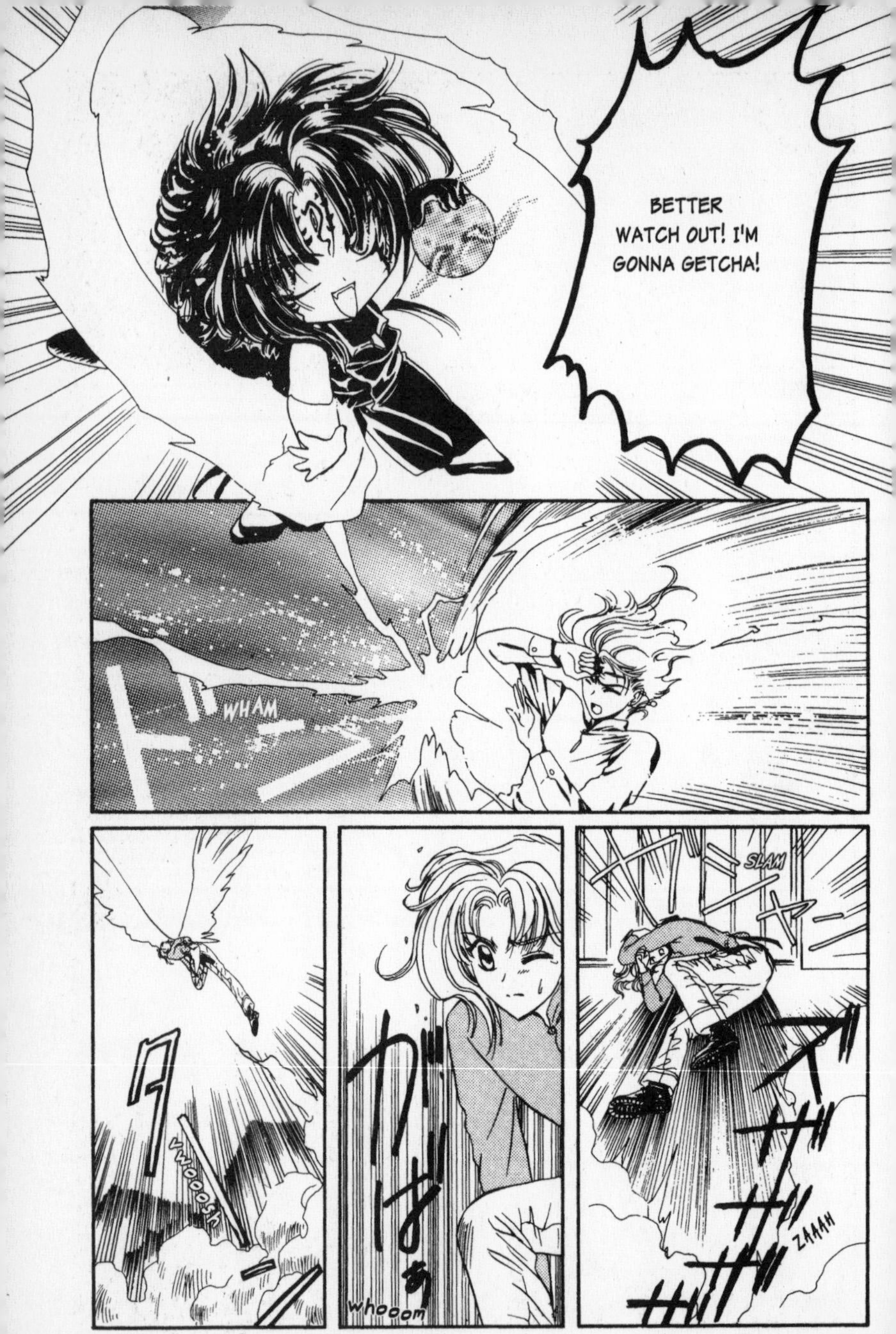
BETTER WATCH OUT! I'M GONNA GETCHA!
WHAM
SLAM
ZAAAH
whooom
VWOOOSH

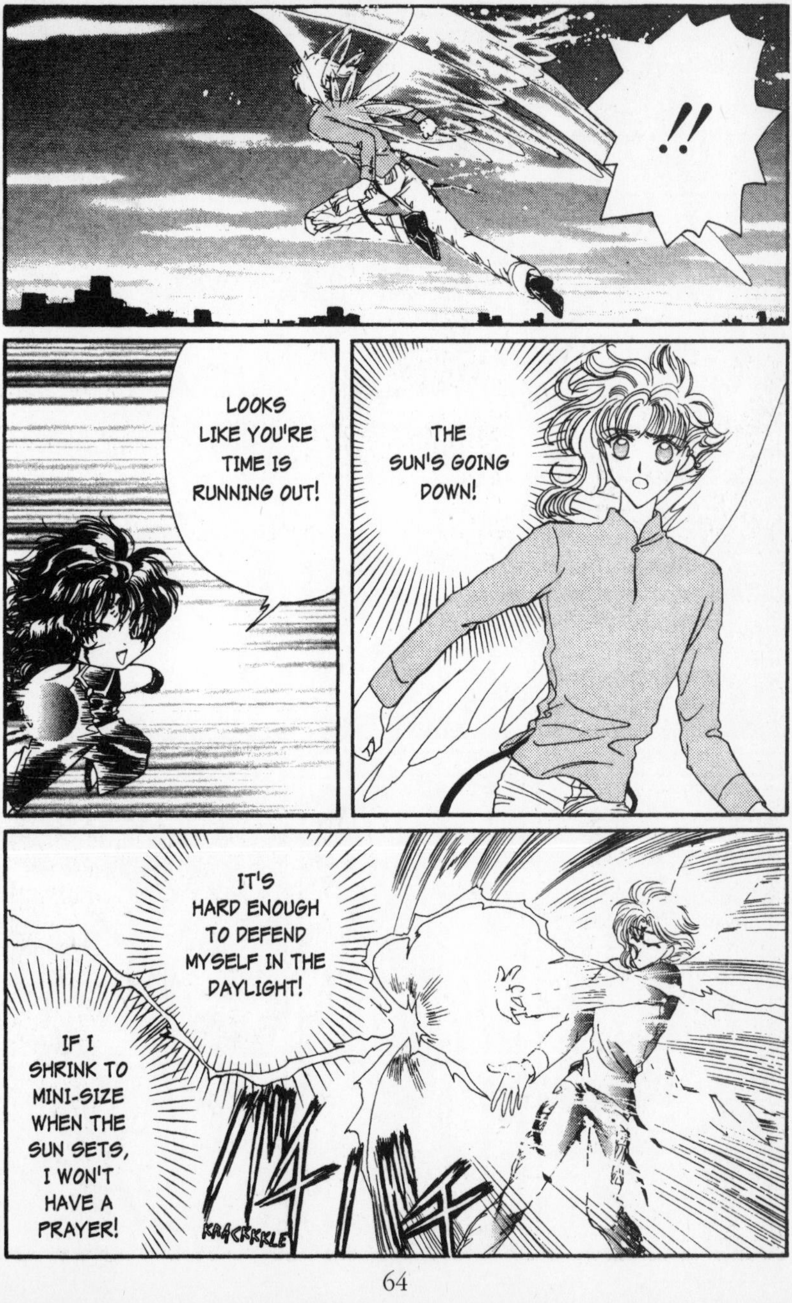
!!
THE SUN'S GOING DOWN!
LOOKS LIKE YOU'RE TIME IS RUNNING OUT!
IT'S HARD ENOUGH TO DEFEND MYSELF IN THE DAYLIGHT!
IF I SHRINK TO MINI-SIZE WHEN THE SUN SETS, I WON'T HAVE A PRAYER!
KRACKKKLE

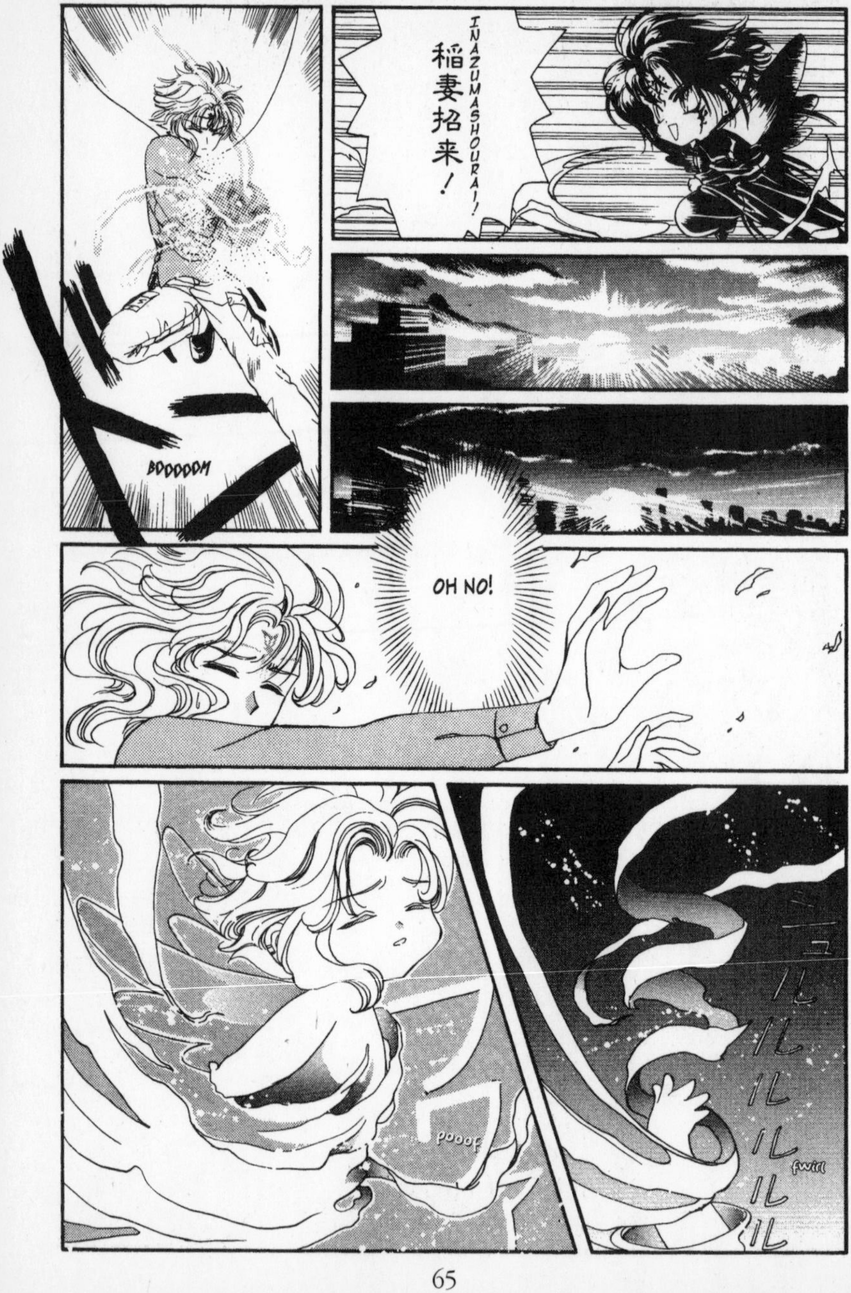
稲妻招来!
INAZUMASHOURAI!
BOOOOOM
OH NO!
シュルルルルル
fwirl
pooof

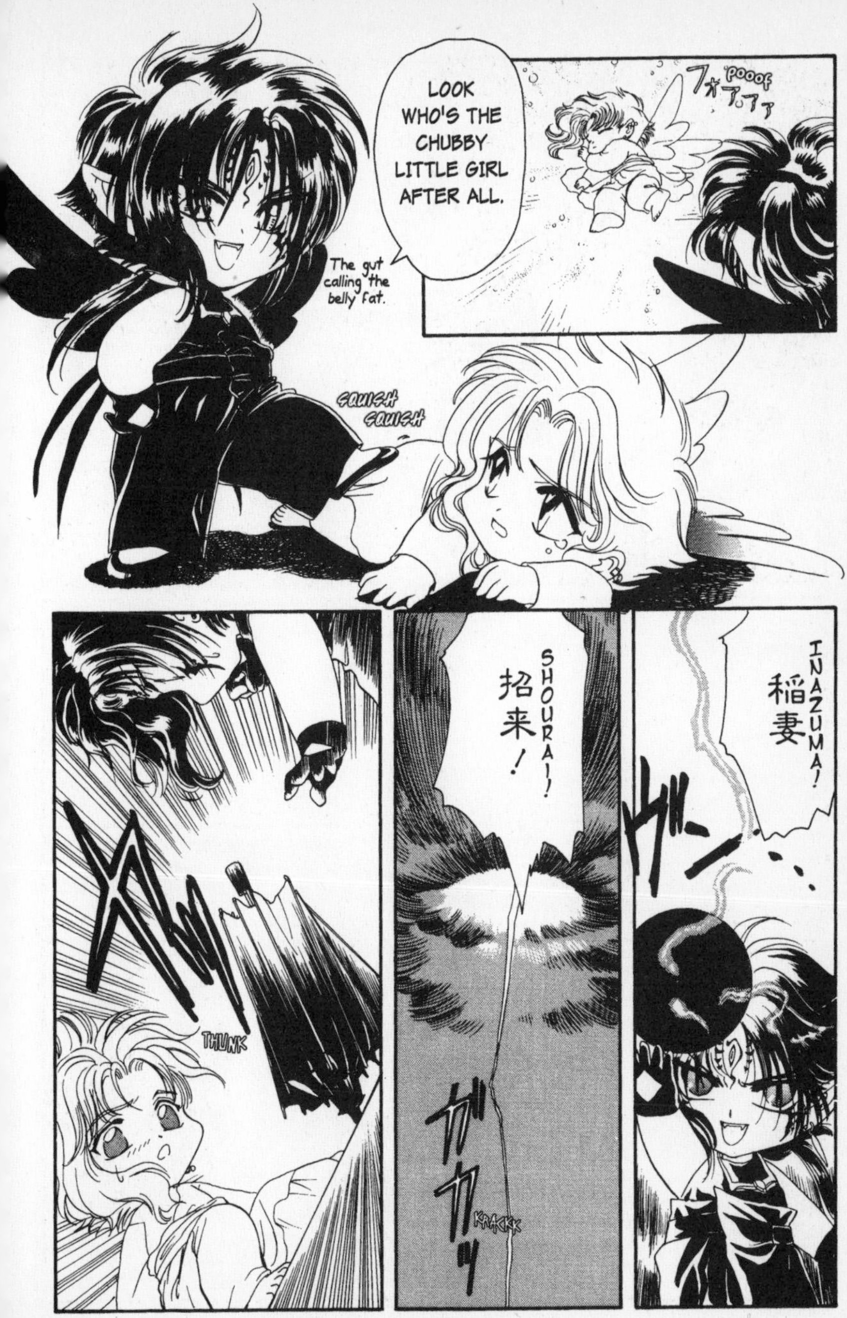
フォアァァ
pooof
LOOK WHO'S THE CHUBBY LITTLE GIRL AFTER ALL.
The gut calling the belly fat.
SQUISH SQUISH
稲妻!
INAZUMA!
招来!
SHOURAI!
KRACKK
THUNK

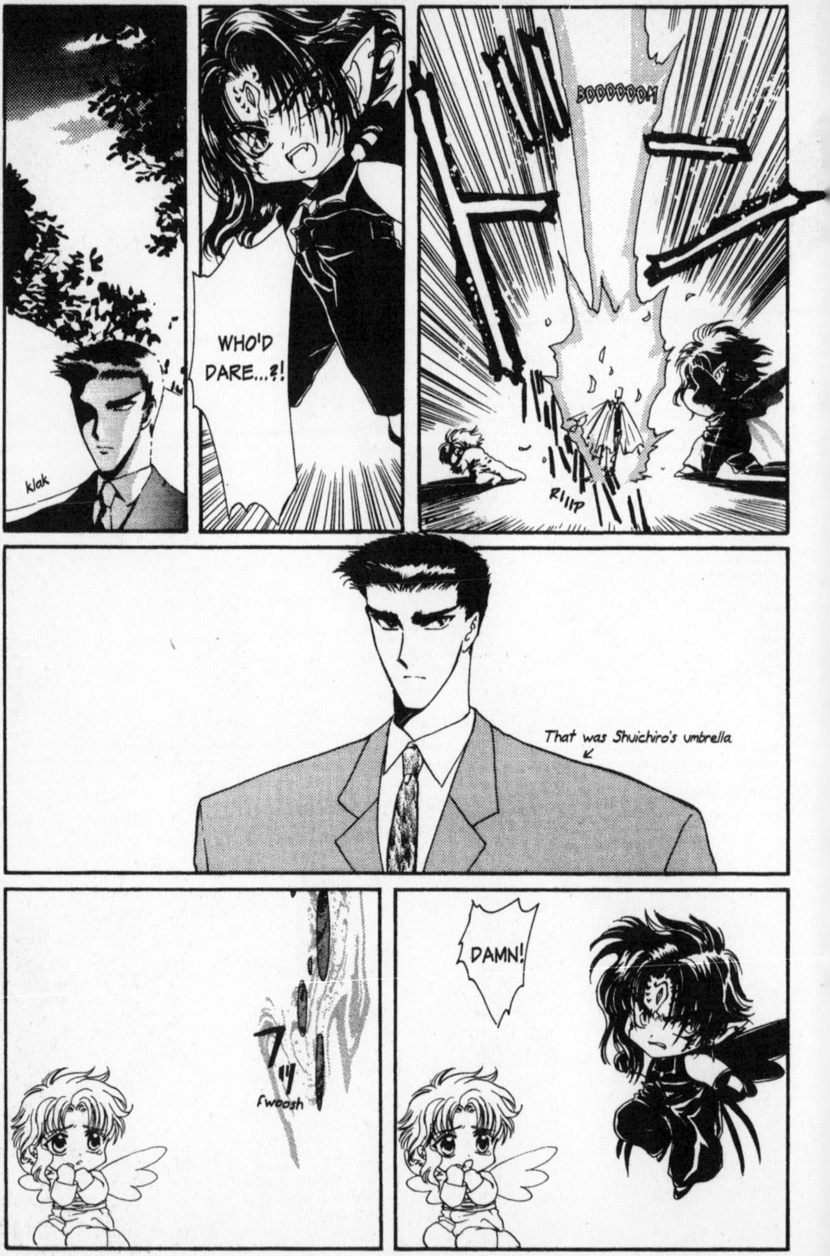
BOOOOOOM
RIIIP
WHO'D DARE...?!
klak
That was Shuichiro's umbrella
DAMN!
fwoosh

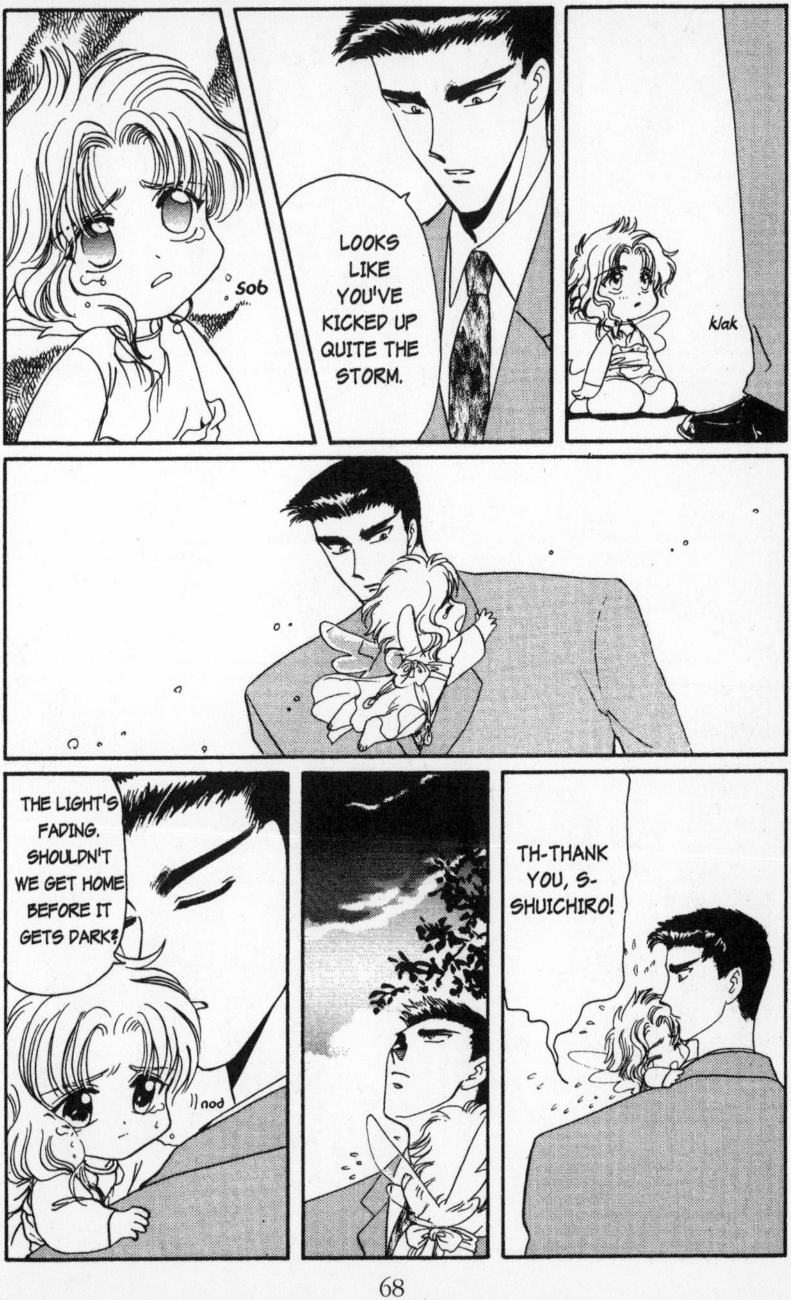
klak
LOOKS LIKE YOU'VE KICKED UP QUITE THE STORM.
sob
TH-THANK YOU, S-SHUICHIRO!
THE LIGHT'S FADING. SHOULDN'T WE GET HOME BEFORE IT GETS DARK?
nod

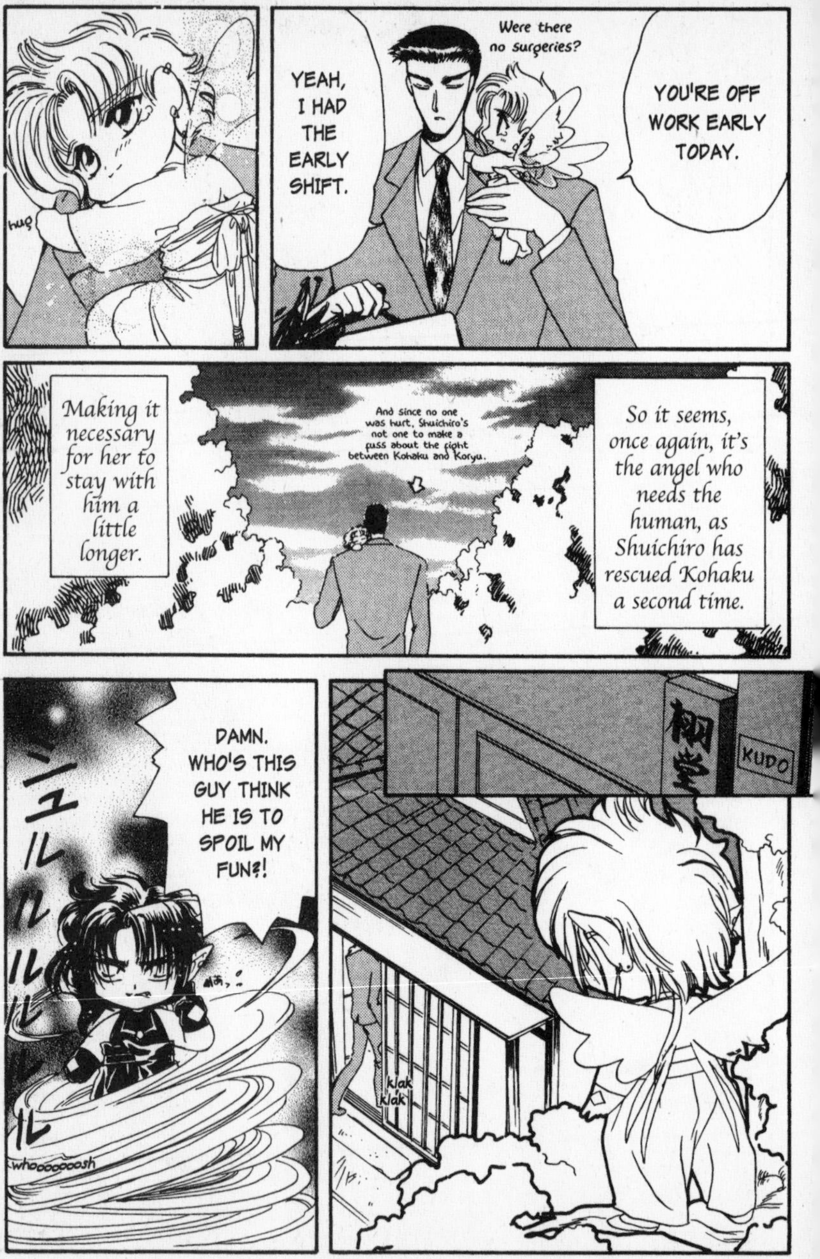
YOU'RE OFF WORK EARLY TODAY.
Were there no surgeries?
YEAH, I HAD THE EARLY SHIFT.
hug
So it seems, once again, it's the angel who needs the human, as Shuichiro has rescued Kohaku a second time.
And since no one was hurt, Shuichiro's not one to make a fuss about the fight between Kohaku and Koryu.
Making it necessary for her to stay with him a little longer.
KUDO
klak
klak
DAMN. WHO'S THIS GUY THINK HE IS TO SPOIL MY FUN?!
whoooooooosh

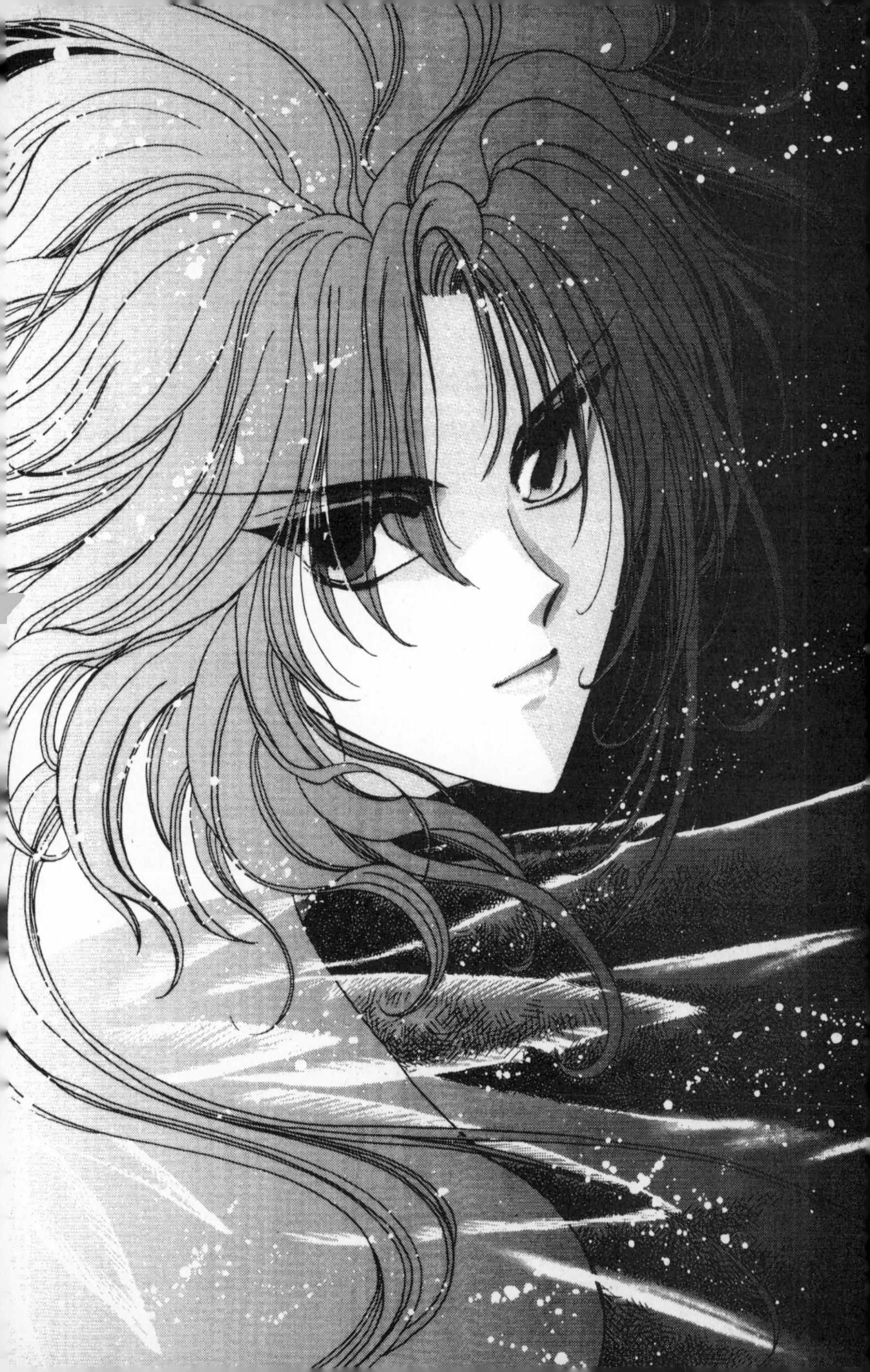

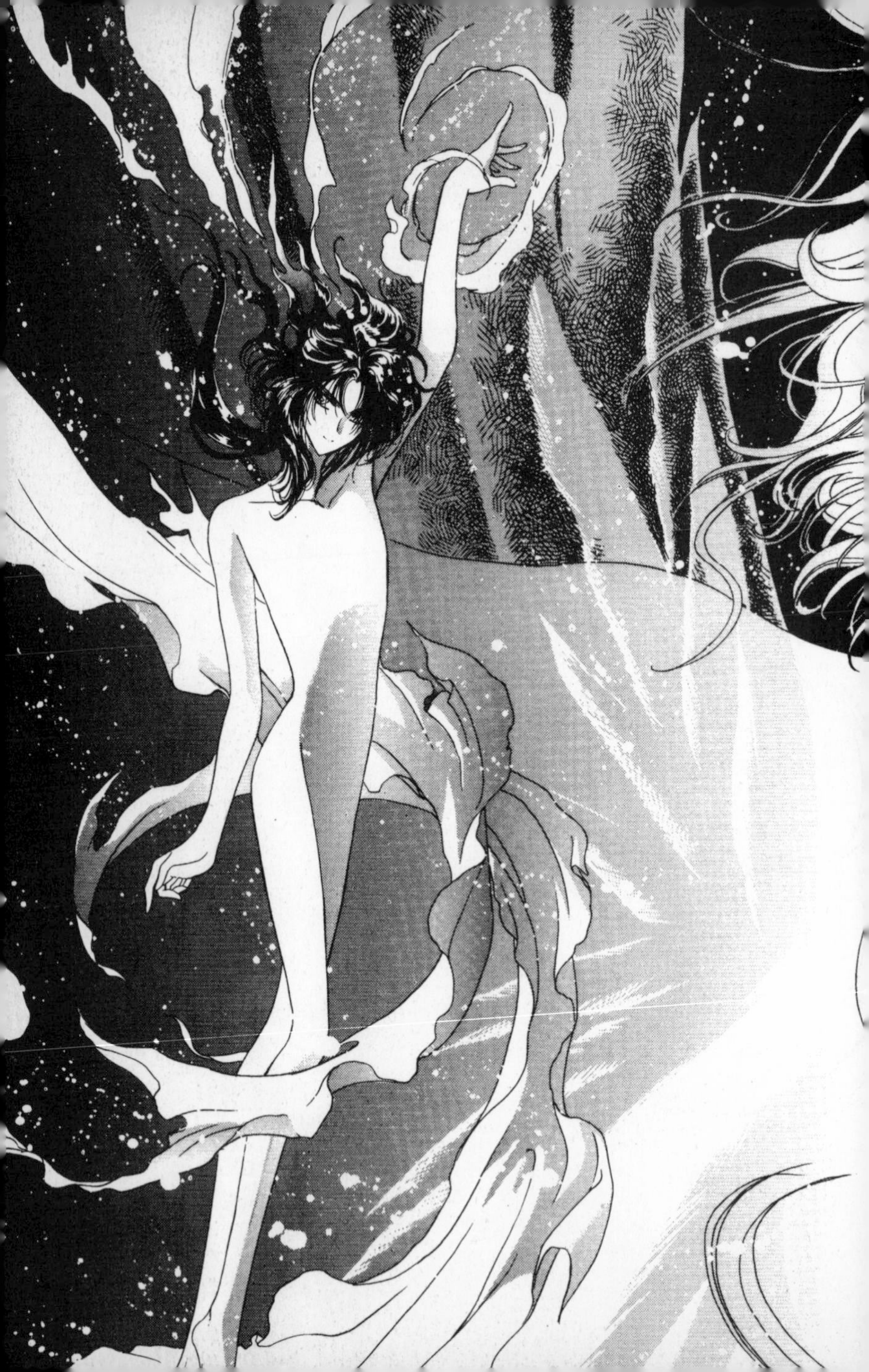

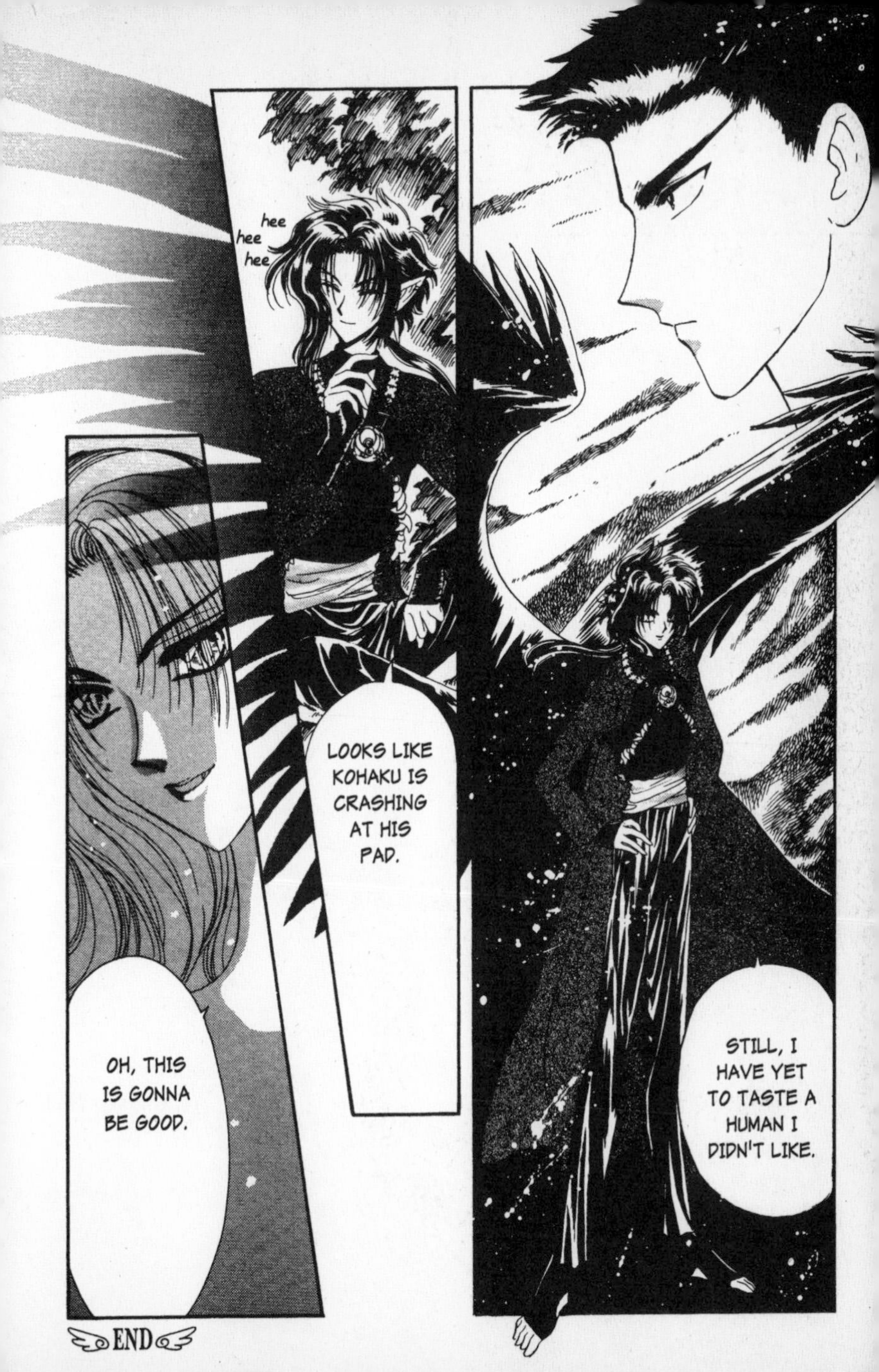
STILL, I HAVE YET TO TASTE A HUMAN I DIDN'T LIKE.
hee hee hee
LOOKS LIKE KOHAKU IS CRASHING AT HIS PAD.
OH, THIS IS GONNA BE GOOD.
END

Contact.3

はじめてのおつかい

HER FIRST CHORE

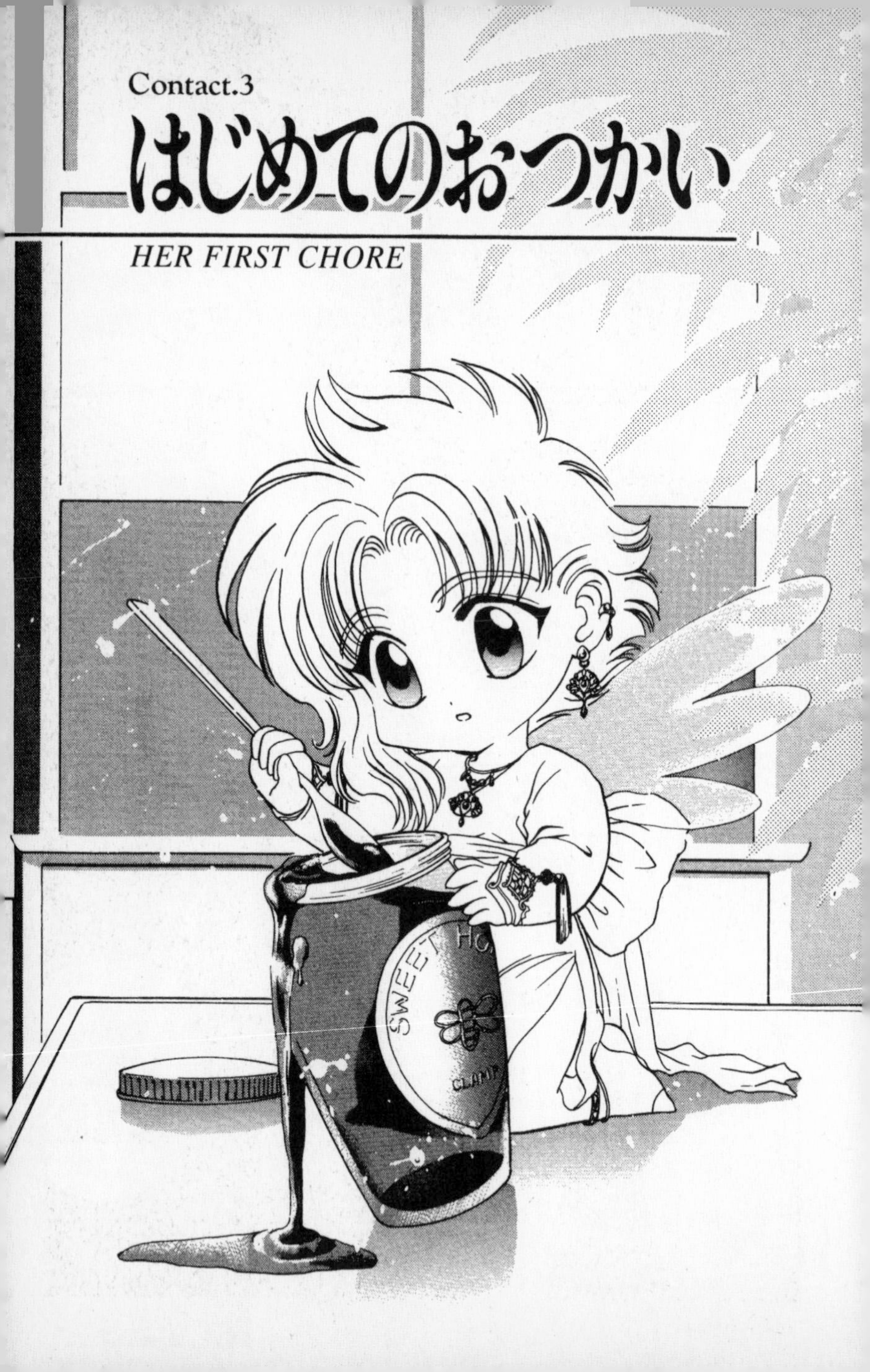

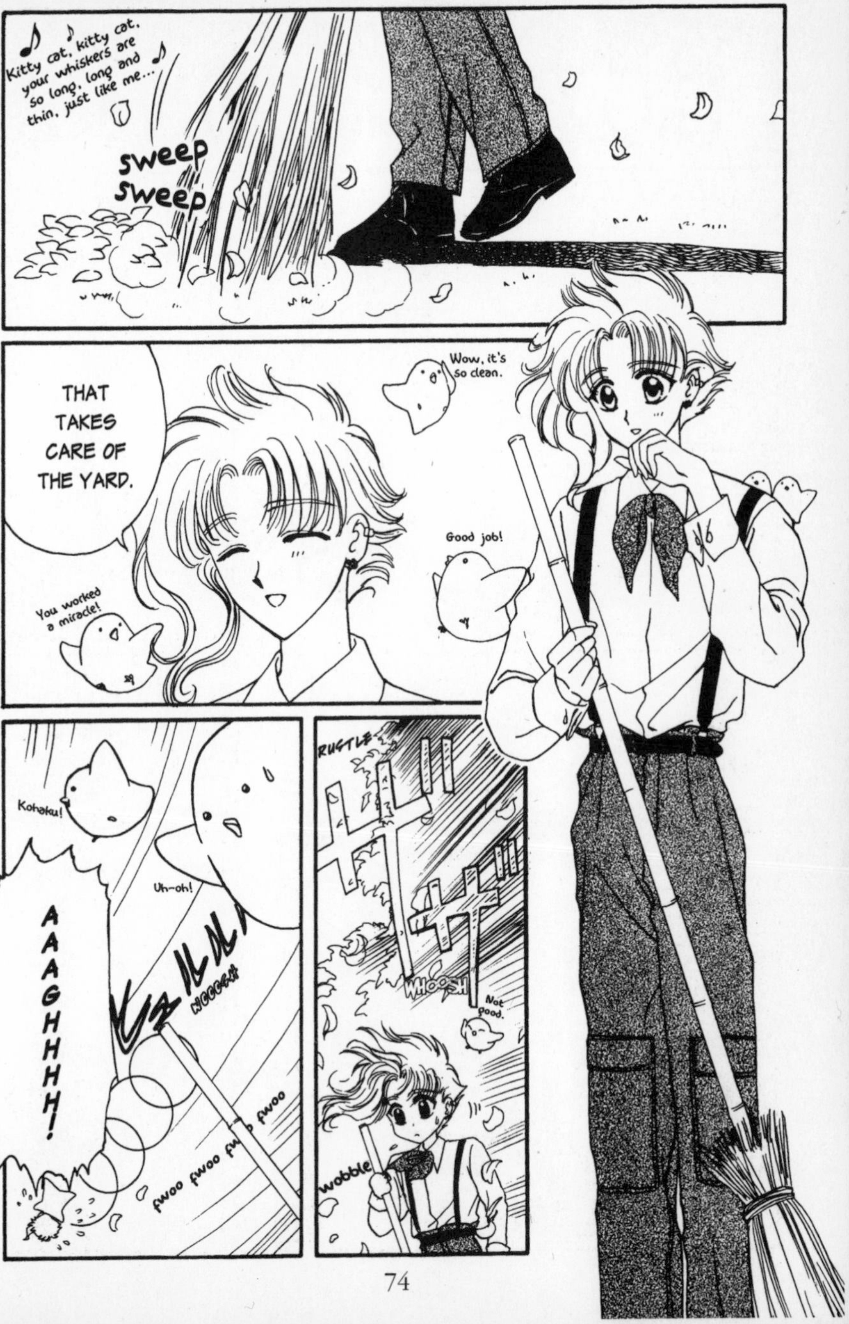
♪ ♪ Kitty cat, kitty cat, your whiskers are so long, long and thin, just like me... ♪
sweep sweep
Wow, it's so clean.
THAT TAKES CARE OF THE YARD.
Good job!
You worked a miracle!
RUSTLE
WHOOSH
Not good.
wobble
Kohaku!
Uh-oh!
WOOOSH
AAAGHHHH!
fwoo fwoo fwoo fwoo

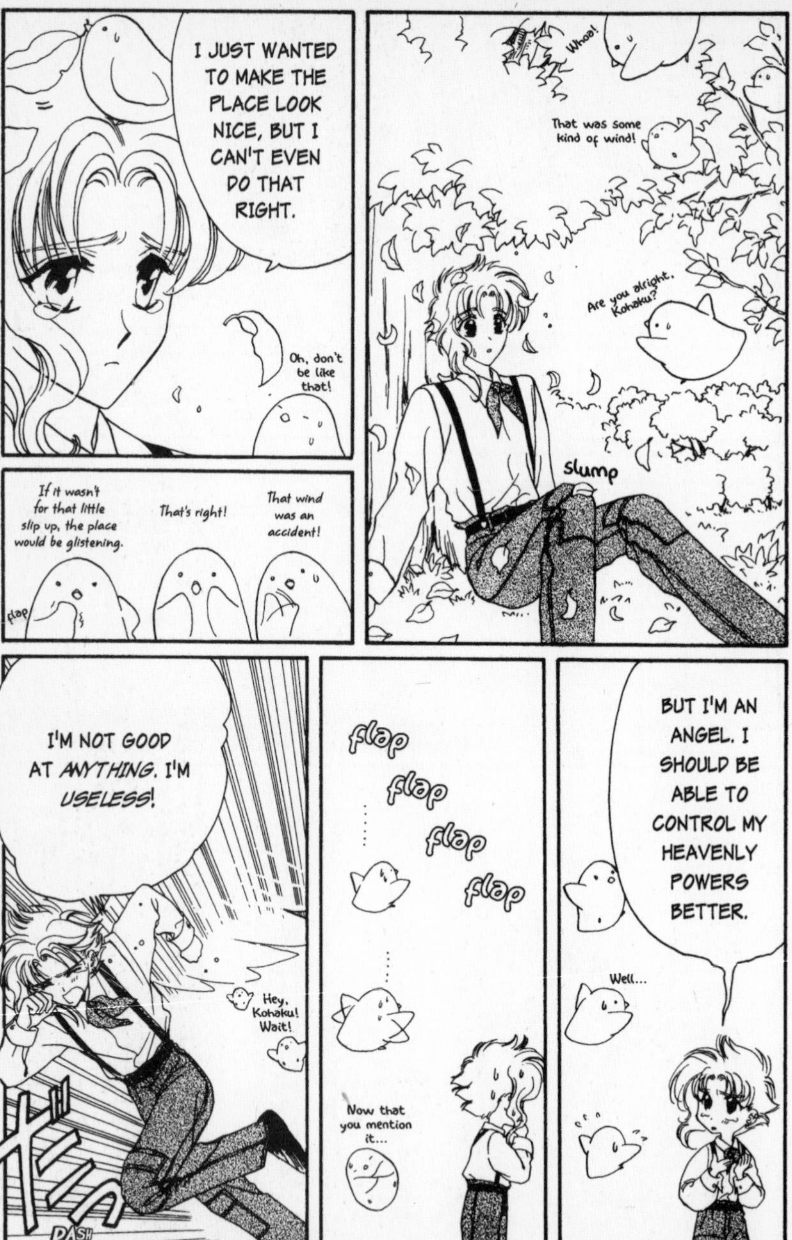
Whoa!
That was some kind of wind!
Are you alright, Kohaku?
slump
I JUST WANTED TO MAKE THE PLACE LOOK NICE, BUT I CAN'T EVEN DO THAT RIGHT.
Oh, don't be like that!
That wind was an accident!
That's right!
If it wasn't for that little slip up, the place would be glistening.
flap
BUT I'M AN ANGEL. I SHOULD BE ABLE TO CONTROL MY HEAVENLY POWERS BETTER.
Well...
flap
flap
flap
flap
......
......
Now that you mention it...
I'M NOT GOOD AT *ANYTHING*. I'M *USELESS*!
Hey, Kohaku! Wait!
DASH

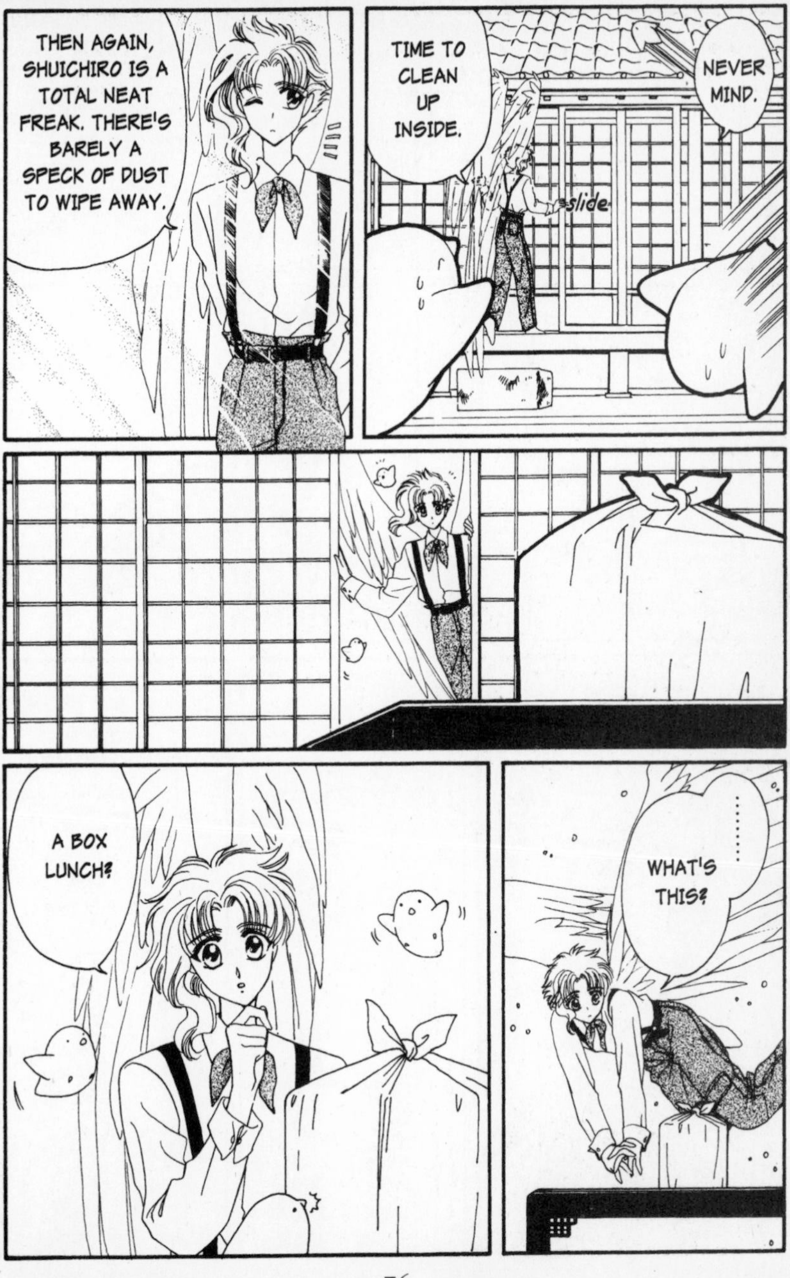
NEVER MIND.
TIME TO CLEAN UP INSIDE.
slide
THEN AGAIN, SHUICHIRO IS A TOTAL NEAT FREAK. THERE'S BARELY A SPECK OF DUST TO WIPE AWAY.
......
WHAT'S THIS?
A BOX LUNCH?

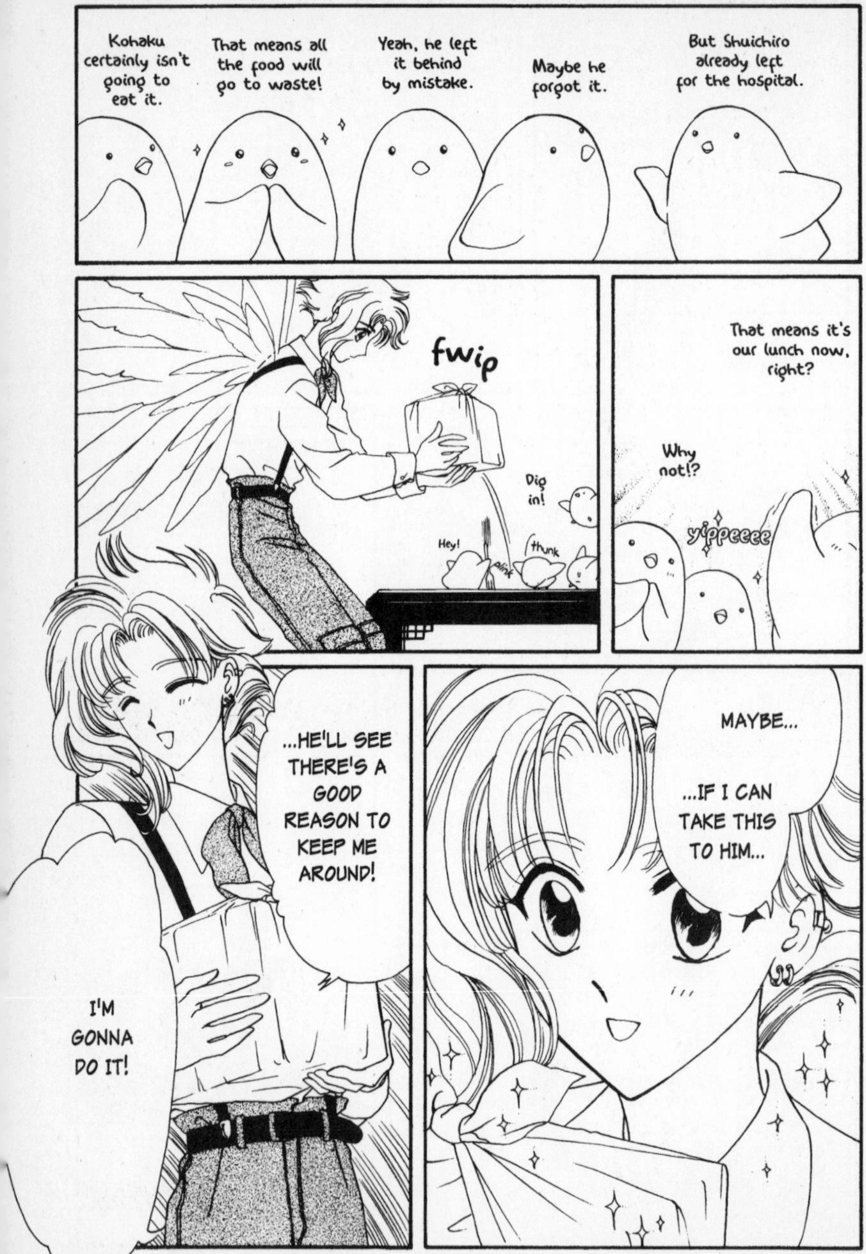
But Shuichiro already left for the hospital.
Maybe he forgot it.
Yeah, he left it behind by mistake.
That means all the food will go to waste!
Kohaku certainly isn't going to eat it.
That means it's our lunch now, right?
Why not!?
yippeeee
fwip
Dig in!
thunk
plink
Hey!
MAYBE...
...IF I CAN TAKE THIS TO HIM...
...HE'LL SEE THERE'S A GOOD REASON TO KEEP ME AROUND!
I'M GONNA DO IT!

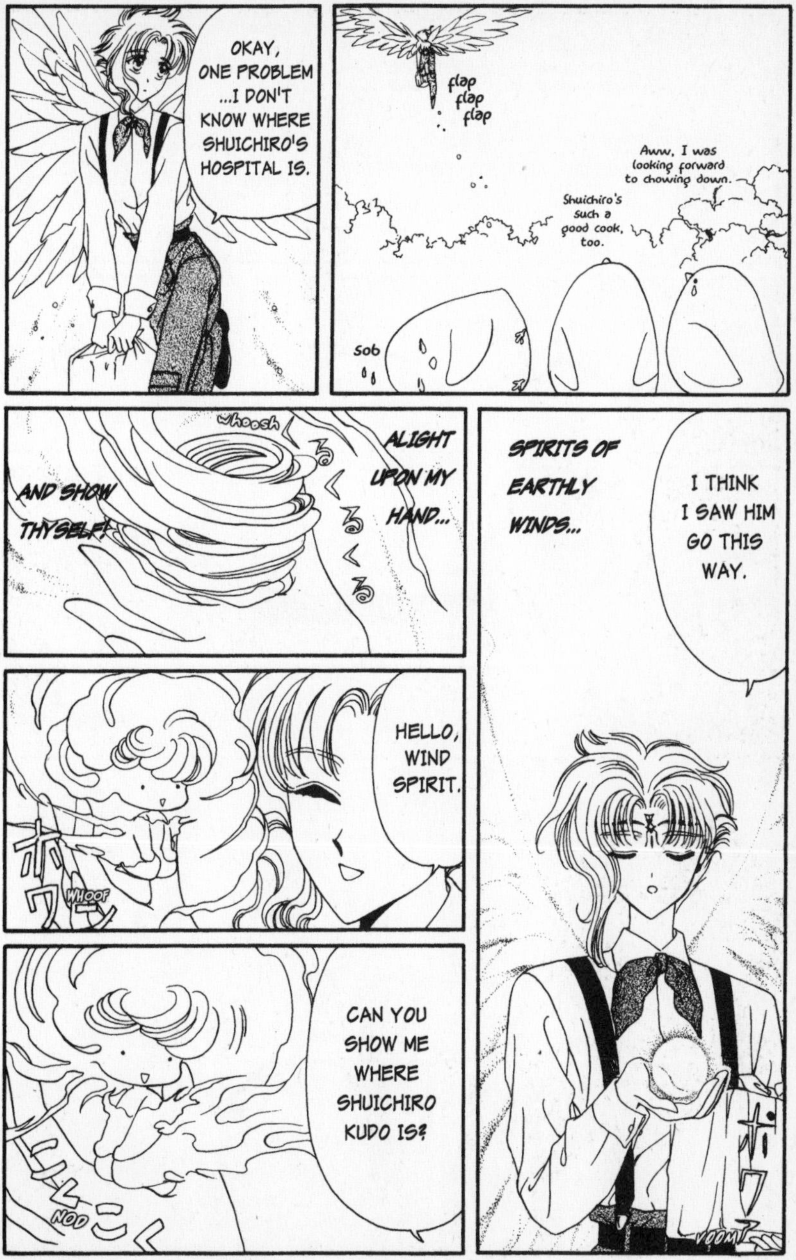
flap flap flap
Aww, I was looking forward to chowing down.
Shuichiro's such a good cook, too.
sob
OKAY, ONE PROBLEM ...I DON'T KNOW WHERE SHUICHIRO'S HOSPITAL IS.
I THINK I SAW HIM GO THIS WAY.
SPIRITS OF EARTHLY WINDS...
VOOM
WHOOSH
ALIGHT UPON MY HAND...
AND SHOW THYSELF!
HELLO, WIND SPIRIT.
WHOOF
CAN YOU SHOW ME WHERE SHUICHIRO KUDO IS?
NOD

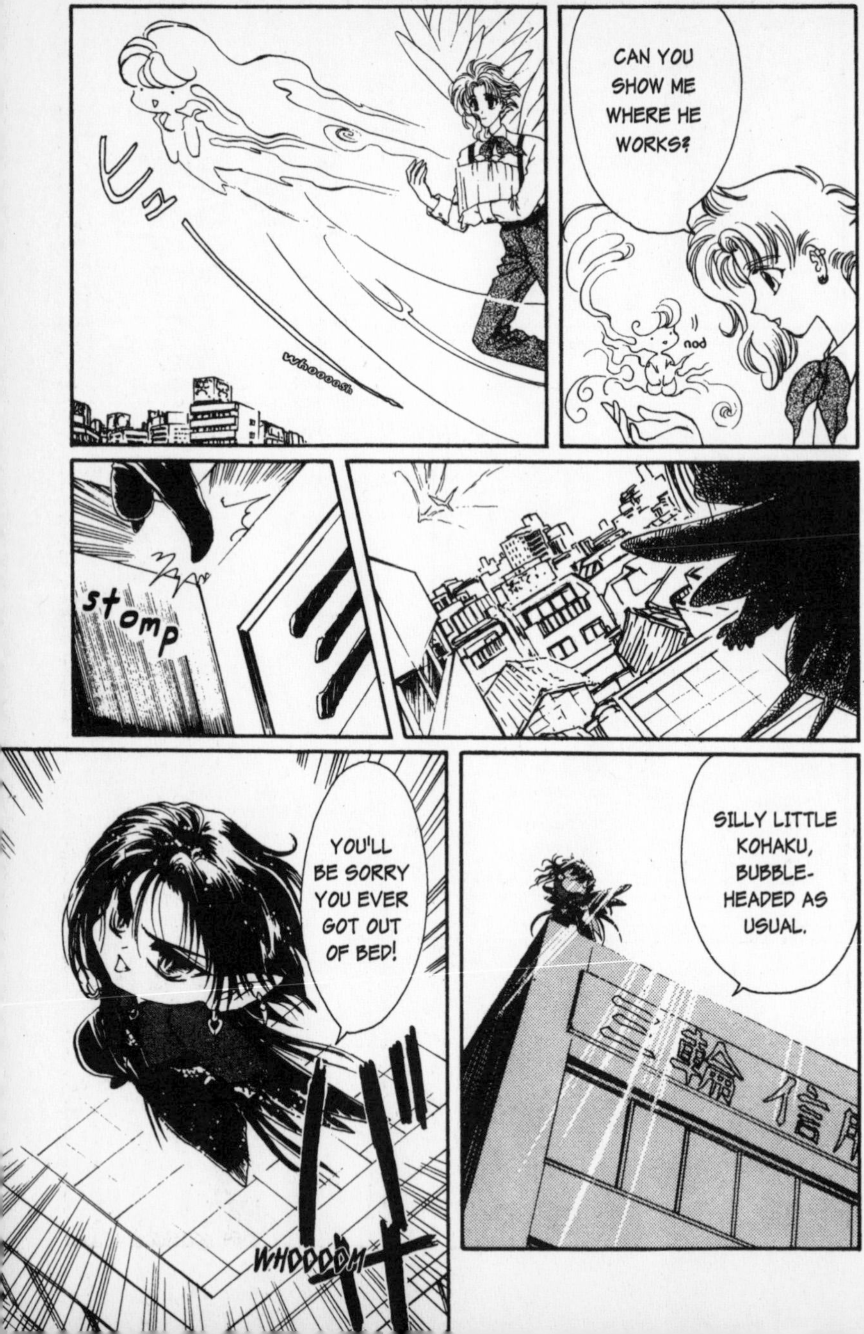
CAN YOU SHOW ME WHERE HE WORKS?
nod
ヒュ
whoooosh
stomp
SILLY LITTLE KOHAKU, BUBBLE-HEADED AS USUAL.
YOU'LL BE SORRY YOU EVER GOT OUT OF BED!
WHOOOOM

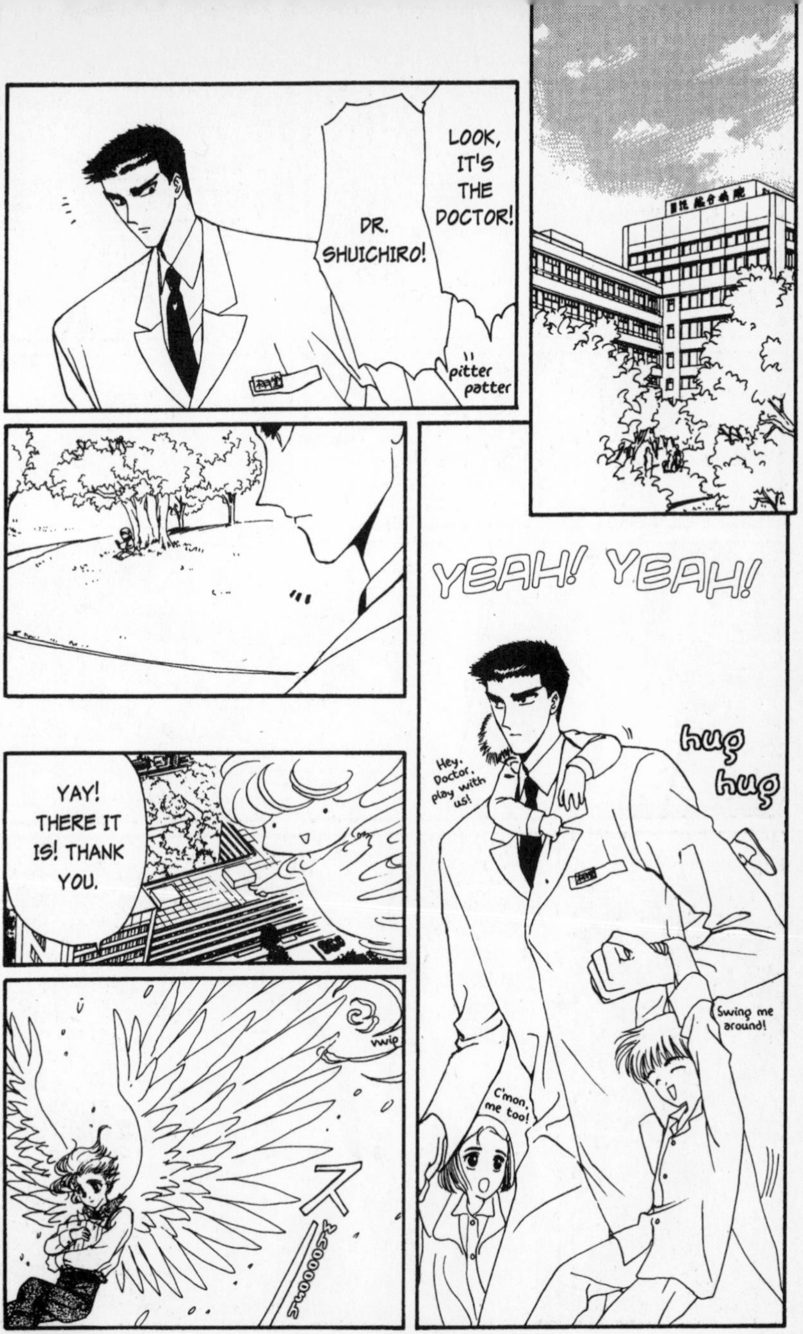
LOOK, IT'S THE DOCTOR!
DR. SHUICHIRO!
pitter patter
YEAH! YEAH!
hug hug
Hey, Doctor, play with us!
Swing me around!
C'mon, me too!
YAY! THERE IT IS! THANK YOU.
vwip
ス

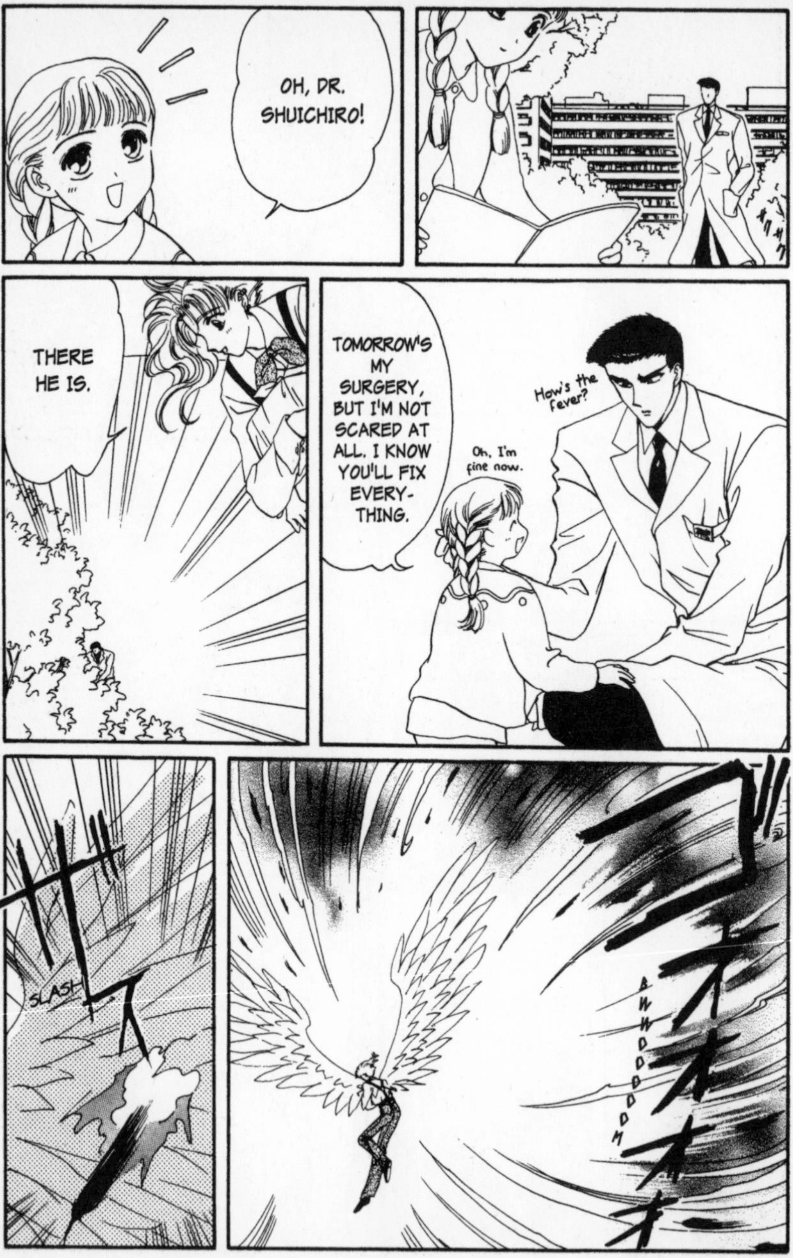
OH, DR. SHUICHIRO!
How's the fever?
Oh, I'm fine now.
TOMORROW'S MY SURGERY, BUT I'M NOT SCARED AT ALL. I KNOW YOU'LL FIX EVERY-THING.
THERE HE IS.
BWWDDDDDM
SLASH

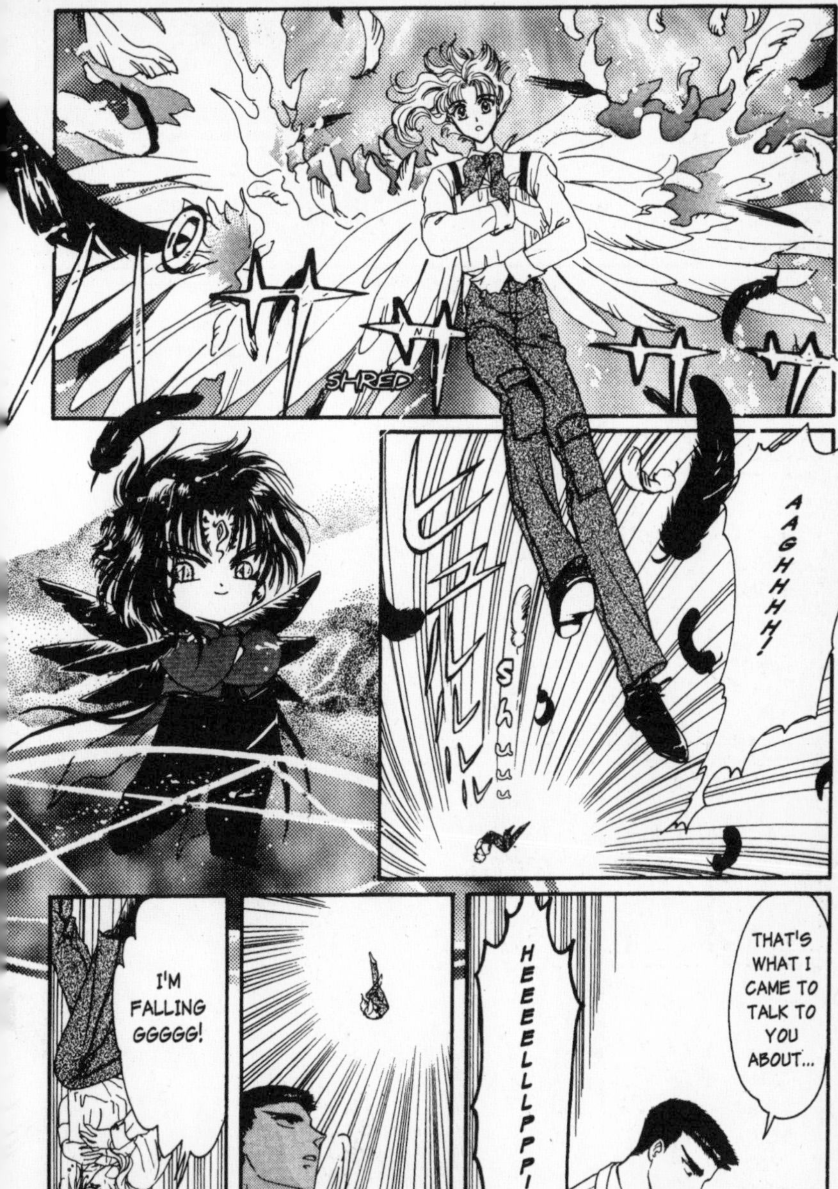
SHRED
AAGHHHH!
shuuuu
THAT'S WHAT I CAME TO TALK TO YOU ABOUT...
HEEEEELLLPPP!
I'M FALLING GGGGG!

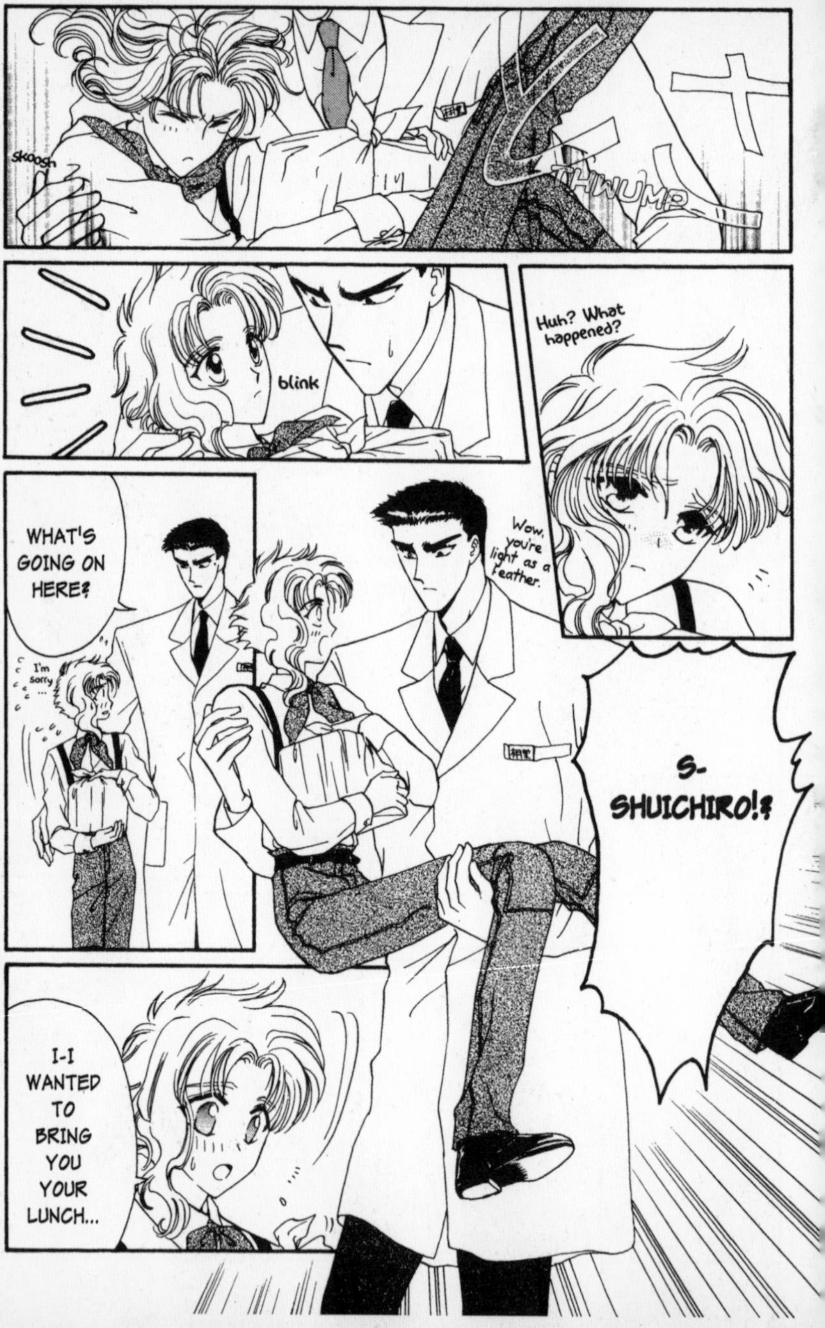
THWUMP
skoosh
Huh? What happened?
blink
S-SHUICHIRO!?
Wow, you're light as a feather.
WHAT'S GOING ON HERE?
I'm sorry...
I-I WANTED TO BRING YOU YOUR LUNCH...

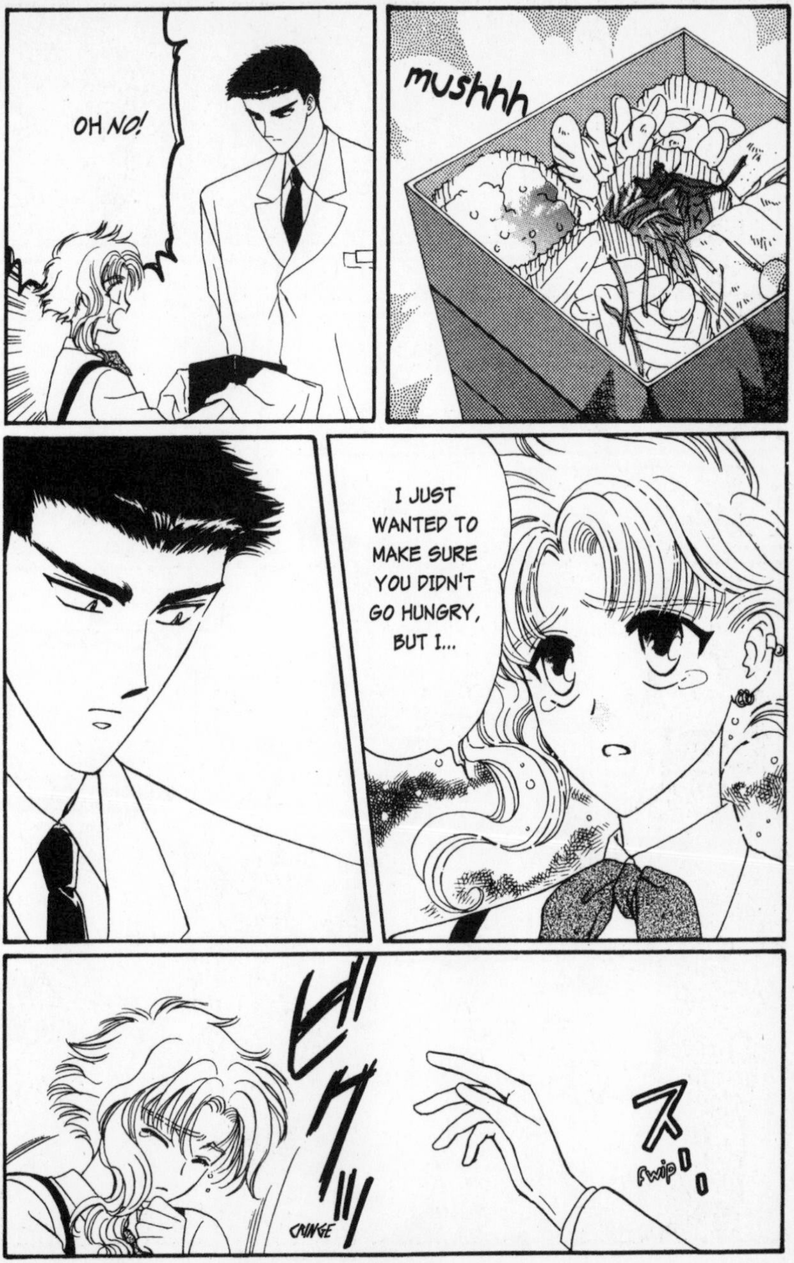
mushhh
OH NO!
I JUST WANTED TO MAKE SURE YOU DIDN'T GO HUNGRY, BUT I...
ス
fwip
CRINGE

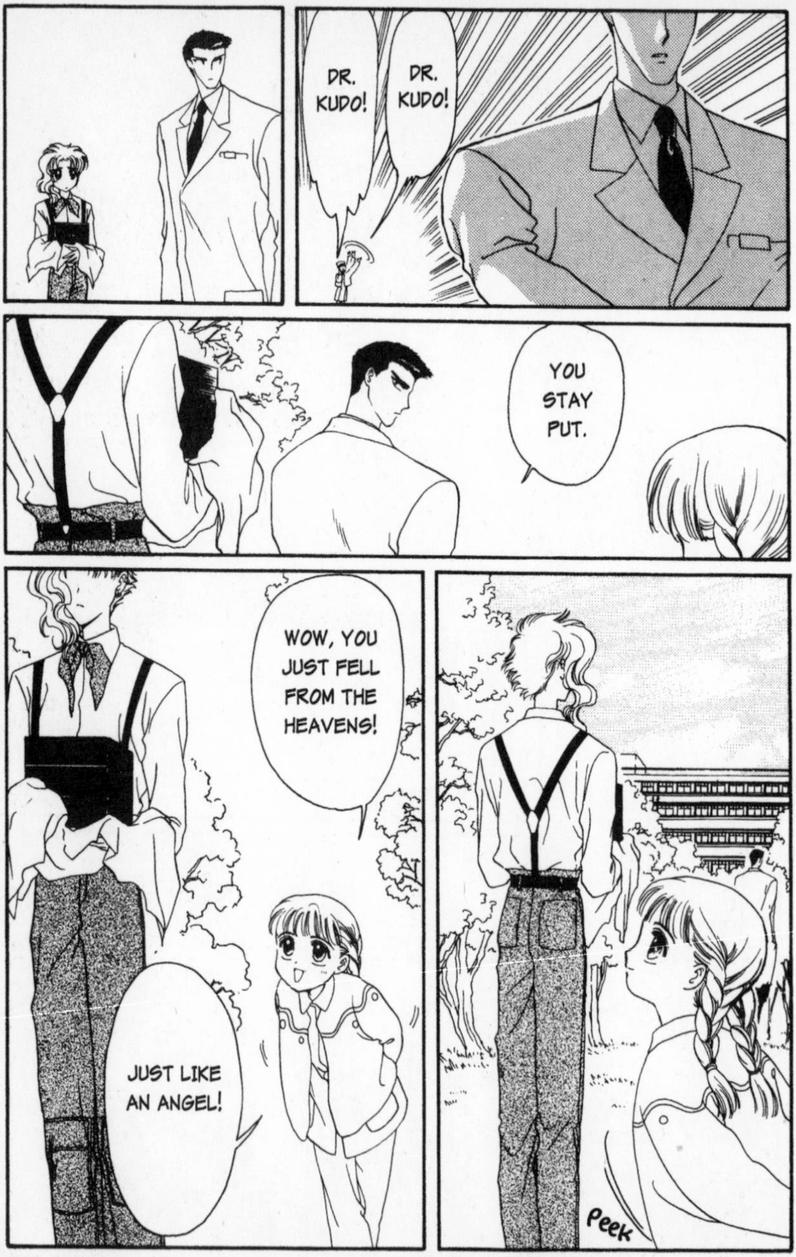
DR. KUDO!
DR. KUDO!
YOU STAY PUT.
Peek
WOW, YOU JUST FELL FROM THE HEAVENS!
JUST LIKE AN ANGEL!

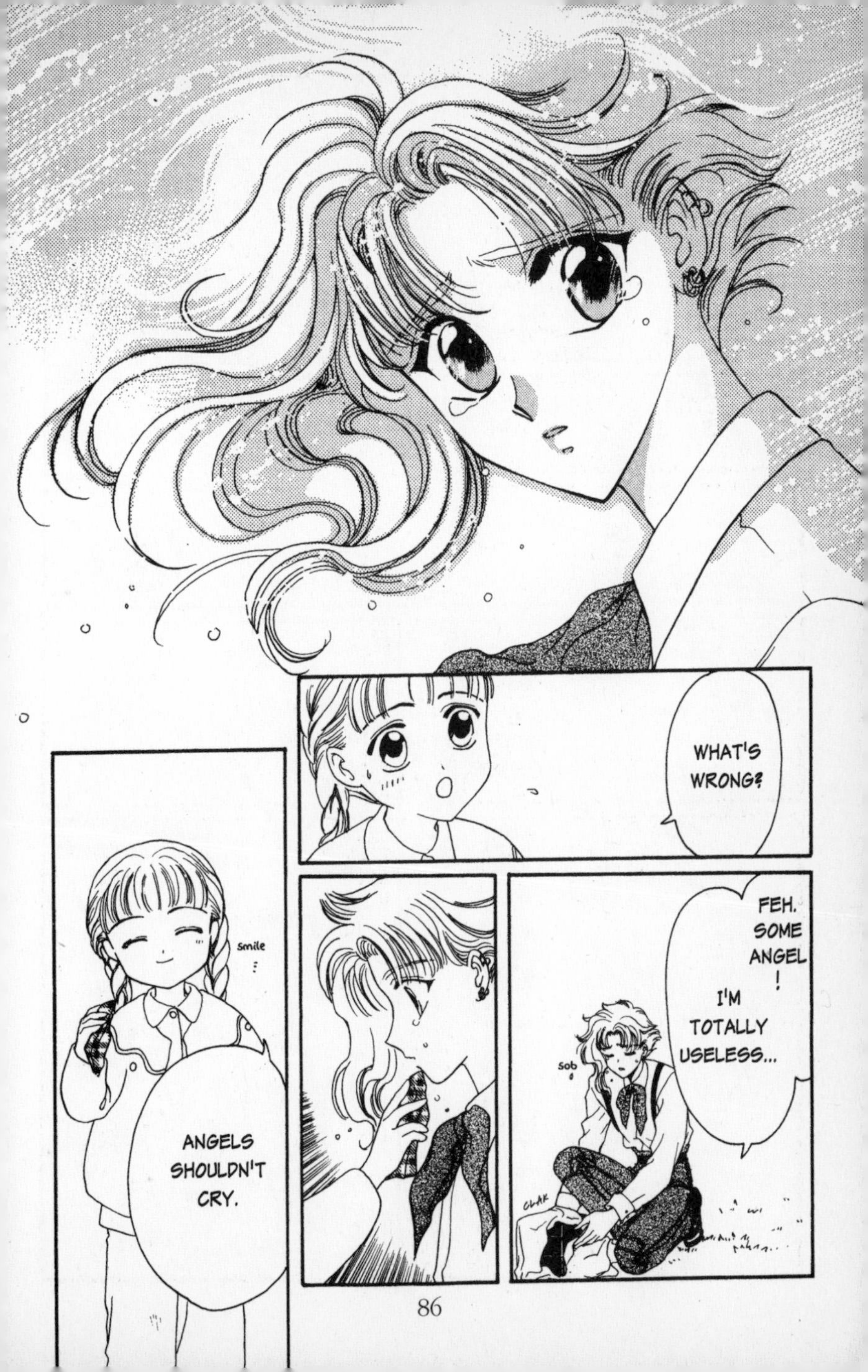
WHAT'S WRONG?
FEH. SOME ANGEL!
I'M TOTALLY USELESS...
sob
CLAK
smile
ANGELS SHOULDN'T CRY.

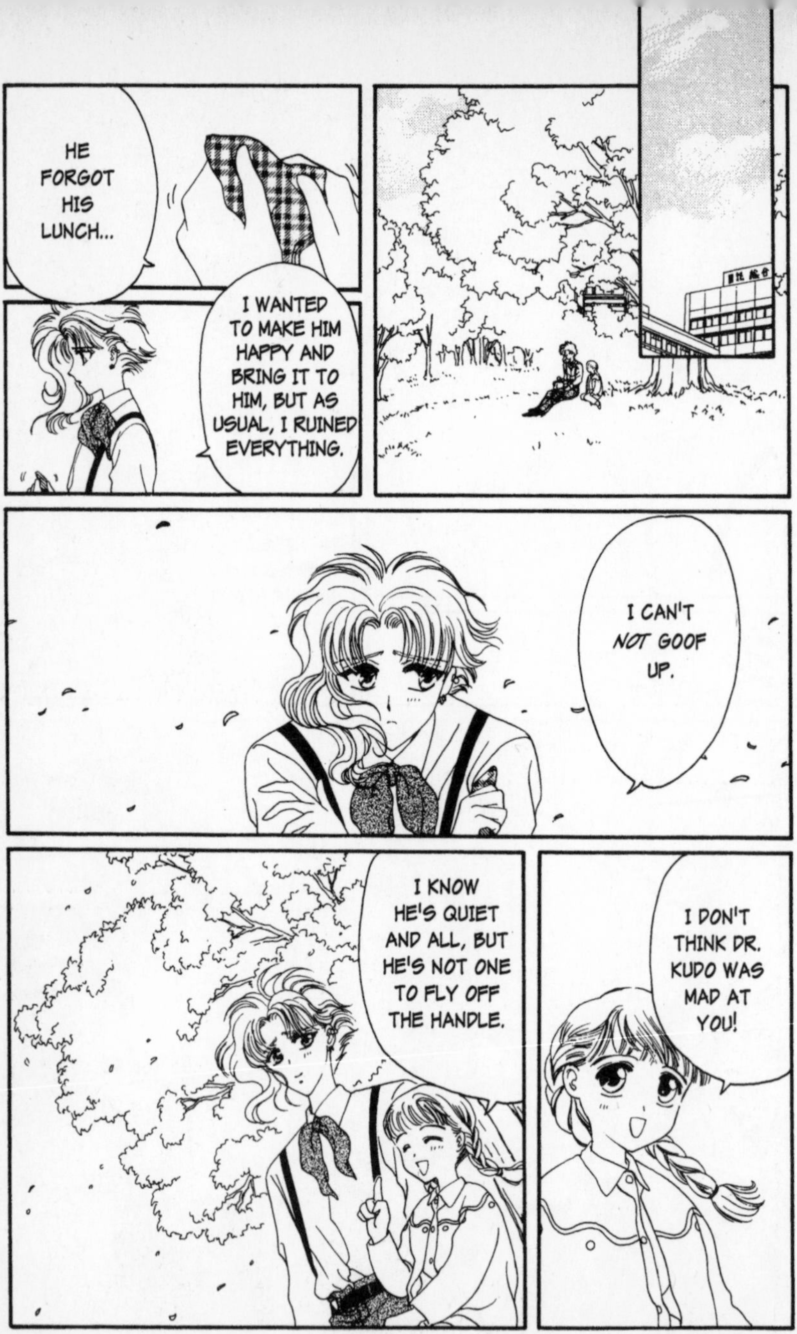
HE FORGOT HIS LUNCH...
I WANTED TO MAKE HIM HAPPY AND BRING IT TO HIM, BUT AS USUAL, I RUINED EVERYTHING.
I CAN'T *NOT* GOOF UP.
I DON'T THINK DR. KUDO WAS MAD AT YOU!
I KNOW HE'S QUIET AND ALL, BUT HE'S NOT ONE TO FLY OFF THE HANDLE.

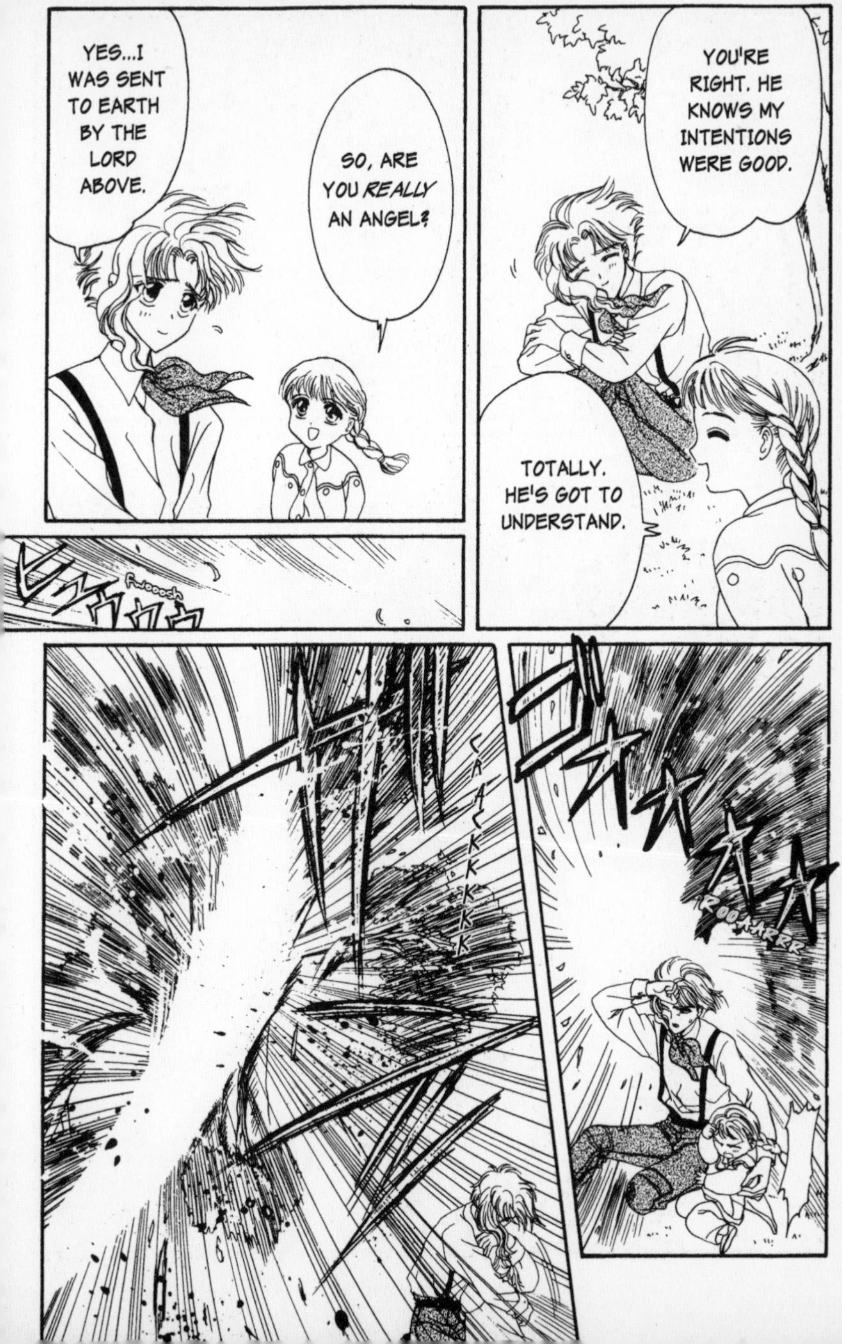
YOU'RE RIGHT. HE KNOWS MY INTENTIONS WERE GOOD.
TOTALLY. HE'S GOT TO UNDERSTAND.
SO, ARE YOU *REALLY* AN ANGEL?
YES...I WAS SENT TO EARTH BY THE LORD ABOVE.
fwooosh
ROOAARRR
CRAACKKKKK

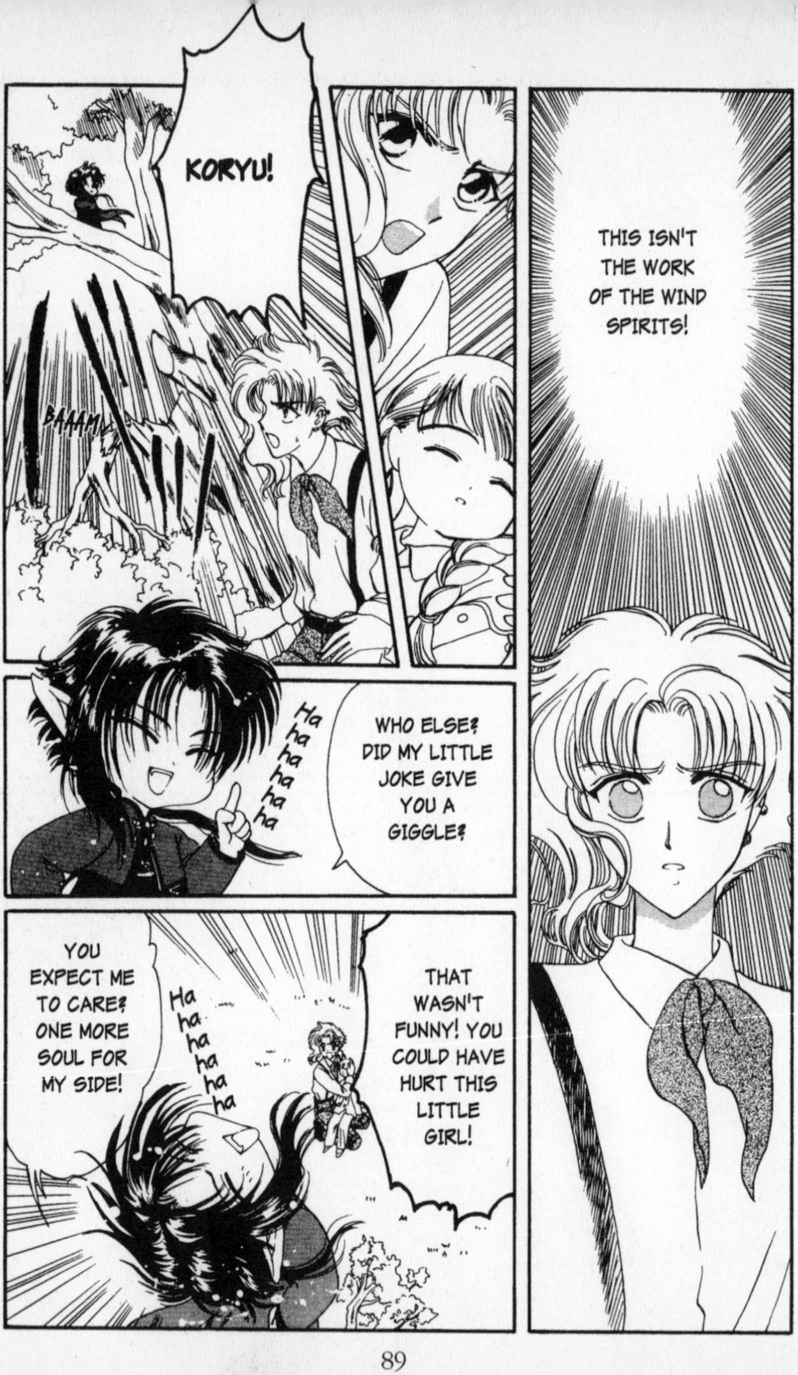
THIS ISN'T THE WORK OF THE WIND SPIRITS!
KORYU!
BAAAM
WHO ELSE? DID MY LITTLE JOKE GIVE YOU A GIGGLE?
Ha ha ha ha ha ha ha
THAT WASN'T FUNNY! YOU COULD HAVE HURT THIS LITTLE GIRL!
Ha ha ha ha ha ha ha
YOU EXPECT ME TO CARE? ONE MORE SOUL FOR MY SIDE!

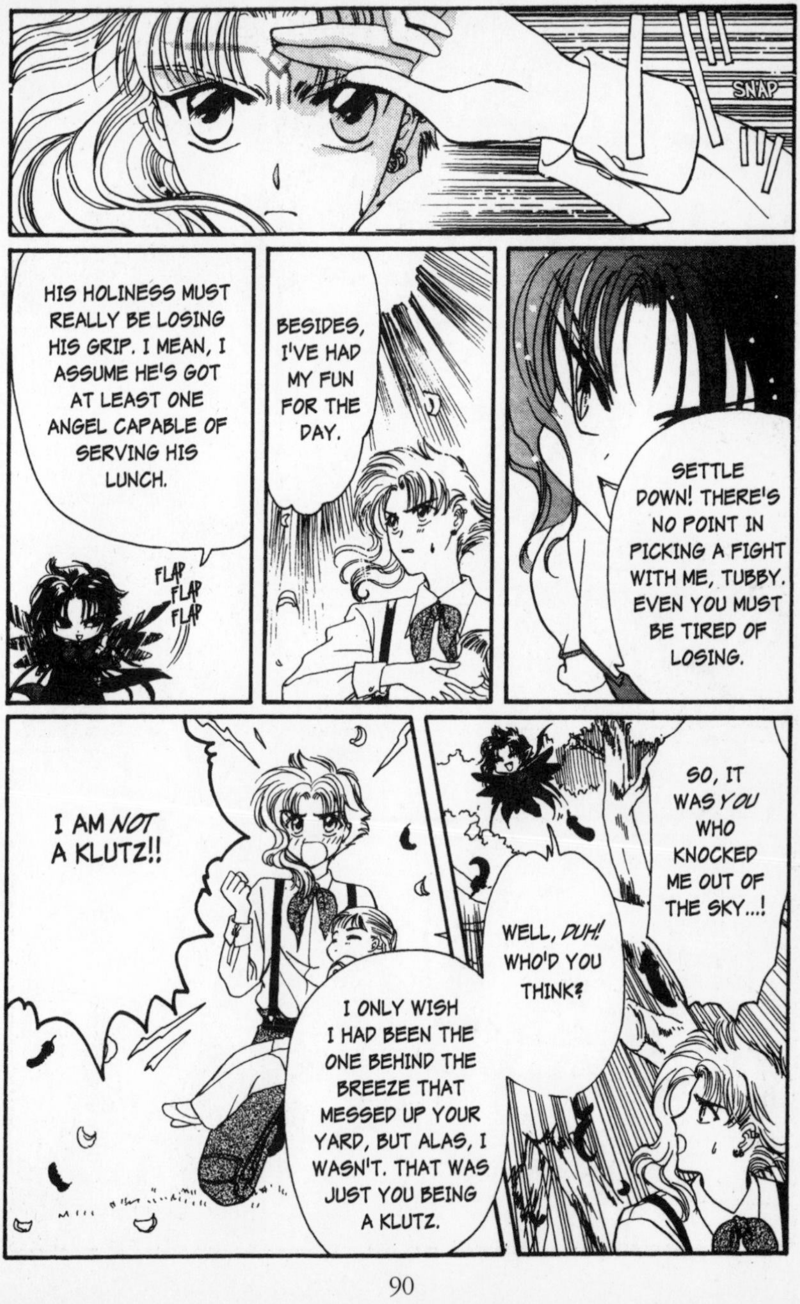
SNAP
SETTLE DOWN! THERE'S NO POINT IN PICKING A FIGHT WITH ME, TUBBY. EVEN YOU MUST BE TIRED OF LOSING.
BESIDES, I'VE HAD MY FUN FOR THE DAY.
HIS HOLINESS MUST REALLY BE LOSING HIS GRIP. I MEAN, I ASSUME HE'S GOT AT LEAST ONE ANGEL CAPABLE OF SERVING HIS LUNCH.
FLAP FLAP FLAP
SO, IT WAS *YOU* WHO KNOCKED ME OUT OF THE SKY...!
WELL, *DUH!* WHO'D YOU THINK?
I ONLY WISH I HAD BEEN THE ONE BEHIND THE BREEZE THAT MESSED UP YOUR YARD, BUT ALAS, I WASN'T. THAT WAS JUST YOU BEING A KLUTZ.
I AM *NOT* A KLUTZ!!

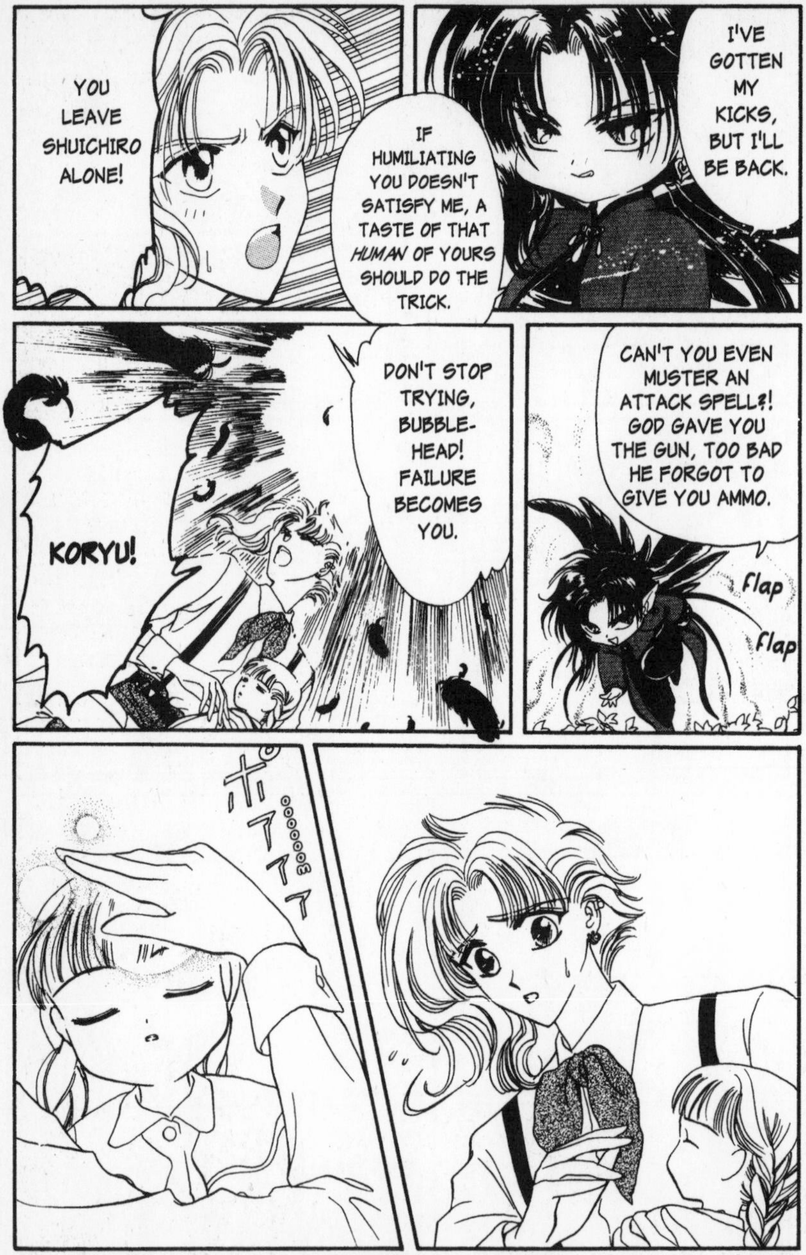
I'VE GOTTEN MY KICKS, BUT I'LL BE BACK.
IF HUMILIATING YOU DOESN'T SATISFY ME, A TASTE OF THAT *HUMAN* OF YOURS SHOULD DO THE TRICK.
YOU LEAVE SHUICHIRO ALONE!
CAN'T YOU EVEN MUSTER AN ATTACK SPELL?! GOD GAVE YOU THE GUN, TOO BAD HE FORGOT TO GIVE YOU AMMO.
Flap
Flap
DON'T STOP TRYING, BUBBLE-HEAD! FAILURE BECOMES YOU.
KORYU!
ポアアア
oooooom

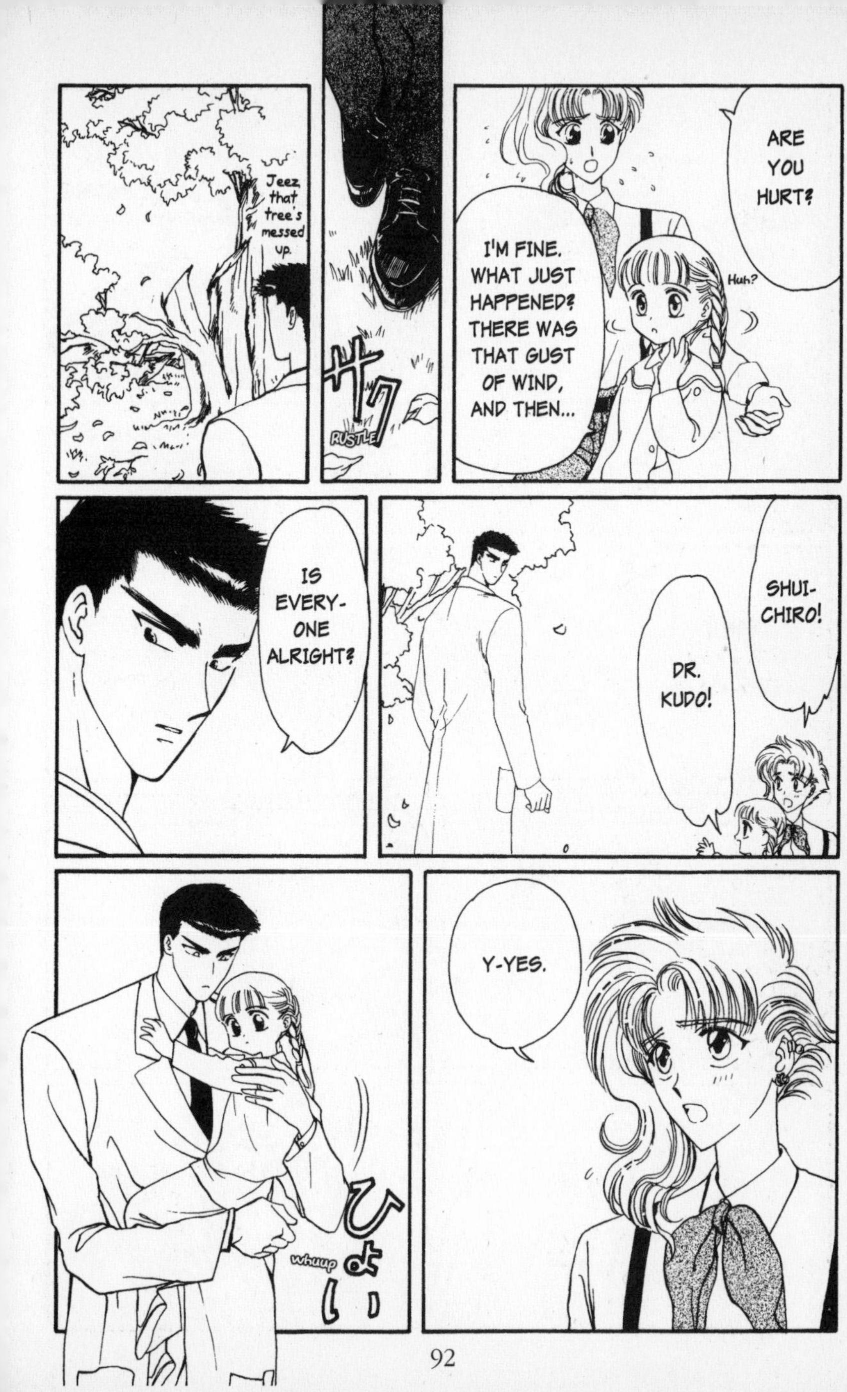
ARE YOU HURT?
Huh?
I'M FINE. WHAT JUST HAPPENED? THERE WAS THAT GUST OF WIND, AND THEN...
サク
RUSTLE
Jeez that tree's messed up.
SHUI-CHIRO!
DR. KUDO!
IS EVERY-ONE ALRIGHT?
Y-YES.
ひょい
whuup

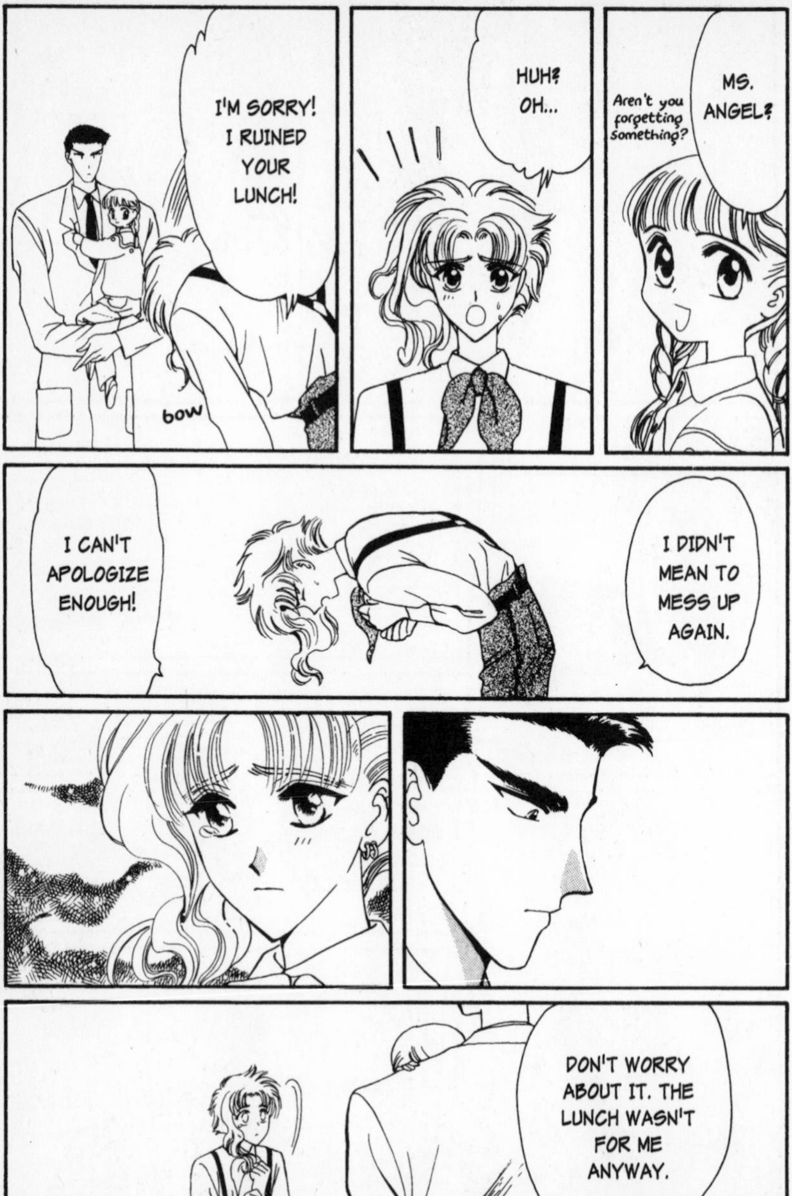
MS. ANGEL?
Aren't you forgetting something?
HUH? OH...
I'M SORRY! I RUINED YOUR LUNCH!
bow
I DIDN'T MEAN TO MESS UP AGAIN.
I CAN'T APOLOGIZE ENOUGH!
DON'T WORRY ABOUT IT. THE LUNCH WASN'T FOR ME ANYWAY.

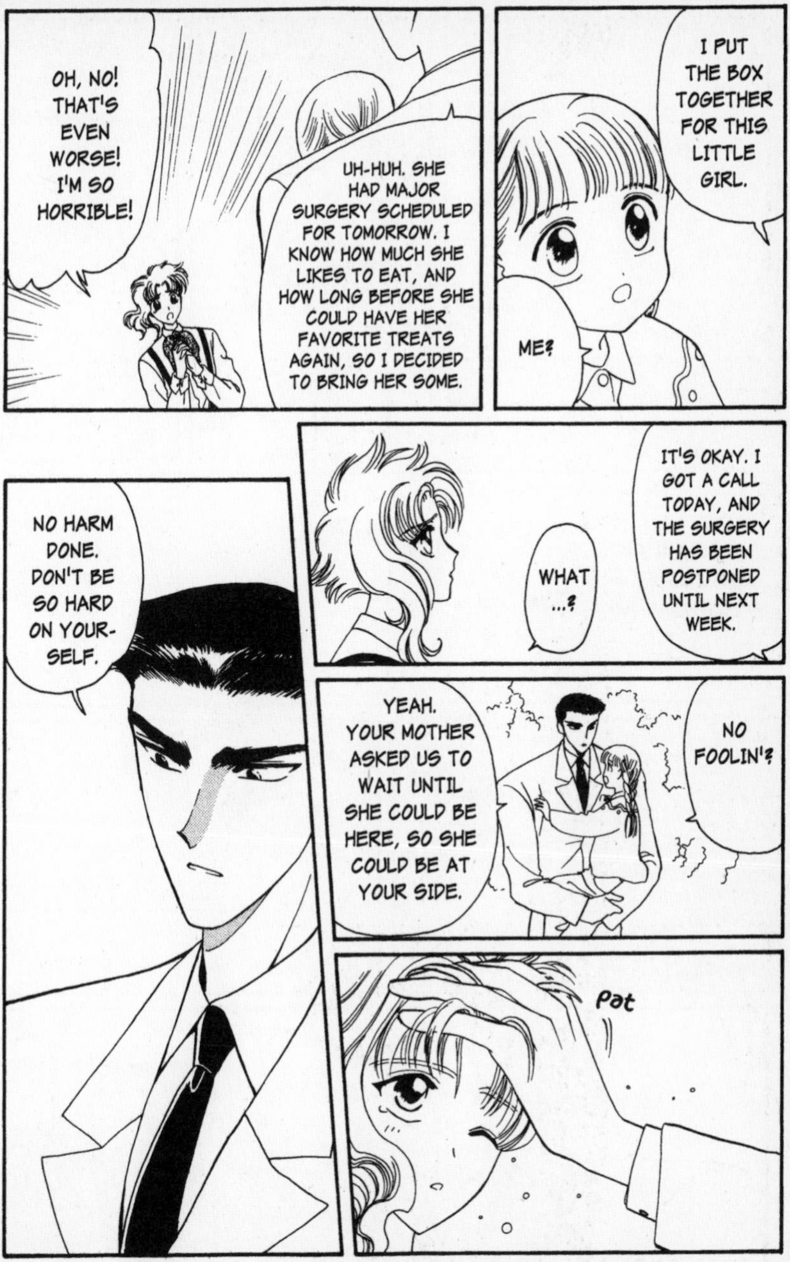
I PUT THE BOX TOGETHER FOR THIS LITTLE GIRL.
ME?
UH-HUH. SHE HAD MAJOR SURGERY SCHEDULED FOR TOMORROW. I KNOW HOW MUCH SHE LIKES TO EAT, AND HOW LONG BEFORE SHE COULD HAVE HER FAVORITE TREATS AGAIN, SO I DECIDED TO BRING HER SOME.
OH, NO! THAT'S EVEN WORSE! I'M SO HORRIBLE!
IT'S OKAY. I GOT A CALL TODAY, AND THE SURGERY HAS BEEN POSTPONED UNTIL NEXT WEEK.
WHAT ...?
NO FOOLIN'?
YEAH. YOUR MOTHER ASKED US TO WAIT UNTIL SHE COULD BE HERE, SO SHE COULD BE AT YOUR SIDE.
Pat
NO HARM DONE. DON'T BE SO HARD ON YOURSELF.

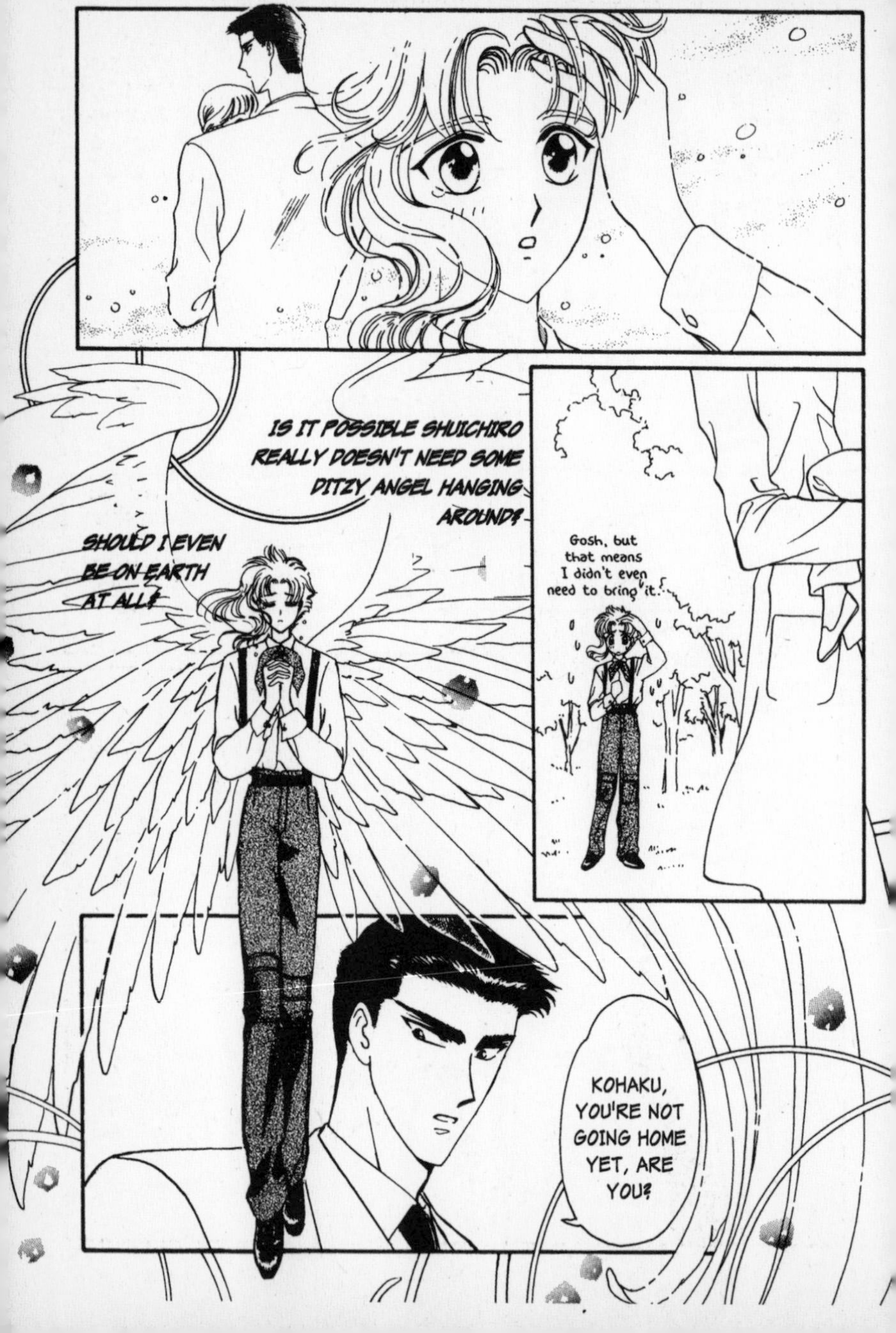
Gosh, but that means I didn't even need to bring it.
IS IT POSSIBLE SHUICHIRO REALLY DOESN'T NEED SOME DITZY ANGEL HANGING AROUND?
SHOULD I EVEN BE ON EARTH AT ALL?
KOHAKU, YOU'RE NOT GOING HOME YET, ARE YOU?

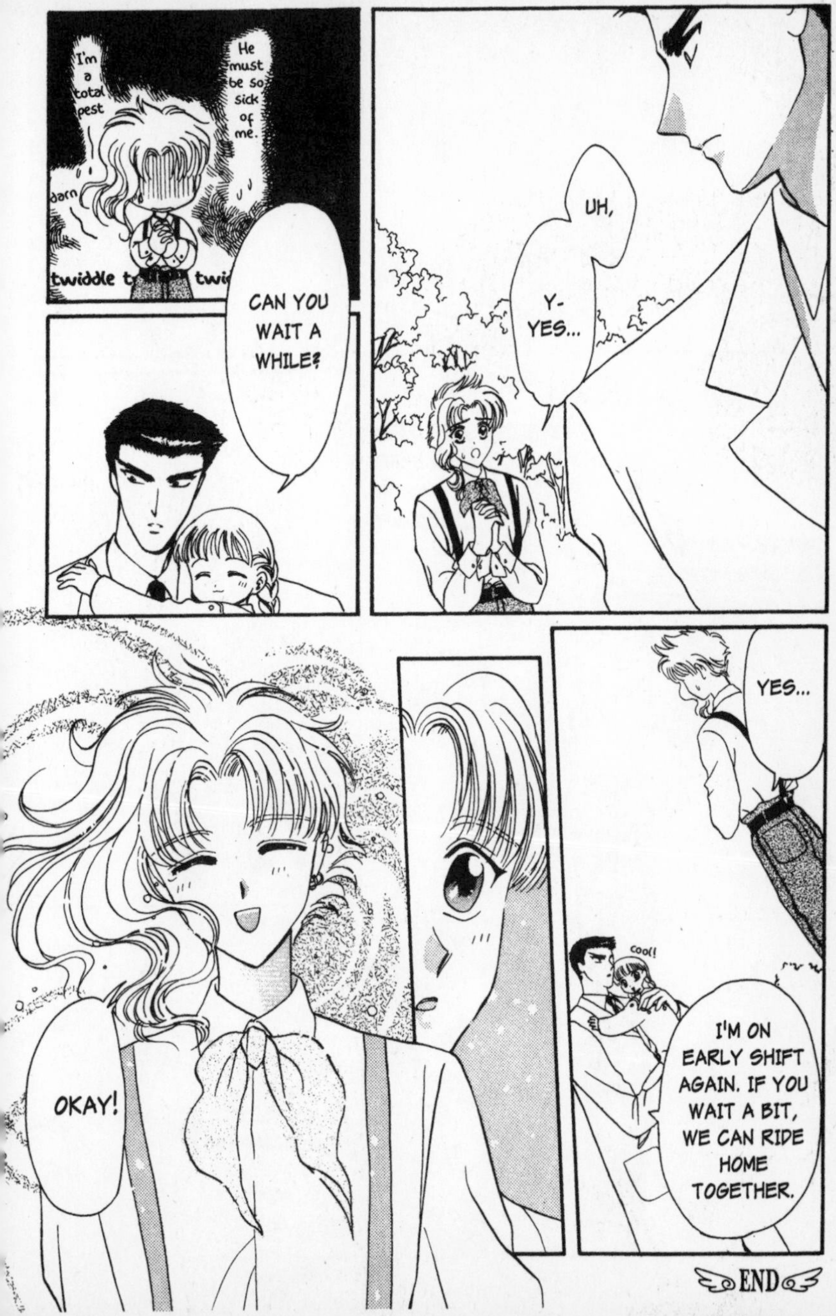
UH,
Y-YES...
I'm a total pest
He must be so sick of me.
darn
twiddle t
twid
CAN YOU WAIT A WHILE?
YES...
cool!
I'M ON EARLY SHIFT AGAIN. IF YOU WAIT A BIT, WE CAN RIDE HOME TOGETHER.
OKAY!
END

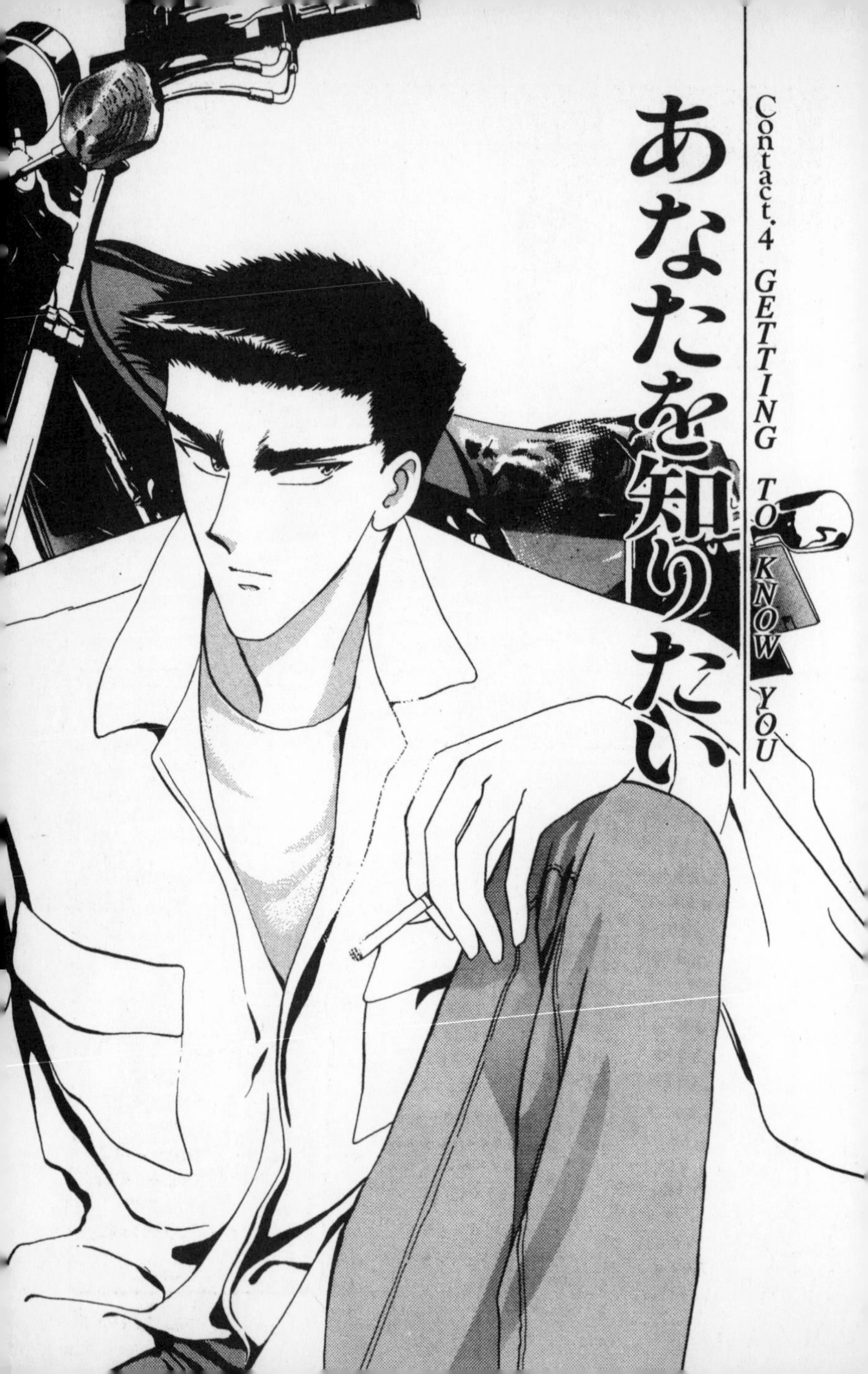
あなたを知りたい
Contact.4 GETTING TO KNOW YOU

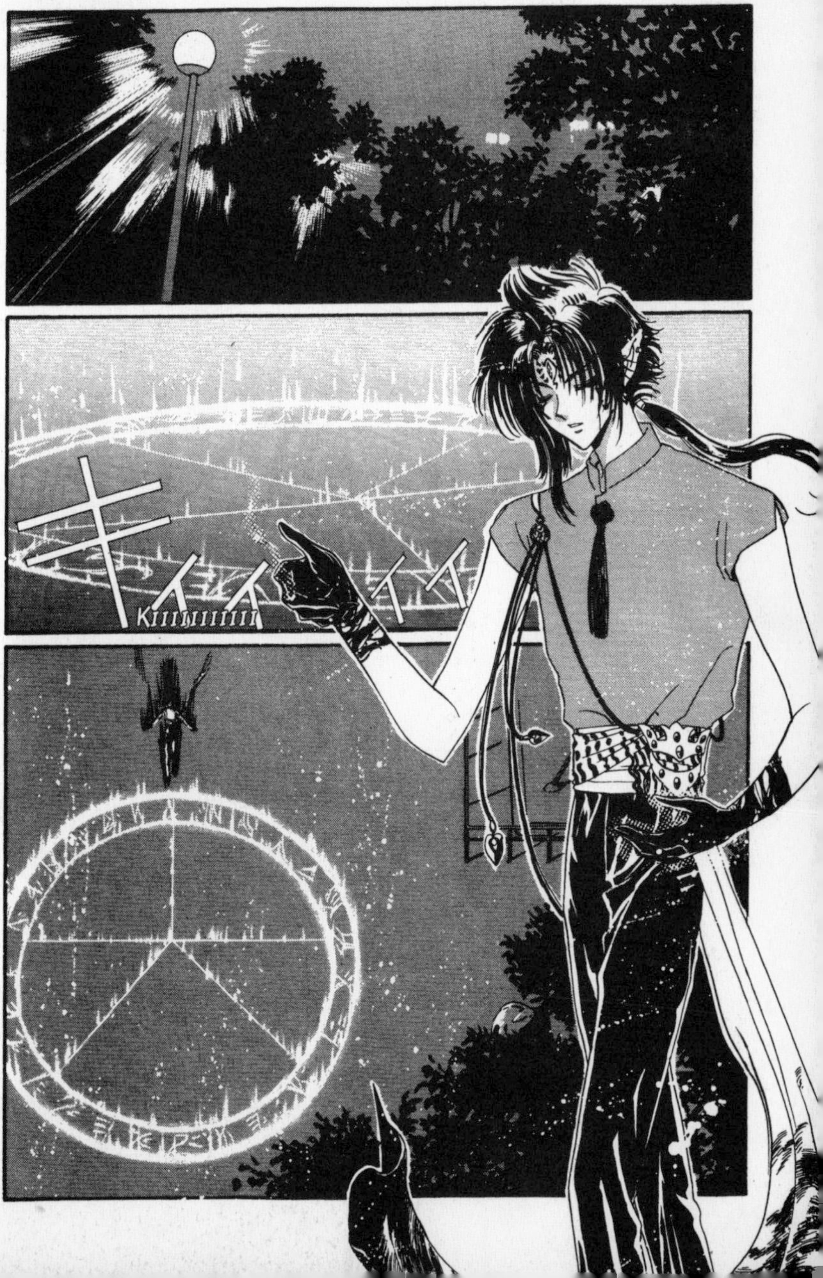
キイイイイ
KIIIIIIIIIII

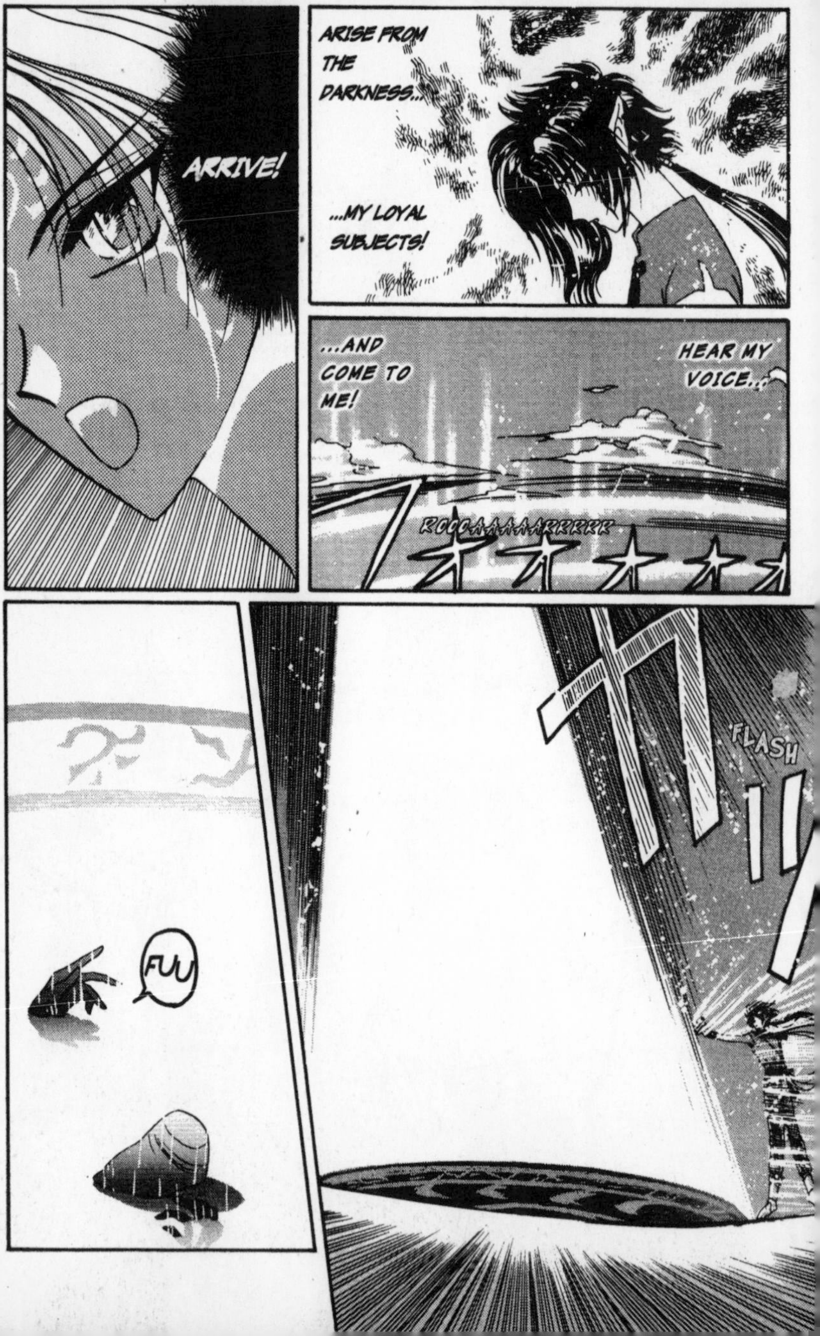
ARISE FROM THE DARKNESS...
...MY LOYAL SUBJECTS!
HEAR MY VOICE...
...AND COME TO ME!
ROOOAAAAAARRRRRR
ARRIVE!
FLASH
FUU

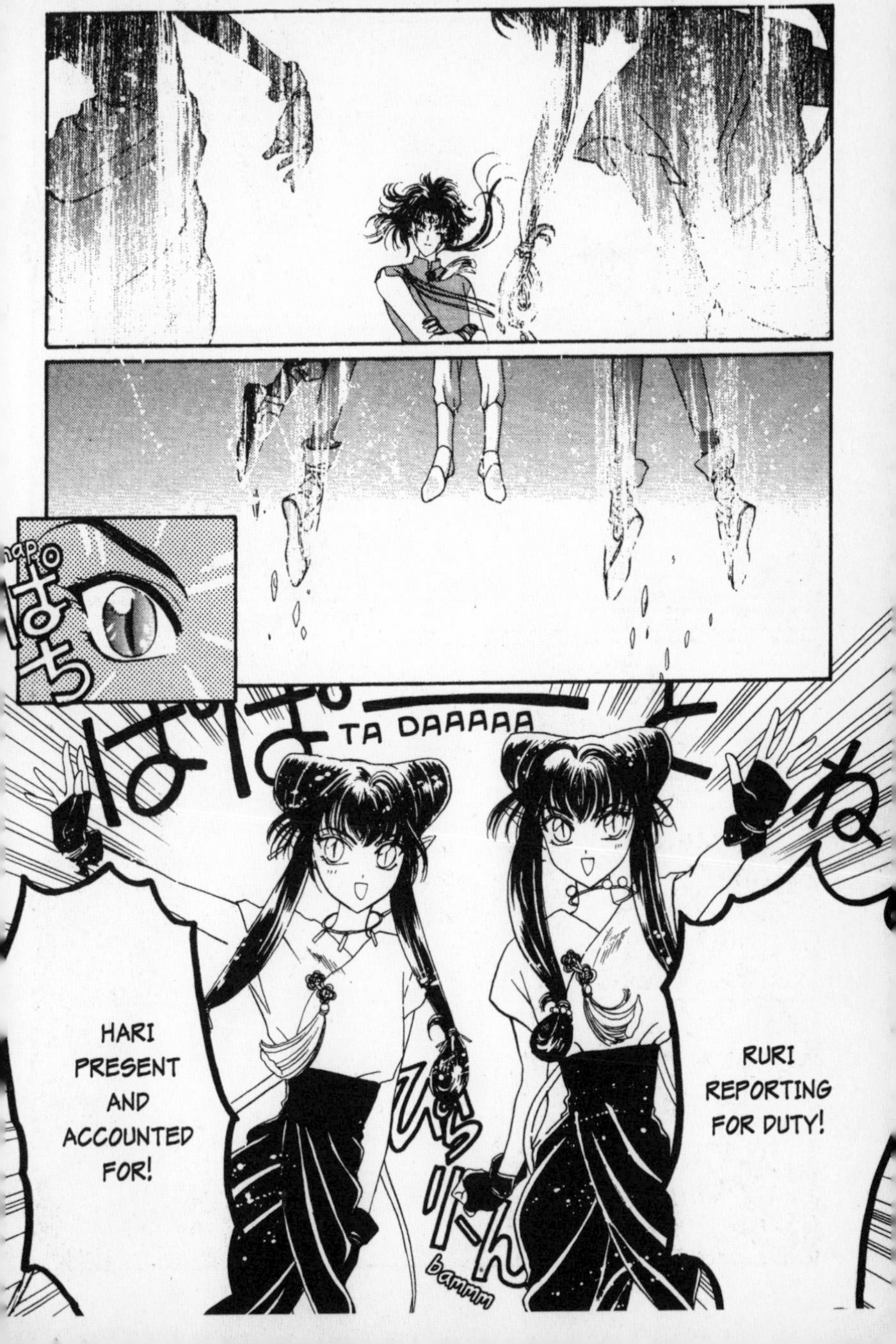
TA DAAAAA
RURI REPORTING FOR DUTY!
HARI PRESENT AND ACCOUNTED FOR!
bammm

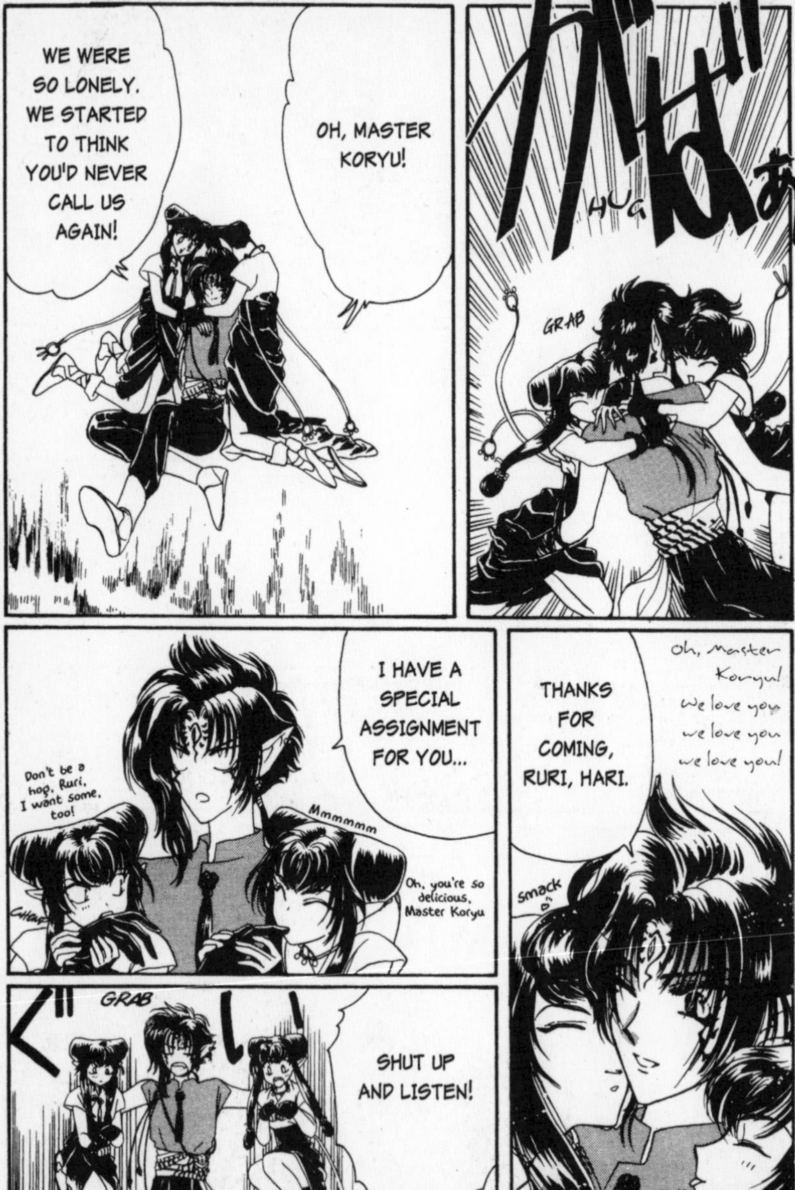
がばあ
HUG
GRAB
OH, MASTER KORYU!
WE WERE SO LONELY. WE STARTED TO THINK YOU'D NEVER CALL US AGAIN!
THANKS FOR COMING, RURI, HARI.
Oh, Master Koryu! We love you we love you we love you!
smack
purr
I HAVE A SPECIAL ASSIGNMENT FOR YOU...
Mmmmmm
Oh, you're so delicious, Master Koryu
Don't be a hog, Ruri, I want some, too!
GRAB
SHUT UP AND LISTEN!

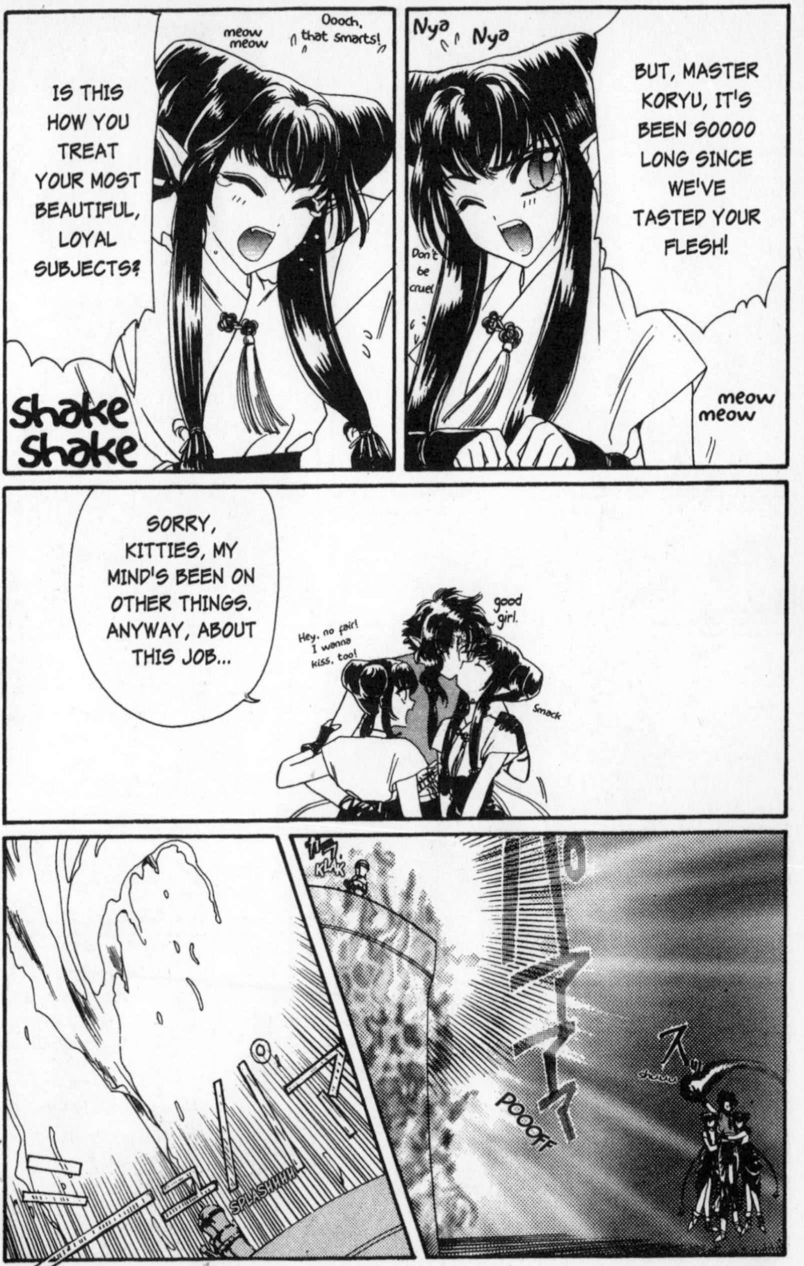
Nya Nya
BUT, MASTER KORYU, IT'S BEEN SOOOO LONG SINCE WE'VE TASTED YOUR FLESH!
Don't be cruel
meow meow
Oooch, that smarts!
meow meow
IS THIS HOW YOU TREAT YOUR MOST BEAUTIFUL, LOYAL SUBJECTS?
Shake Shake
good girl.
Smack
Hey, no fair! I wanna kiss, too!
SORRY, KITTIES, MY MIND'S BEEN ON OTHER THINGS. ANYWAY, ABOUT THIS JOB...
KLAK
POOOFF
SPLASHHH

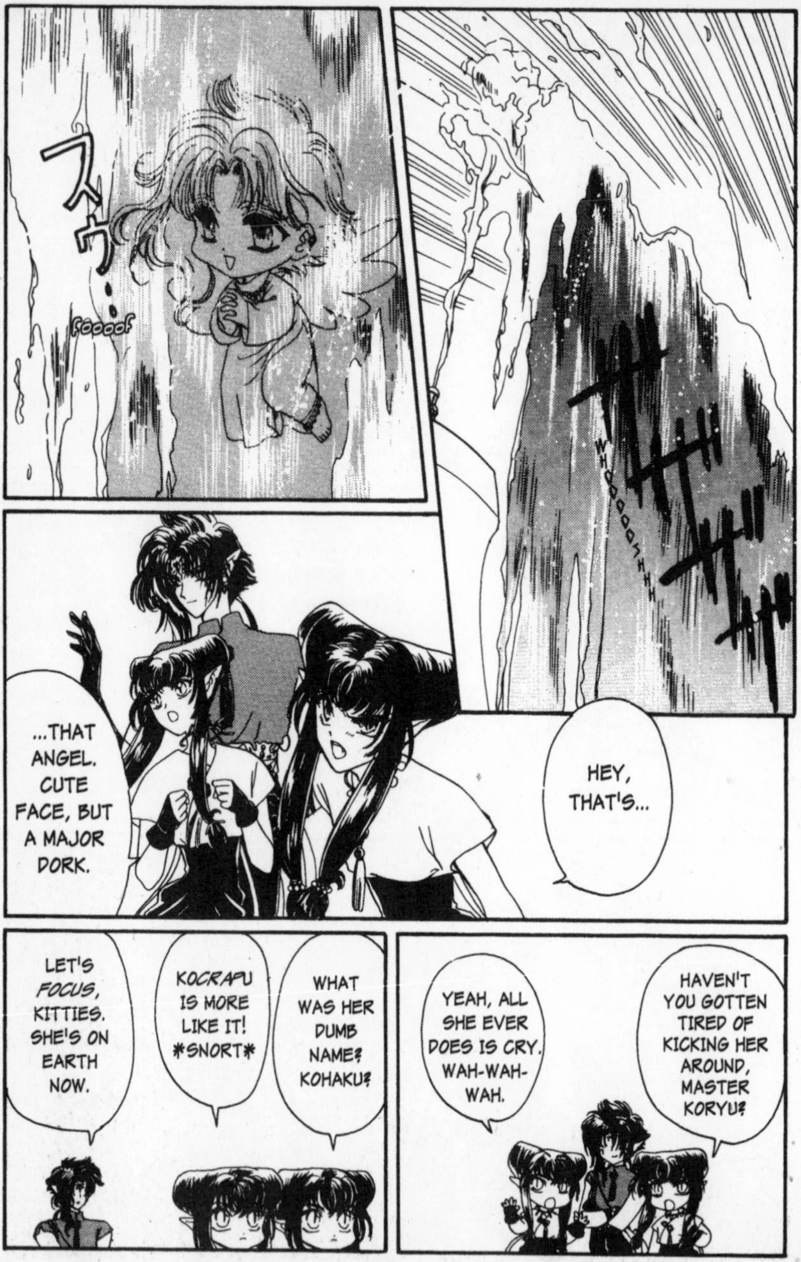
WHOOOOOSHHH
スゥ…
FOOOOF
HEY, THAT'S...
...THAT ANGEL. CUTE FACE, BUT A MAJOR DORK.
HAVEN'T YOU GOTTEN TIRED OF KICKING HER AROUND, MASTER KORYU?
YEAH, ALL SHE EVER DOES IS CRY. WAH-WAH-WAH.
WHAT WAS HER DUMB NAME? KOHAKU?
KOCRAPU IS MORE LIKE IT! *SNORT*
LET'S *FOCUS*, KITTIES. SHE'S ON EARTH NOW.

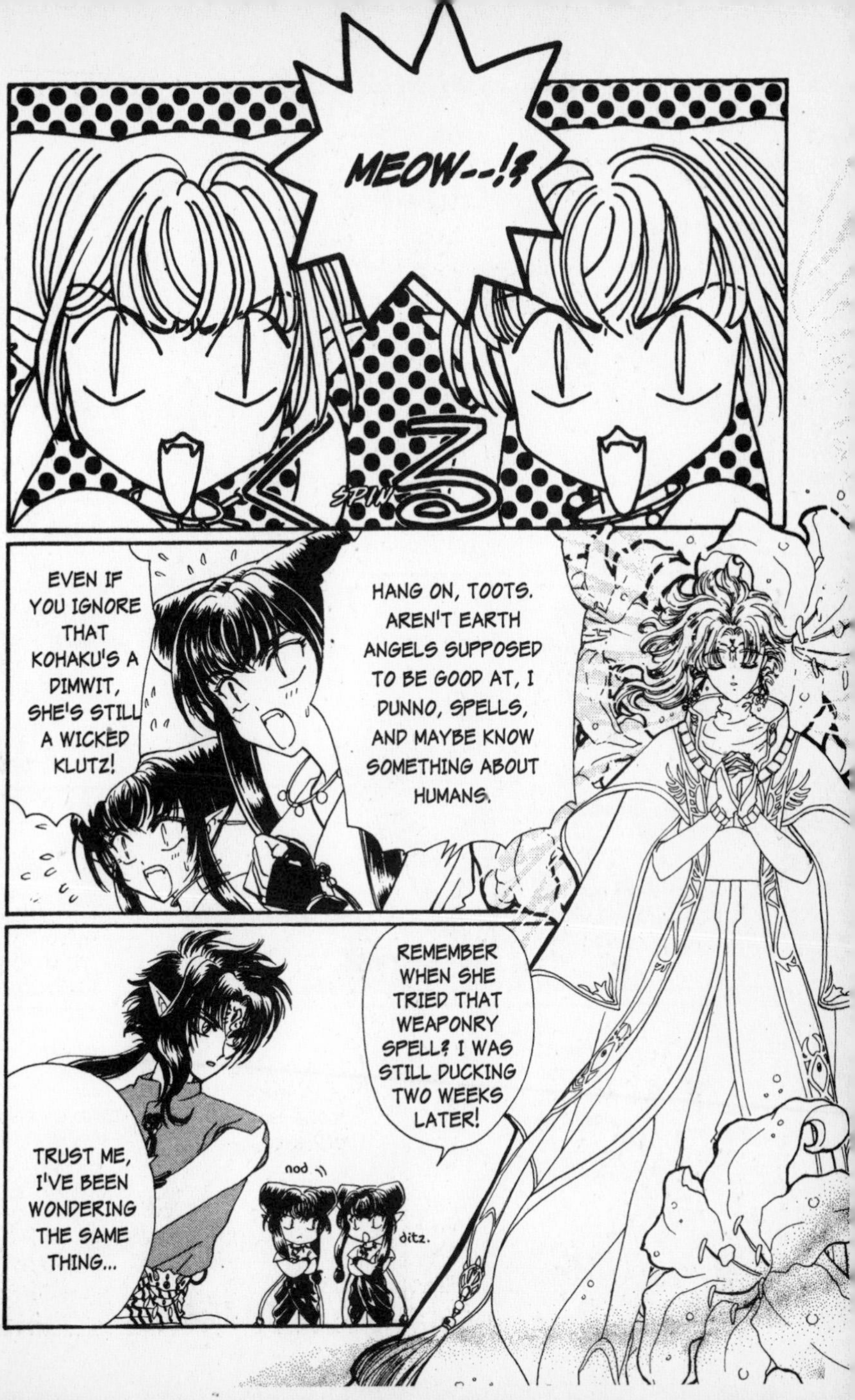
MEOW--!?
SPIN
HANG ON, TOOTS. AREN'T EARTH ANGELS SUPPOSED TO BE GOOD AT, I DUNNO, SPELLS, AND MAYBE KNOW SOMETHING ABOUT HUMANS.
EVEN IF YOU IGNORE THAT KOHAKU'S A DIMWIT, SHE'S STILL A WICKED KLUTZ!
REMEMBER WHEN SHE TRIED THAT WEAPONRY SPELL? I WAS STILL DUCKING TWO WEEKS LATER!
nod
ditz.
TRUST ME, I'VE BEEN WONDERING THE SAME THING...

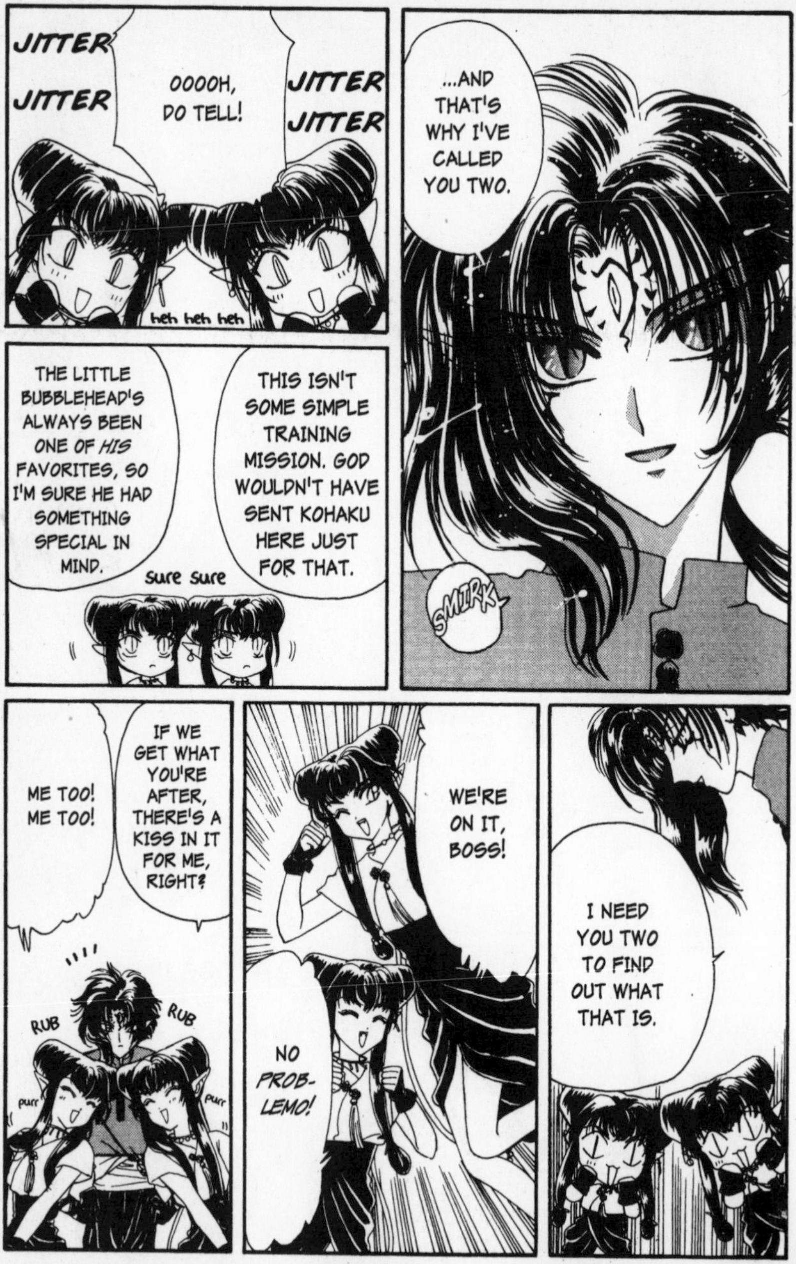
...AND THAT'S WHY I'VE CALLED YOU TWO.
SMIRK
JITTER JITTER
OOOOH, DO TELL!
JITTER JITTER
heh heh heh
THIS ISN'T SOME SIMPLE TRAINING MISSION. GOD WOULDN'T HAVE SENT KOHAKU HERE JUST FOR THAT.
THE LITTLE BUBBLEHEAD'S ALWAYS BEEN ONE OF *HIS* FAVORITES, SO I'M SURE HE HAD SOMETHING SPECIAL IN MIND.
sure sure
I NEED YOU TWO TO FIND OUT WHAT THAT IS.
WE'RE ON IT, BOSS!
NO PROB-LEMO!
IF WE GET WHAT YOU'RE AFTER, THERE'S A KISS IN IT FOR ME, RIGHT?
ME TOO! ME TOO!
RUB
RUB
purr
purr

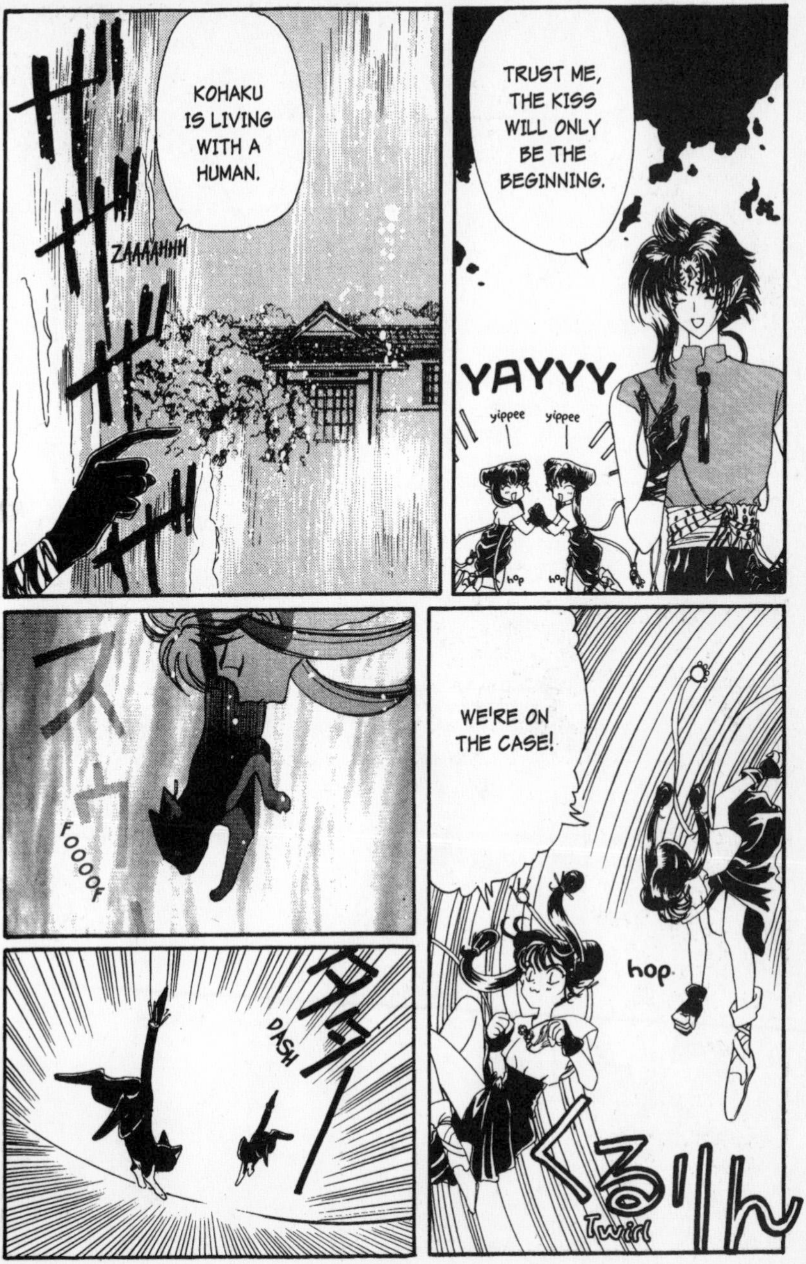
TRUST ME, THE KISS WILL ONLY BE THE BEGINNING.
YAYYY
yippee
yippee
hop
hop
KOHAKU IS LIVING WITH A HUMAN.
ZAAAAHHH
WE'RE ON THE CASE!
hop
Twirl
FOOOOF
DASH

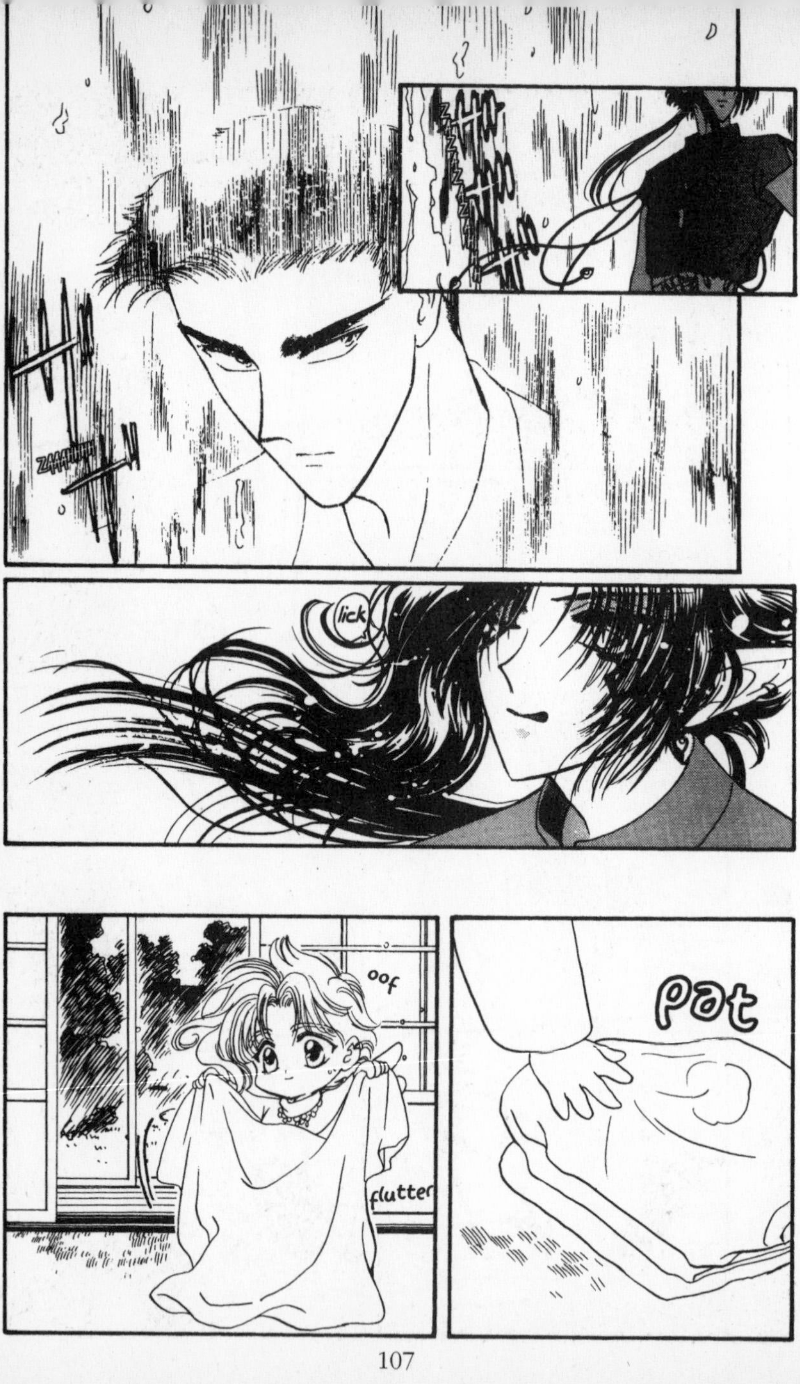
ZAAAHHHH
lick
pat
oof
flutter

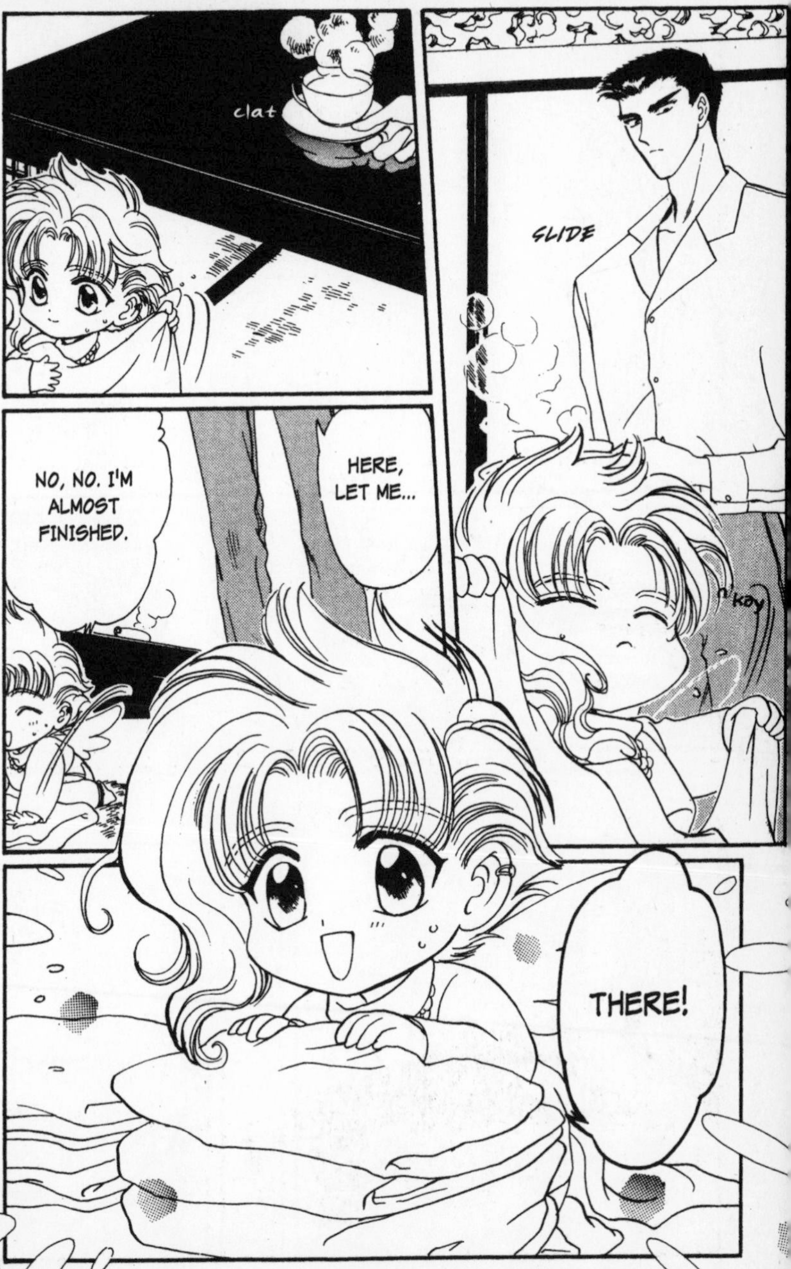
SLIDE
n'kay
clat
HERE, LET ME...
NO, NO. I'M ALMOST FINISHED.
THERE!

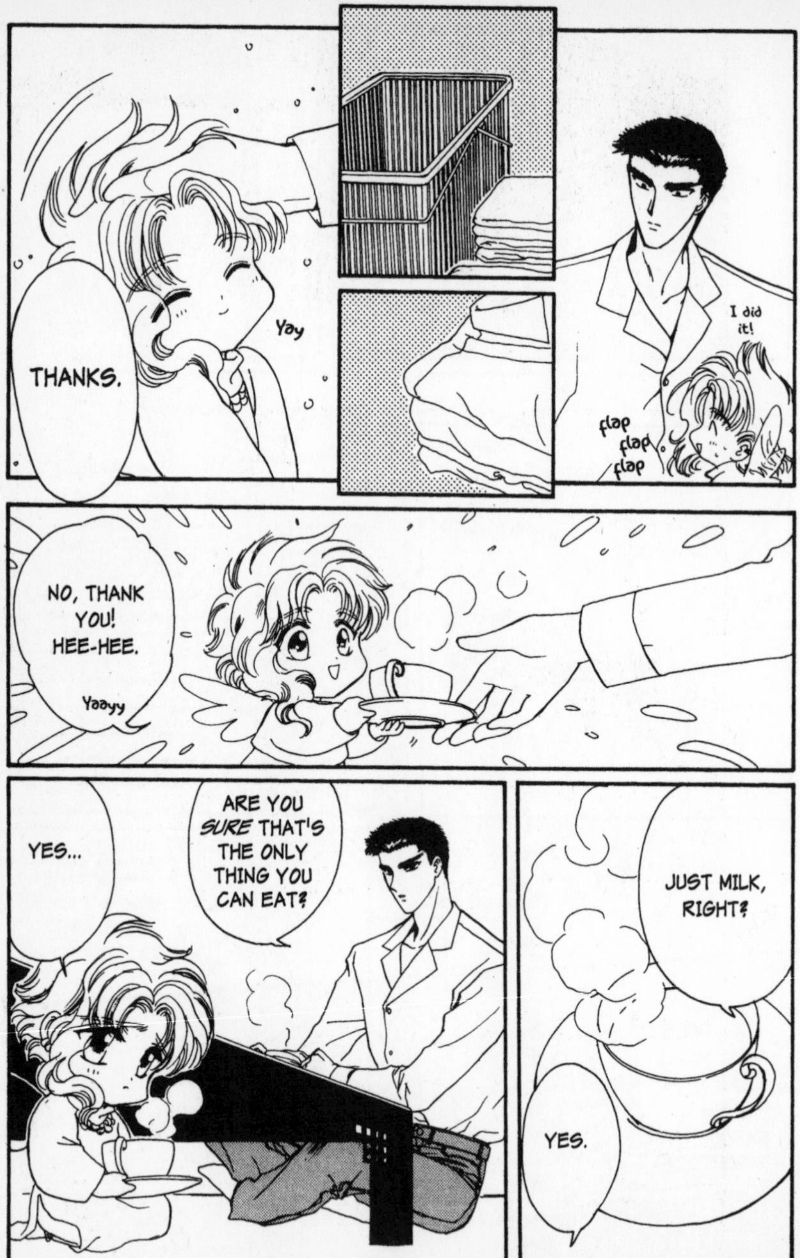
I did it!
flap flap flap
Yay
THANKS.
NO, THANK YOU! HEE-HEE.
Yaayy
JUST MILK, RIGHT?
YES.
ARE YOU *SURE* THAT'S THE ONLY THING YOU CAN EAT?
YES...

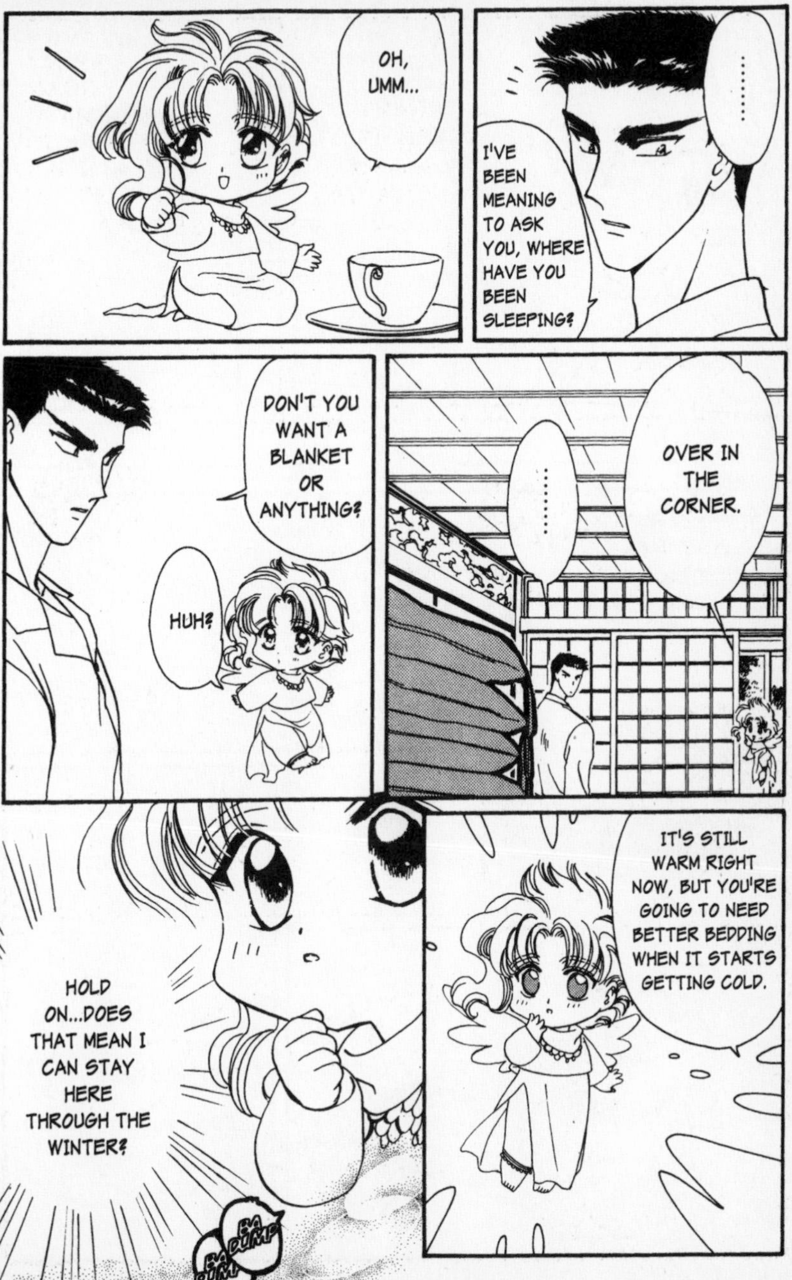
......
I'VE BEEN MEANING TO ASK YOU, WHERE HAVE YOU BEEN SLEEPING?
OH, UMM...
OVER IN THE CORNER.
......
DON'T YOU WANT A BLANKET OR ANYTHING?
HUH?
IT'S STILL WARM RIGHT NOW, BUT YOU'RE GOING TO NEED BETTER BEDDING WHEN IT STARTS GETTING COLD.
HOLD ON...DOES THAT MEAN I CAN STAY HERE THROUGH THE WINTER?
BA DUMP
BA DUMP

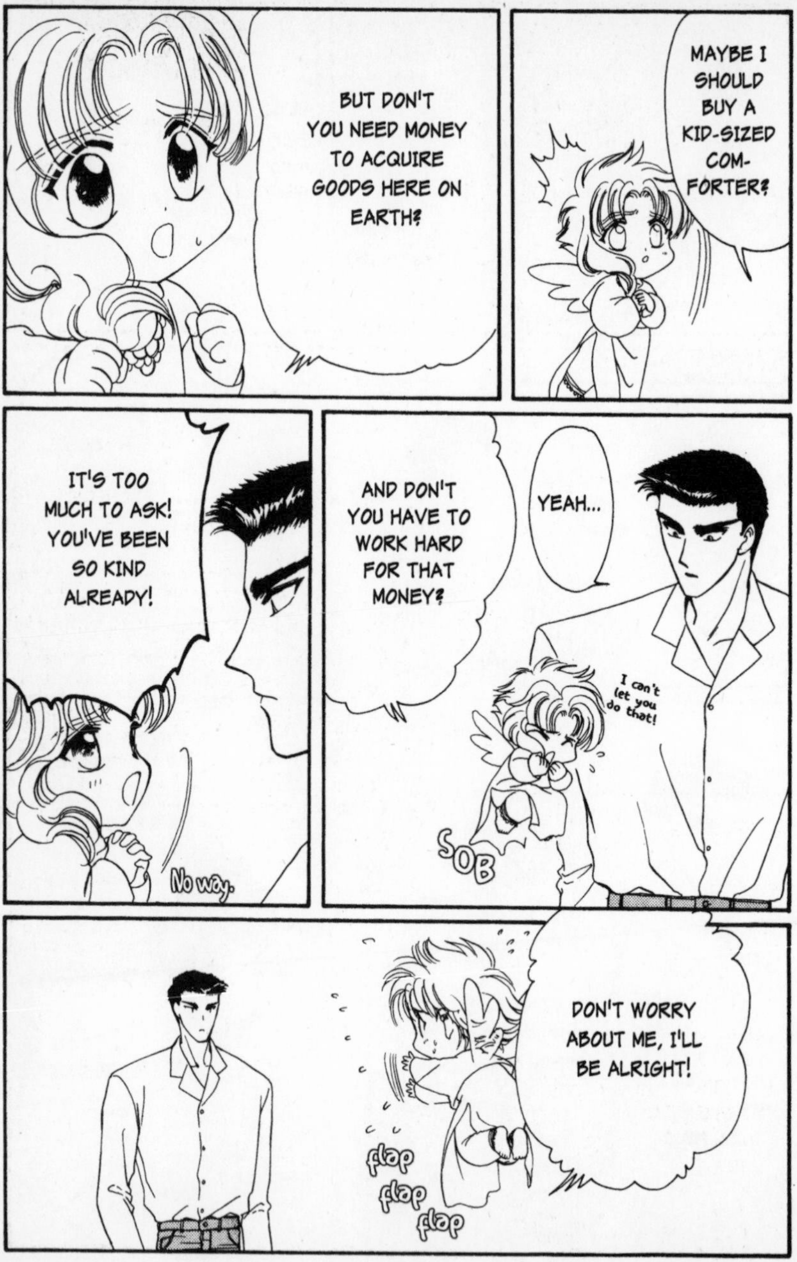

MAYBE I SHOULD BUY A KID-SIZED COM-FORTER?
BUT DON'T YOU NEED MONEY TO ACQUIRE GOODS HERE ON EARTH?
YEAH...
AND DON'T YOU HAVE TO WORK HARD FOR THAT MONEY?
I can't let you do that!
SOB
IT'S TOO MUCH TO ASK! YOU'VE BEEN SO KIND ALREADY!
No way.
DON'T WORRY ABOUT ME, I'LL BE ALRIGHT!
flap
flap
flap

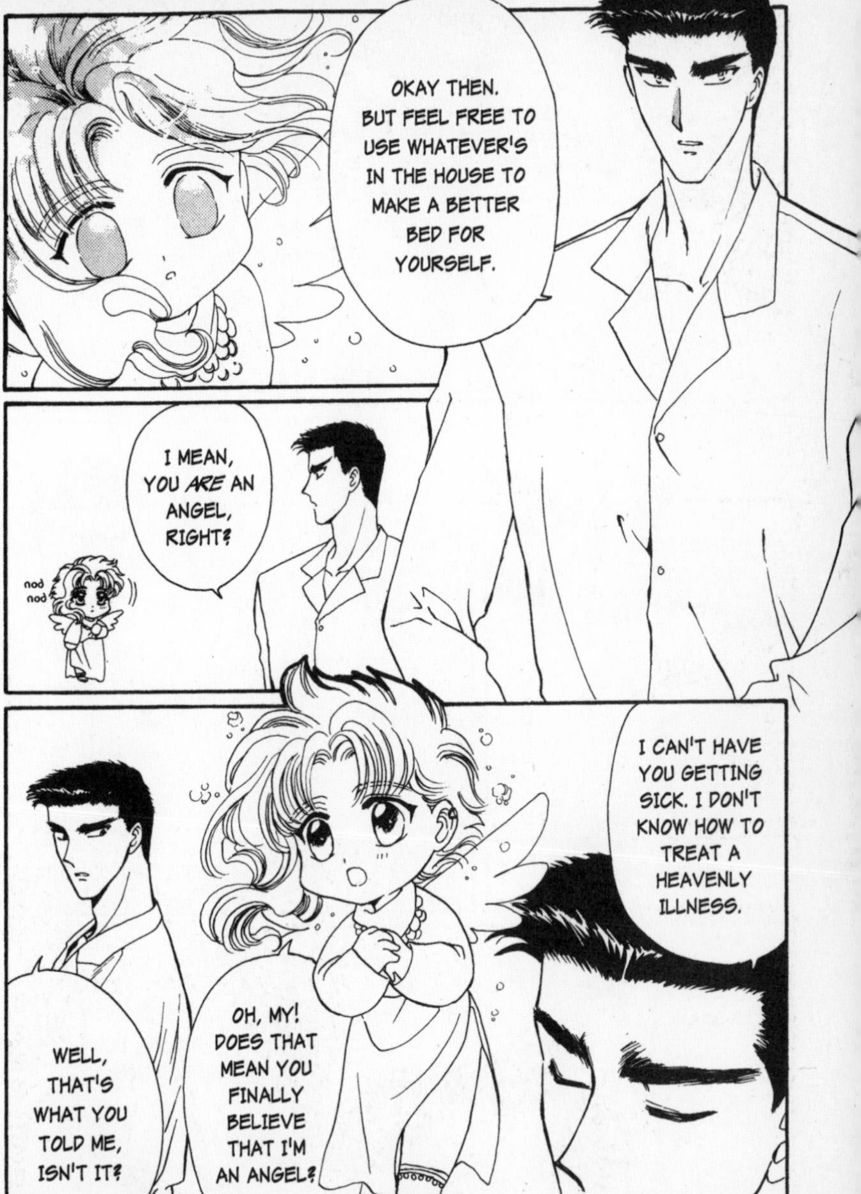
OKAY THEN. BUT FEEL FREE TO USE WHATEVER'S IN THE HOUSE TO MAKE A BETTER BED FOR YOURSELF.
I MEAN, YOU *ARE* AN ANGEL, RIGHT?
nod nod
I CAN'T HAVE YOU GETTING SICK. I DON'T KNOW HOW TO TREAT A HEAVENLY ILLNESS.
OH, MY! DOES THAT MEAN YOU FINALLY BELIEVE THAT I'M AN ANGEL?
WELL, THAT'S WHAT YOU TOLD ME, ISN'T IT?

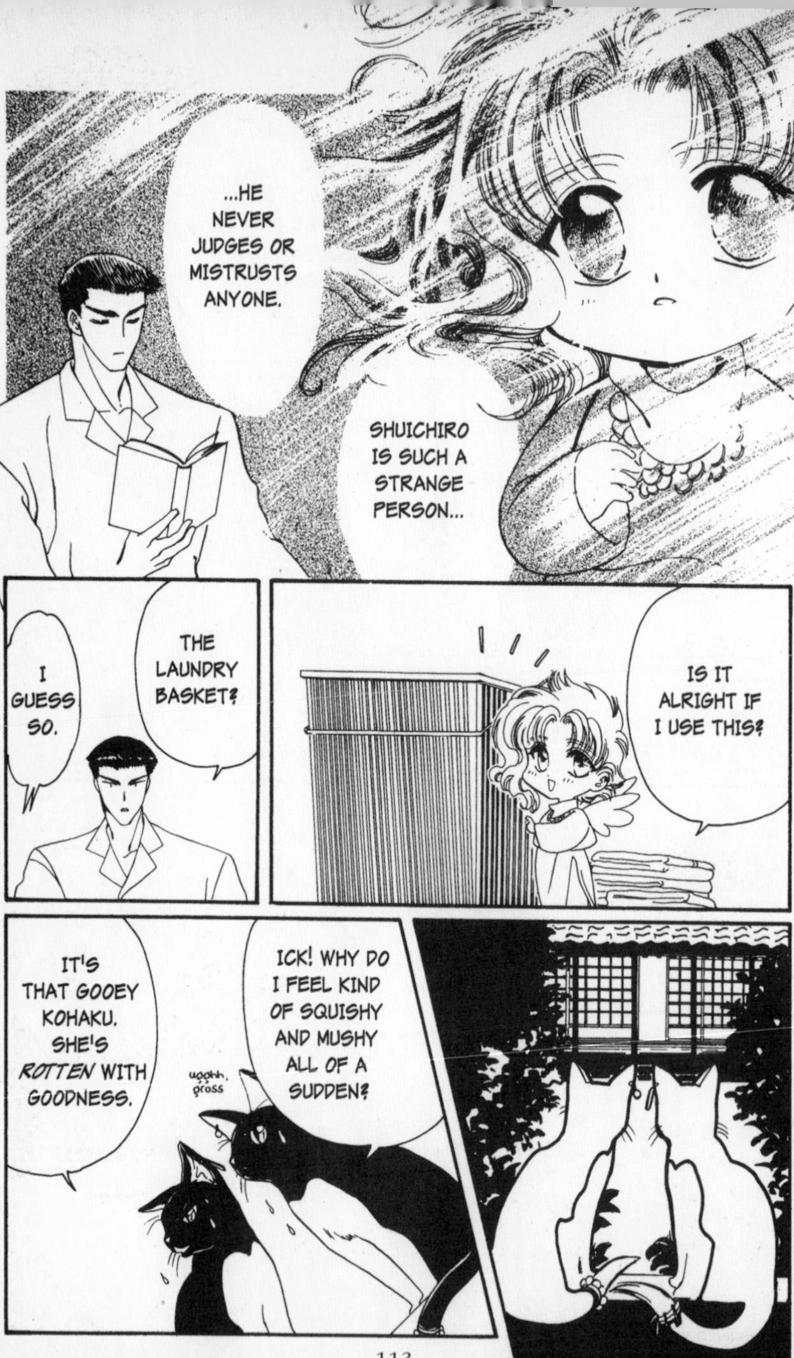
SHUICHIRO IS SUCH A STRANGE PERSON...
...HE NEVER JUDGES OR MISTRUSTS ANYONE.
IS IT ALRIGHT IF I USE THIS?
THE LAUNDRY BASKET?
I GUESS SO.
ICK! WHY DO I FEEL KIND OF SQUISHY AND MUSHY ALL OF A SUDDEN?
ugghh, gross
IT'S THAT GOOEY KOHAKU. SHE'S *ROTTEN* WITH GOODNESS.

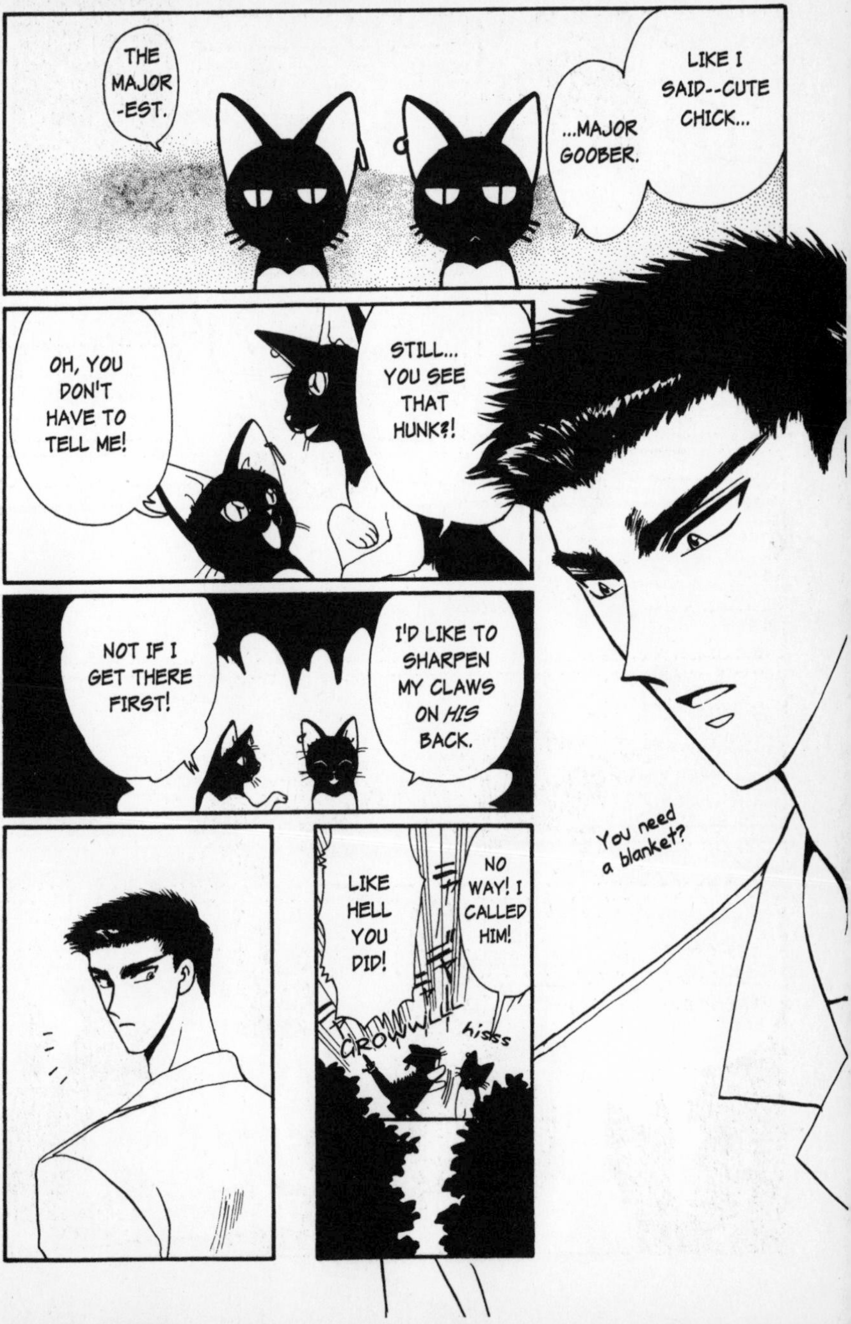
LIKE I SAID--CUTE CHICK...
...MAJOR GOOBER.
THE MAJOR-EST.
You need a blanket?
STILL... YOU SEE THAT HUNK?!
OH, YOU DON'T HAVE TO TELL ME!
I'D LIKE TO SHARPEN MY CLAWS ON *HIS* BACK.
NOT IF I GET THERE FIRST!
NO WAY! I CALLED HIM!
LIKE HELL YOU DID!
hisss
GROWWL

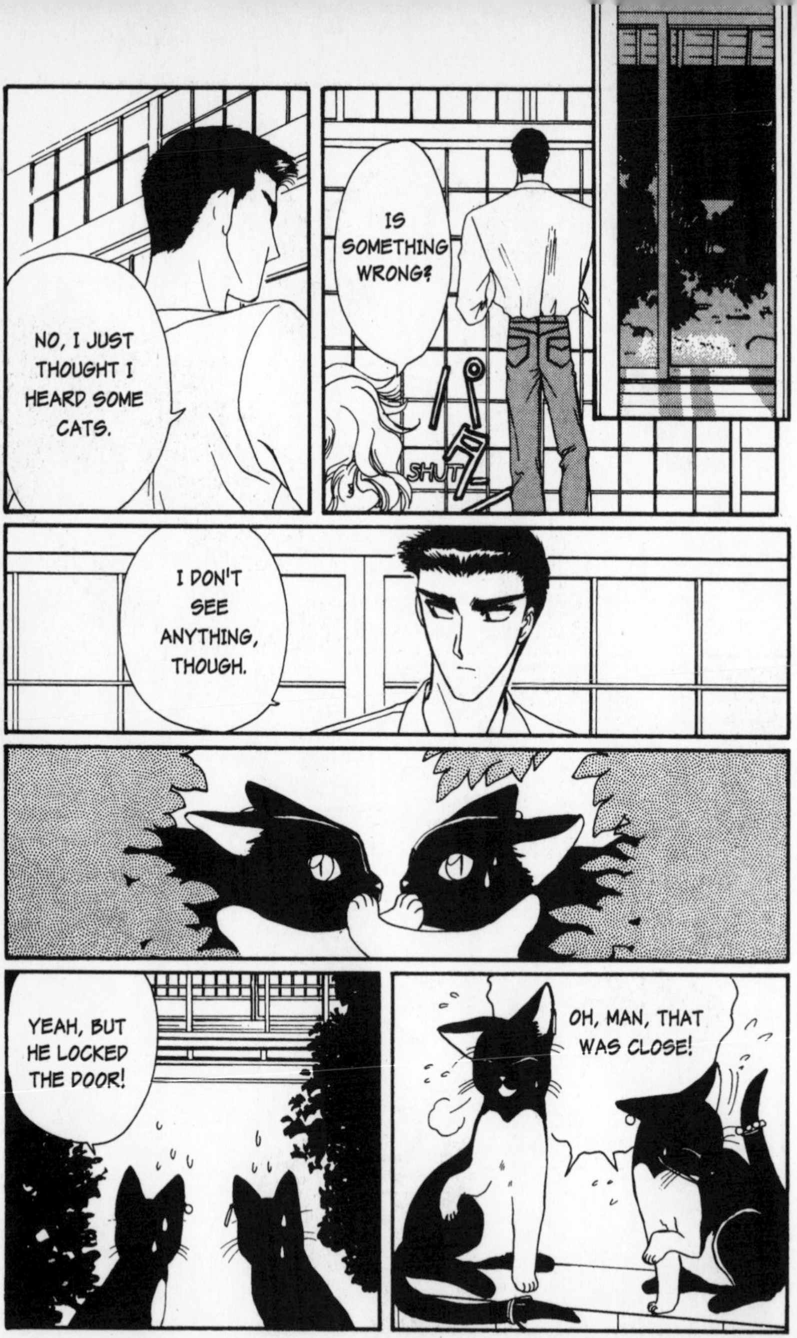
SHUT
IS SOMETHING WRONG?
NO, I JUST THOUGHT I HEARD SOME CATS.
I DON'T SEE ANYTHING, THOUGH.
OH, MAN, THAT WAS CLOSE!
YEAH, BUT HE LOCKED THE DOOR!

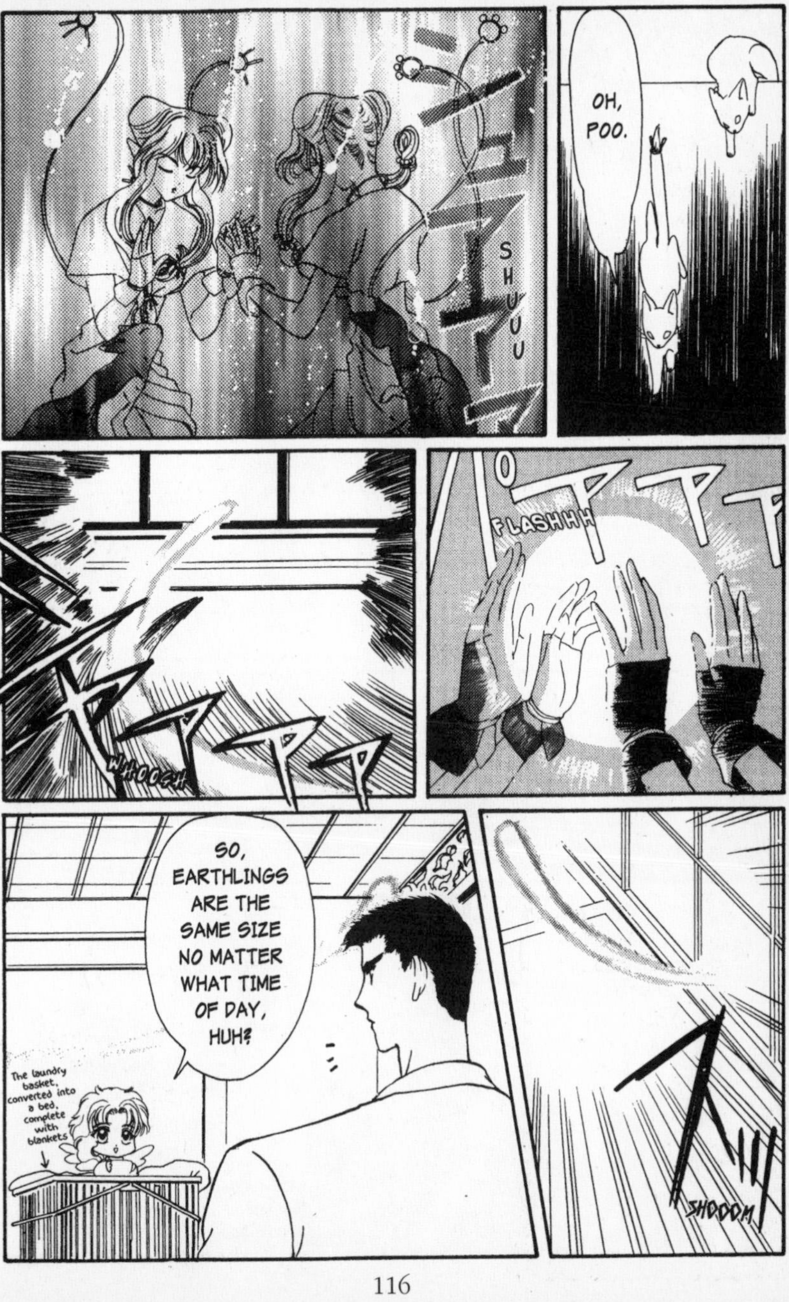
OH, POO.
SHUUU
FLASHHH
WHOOSH
SHOOOM
SO, EARTHLINGS ARE THE SAME SIZE NO MATTER WHAT TIME OF DAY, HUH?
...
The laundry basket, converted into a bed, complete with blankets

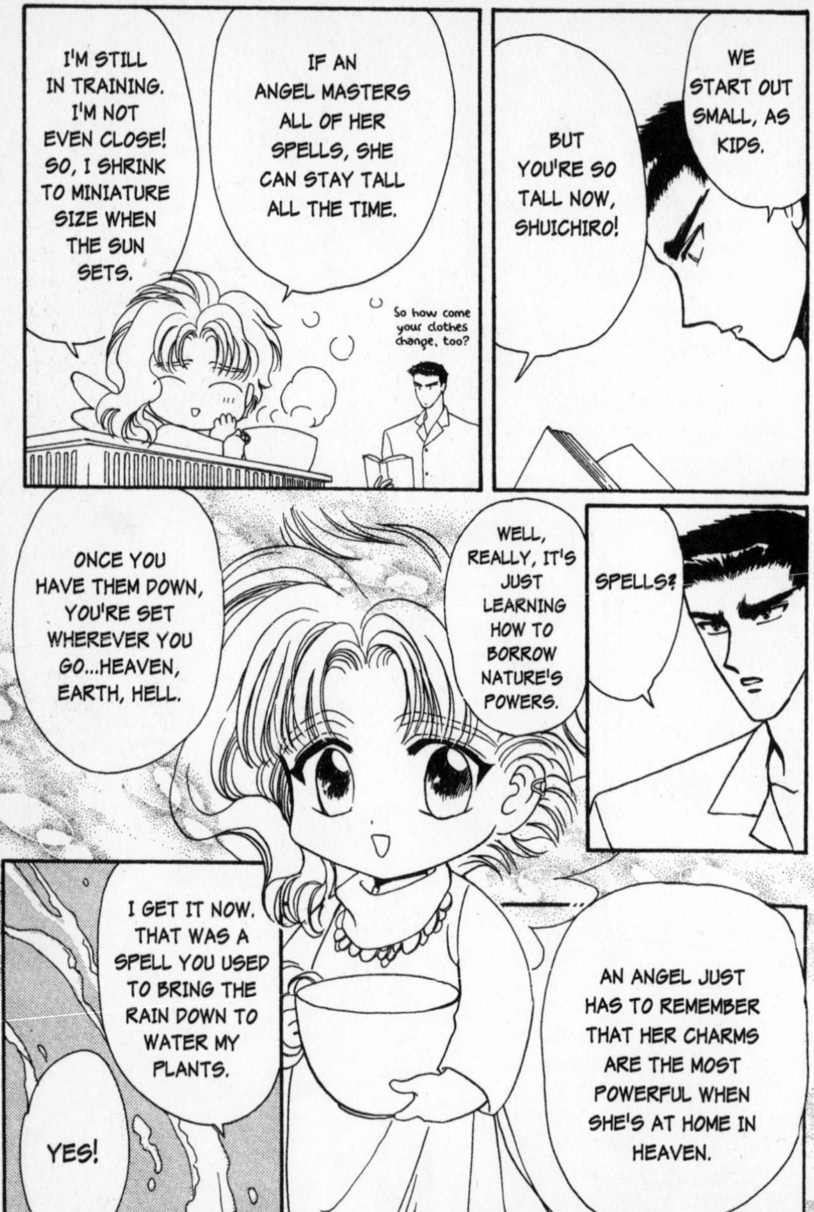
WE START OUT SMALL, AS KIDS.
BUT YOU'RE SO TALL NOW, SHUICHIRO!
IF AN ANGEL MASTERS ALL OF HER SPELLS, SHE CAN STAY TALL ALL THE TIME.
I'M STILL IN TRAINING. I'M NOT EVEN CLOSE! SO, I SHRINK TO MINIATURE SIZE WHEN THE SUN SETS.
So how come your clothes change, too?
SPELLS?
WELL, REALLY, IT'S JUST LEARNING HOW TO BORROW NATURE'S POWERS.
ONCE YOU HAVE THEM DOWN, YOU'RE SET WHEREVER YOU GO...HEAVEN, EARTH, HELL.
——...
AN ANGEL JUST HAS TO REMEMBER THAT HER CHARMS ARE THE MOST POWERFUL WHEN SHE'S AT HOME IN HEAVEN.
I GET IT NOW. THAT WAS A SPELL YOU USED TO BRING THE RAIN DOWN TO WATER MY PLANTS.
YES!

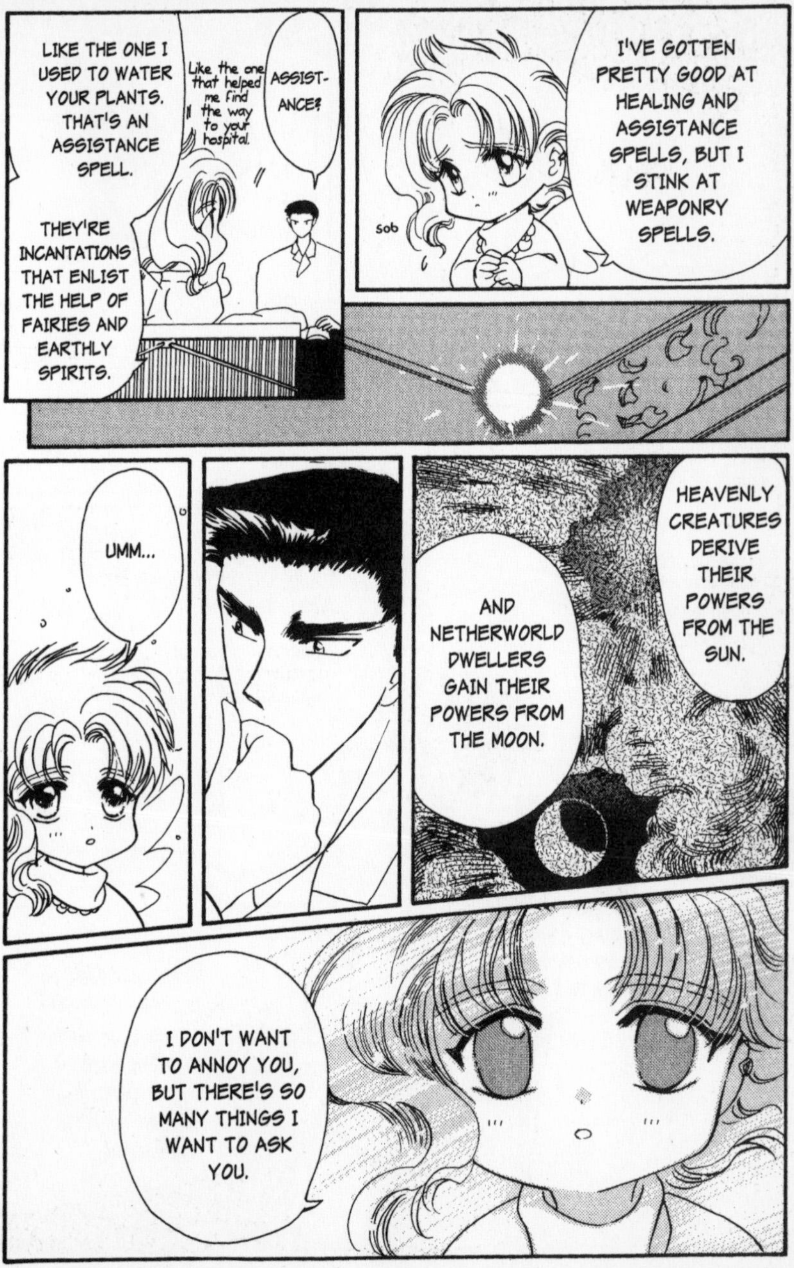
I'VE GOTTEN PRETTY GOOD AT HEALING AND ASSISTANCE SPELLS, BUT I STINK AT WEAPONRY SPELLS.
sob
ASSIST-ANCE?
Like the one that helped me find the way to your hospital.
LIKE THE ONE I USED TO WATER YOUR PLANTS. THAT'S AN ASSISTANCE SPELL.
THEY'RE INCANTATIONS THAT ENLIST THE HELP OF FAIRIES AND EARTHLY SPIRITS.
HEAVENLY CREATURES DERIVE THEIR POWERS FROM THE SUN.
AND NETHERWORLD DWELLERS GAIN THEIR POWERS FROM THE MOON.
UMM...
I DON'T WANT TO ANNOY YOU, BUT THERE'S SO MANY THINGS I WANT TO ASK YOU.

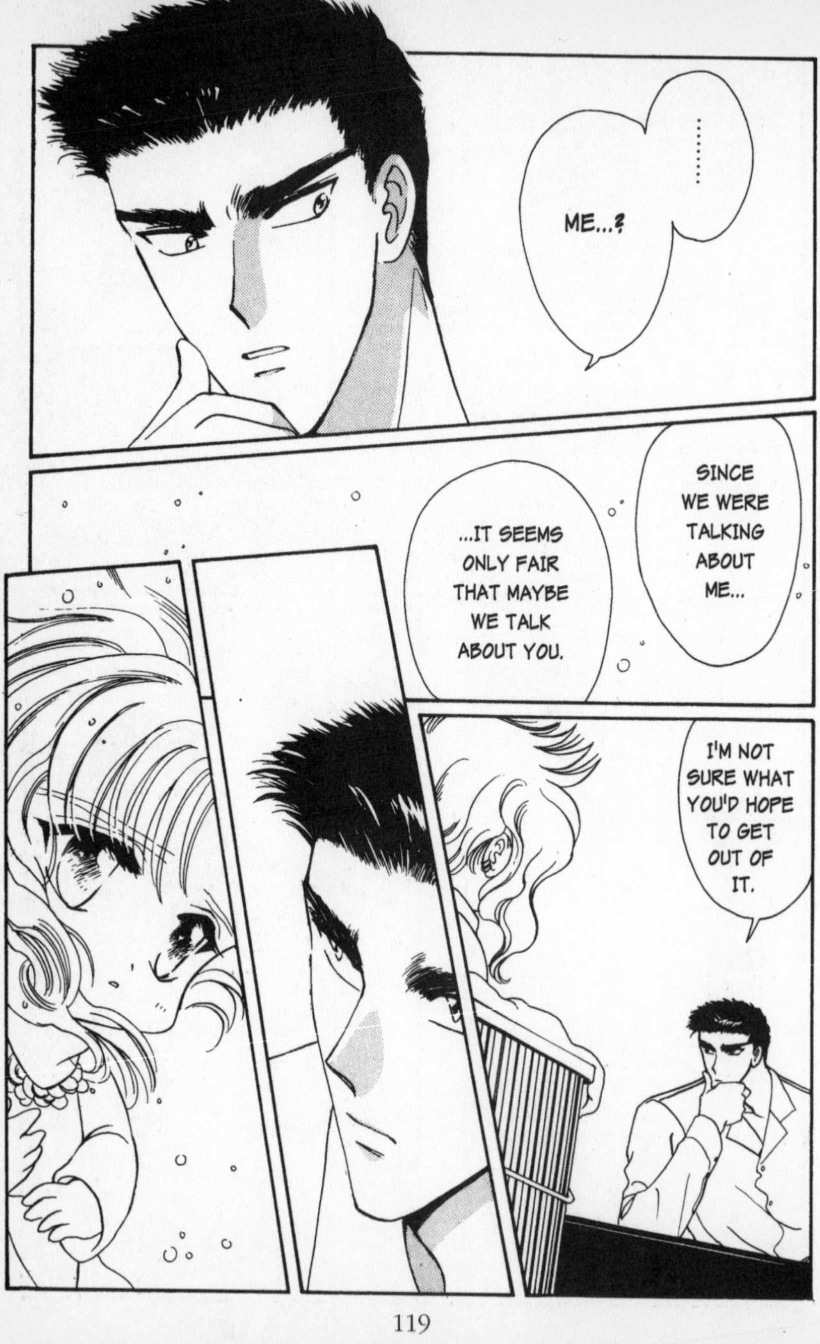
......
ME...?
SINCE WE WERE TALKING ABOUT ME...
...IT SEEMS ONLY FAIR THAT MAYBE WE TALK ABOUT YOU.
I'M NOT SURE WHAT YOU'D HOPE TO GET OUT OF IT.

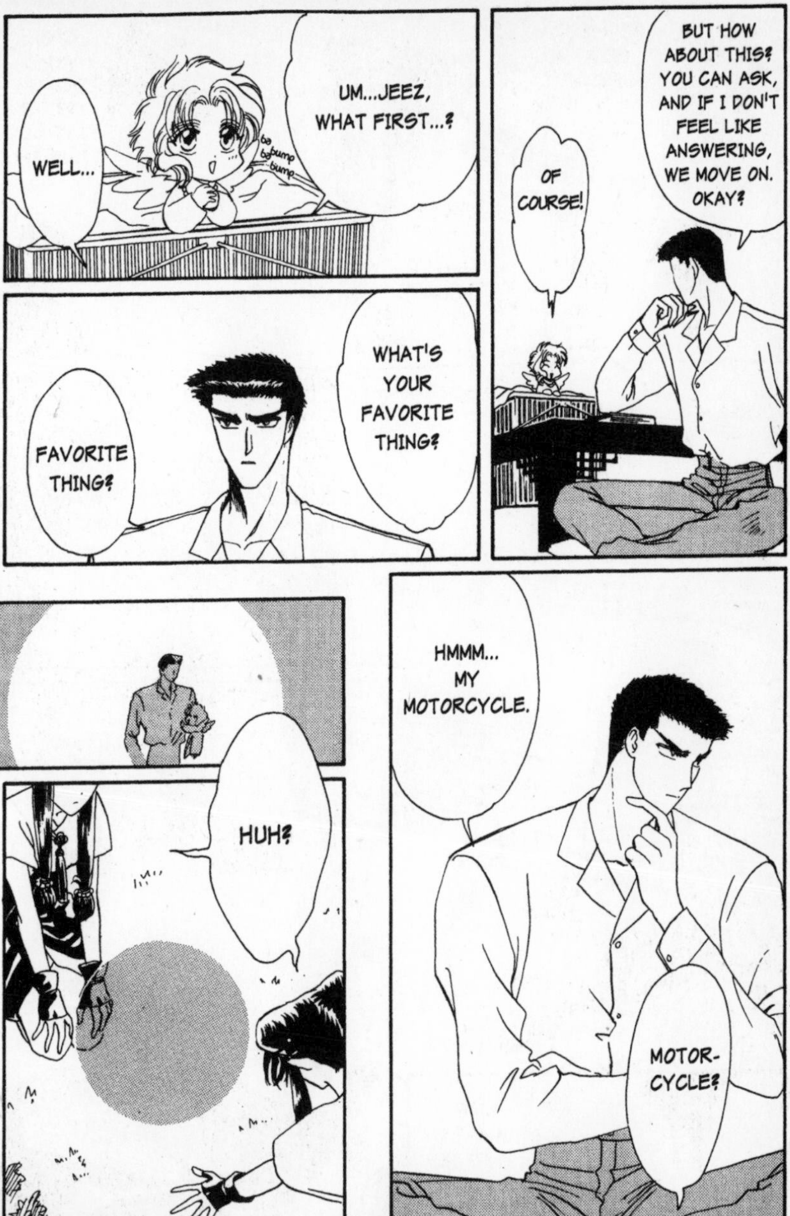

BUT HOW ABOUT THIS? YOU CAN ASK, AND IF I DON'T FEEL LIKE ANSWERING, WE MOVE ON. OKAY?
OF COURSE!
UM...JEEZ, WHAT FIRST...?
ba bump ba bump
WELL...
WHAT'S YOUR FAVORITE THING?
FAVORITE THING?
HMMM... MY MOTORCYCLE.
MOTOR-CYCLE?
HUH?

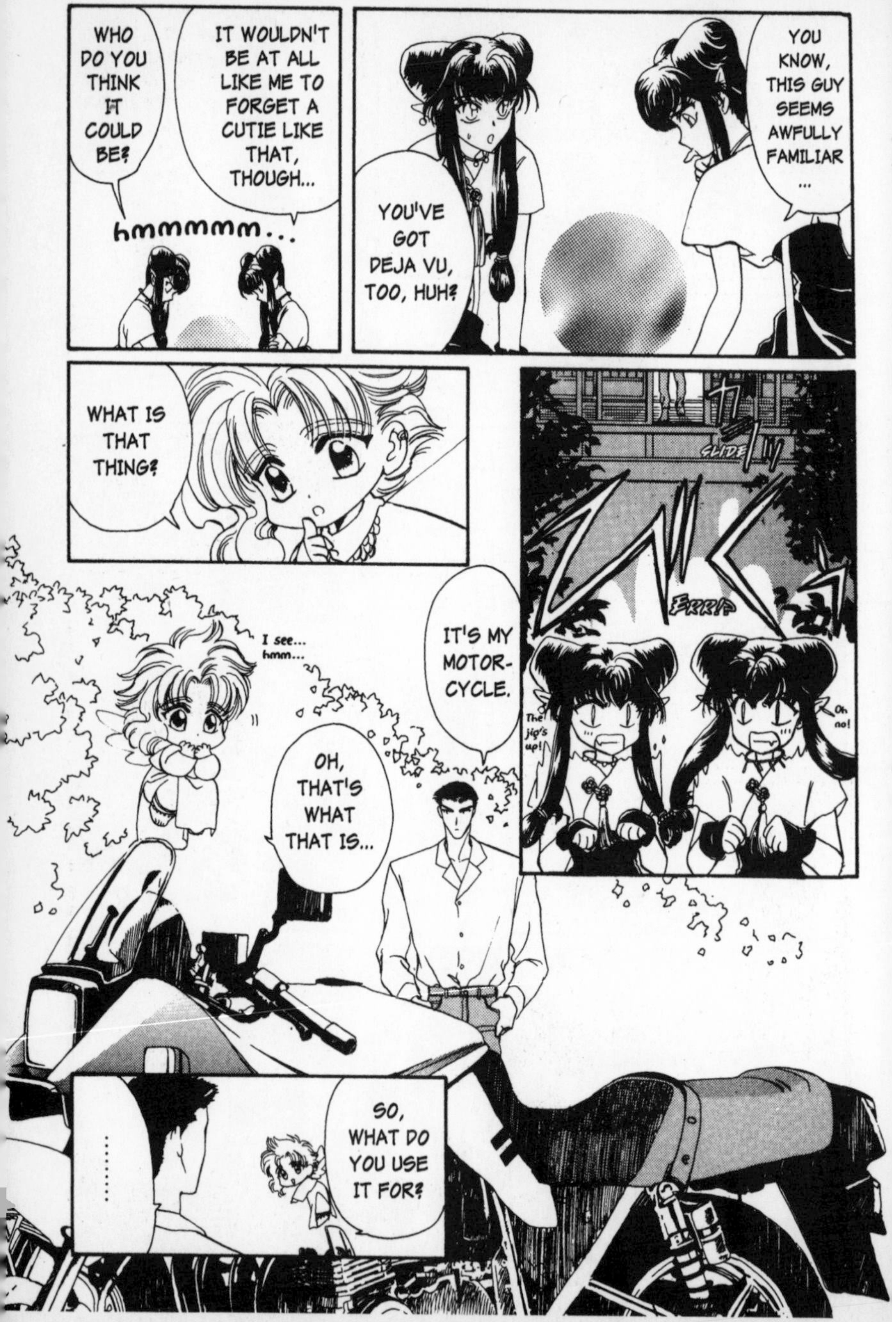
YOU KNOW, THIS GUY SEEMS AWFULLY FAMILIAR...
YOU'VE GOT DEJA VU, TOO, HUH?
IT WOULDN'T BE AT ALL LIKE ME TO FORGET A CUTIE LIKE THAT, THOUGH...
WHO DO YOU THINK IT COULD BE?
hmmmmm...
SLIDE
ERR!?
Oh no!
The jig's up!
WHAT IS THAT THING?
IT'S MY MOTORCYCLE.
OH, THAT'S WHAT THAT IS...
I see... hmm...
SO, WHAT DO YOU USE IT FOR?
....

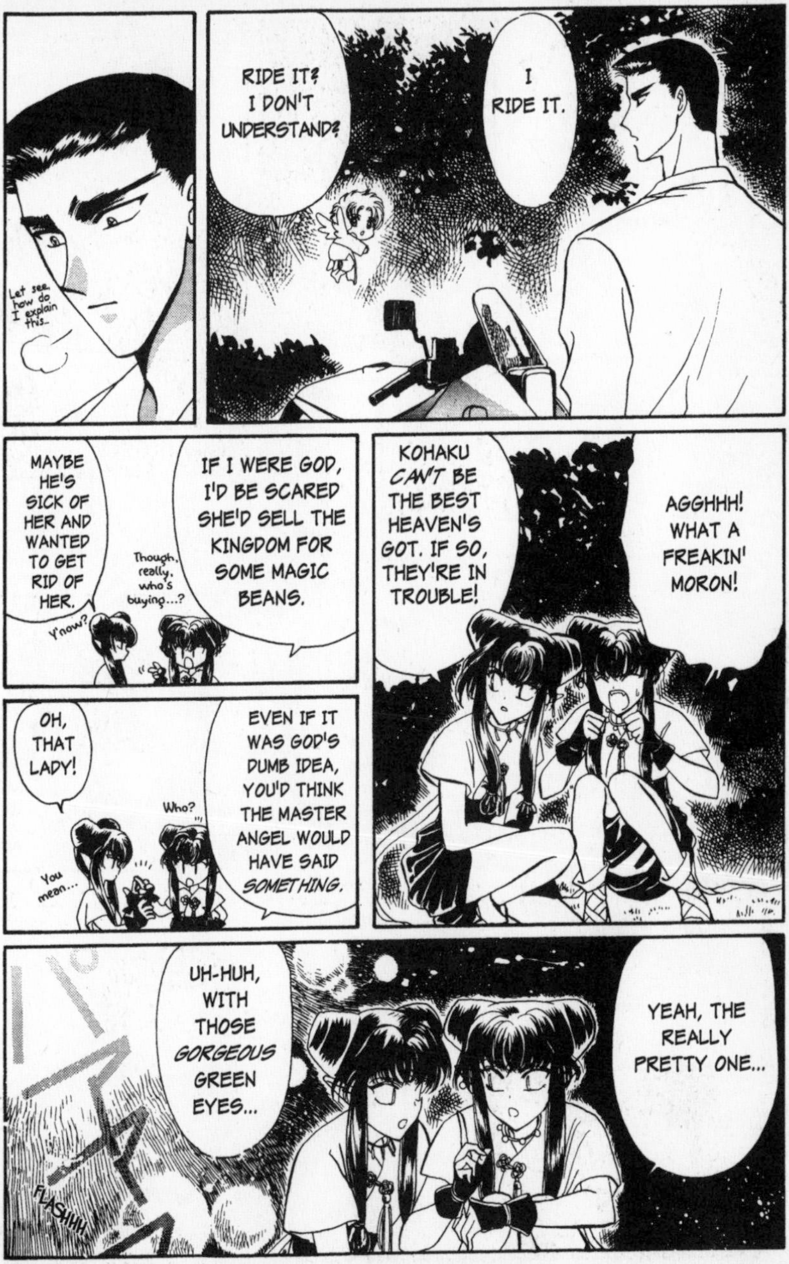
I RIDE IT.
RIDE IT? I DON'T UNDERSTAND?
Let see how do I explain this...
AGGHHH! WHAT A FREAKIN' MORON!
KOHAKU *CAN'T* BE THE BEST HEAVEN'S GOT. IF SO, THEY'RE IN TROUBLE!
IF I WERE GOD, I'D BE SCARED SHE'D SELL THE KINGDOM FOR SOME MAGIC BEANS.
Though, really, who's buying...?
MAYBE HE'S SICK OF HER AND WANTED TO GET RID OF HER.
Y'now?
EVEN IF IT WAS GOD'S DUMB IDEA, YOU'D THINK THE MASTER ANGEL WOULD HAVE SAID *SOMETHING*.
Who?
OH, THAT LADY!
You mean...
YEAH, THE REALLY PRETTY ONE...
UH-HUH, WITH THOSE *GORGEOUS* GREEN EYES...
FLASHHH

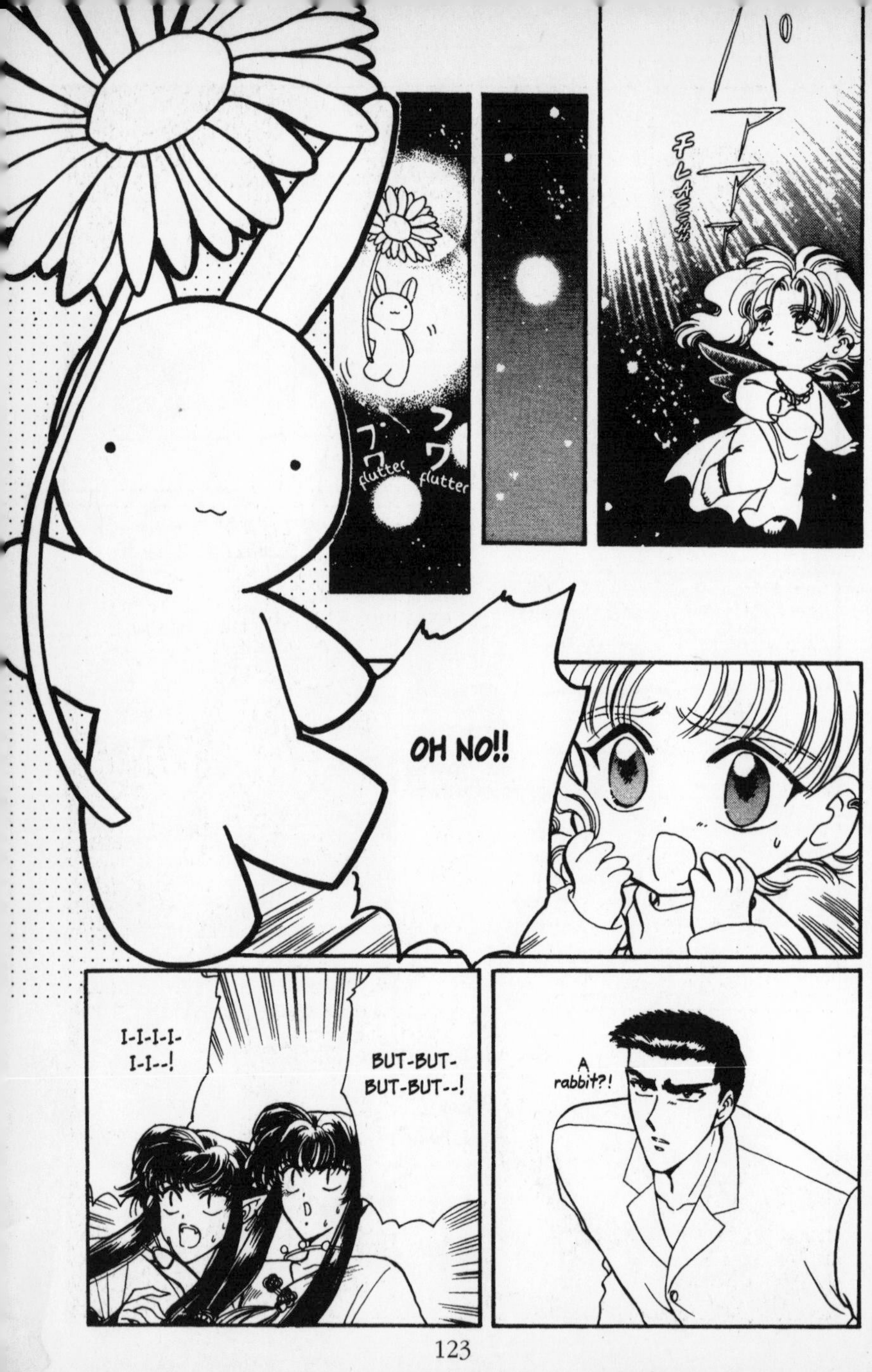

パァァァァ
フワ
flutter
フワ
flutter
OH NO!!
A rabbit?!
BUT-BUT-
BUT-BUT--!
I-I-I-I-
I-I--!

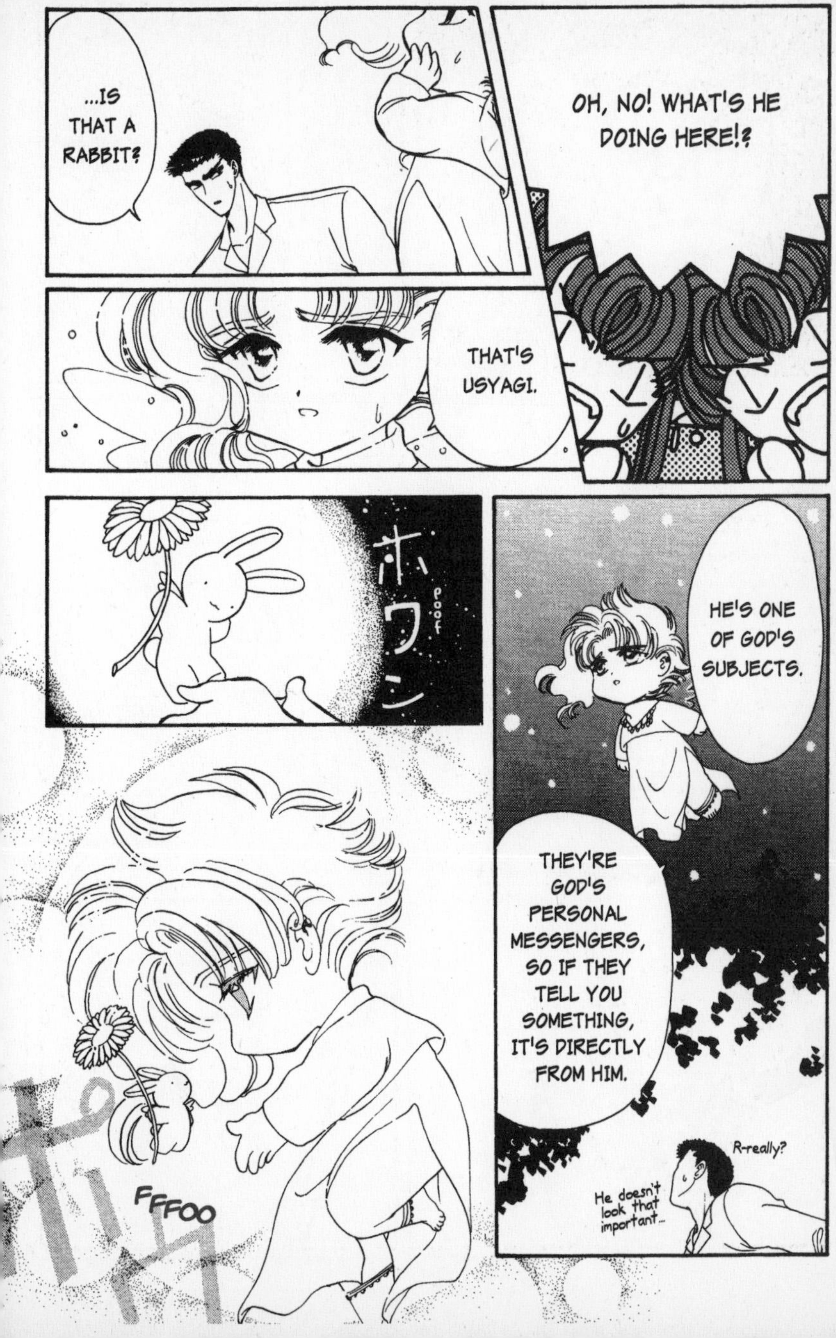
OH, NO! WHAT'S HE DOING HERE!?
...IS THAT A RABBIT?
THAT'S USYAGI.
HE'S ONE OF GOD'S SUBJECTS.
THEY'RE GOD'S PERSONAL MESSENGERS, SO IF THEY TELL YOU SOMETHING, IT'S DIRECTLY FROM HIM.
R-really?
He doesn't look that important...
ホワン
poof
FFFOO

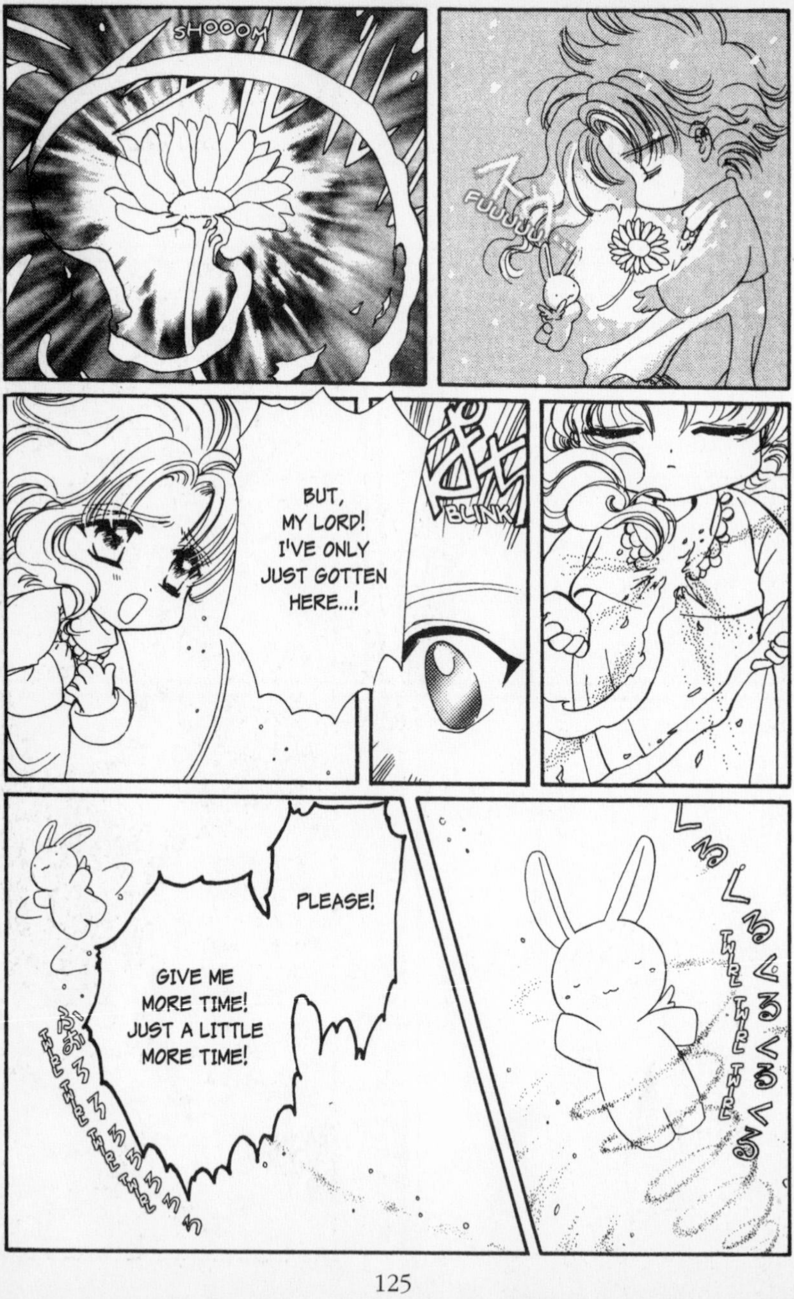
FUUUUU
SHOOOM
BLINK
BUT, MY LORD! I'VE ONLY JUST GOTTEN HERE...!
TWIRL TWIRL TWIRL
PLEASE!
GIVE ME MORE TIME! JUST A LITTLE MORE TIME!
TWIRL TWIRL TWIRL

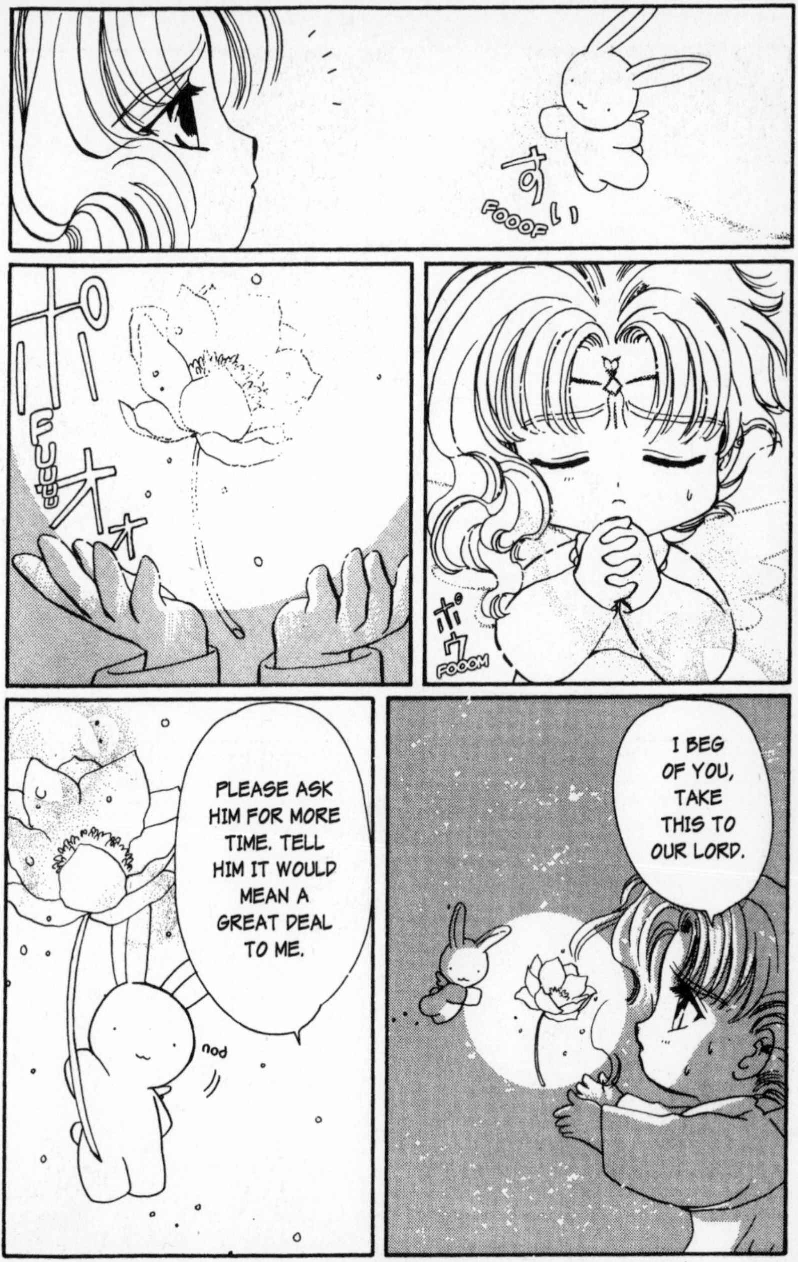
すぃ
FOOOF
ポゥ
FOOOM
ポーーオォ
FUUU
I BEG OF YOU, TAKE THIS TO OUR LORD.
PLEASE ASK HIM FOR MORE TIME. TELL HIM IT WOULD MEAN A GREAT DEAL TO ME.
nod

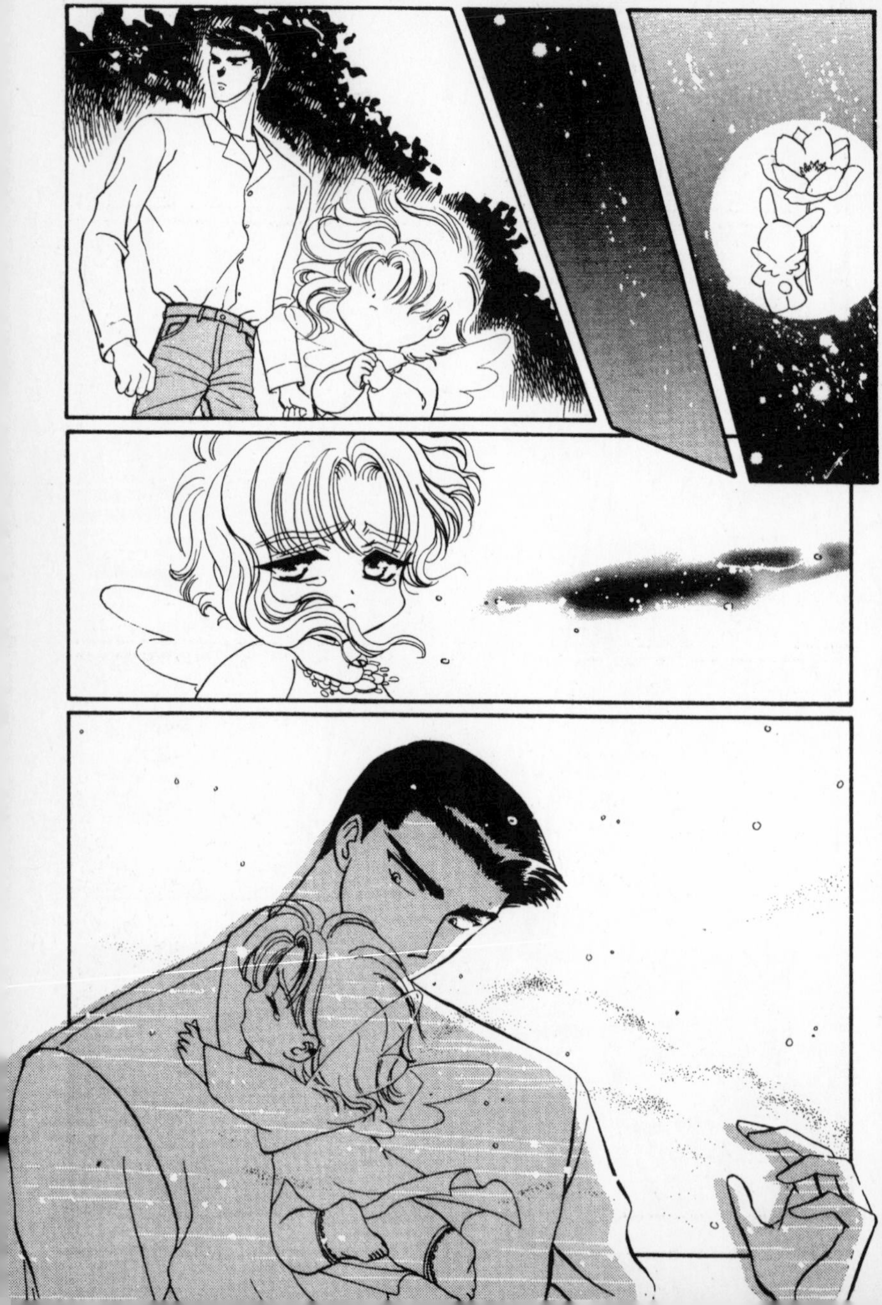

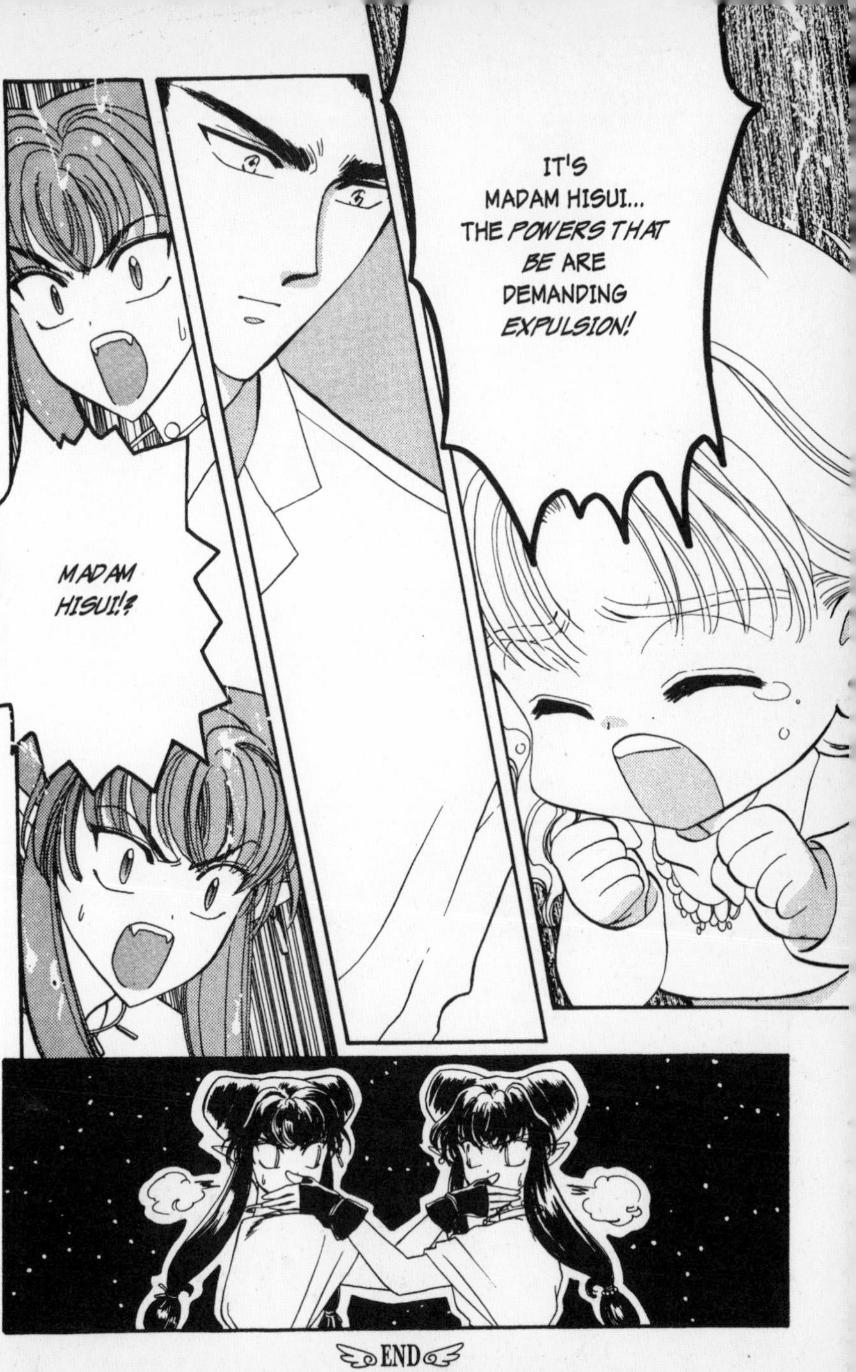
IT'S MADAM HISUI... THE *POWERS THAT BE* ARE DEMANDING *EXPULSION!*
MADAM HISUI!?

END

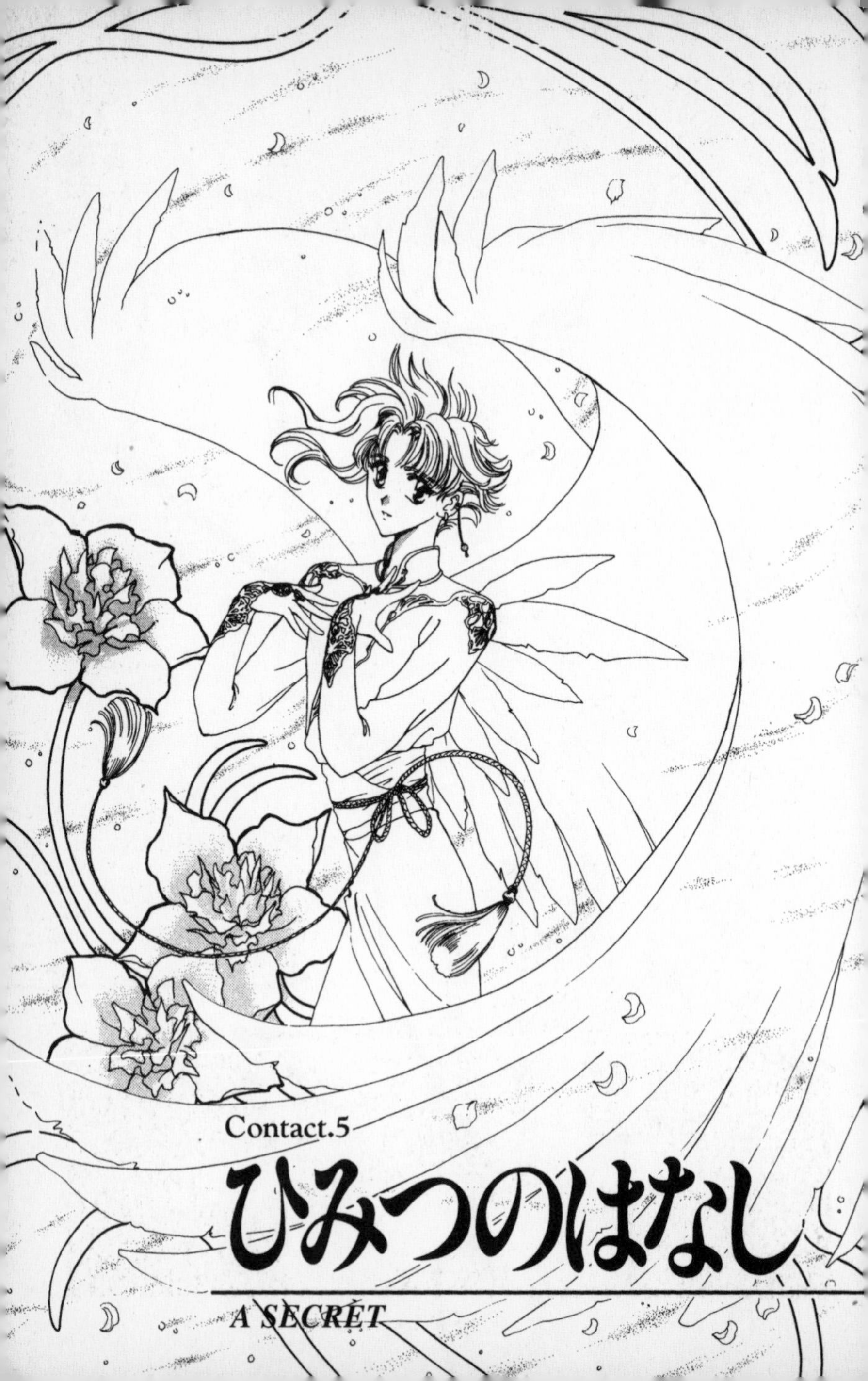
Contact.5
ひみつのはなし
A SECRET

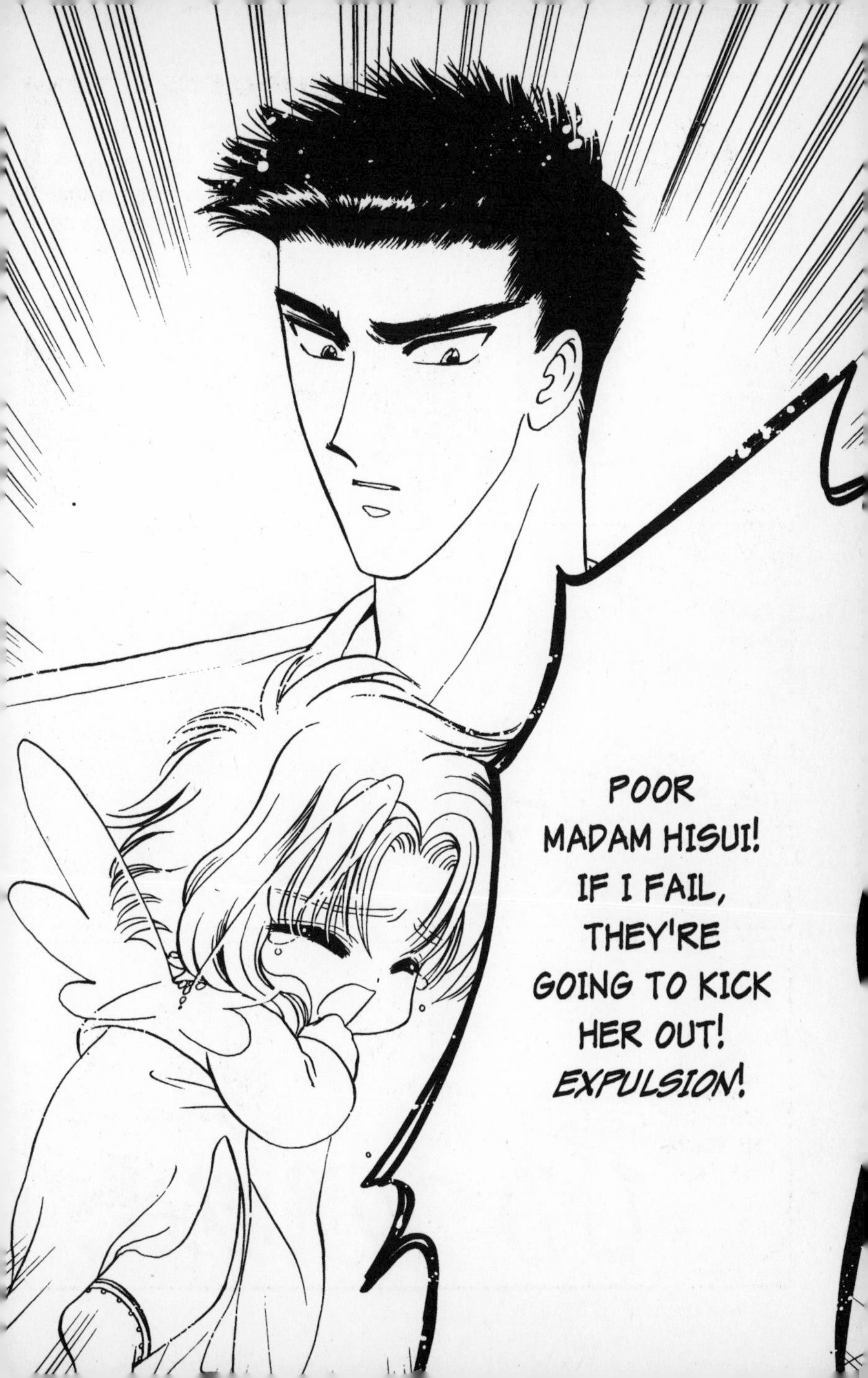
POOR MADAM HISUI! IF I FAIL, THEY'RE GOING TO KICK HER OUT! *EXPULSION*!

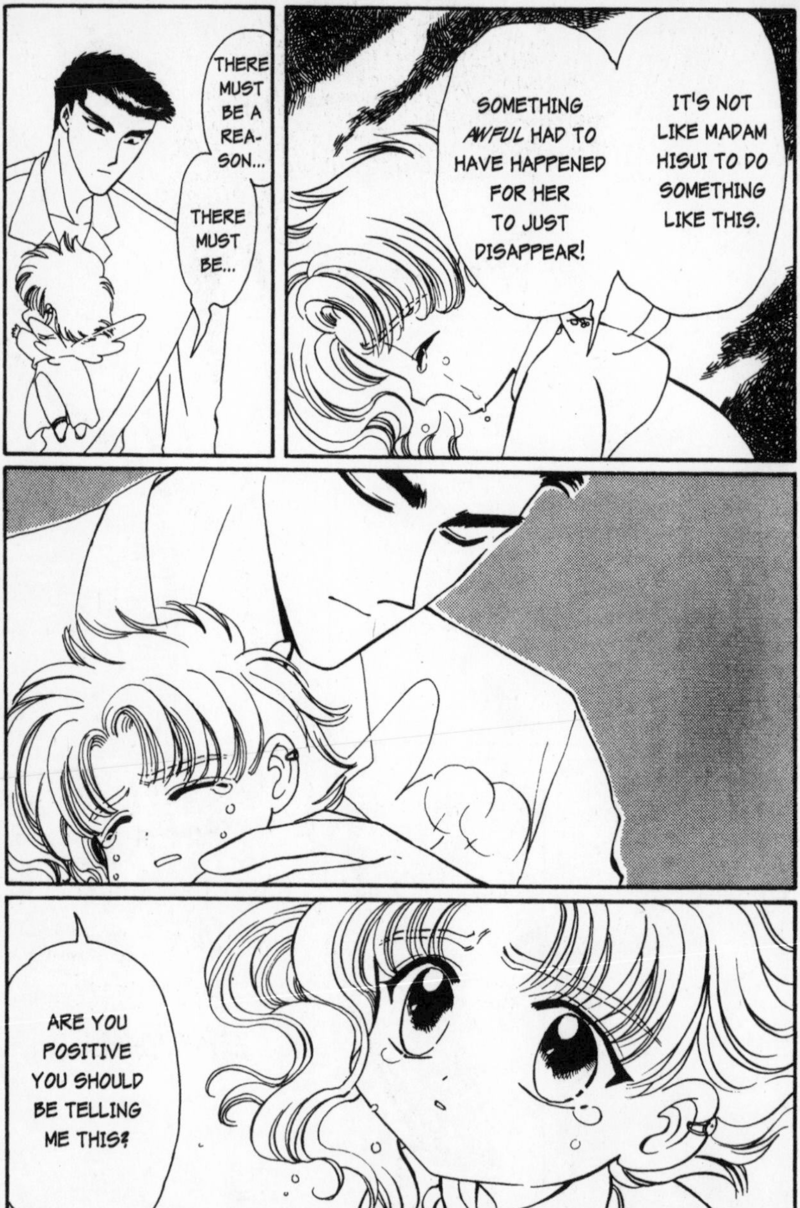
IT'S NOT LIKE MADAM HISUI TO DO SOMETHING LIKE THIS.
SOMETHING AWFUL HAD TO HAVE HAPPENED FOR HER TO JUST DISAPPEAR!
THERE MUST BE A REA-SON...
THERE MUST BE...
ARE YOU POSITIVE YOU SHOULD BE TELLING ME THIS?

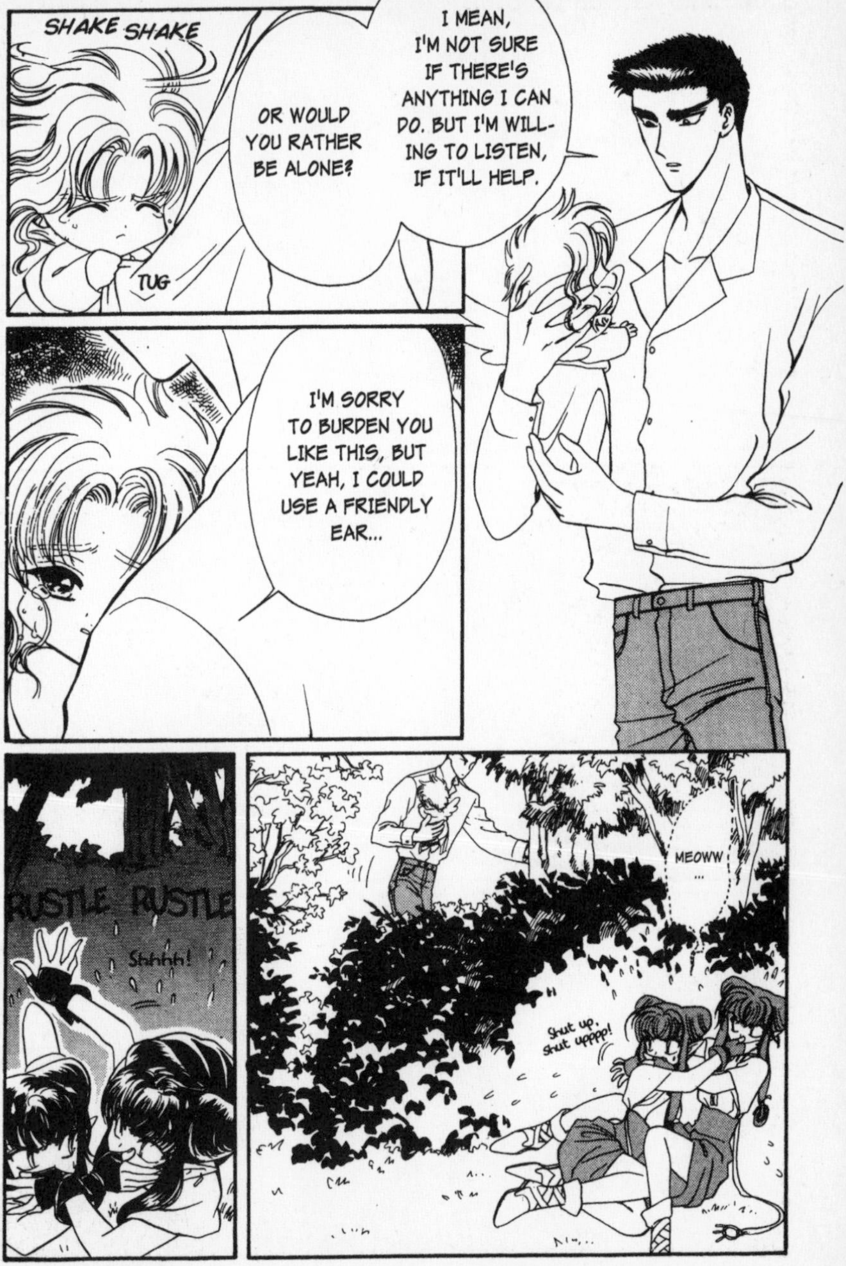
I MEAN, I'M NOT SURE IF THERE'S ANYTHING I CAN DO. BUT I'M WILL-ING TO LISTEN, IF IT'LL HELP.
OR WOULD YOU RATHER BE ALONE?
SHAKE SHAKE
TUG
I'M SORRY TO BURDEN YOU LIKE THIS, BUT YEAH, I COULD USE A FRIENDLY EAR...
MEOWW ...
Shut up, shut upppp!
RUSTLE RUSTLE
Shhhh!

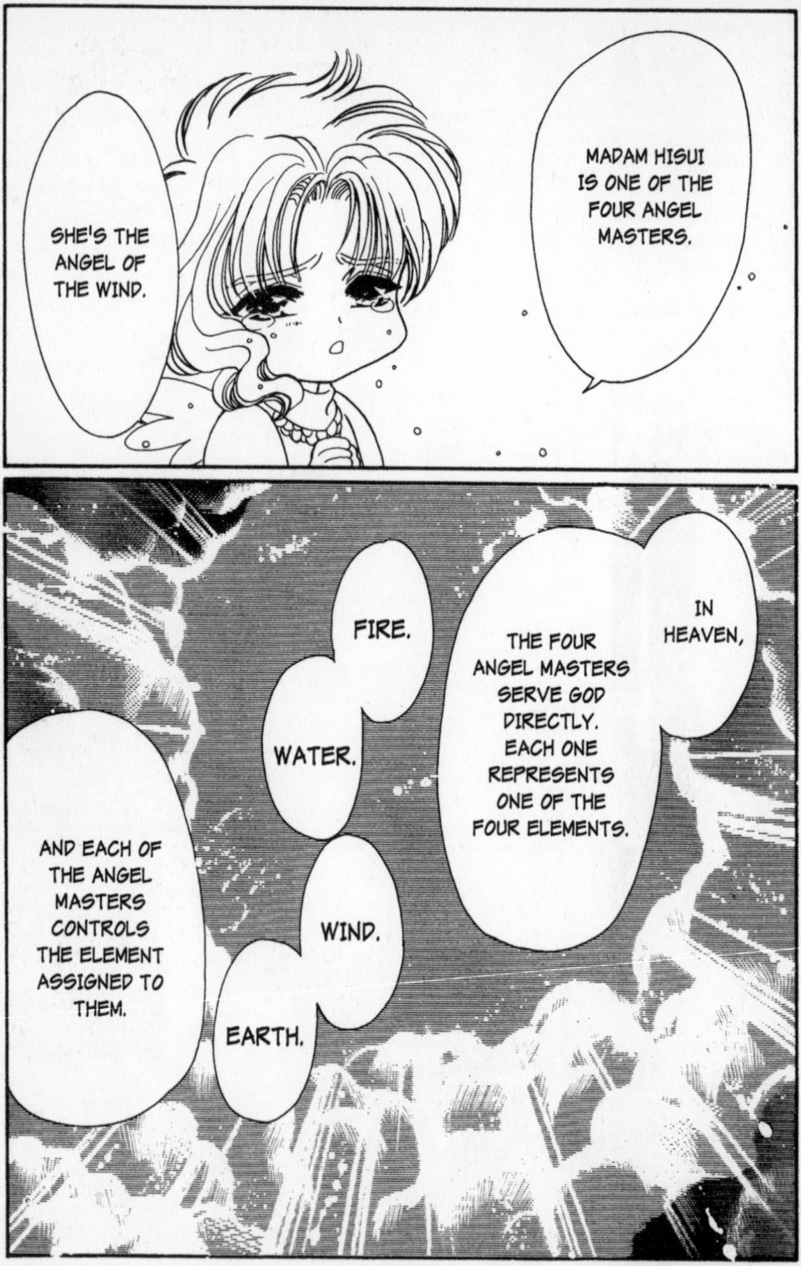
MADAM HISUI IS ONE OF THE FOUR ANGEL MASTERS.
SHE'S THE ANGEL OF THE WIND.
IN HEAVEN,
THE FOUR ANGEL MASTERS SERVE GOD DIRECTLY. EACH ONE REPRESENTS ONE OF THE FOUR ELEMENTS.
FIRE.
WATER.
WIND.
EARTH.
AND EACH OF THE ANGEL MASTERS CONTROLS THE ELEMENT ASSIGNED TO THEM.

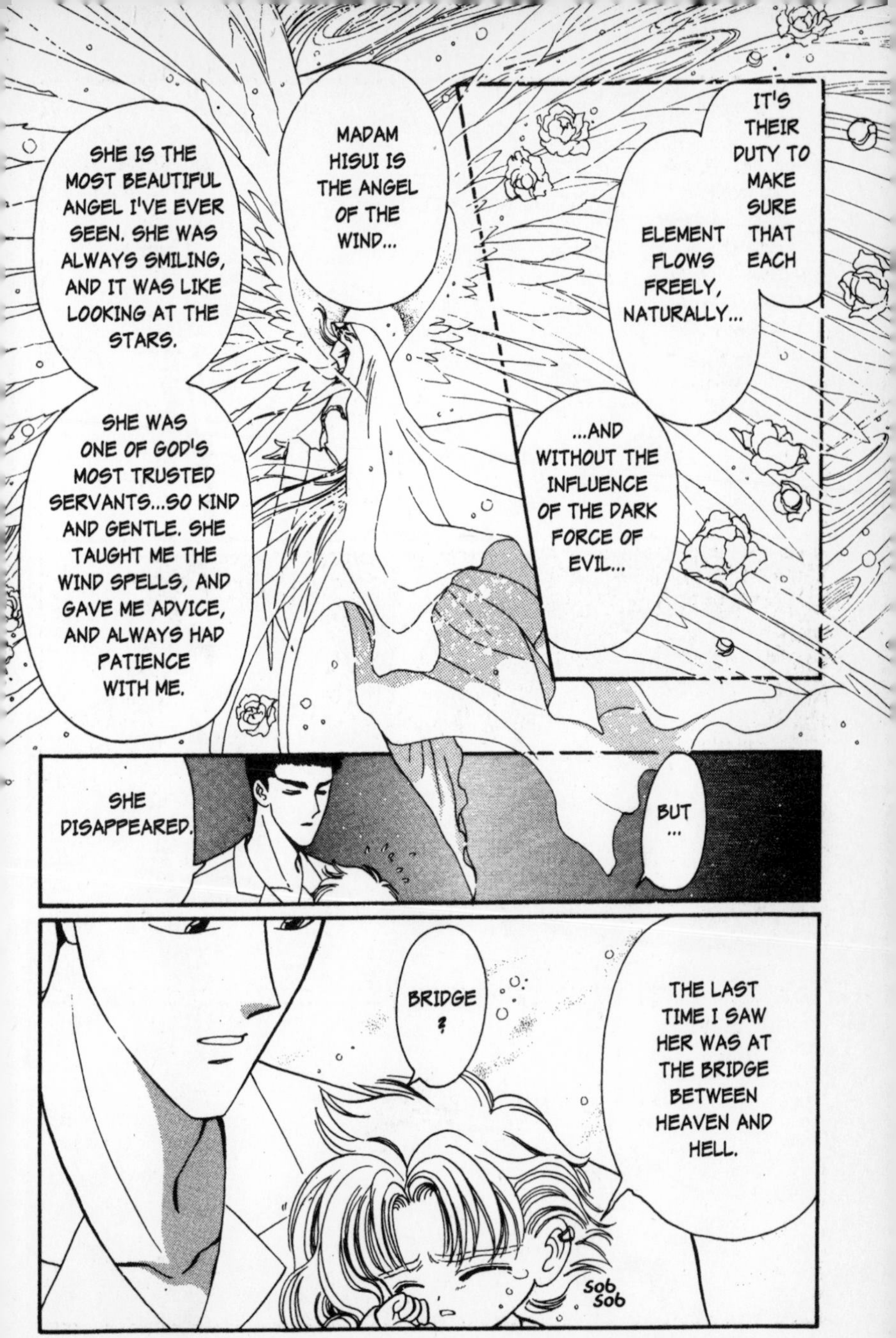
MADAM HISUI IS THE ANGEL OF THE WIND...
IT'S THEIR DUTY TO MAKE SURE THAT EACH ELEMENT FLOWS FREELY, NATURALLY...
...AND WITHOUT THE INFLUENCE OF THE DARK FORCE OF EVIL...
SHE IS THE MOST BEAUTIFUL ANGEL I'VE EVER SEEN. SHE WAS ALWAYS SMILING, AND IT WAS LIKE LOOKING AT THE STARS.
SHE WAS ONE OF GOD'S MOST TRUSTED SERVANTS...SO KIND AND GENTLE. SHE TAUGHT ME THE WIND SPELLS, AND GAVE ME ADVICE, AND ALWAYS HAD PATIENCE WITH ME.
BUT...
SHE DISAPPEARED.
THE LAST TIME I SAW HER WAS AT THE BRIDGE BETWEEN HEAVEN AND HELL.
BRIDGE?
Sob Sob

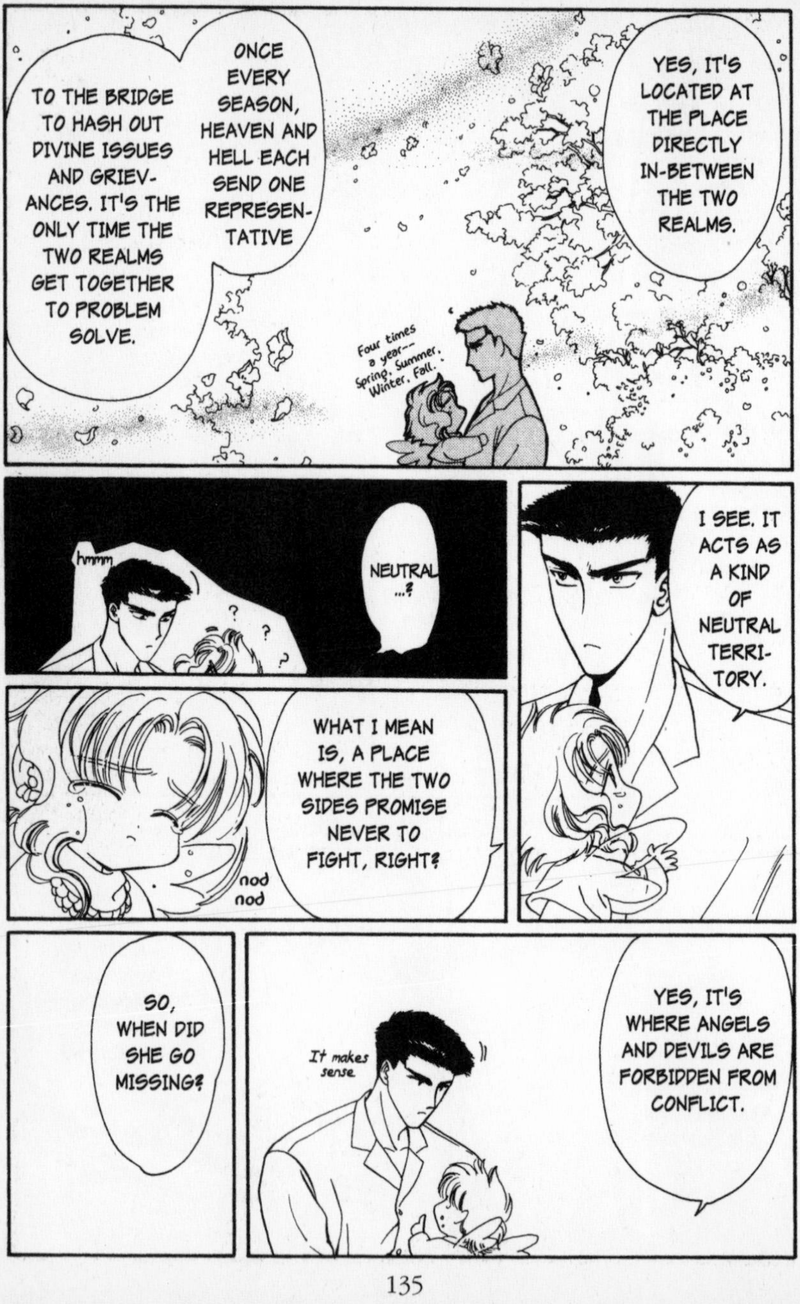
YES, IT'S LOCATED AT THE PLACE DIRECTLY IN-BETWEEN THE TWO REALMS.
ONCE EVERY SEASON, HEAVEN AND HELL EACH SEND ONE REPRESEN-TATIVE
TO THE BRIDGE TO HASH OUT DIVINE ISSUES AND GRIEV-ANCES. IT'S THE ONLY TIME THE TWO REALMS GET TOGETHER TO PROBLEM SOLVE.
Four times a year-- Spring, Summer, Winter, Fall.
I SEE. IT ACTS AS A KIND OF NEUTRAL TERRI-TORY.
NEUTRAL ...?
hmmm
WHAT I MEAN IS, A PLACE WHERE THE TWO SIDES PROMISE NEVER TO FIGHT, RIGHT?
nod nod
YES, IT'S WHERE ANGELS AND DEVILS ARE FORBIDDEN FROM CONFLICT.
It makes sense
SO, WHEN DID SHE GO MISSING?

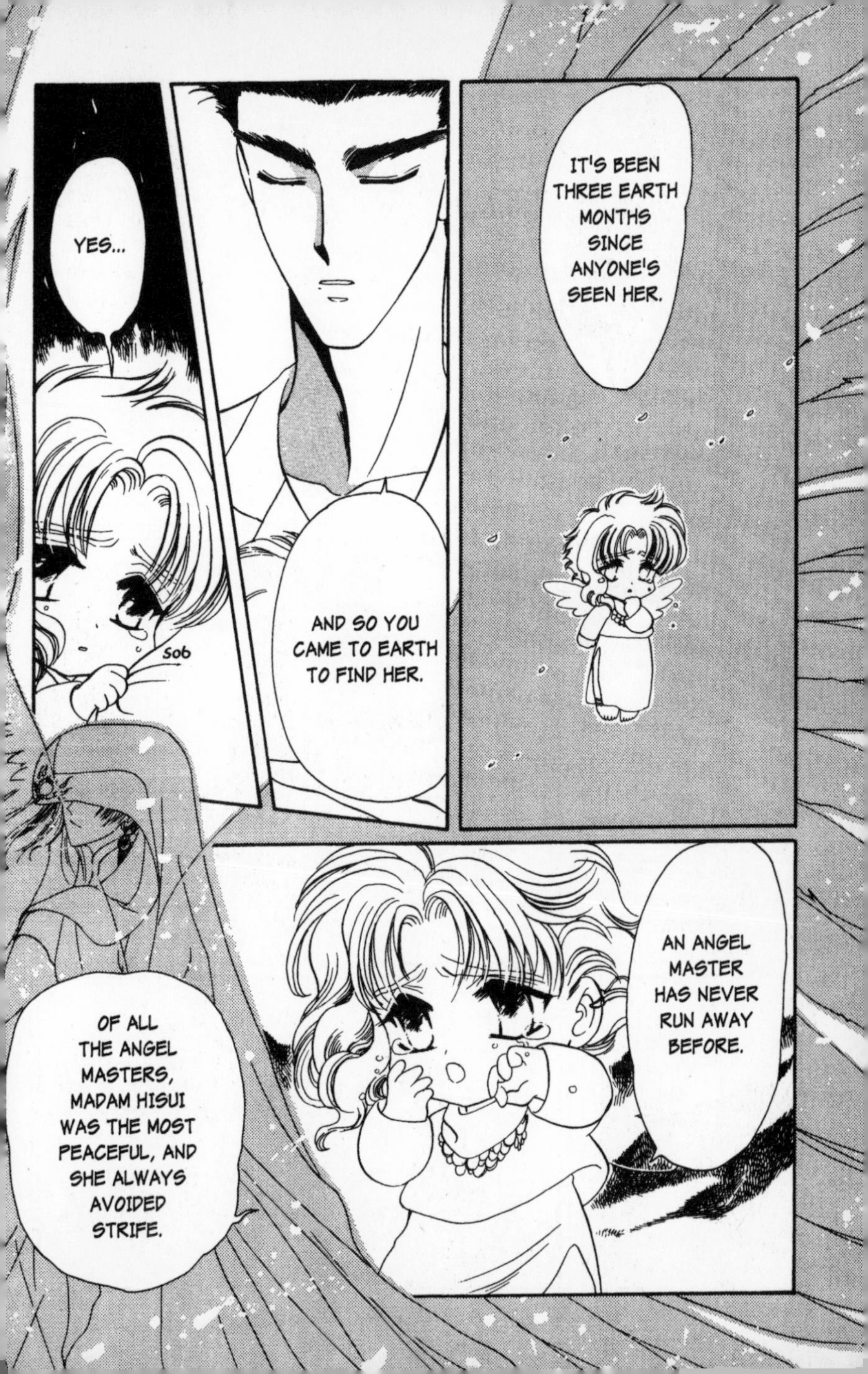
IT'S BEEN THREE EARTH MONTHS SINCE ANYONE'S SEEN HER.
AND SO YOU CAME TO EARTH TO FIND HER.
YES...
Sob
AN ANGEL MASTER HAS NEVER RUN AWAY BEFORE.
OF ALL THE ANGEL MASTERS, MADAM HISUI WAS THE MOST PEACEFUL, AND SHE ALWAYS AVOIDED STRIFE.

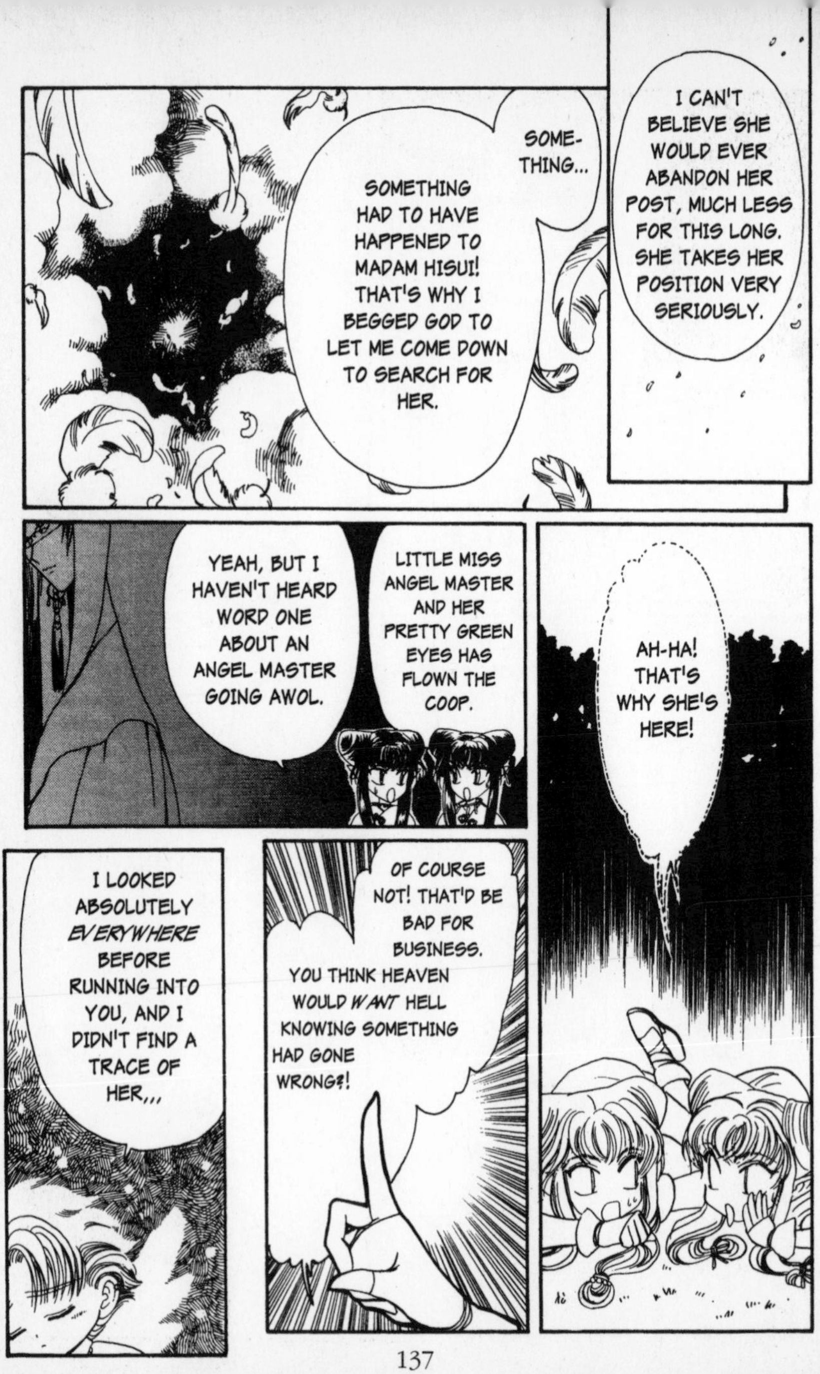
I CAN'T BELIEVE SHE WOULD EVER ABANDON HER POST, MUCH LESS FOR THIS LONG. SHE TAKES HER POSITION VERY SERIOUSLY.
SOME-THING...
SOMETHING HAD TO HAVE HAPPENED TO MADAM HISUI! THAT'S WHY I BEGGED GOD TO LET ME COME DOWN TO SEARCH FOR HER.
AH-HA! THAT'S WHY SHE'S HERE!
LITTLE MISS ANGEL MASTER AND HER PRETTY GREEN EYES HAS FLOWN THE COOP.
YEAH, BUT I HAVEN'T HEARD WORD ONE ABOUT AN ANGEL MASTER GOING AWOL.
OF COURSE NOT! THAT'D BE BAD FOR BUSINESS.
YOU THINK HEAVEN WOULD *WANT* HELL KNOWING SOMETHING HAD GONE WRONG?!
I LOOKED ABSOLUTELY *EVERYWHERE* BEFORE RUNNING INTO YOU, AND I DIDN'T FIND A TRACE OF HER...

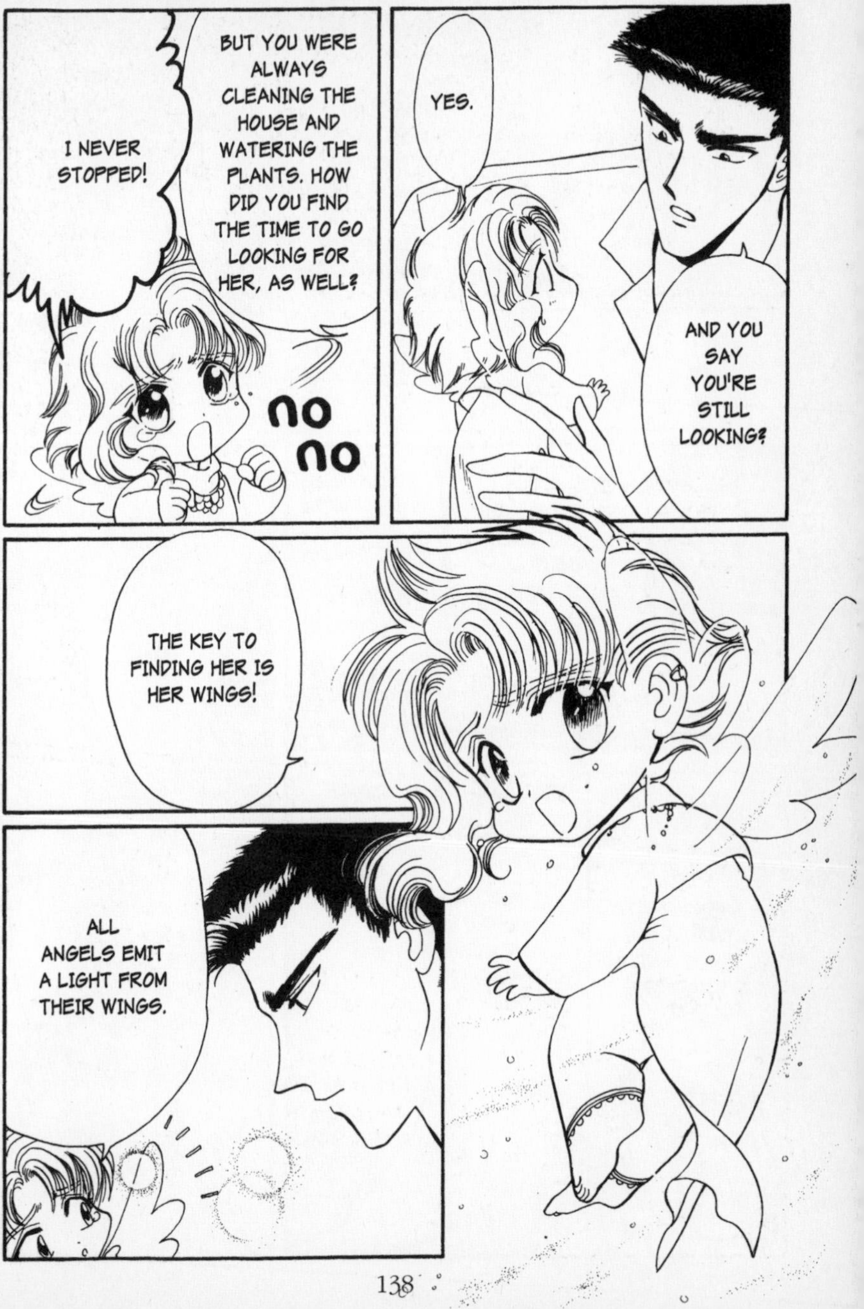
YES.
AND YOU SAY YOU'RE STILL LOOKING?
BUT YOU WERE ALWAYS CLEANING THE HOUSE AND WATERING THE PLANTS. HOW DID YOU FIND THE TIME TO GO LOOKING FOR HER, AS WELL?
I NEVER STOPPED!
no no
THE KEY TO FINDING HER IS HER WINGS!
ALL ANGELS EMIT A LIGHT FROM THEIR WINGS.

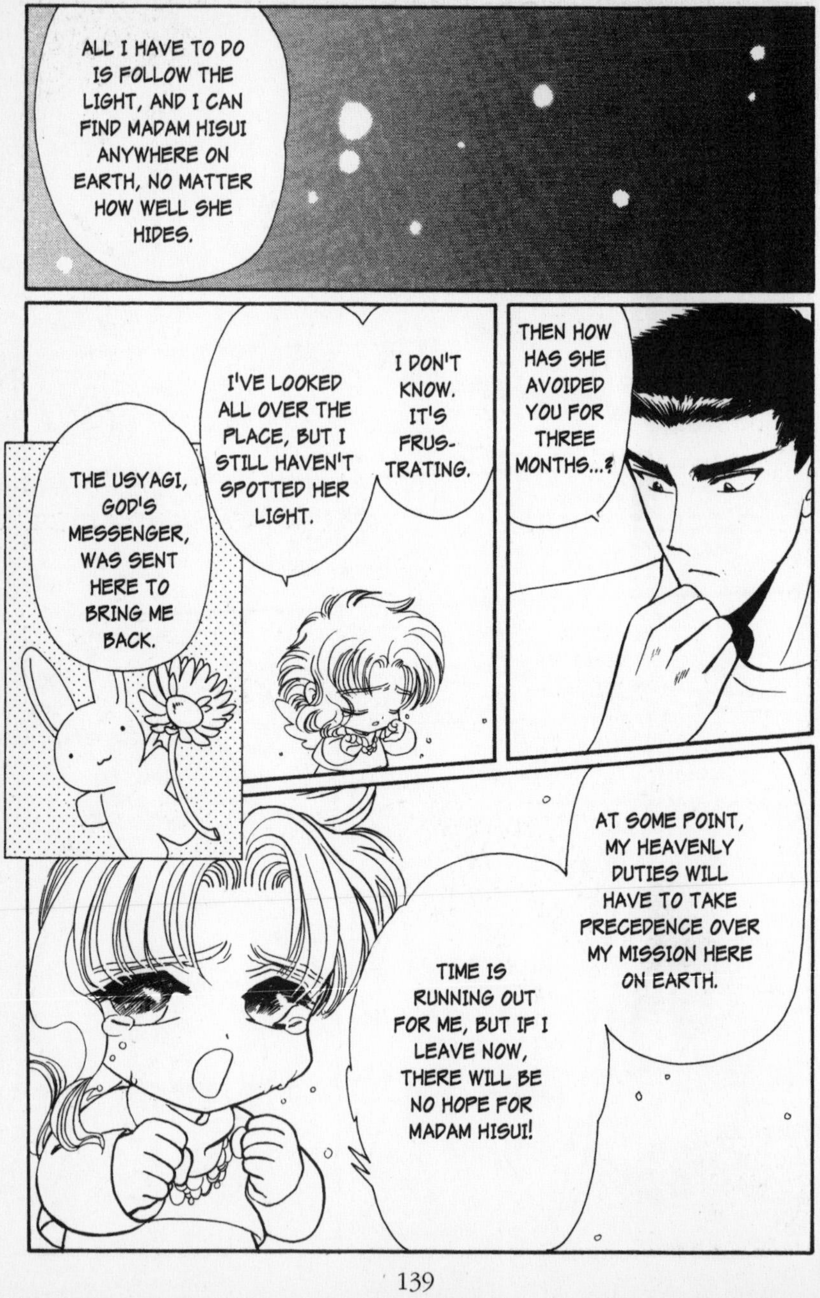
ALL I HAVE TO DO IS FOLLOW THE LIGHT, AND I CAN FIND MADAM HISUI ANYWHERE ON EARTH, NO MATTER HOW WELL SHE HIDES.
THEN HOW HAS SHE AVOIDED YOU FOR THREE MONTHS...?
I DON'T KNOW. IT'S FRUS-TRATING.
I'VE LOOKED ALL OVER THE PLACE, BUT I STILL HAVEN'T SPOTTED HER LIGHT.
THE USYAGI, GOD'S MESSENGER, WAS SENT HERE TO BRING ME BACK.
AT SOME POINT, MY HEAVENLY DUTIES WILL HAVE TO TAKE PRECEDENCE OVER MY MISSION HERE ON EARTH.
TIME IS RUNNING OUT FOR ME, BUT IF I LEAVE NOW, THERE WILL BE NO HOPE FOR MADAM HISUI!

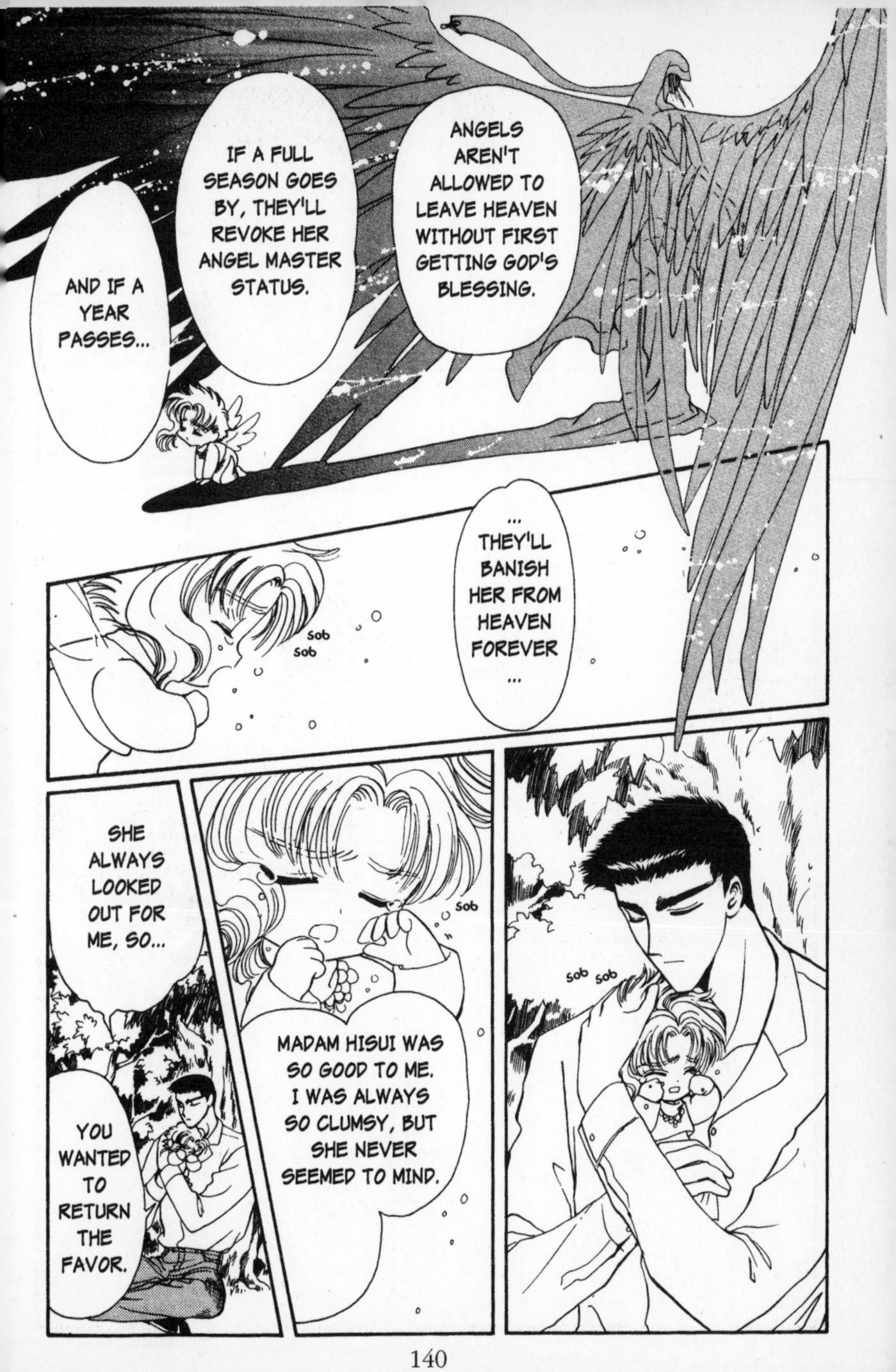
ANGELS AREN'T ALLOWED TO LEAVE HEAVEN WITHOUT FIRST GETTING GOD'S BLESSING.
IF A FULL SEASON GOES BY, THEY'LL REVOKE HER ANGEL MASTER STATUS.
AND IF A YEAR PASSES...
... THEY'LL BANISH HER FROM HEAVEN FOREVER ...
SOB SOB
SOB SOB
SOB
MADAM HISUI WAS SO GOOD TO ME. I WAS ALWAYS SO CLUMSY, BUT SHE NEVER SEEMED TO MIND.
SHE ALWAYS LOOKED OUT FOR ME, SO...
YOU WANTED TO RETURN THE FAVOR.

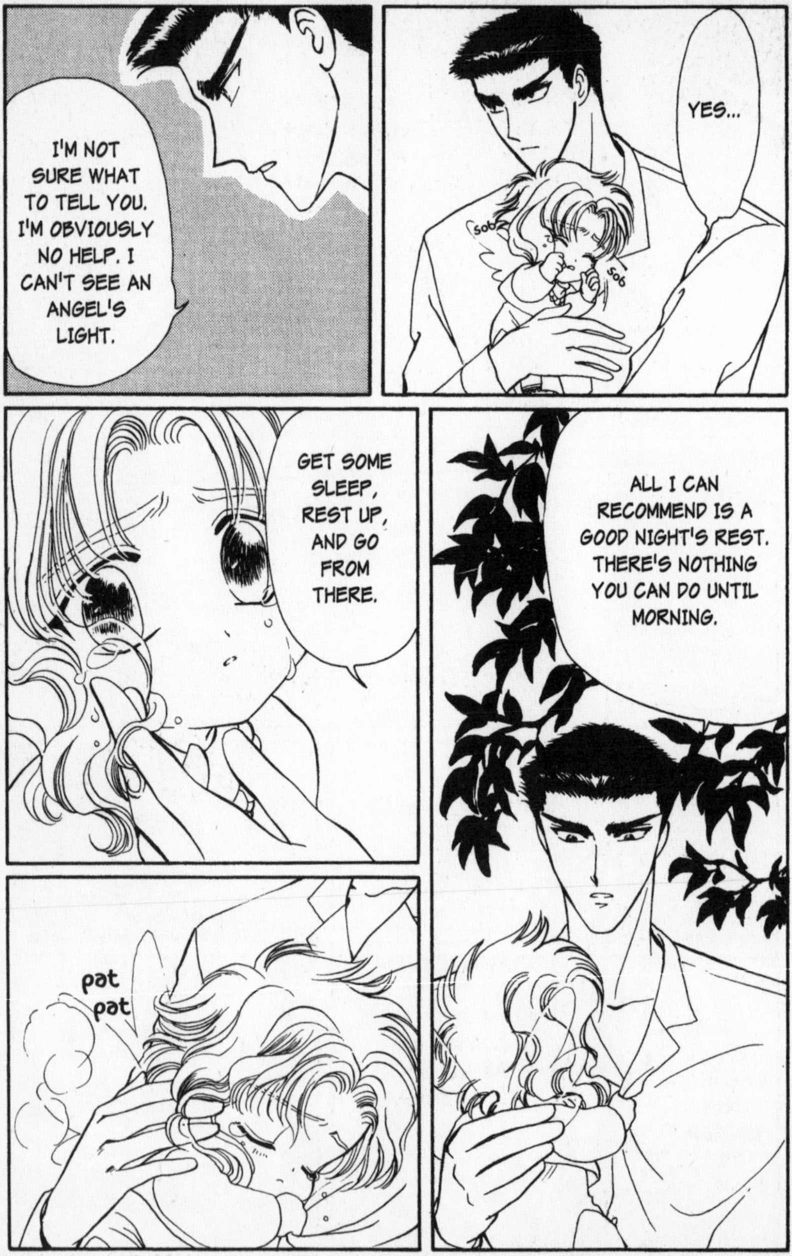
YES...
sob
sob
I'M NOT SURE WHAT TO TELL YOU. I'M OBVIOUSLY NO HELP. I CAN'T SEE AN ANGEL'S LIGHT.
ALL I CAN RECOMMEND IS A GOOD NIGHT'S REST. THERE'S NOTHING YOU CAN DO UNTIL MORNING.
GET SOME SLEEP, REST UP, AND GO FROM THERE.
pat pat

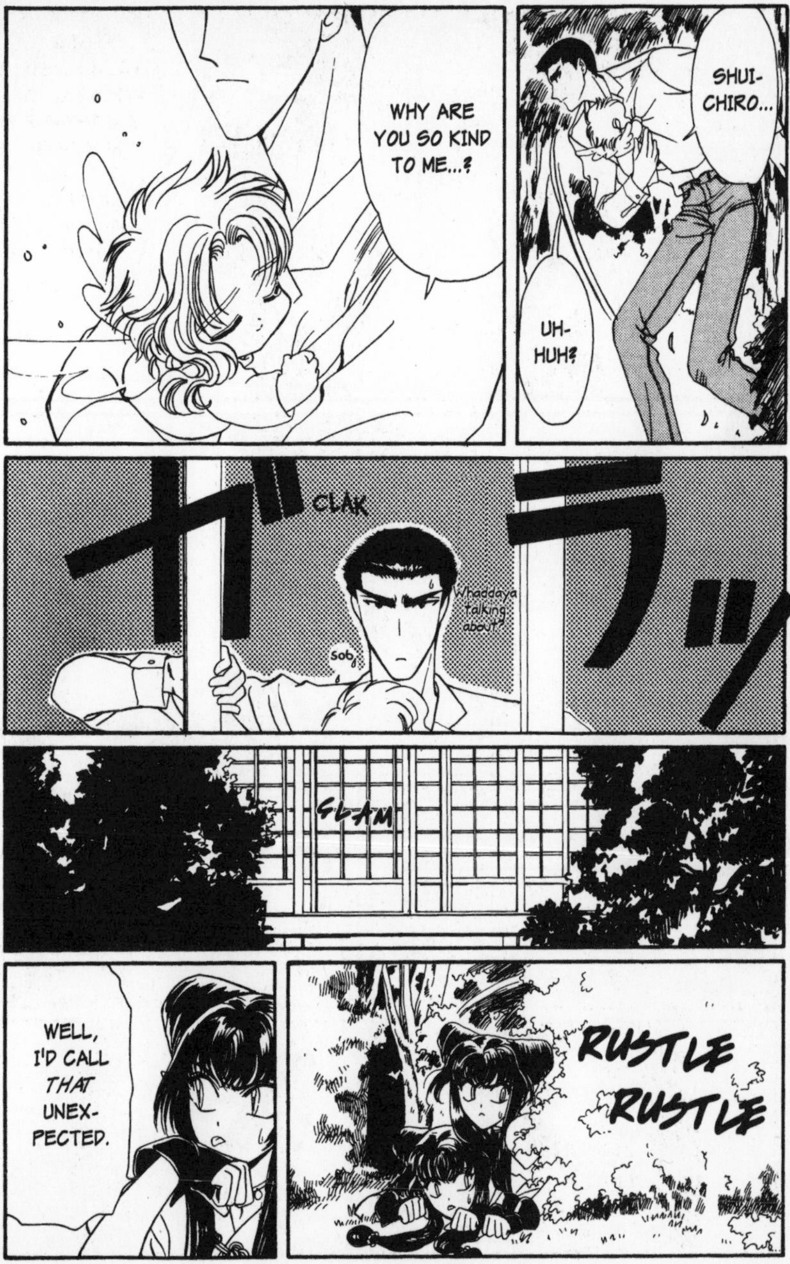
SHUI-CHIRO...
UH-HUH?
WHY ARE YOU SO KIND TO ME...?
ガラッ
CLAK
Whaddaya talking about?
sob
SLAM
RUSTLE RUSTLE
WELL, I'D CALL *THAT* UNEXPECTED.

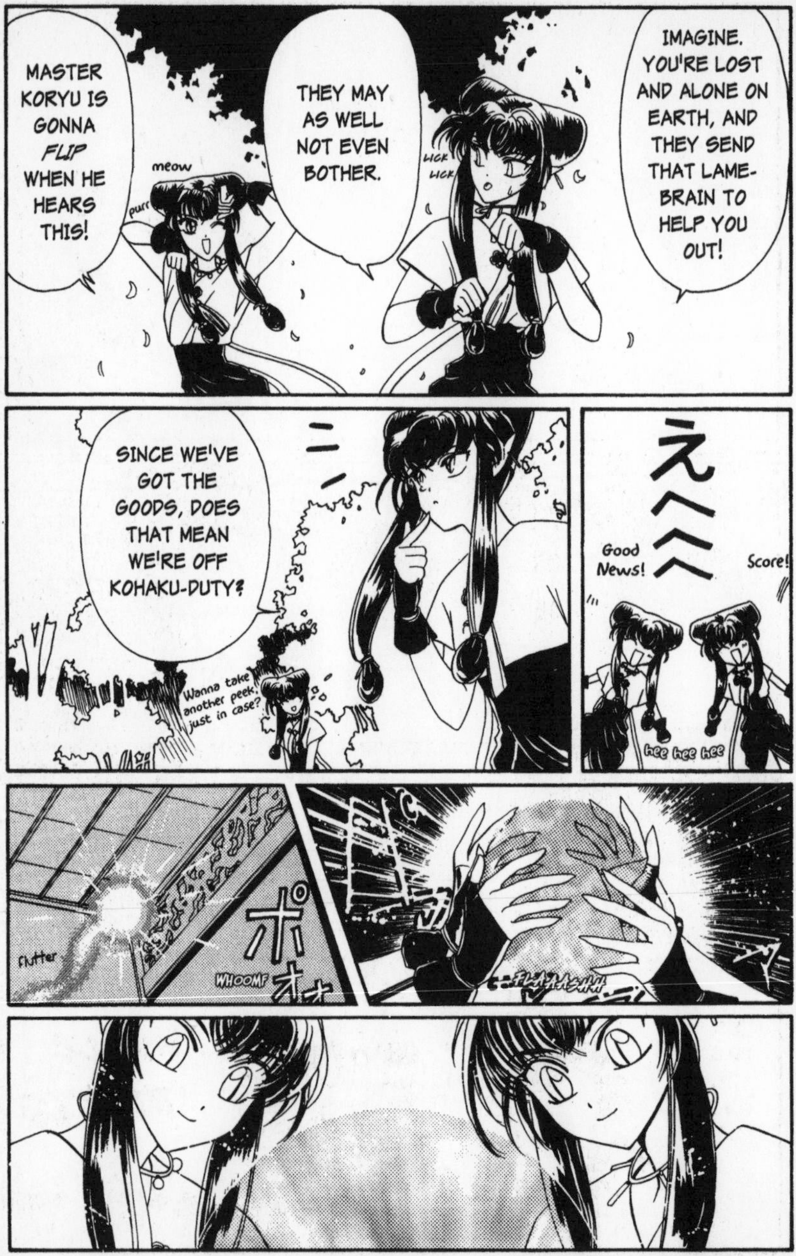

IMAGINE. YOU'RE LOST AND ALONE ON EARTH, AND THEY SEND THAT LAME-BRAIN TO HELP YOU OUT!
LICK LICK
THEY MAY AS WELL NOT EVEN BOTHER.
MASTER KORYU IS GONNA *FLIP* WHEN HE HEARS THIS!
meow
purr
えへへへ
Score!
Good News!
hee hee hee
SINCE WE'VE GOT THE GOODS, DOES THAT MEAN WE'RE OFF KOHAKU-DUTY?
Wanna take another peek, just in case?
ポオオ
WHOOMF
flutter

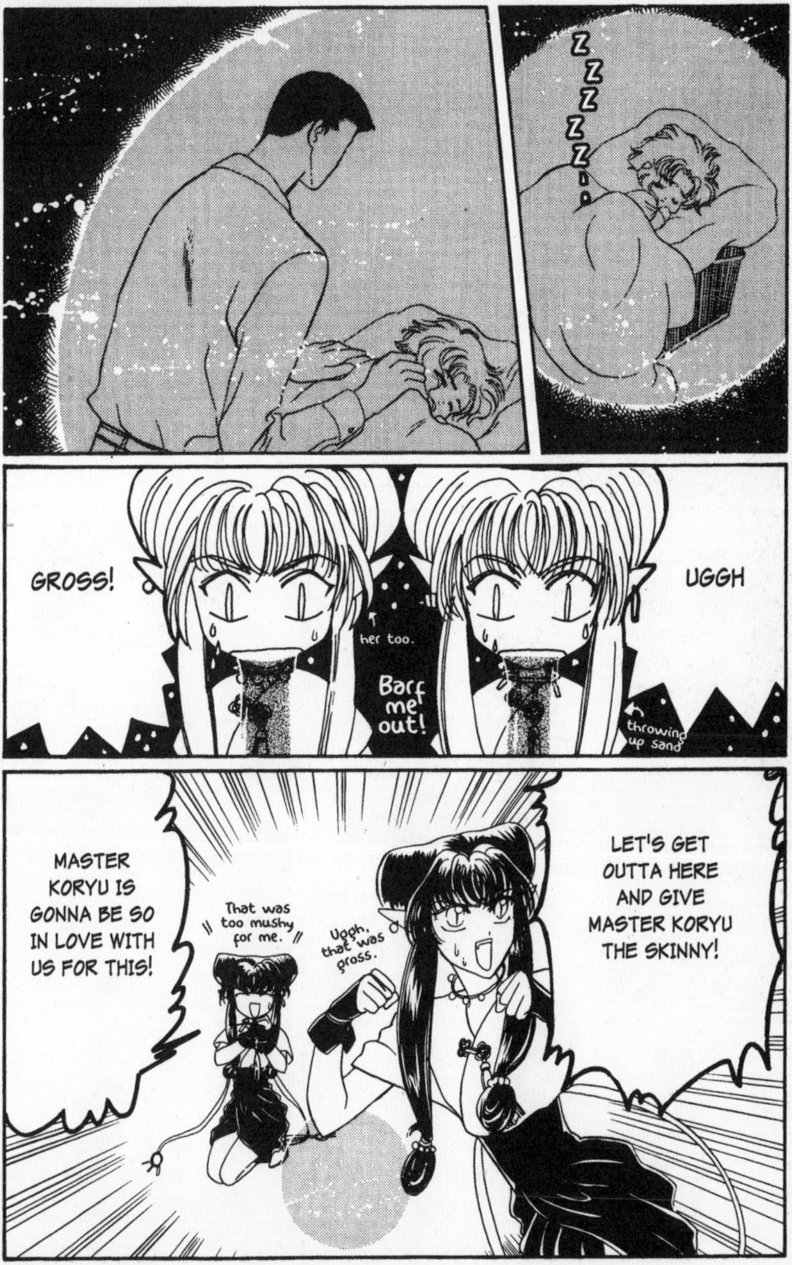
ZZZZZ
UGGH
throwing up sand
her too.
Barf me out!
GROSS!
LET'S GET OUTTA HERE AND GIVE MASTER KORYU THE SKINNY!
Uggh, that was gross.
That was too mushy for me.
MASTER KORYU IS GONNA BE SO IN LOVE WITH US FOR THIS!

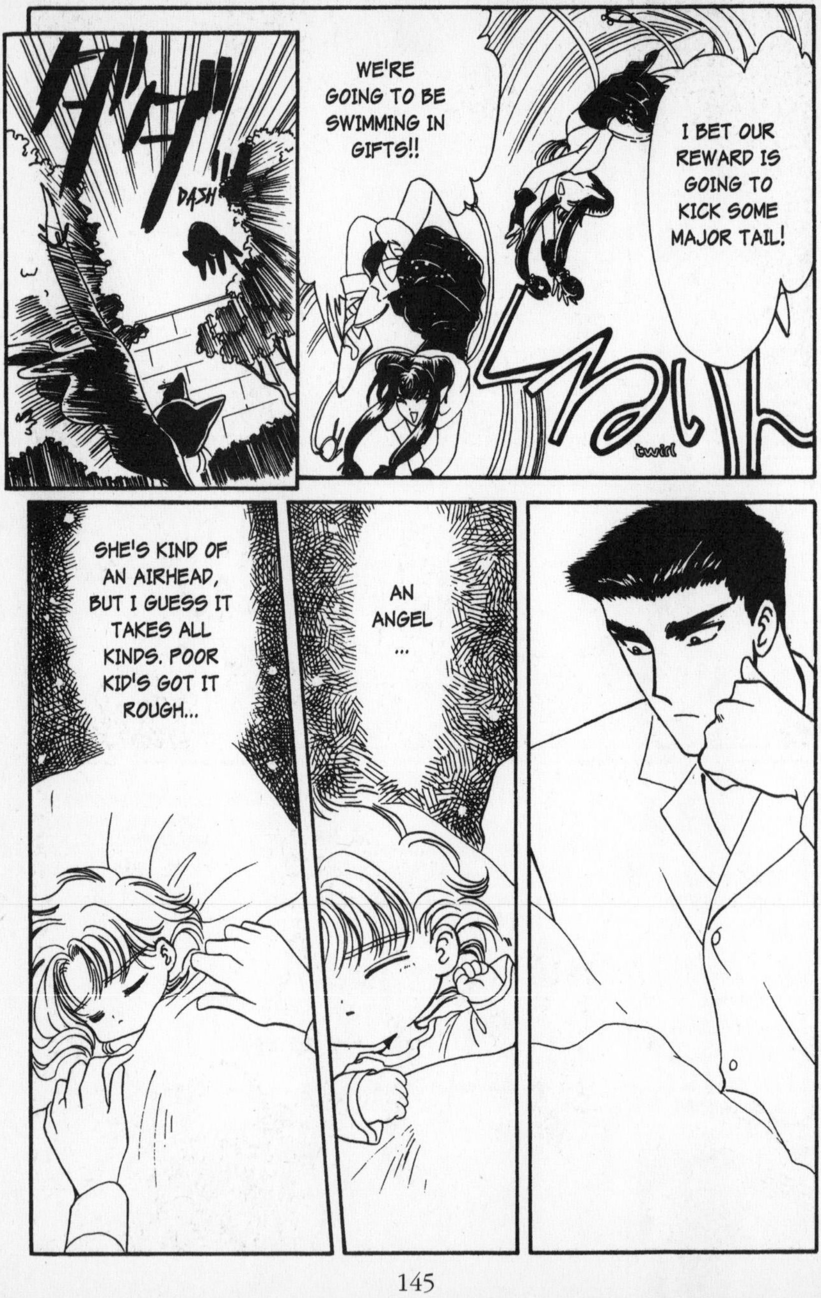
I BET OUR REWARD IS GOING TO KICK SOME MAJOR TAIL!
WE'RE GOING TO BE SWIMMING IN GIFTS!!
twirl
DASH
AN ANGEL ...
SHE'S KIND OF AN AIRHEAD, BUT I GUESS IT TAKES ALL KINDS. POOR KID'S GOT IT ROUGH...

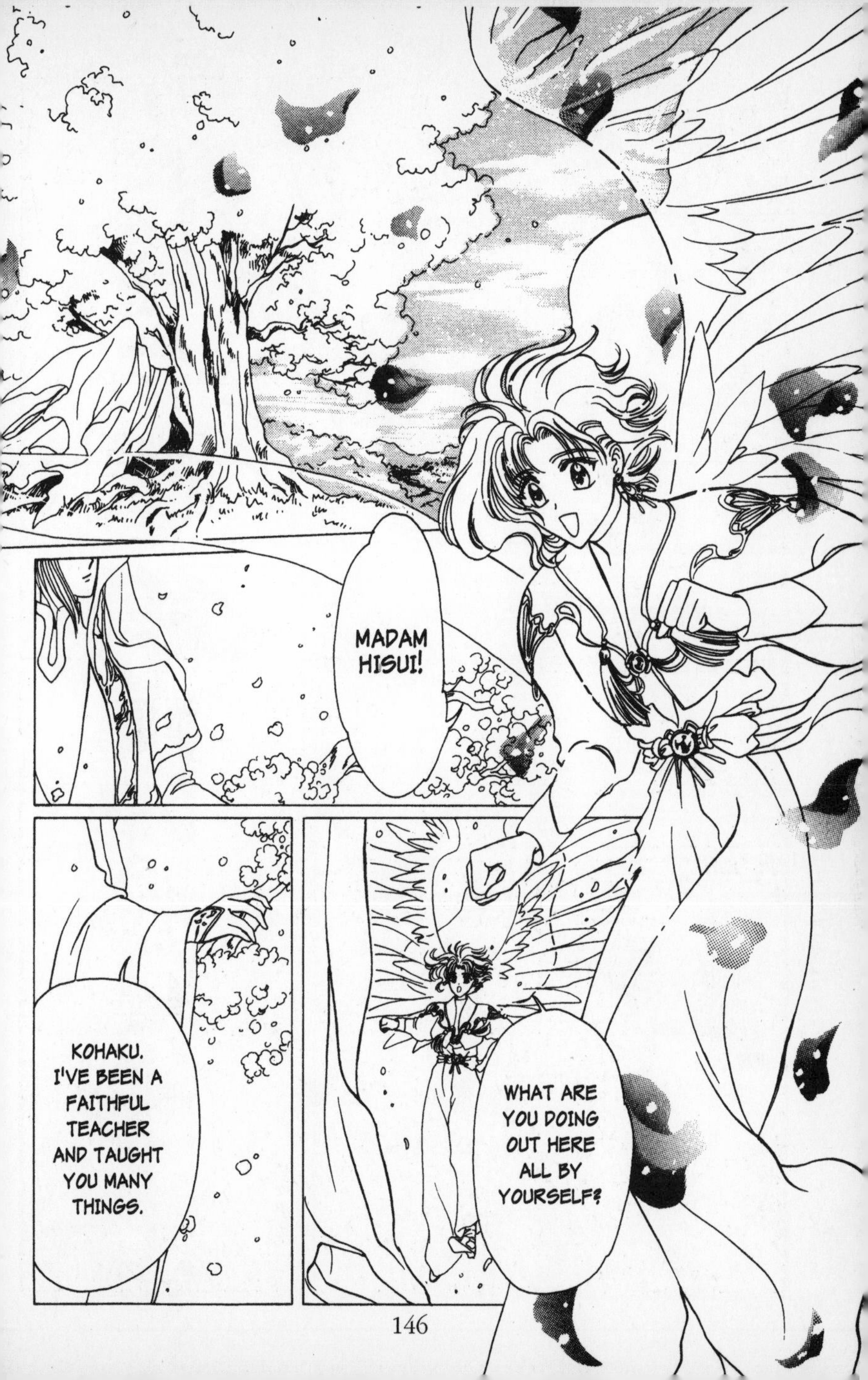
MADAM HISUI!
WHAT ARE YOU DOING OUT HERE ALL BY YOURSELF?
KOHAKU. I'VE BEEN A FAITHFUL TEACHER AND TAUGHT YOU MANY THINGS.

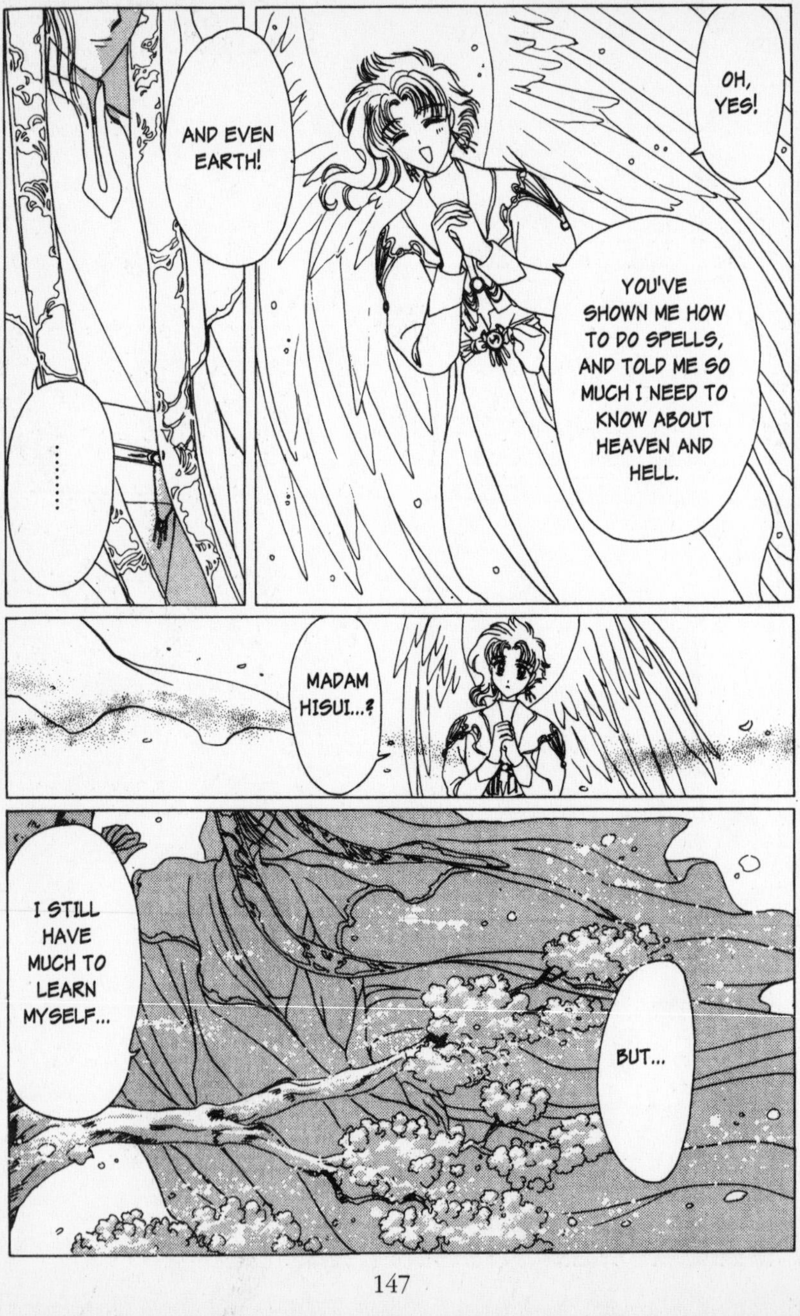
OH, YES!
YOU'VE SHOWN ME HOW TO DO SPELLS, AND TOLD ME SO MUCH I NEED TO KNOW ABOUT HEAVEN AND HELL.
AND EVEN EARTH!
......
MADAM HISUI...?
BUT...
I STILL HAVE MUCH TO LEARN MYSELF...

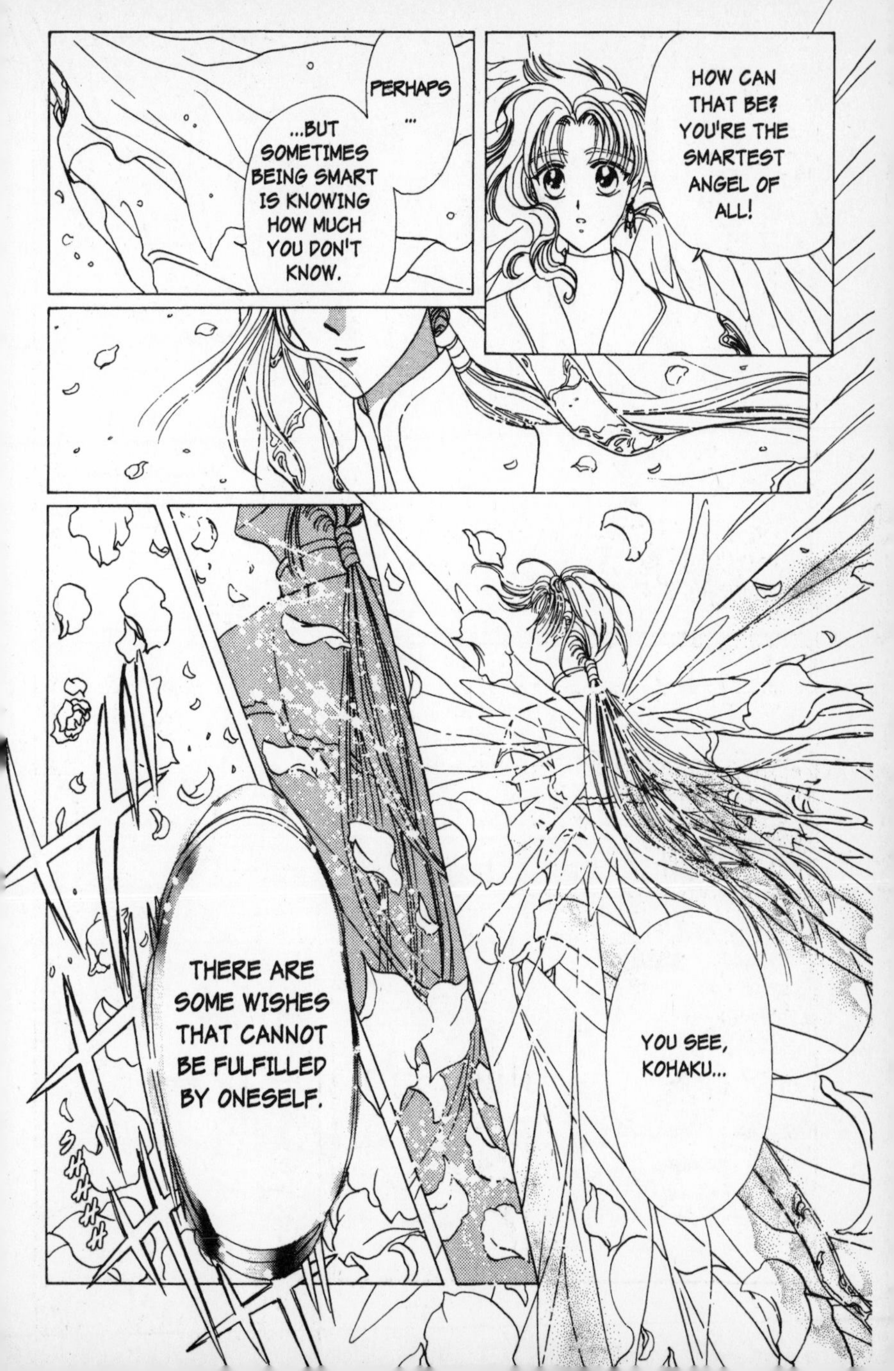
HOW CAN THAT BE? YOU'RE THE SMARTEST ANGEL OF ALL!
PERHAPS ...
...BUT SOMETIMES BEING SMART IS KNOWING HOW MUCH YOU DON'T KNOW.
YOU SEE, KOHAKU...
THERE ARE SOME WISHES THAT CANNOT BE FULFILLED BY ONESELF.
SHHHHH

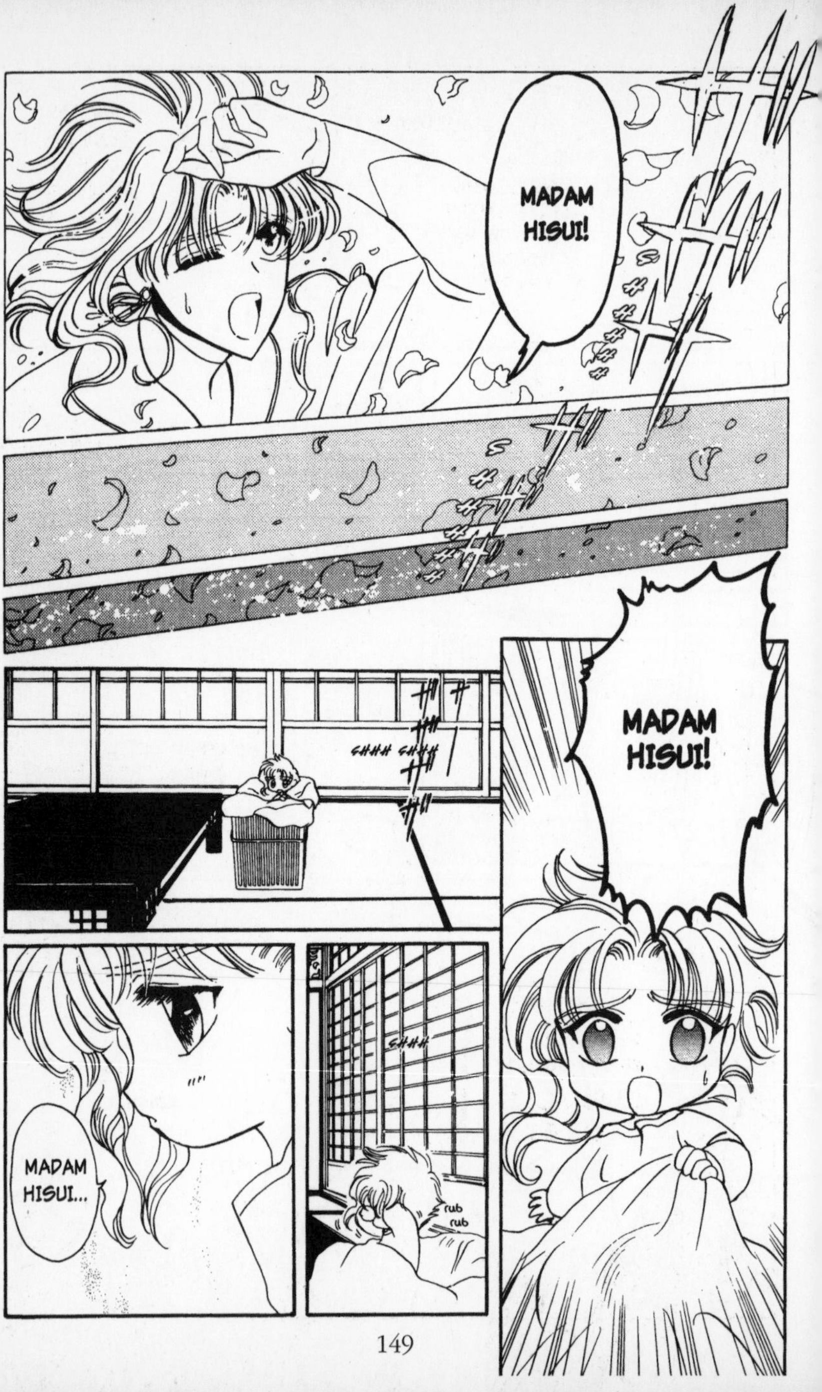
MADAM HISUI!
MADAM HISUI!
SHHH SHHH
SHHH
rub rub
MADAM HISUI...

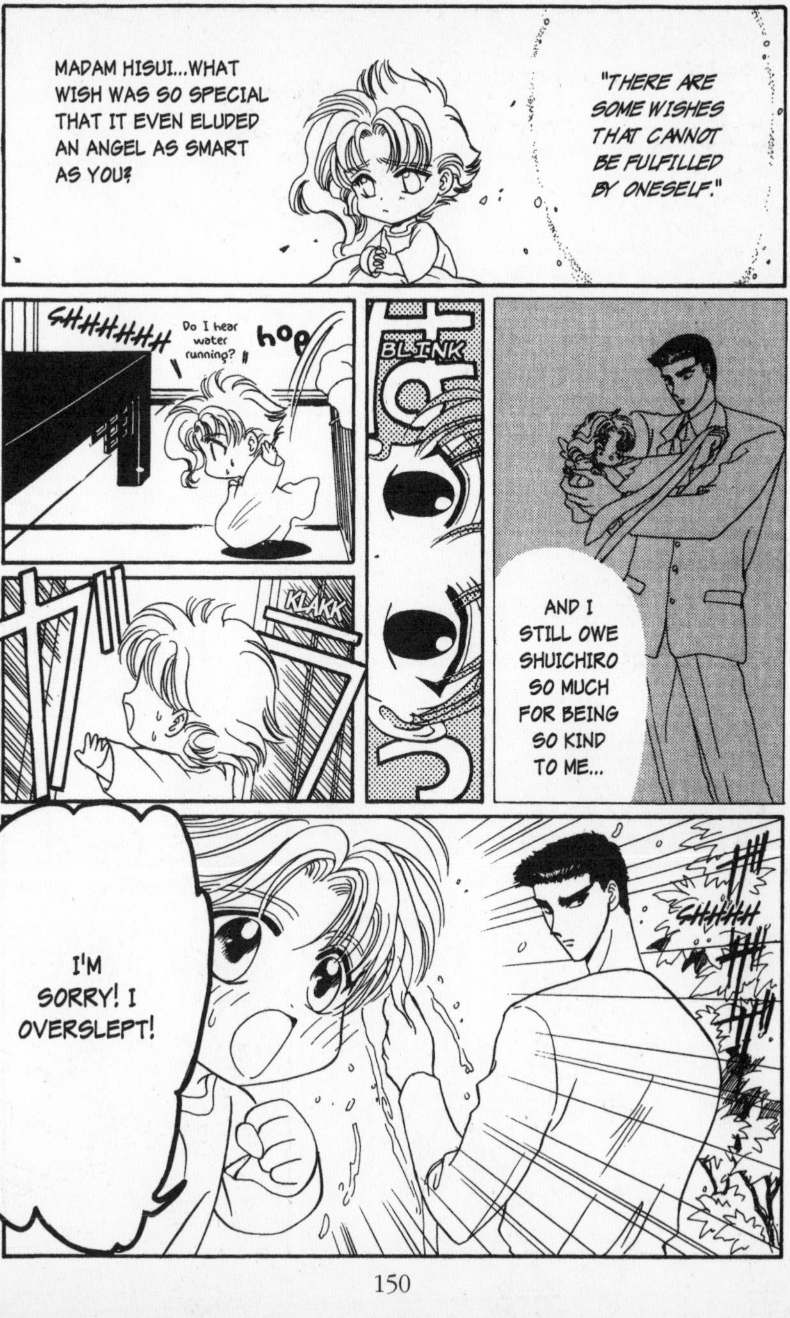
"THERE ARE SOME WISHES THAT CANNOT BE FULFILLED BY ONESELF."
MADAM HISUI...WHAT WISH WAS SO SPECIAL THAT IT EVEN ELUDED AN ANGEL AS SMART AS YOU?
AND I STILL OWE SHUICHIRO SO MUCH FOR BEING SO KIND TO ME...
BLINK
hop
Do I hear water running?
SHHHHHHH
KLAKK
SHHHH
I'M SORRY! I OVERSLEPT!

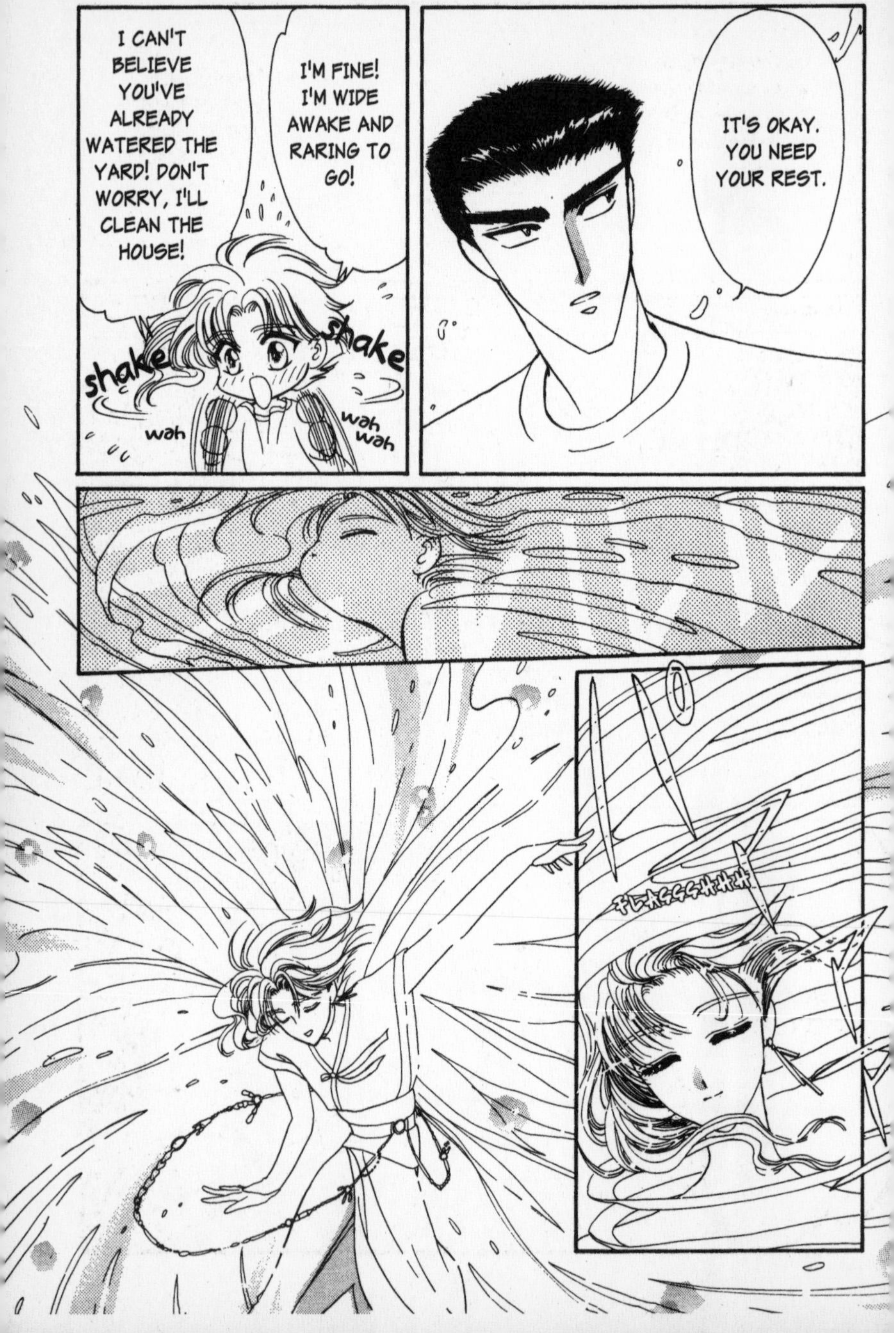
IT'S OKAY. YOU NEED YOUR REST.
I'M FINE! I'M WIDE AWAKE AND RARING TO GO!
I CAN'T BELIEVE YOU'VE ALREADY WATERED THE YARD! DON'T WORRY, I'LL CLEAN THE HOUSE!
shake
shake
wah wah
wah
FLASSSHHH

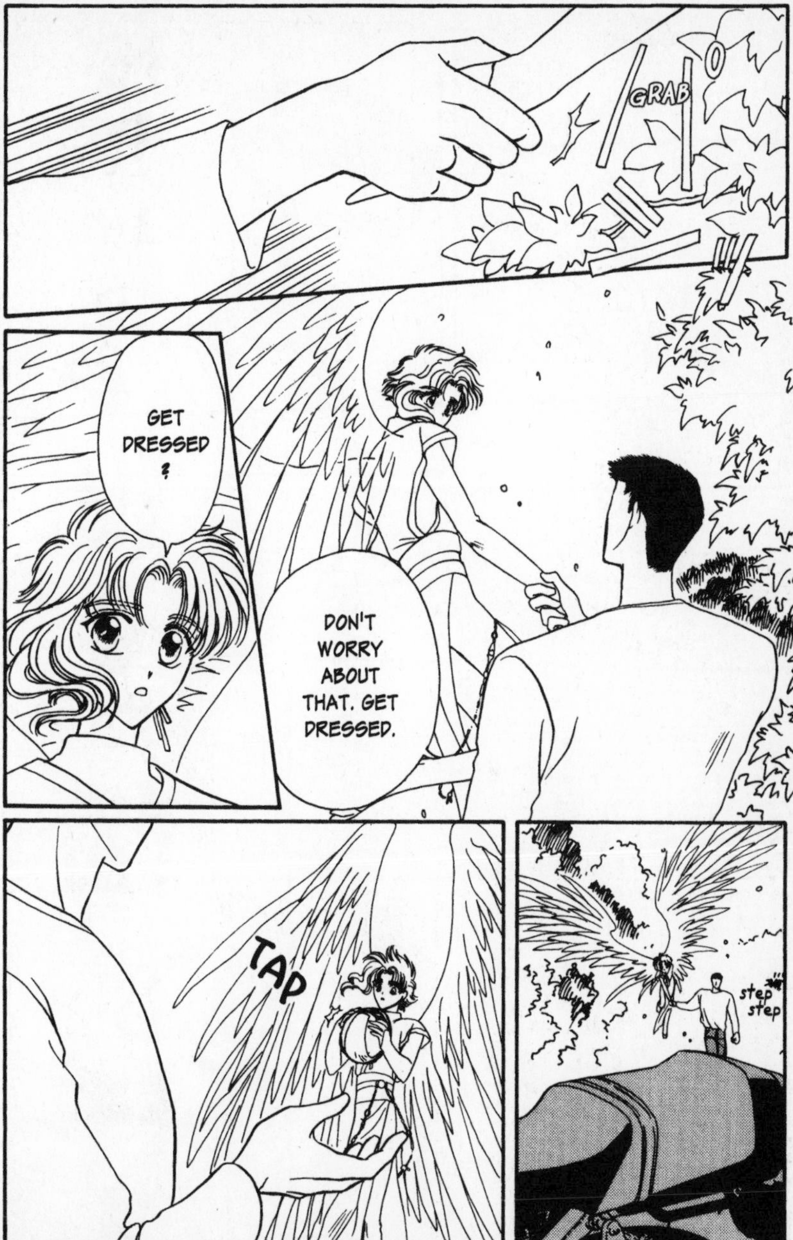
GRAB
DON'T WORRY ABOUT THAT. GET DRESSED.
GET DRESSED?
step step
TAP

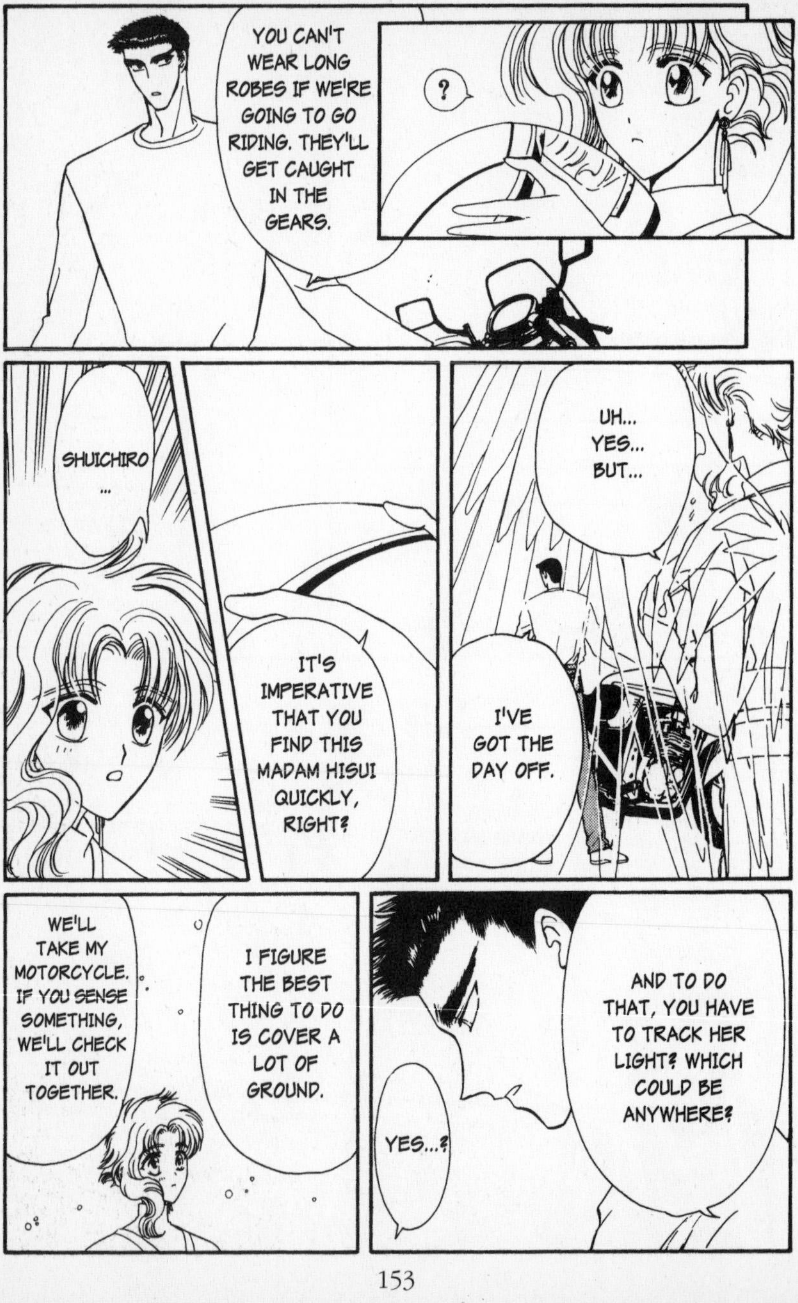
?
YOU CAN'T WEAR LONG ROBES IF WE'RE GOING TO GO RIDING. THEY'LL GET CAUGHT IN THE GEARS.
UH... YES... BUT...
I'VE GOT THE DAY OFF.
IT'S IMPERATIVE THAT YOU FIND THIS MADAM HISUI QUICKLY, RIGHT?
SHUICHIRO ...
AND TO DO THAT, YOU HAVE TO TRACK HER LIGHT? WHICH COULD BE ANYWHERE?
YES...?
I FIGURE THE BEST THING TO DO IS COVER A LOT OF GROUND.
WE'LL TAKE MY MOTORCYCLE. IF YOU SENSE SOMETHING, WE'LL CHECK IT OUT TOGETHER.

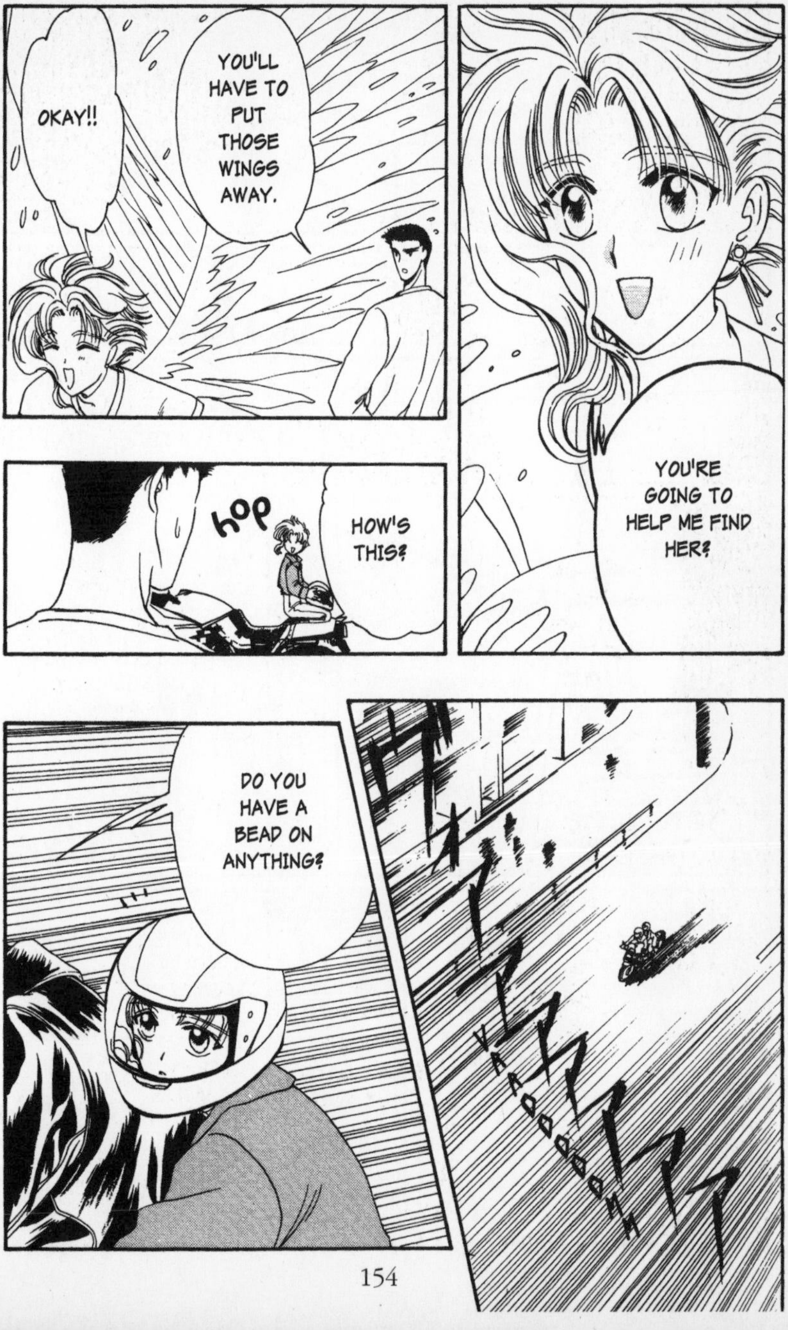
YOU'RE GOING TO HELP ME FIND HER?
YOU'LL HAVE TO PUT THOSE WINGS AWAY.
OKAY!!
HOW'S THIS?
hop
VAROOOOOM
DO YOU HAVE A BEAD ON ANYTHING?

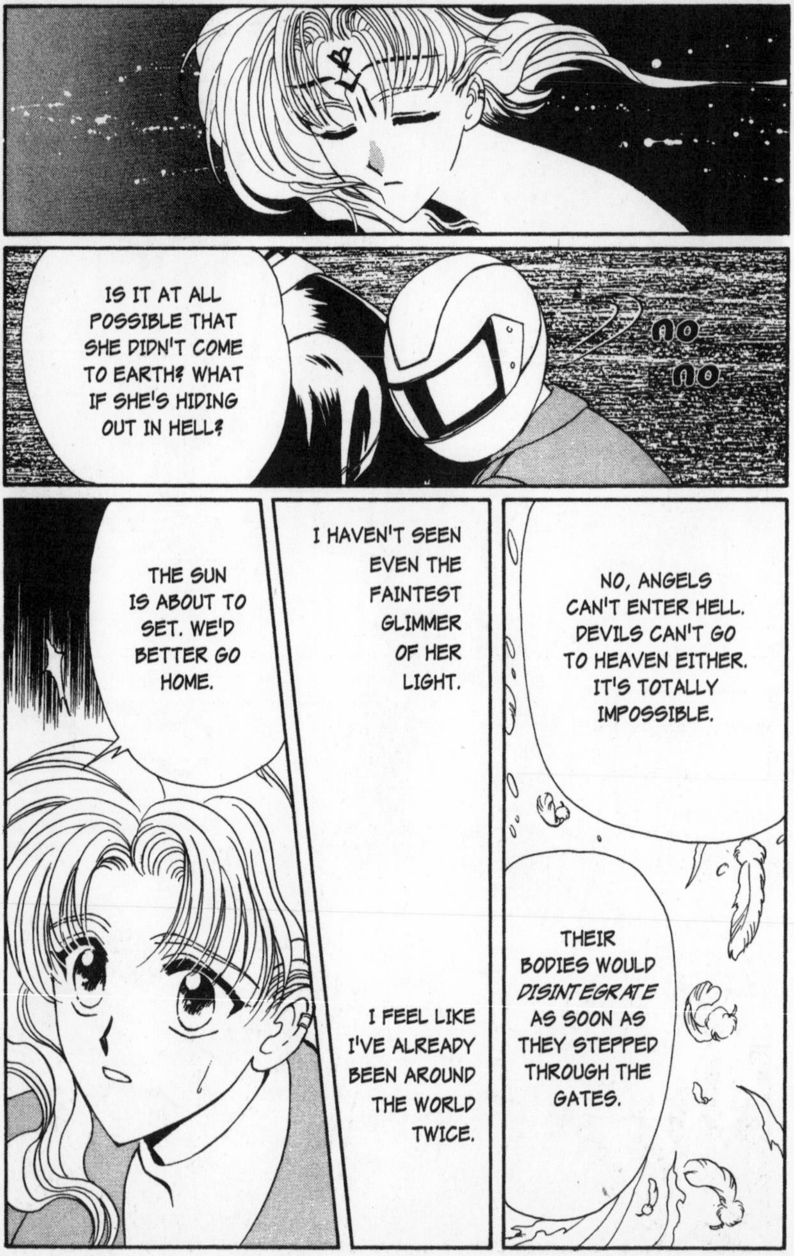
IS IT AT ALL POSSIBLE THAT SHE DIDN'T COME TO EARTH? WHAT IF SHE'S HIDING OUT IN HELL?
NO
NO
NO, ANGELS CAN'T ENTER HELL. DEVILS CAN'T GO TO HEAVEN EITHER. IT'S TOTALLY IMPOSSIBLE.
THEIR BODIES WOULD *DISINTEGRATE* AS SOON AS THEY STEPPED THROUGH THE GATES.
I HAVEN'T SEEN EVEN THE FAINTEST GLIMMER OF HER LIGHT.
I FEEL LIKE I'VE ALREADY BEEN AROUND THE WORLD TWICE.
THE SUN IS ABOUT TO SET. WE'D BETTER GO HOME.

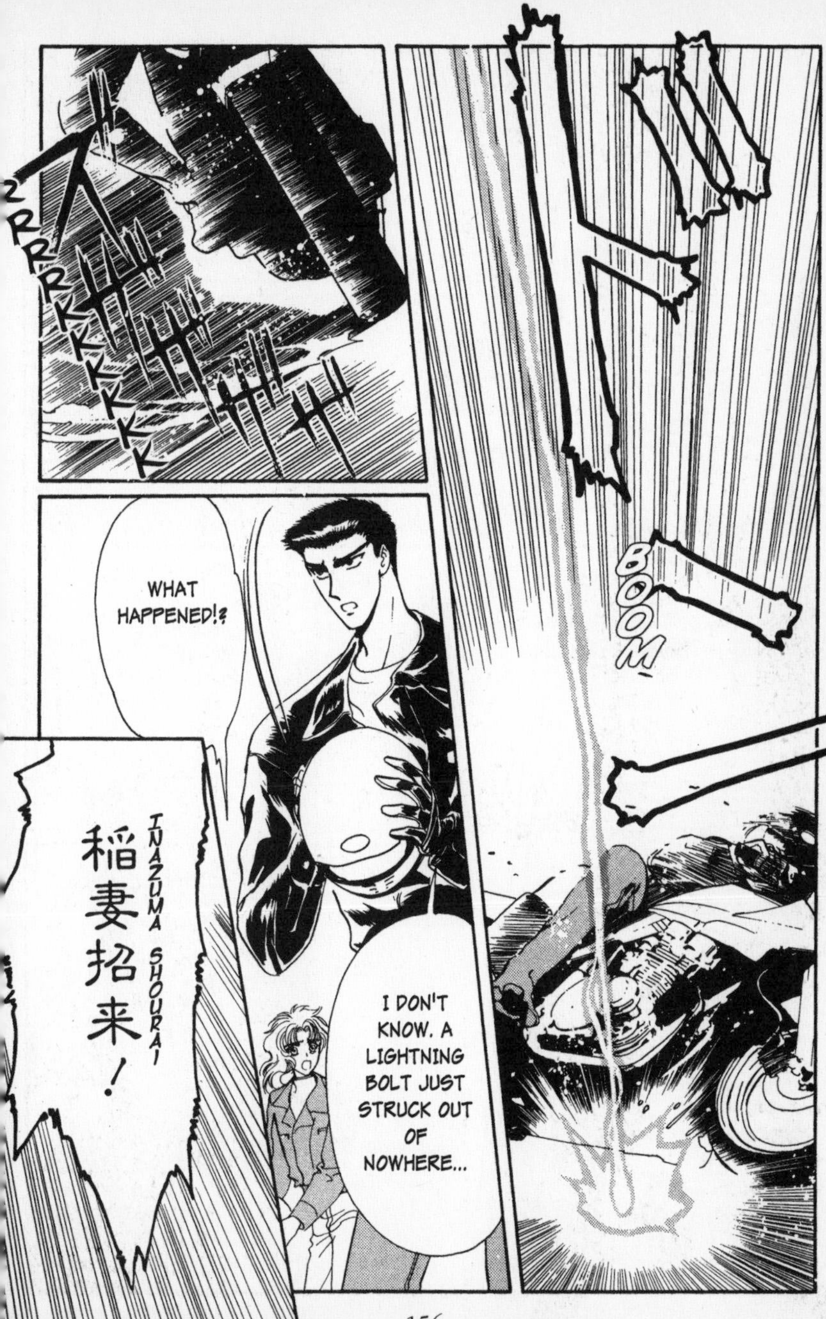
BOOM
ZRRRKKKKKKK
WHAT HAPPENED!?
I DON'T KNOW. A LIGHTNING BOLT JUST STRUCK OUT OF NOWHERE...
稲妻招来!
INAZUMA SHOURAI

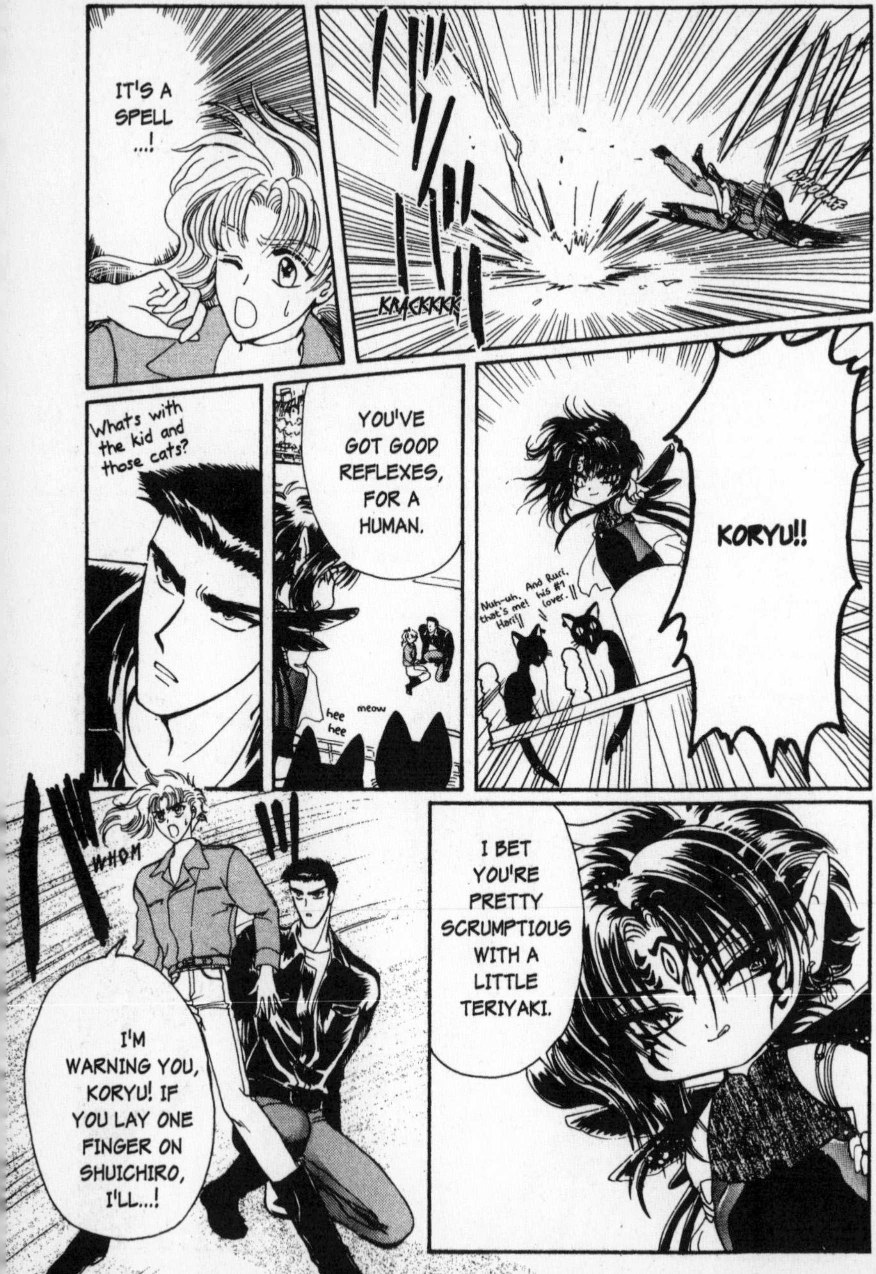
WHOOMF
KRACKKKK
IT'S A SPELL ...!
KORYU!!
And Ruri, his #1 lover.
Nuh-uh, that's me! Hori!
YOU'VE GOT GOOD REFLEXES, FOR A HUMAN.
meow
hee hee
Whats with the kid and those cats?
I BET YOU'RE PRETTY SCRUMPTIOUS WITH A LITTLE TERIYAKI.
WHOM
I'M WARNING YOU, KORYU! IF YOU LAY ONE FINGER ON SHUICHIRO, I'LL...!

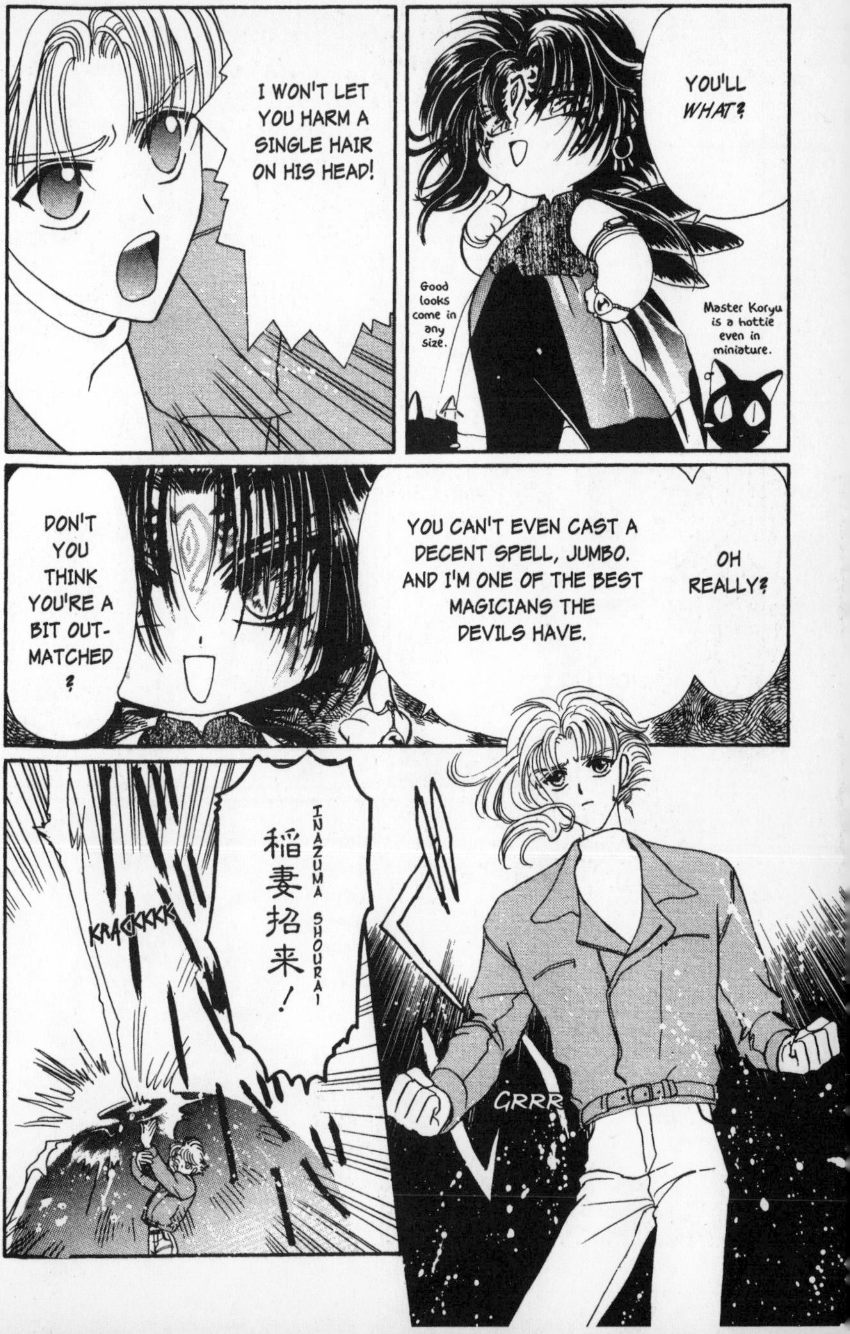
YOU'LL WHAT?
Master Koryu is a hottie even in miniature.
Good looks come in any size.
I WON'T LET YOU HARM A SINGLE HAIR ON HIS HEAD!
OH REALLY?
YOU CAN'T EVEN CAST A DECENT SPELL, JUMBO. AND I'M ONE OF THE BEST MAGICIANS THE DEVILS HAVE.
DON'T YOU THINK YOU'RE A BIT OUT-MATCHED?
GRRR
稲妻招来!
INAZUMA SHOURAI
KRACKKKK

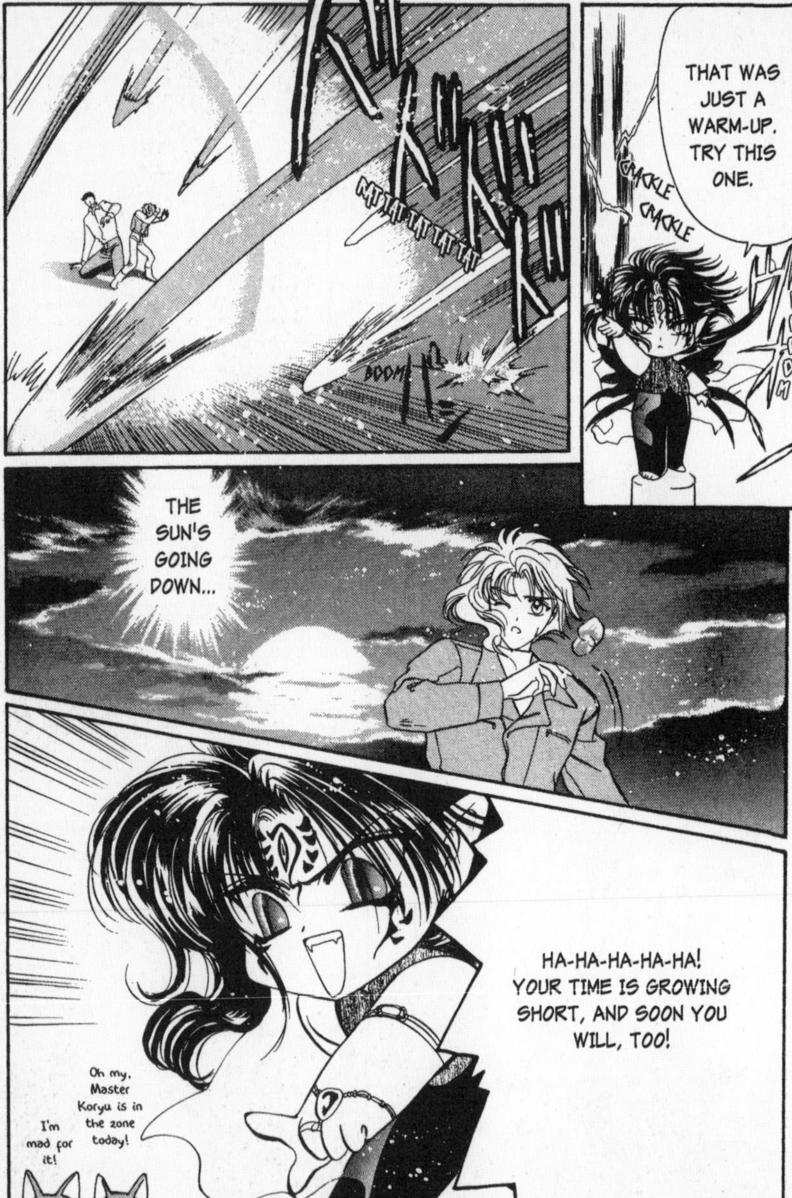
THAT WAS JUST A WARM-UP. TRY THIS ONE.
CRACKLE CRACKLE
VOOOOM
RAT TAT TAT TAT TAT
BOOM
THE SUN'S GOING DOWN...
HA-HA-HA-HA-HA! YOUR TIME IS GROWING SHORT, AND SOON YOU WILL, TOO!
Oh my, Master Koryu is in the zone today!
I'm mad for it!

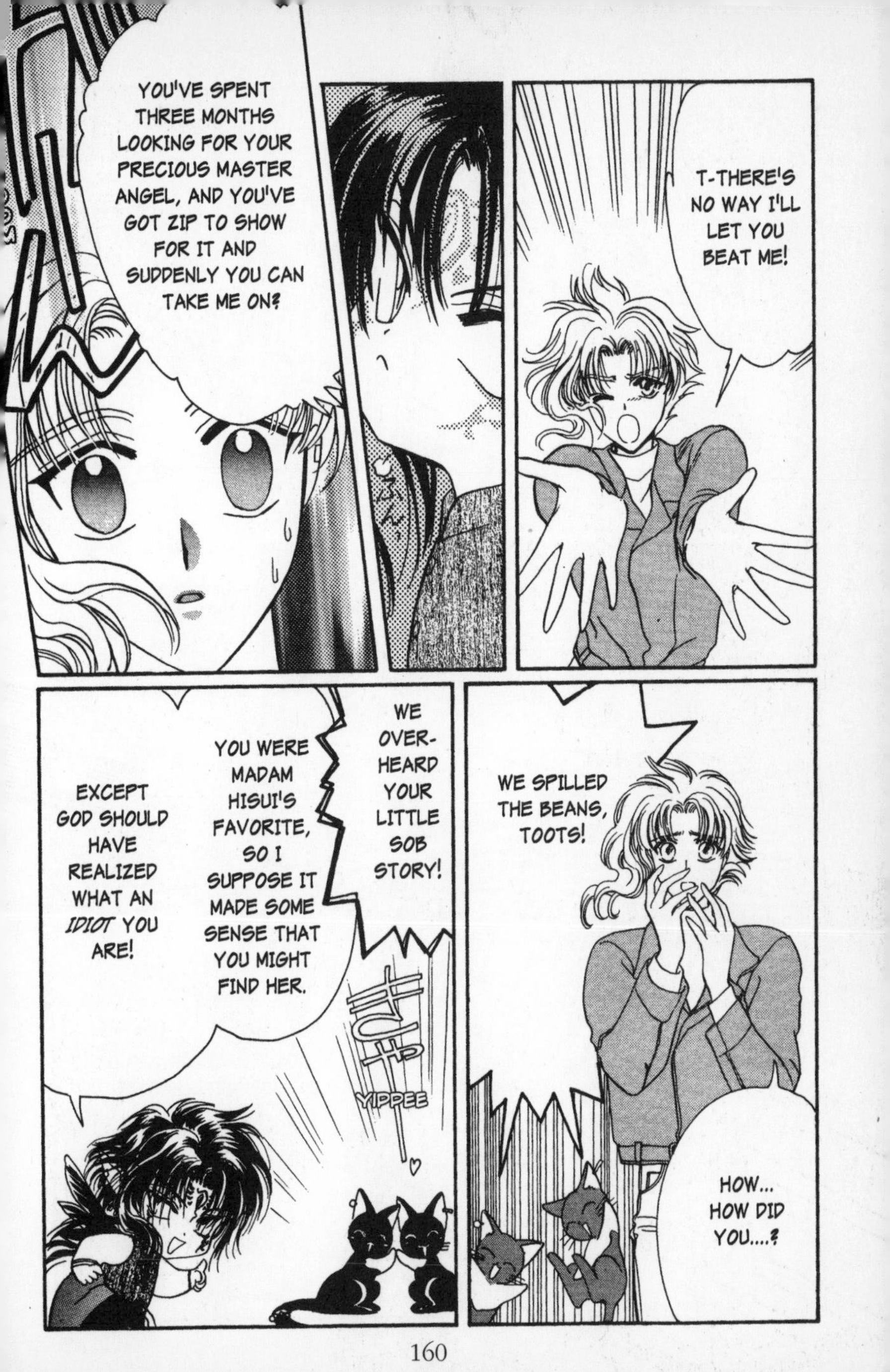
T-THERE'S NO WAY I'LL LET YOU BEAT ME!
YOU'VE SPENT THREE MONTHS LOOKING FOR YOUR PRECIOUS MASTER ANGEL, AND YOU'VE GOT ZIP TO SHOW FOR IT AND SUDDENLY YOU CAN TAKE ME ON?
HOW... HOW DID YOU....?
WE SPILLED THE BEANS, TOOTS!
WE OVER-HEARD YOUR LITTLE SOB STORY!
YIPPEE
YOU WERE MADAM HISUI'S FAVORITE, SO I SUPPOSE IT MADE SOME SENSE THAT YOU MIGHT FIND HER.
EXCEPT GOD SHOULD HAVE REALIZED WHAT AN *IDIOT* YOU ARE!

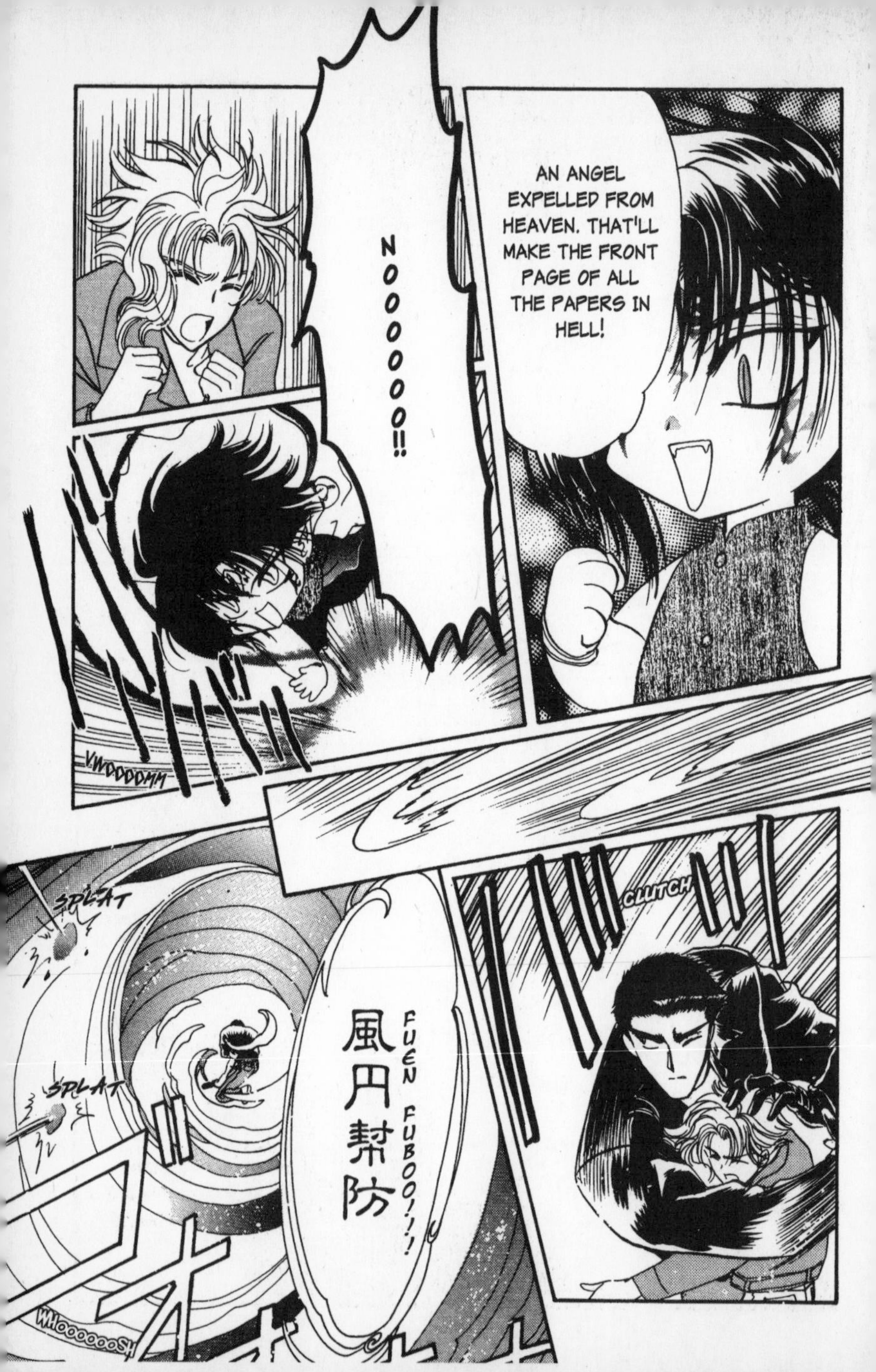
AN ANGEL EXPELLED FROM HEAVEN. THAT'LL MAKE THE FRONT PAGE OF ALL THE PAPERS IN HELL!
NOOOOOOOO!!
VWOOOOMM
CLUTCH
風円帮防
FUEN FUBOO!!!
SPLAT
SPLAT
WHOOOOOOSH

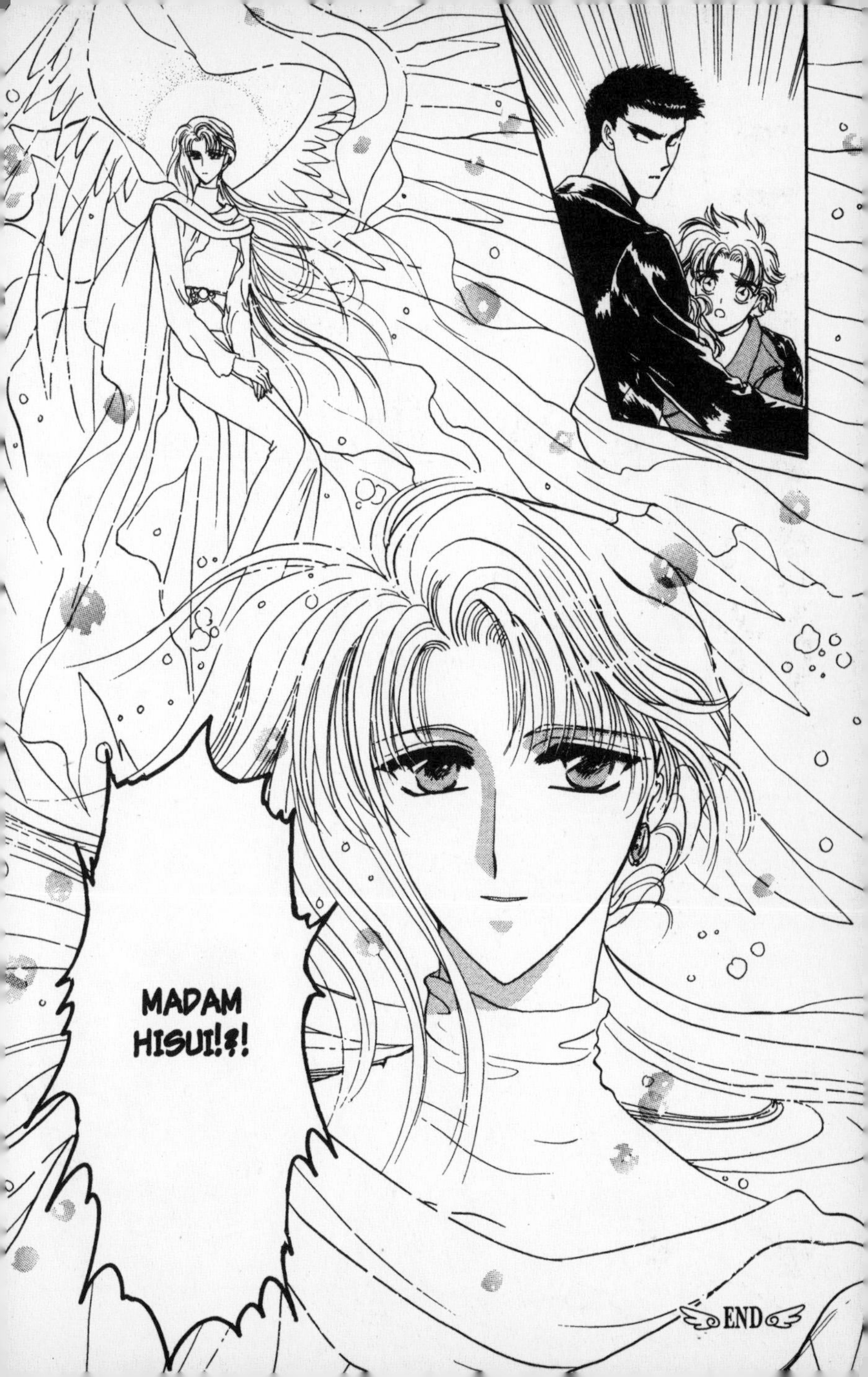
MADAM HISUI!?!
END

こころのわけ

Contact.6 A MATTER OF THE HEART

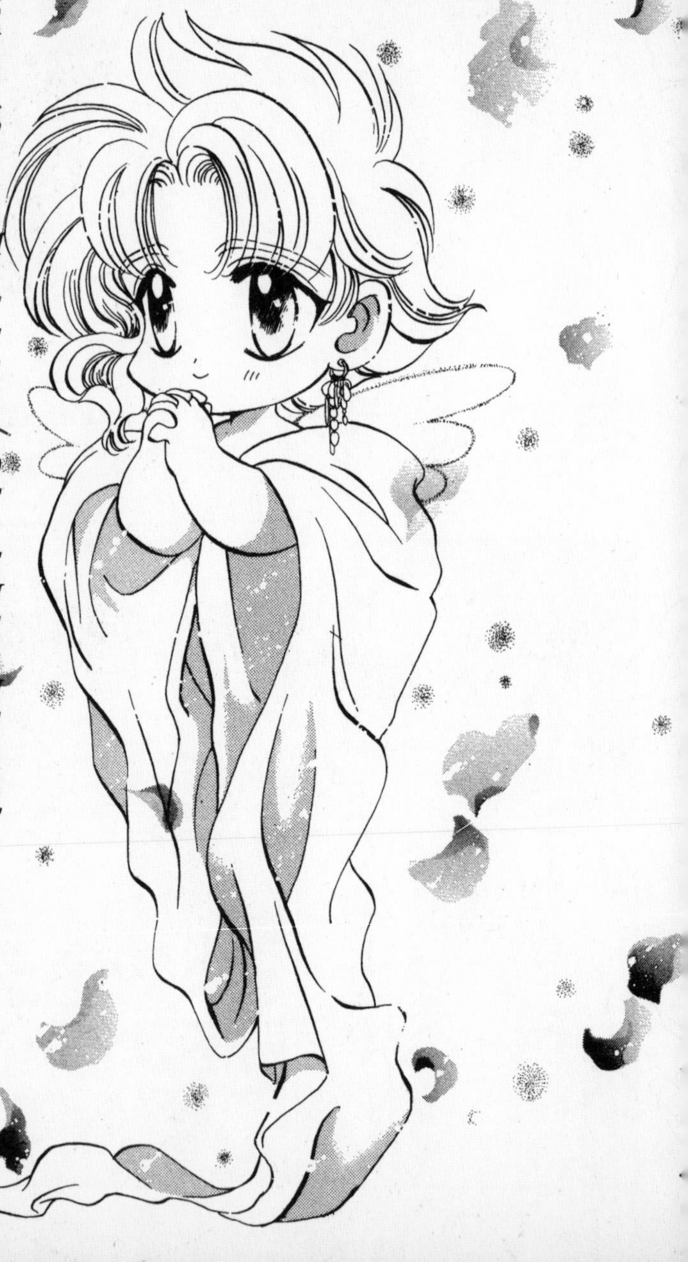

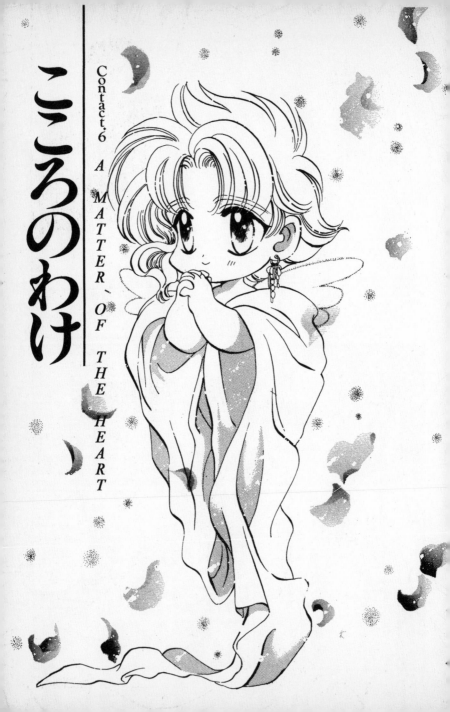

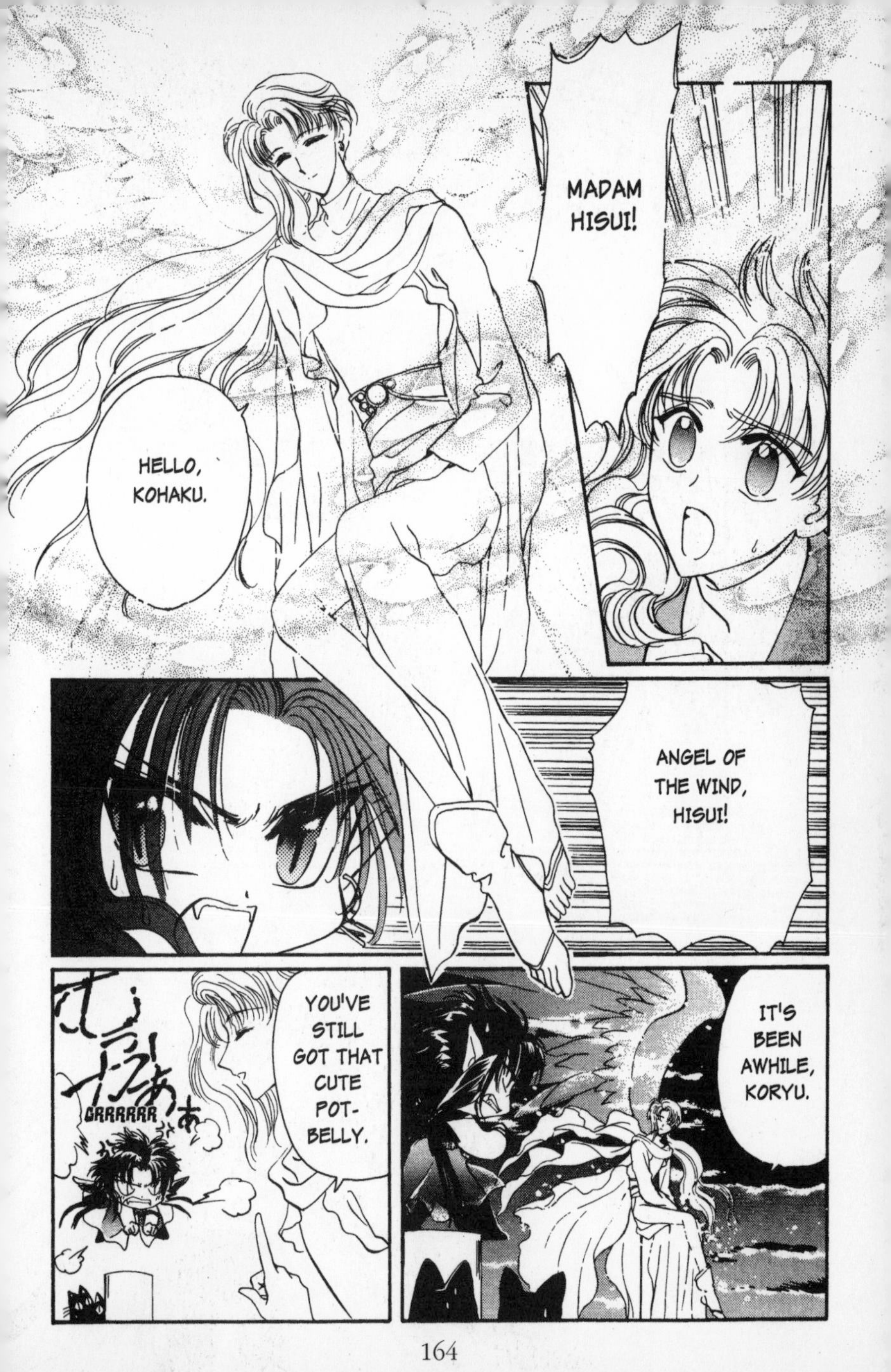
MADAM HISUI!
HELLO, KOHAKU.
ANGEL OF THE WIND, HISUI!
IT'S BEEN AWHILE, KORYU.
YOU'VE STILL GOT THAT CUTE POT-BELLY.
GRRRRRRR

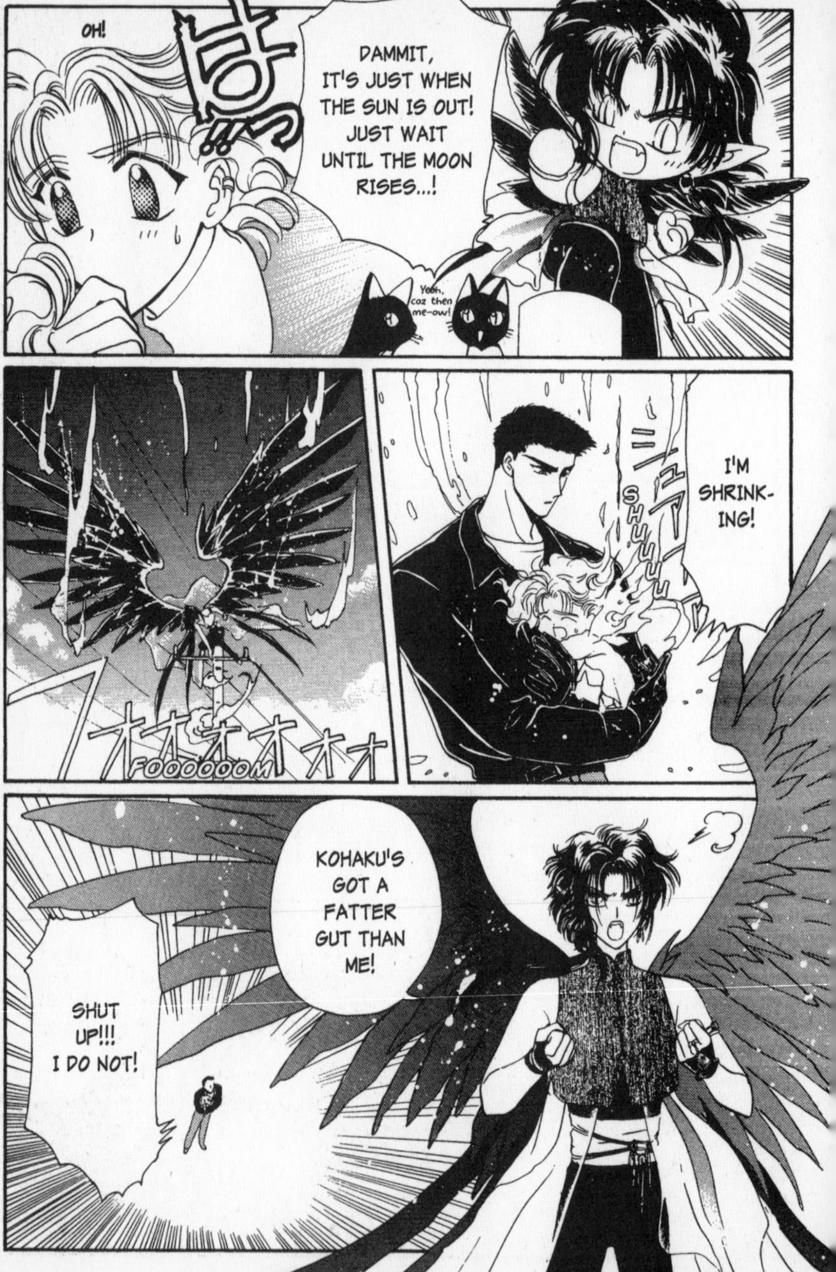
DAMMIT, IT'S JUST WHEN THE SUN IS OUT! JUST WAIT UNTIL THE MOON RISES...!
はっ!!
OH!
Yeah, coz then me-ow!
シュー
SHUUUU
I'M SHRINK-ING!
オオオオオオ
FOOOOOOM
KOHAKU'S GOT A FATTER GUT THAN ME!
SHUT UP!!! I DO NOT!

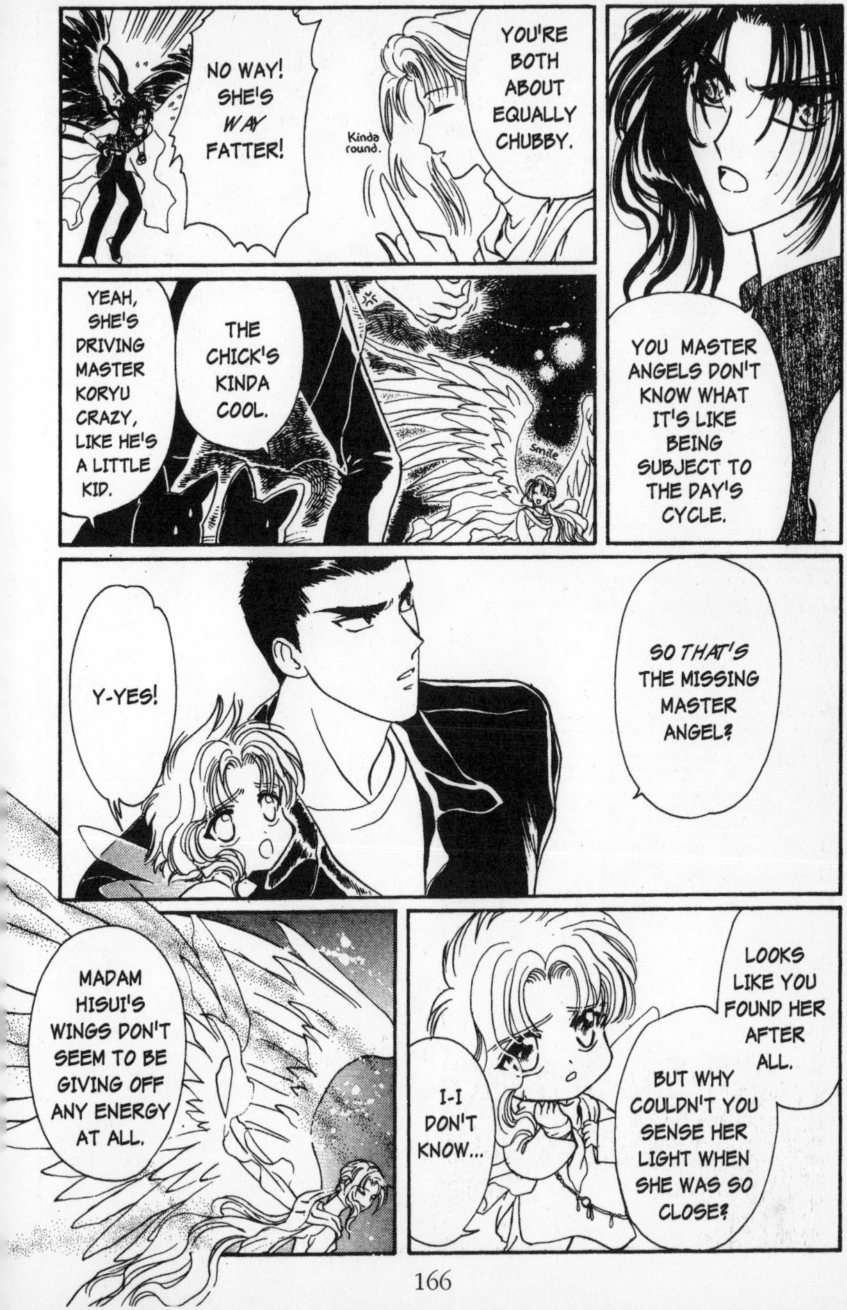
YOU MASTER ANGELS DON'T KNOW WHAT IT'S LIKE BEING SUBJECT TO THE DAY'S CYCLE.
YOU'RE BOTH ABOUT EQUALLY CHUBBY.
Kinda round.
NO WAY! SHE'S *WAY* FATTER!
Smile
THE CHICK'S KINDA COOL.
YEAH, SHE'S DRIVING MASTER KORYU CRAZY, LIKE HE'S A LITTLE KID.
SO *THAT'S* THE MISSING MASTER ANGEL?
Y-YES!
LOOKS LIKE YOU FOUND HER AFTER ALL.
BUT WHY COULDN'T YOU SENSE HER LIGHT WHEN SHE WAS SO CLOSE?
I-I DON'T KNOW...
MADAM HISUI'S WINGS DON'T SEEM TO BE GIVING OFF ANY ENERGY AT ALL.

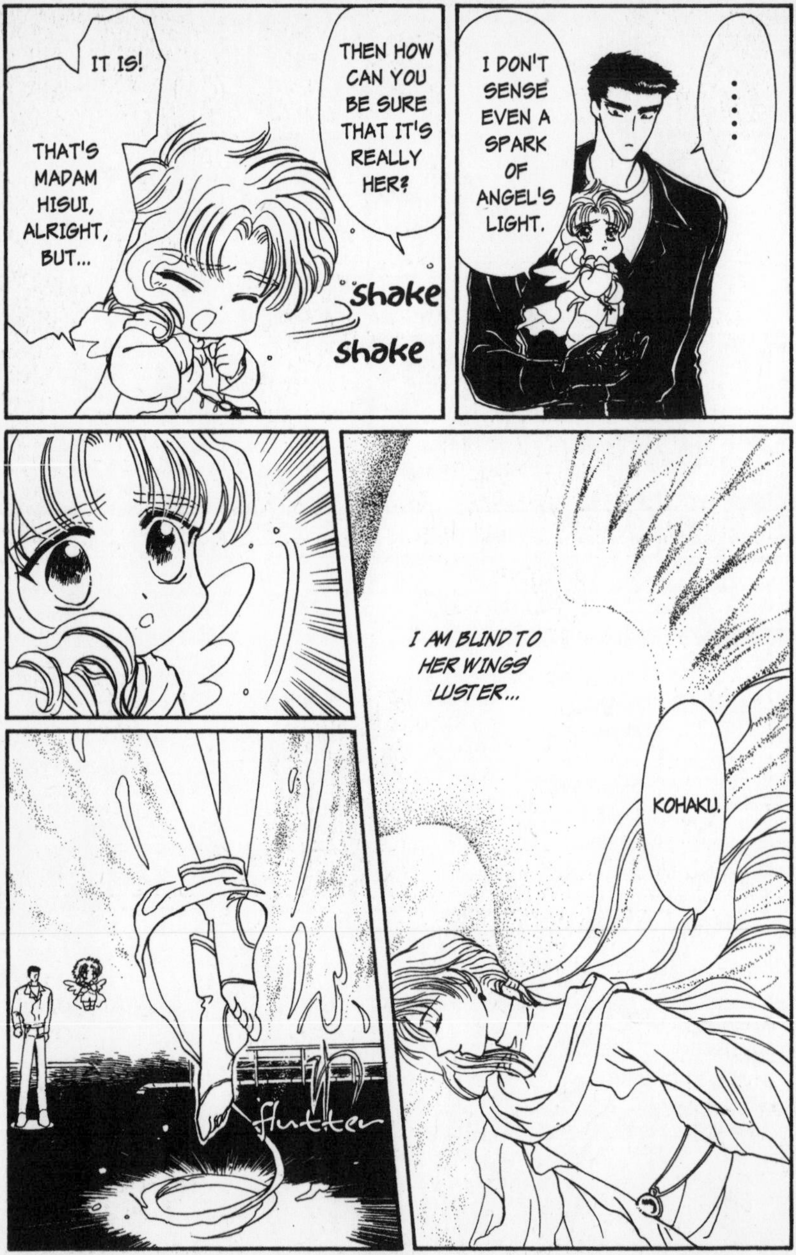
......
I DON'T SENSE EVEN A SPARK OF ANGEL'S LIGHT.
THEN HOW CAN YOU BE SURE THAT IT'S REALLY HER?
IT IS!
THAT'S MADAM HISUI, ALRIGHT, BUT...
Shake
Shake
I AM BLIND TO HER WINGS' LUSTER...
KOHAKU.
flutter

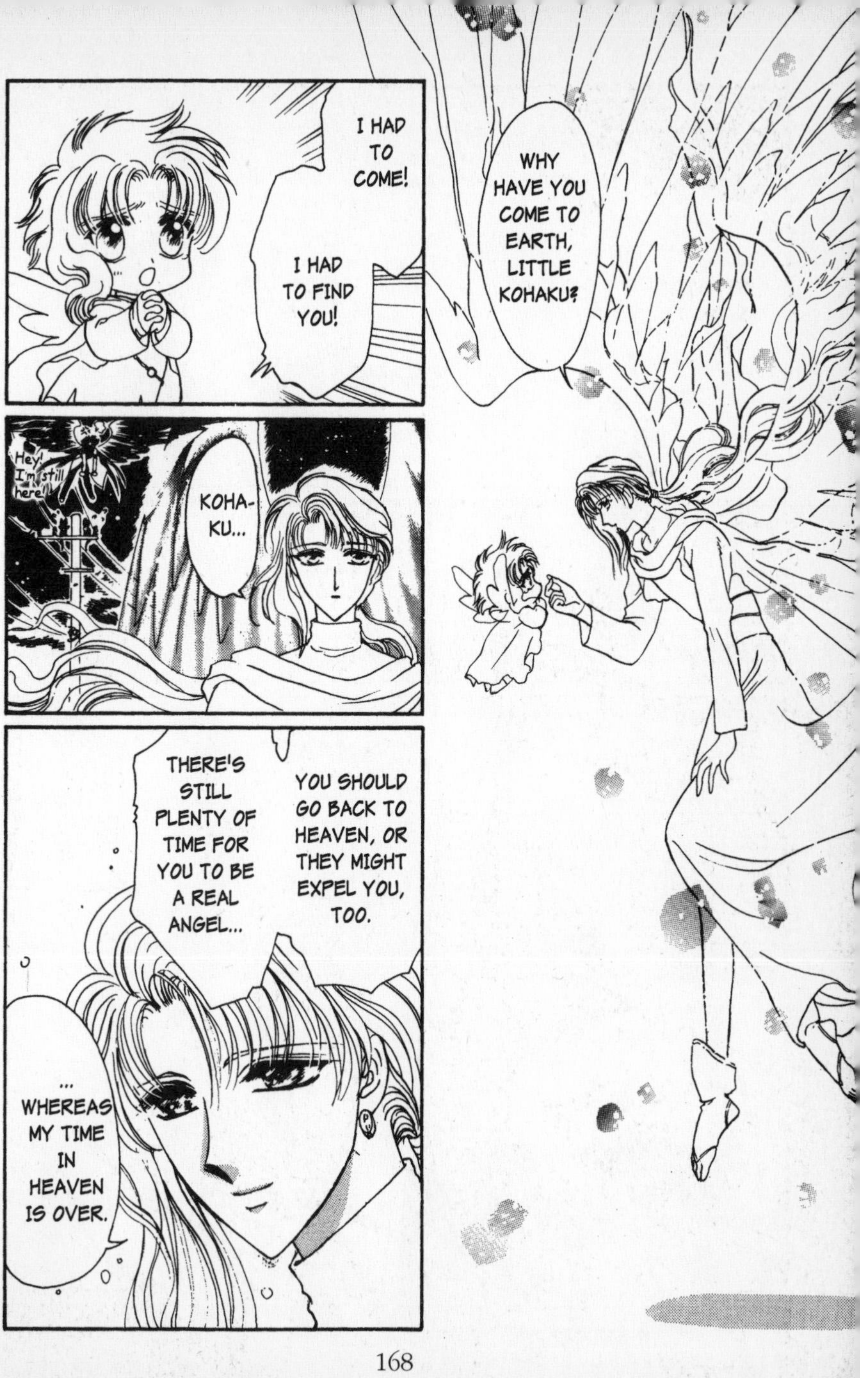
WHY HAVE YOU COME TO EARTH, LITTLE KOHAKU?
I HAD TO COME!
I HAD TO FIND YOU!
KOHA-KU...
Hey! I'm still here!
YOU SHOULD GO BACK TO HEAVEN, OR THEY MIGHT EXPEL YOU, TOO.
THERE'S STILL PLENTY OF TIME FOR YOU TO BE A REAL ANGEL...
...WHEREAS MY TIME IN HEAVEN IS OVER.

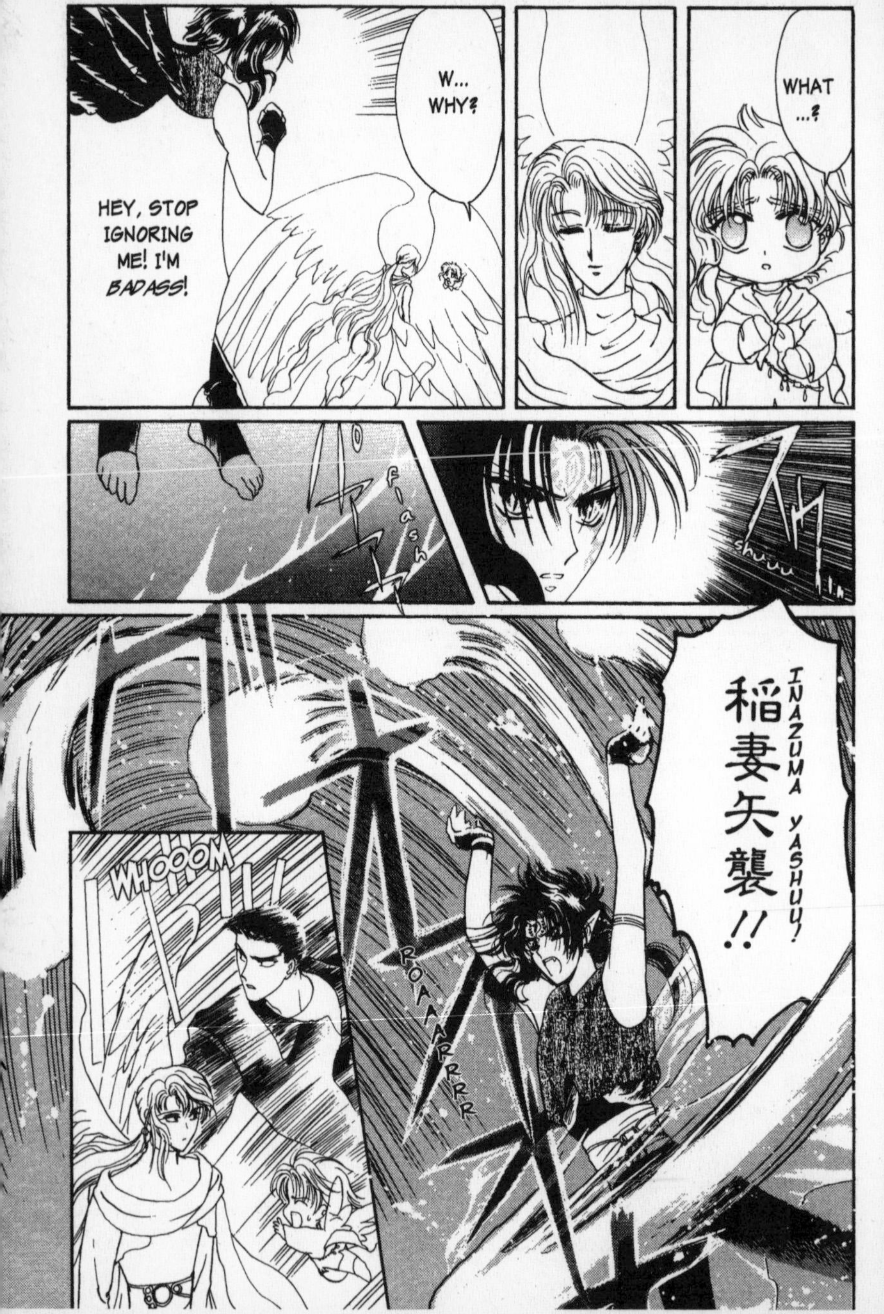
WHAT ...?
W... WHY?
HEY, STOP IGNORING ME! I'M BADASS!
shuuu
flash
稲妻矢襲!!
INAZUMA YASHUU!
ROAAARRRR
WHOOOM

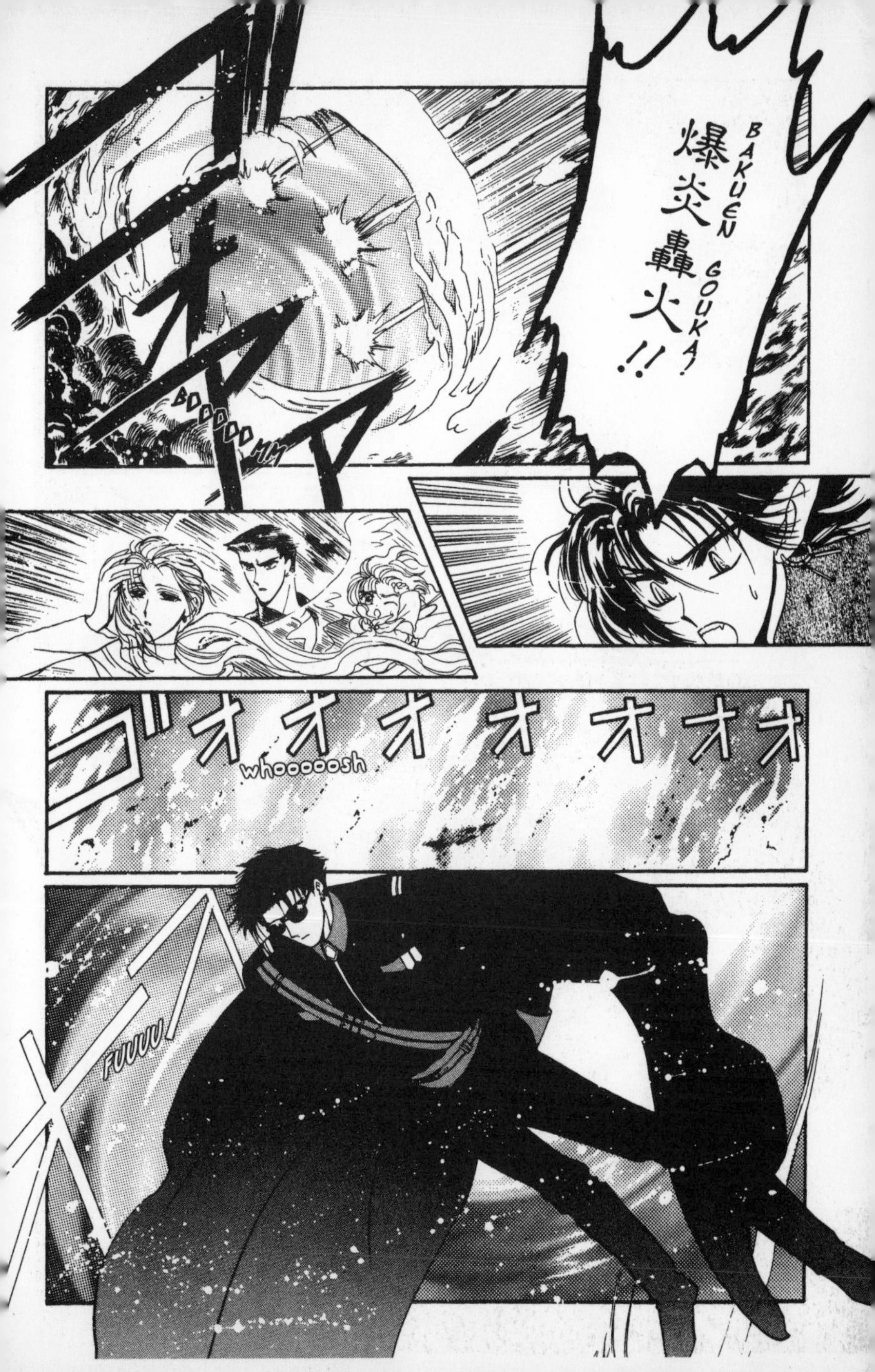
爆炎轟火!!
BAKUEN GOUKA!
BOOOOOMM
ゴオオオオオオ
whoooooosh
FUUUU

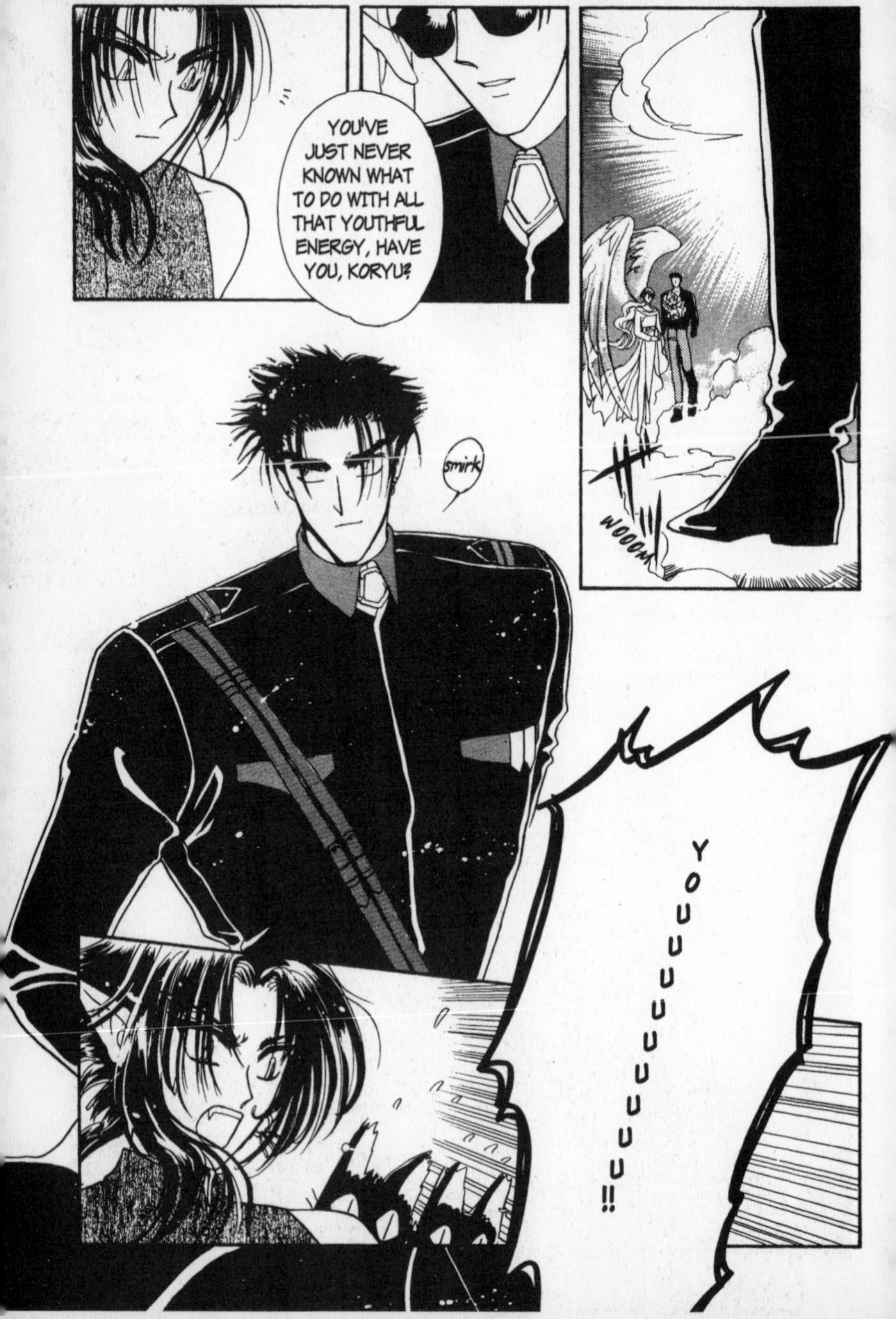
WOOOH
YOU'VE JUST NEVER KNOWN WHAT TO DO WITH ALL THAT YOUTHFUL ENERGY, HAVE YOU, KORYU?
smirk
YOUUUUUUUUUUUUU!!

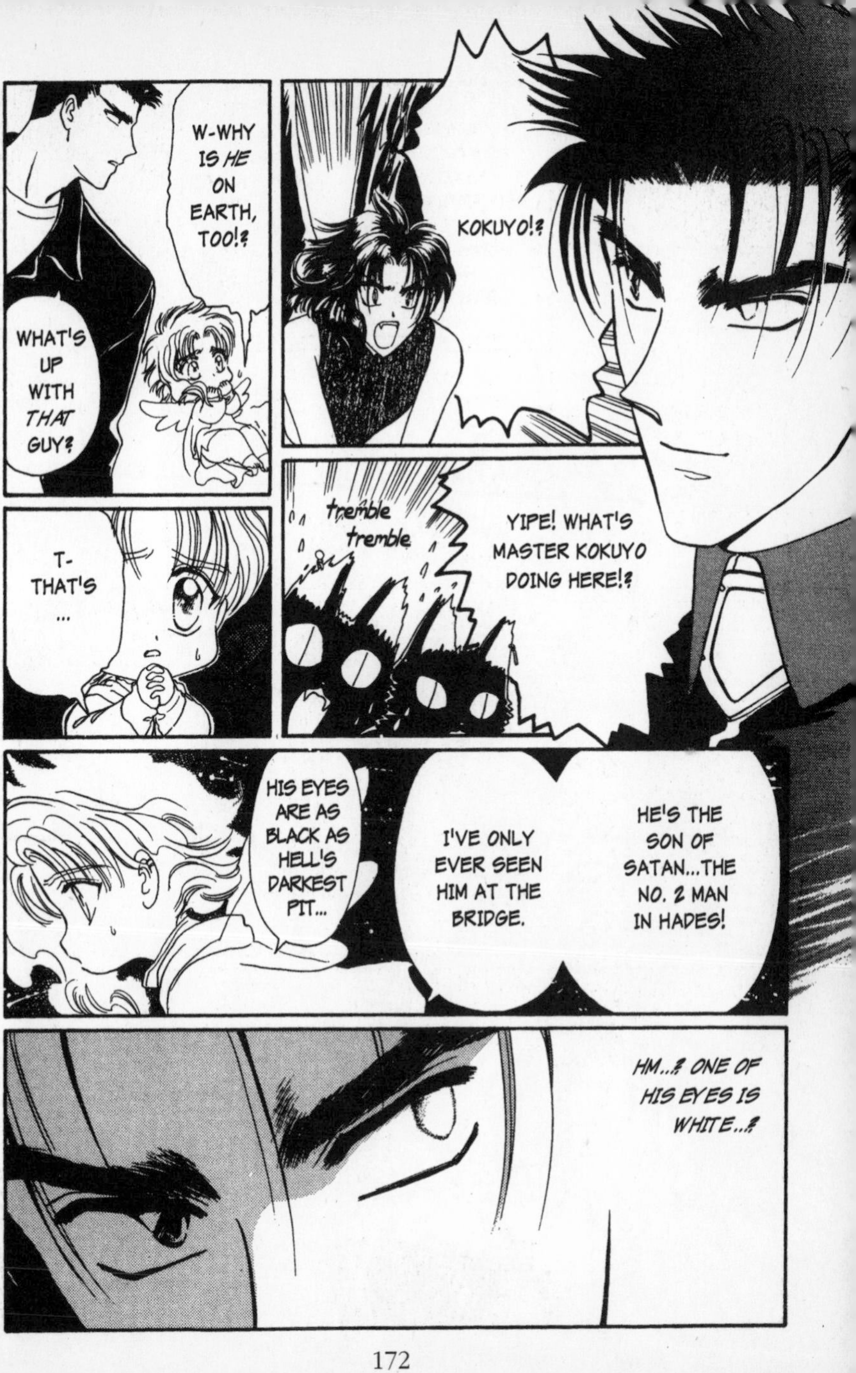
KOKUYO!?
W-WHY IS HE ON EARTH, TOO!?
WHAT'S UP WITH THAT GUY?
tremble tremble
YIPE! WHAT'S MASTER KOKUYO DOING HERE!?
T-THAT'S ...
HE'S THE SON OF SATAN...THE NO. 2 MAN IN HADES!
I'VE ONLY EVER SEEN HIM AT THE BRIDGE.
HIS EYES ARE AS BLACK AS HELL'S DARKEST PIT...
HM...!? ONE OF HIS EYES IS WHITE...!?

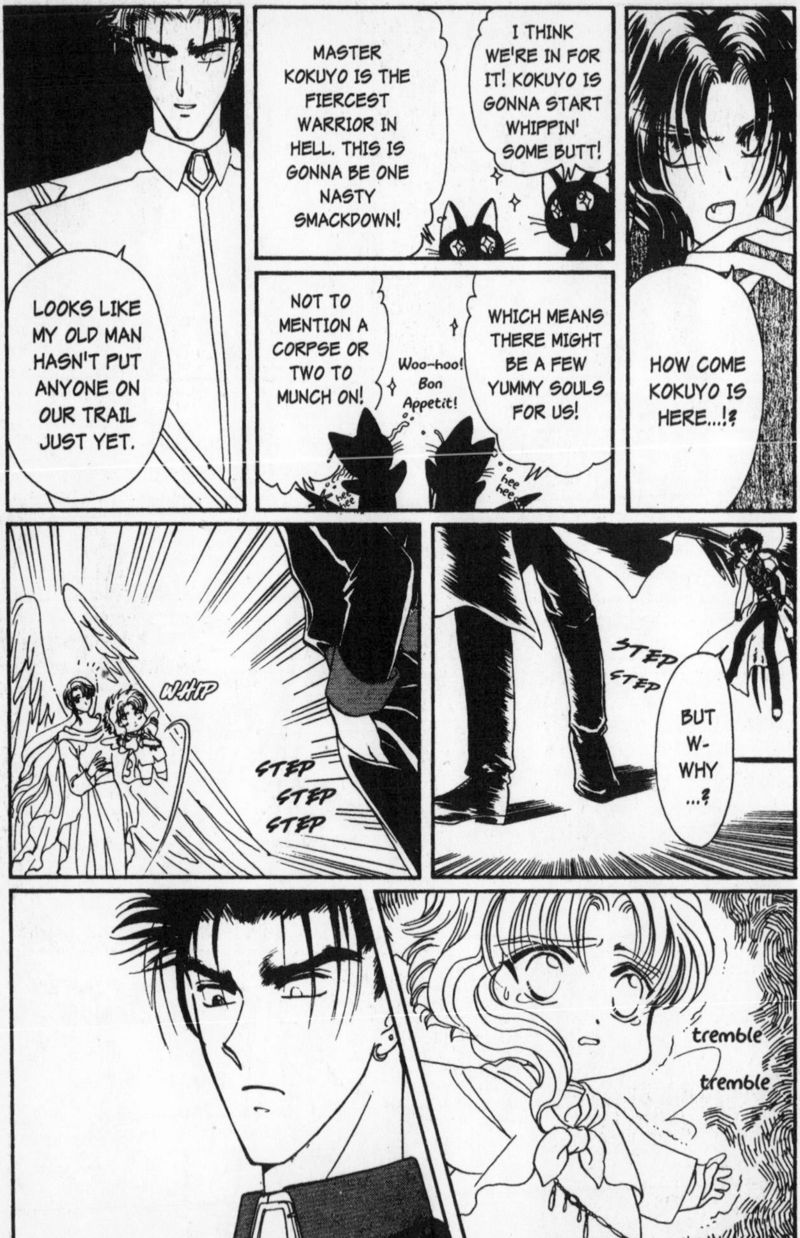
HOW COME KOKUYO IS HERE...!?
I THINK WE'RE IN FOR IT! KOKUYO IS GONNA START WHIPPIN' SOME BUTT!
MASTER KOKUYO IS THE FIERCEST WARRIOR IN HELL. THIS IS GONNA BE ONE NASTY SMACKDOWN!
WHICH MEANS THERE MIGHT BE A FEW YUMMY SOULS FOR US!
NOT TO MENTION A CORPSE OR TWO TO MUNCH ON!
Woo-hoo! Bon Appetit!
hee hee
hee hee
LOOKS LIKE MY OLD MAN HASN'T PUT ANYONE ON OUR TRAIL JUST YET.
STEP STEP
BUT W-WHY ...?
WHIP
STEP STEP STEP
tremble
tremble

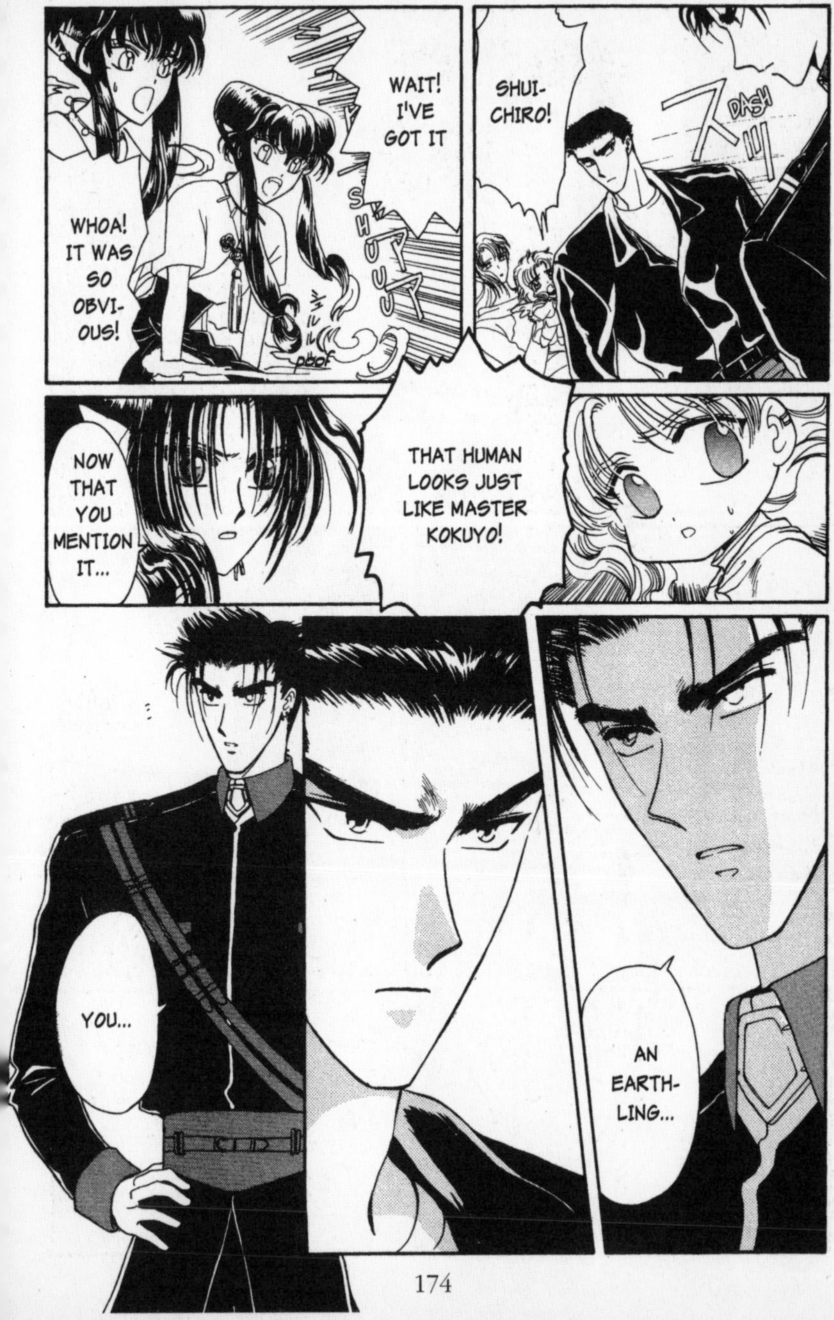
SHUI-CHIRO!
DASH
SHUUU
WAIT! I'VE GOT IT
WHOA! IT WAS SO OBVIOUS!
poof
THAT HUMAN LOOKS JUST LIKE MASTER KOKUYO!
NOW THAT YOU MENTION IT...
AN EARTH-LING...
YOU...

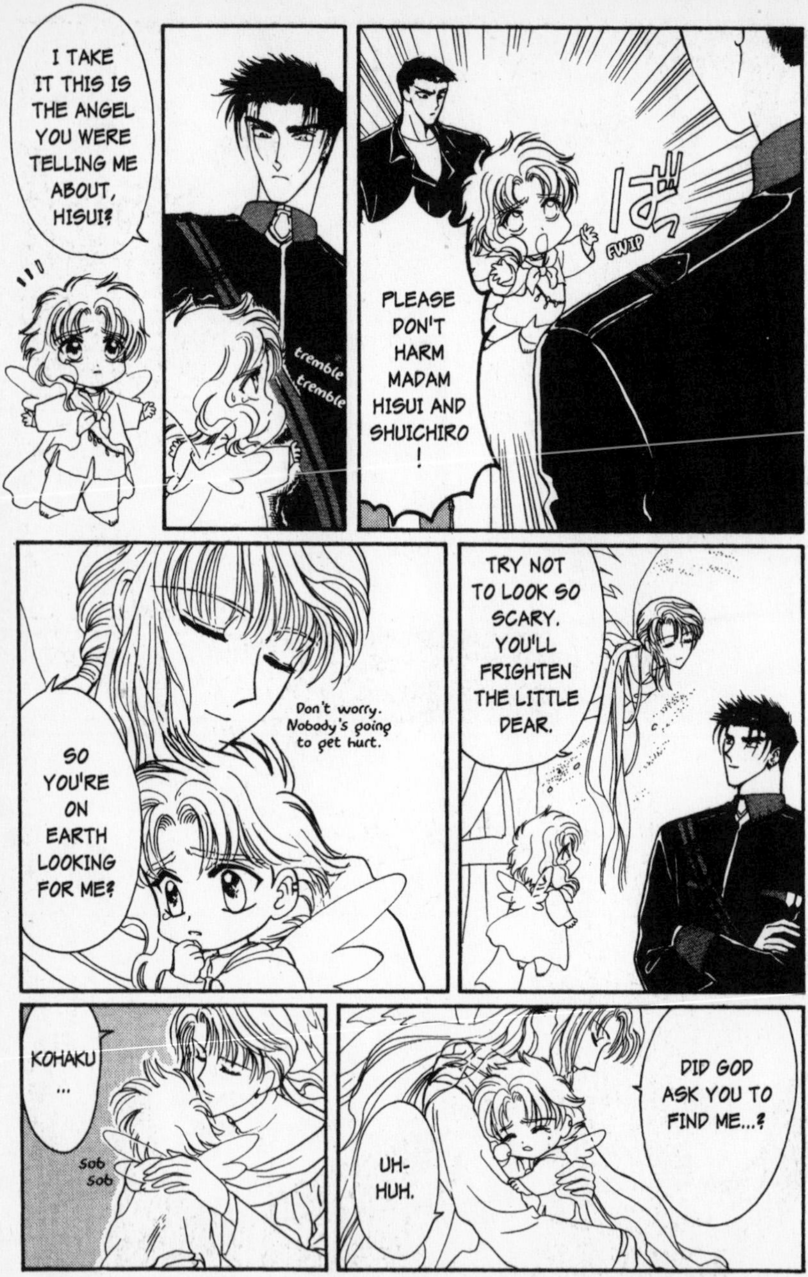
ばっ
FWIP
PLEASE DON'T HARM MADAM HISUI AND SHUICHIRO!
tremble tremble
I TAKE IT THIS IS THE ANGEL YOU WERE TELLING ME ABOUT, HISUI?
TRY NOT TO LOOK SO SCARY. YOU'LL FRIGHTEN THE LITTLE DEAR.
Don't worry. Nobody's going to get hurt.
SO YOU'RE ON EARTH LOOKING FOR ME?
DID GOD ASK YOU TO FIND ME...?
UH-HUH.
KOHAKU ...
Sob Sob

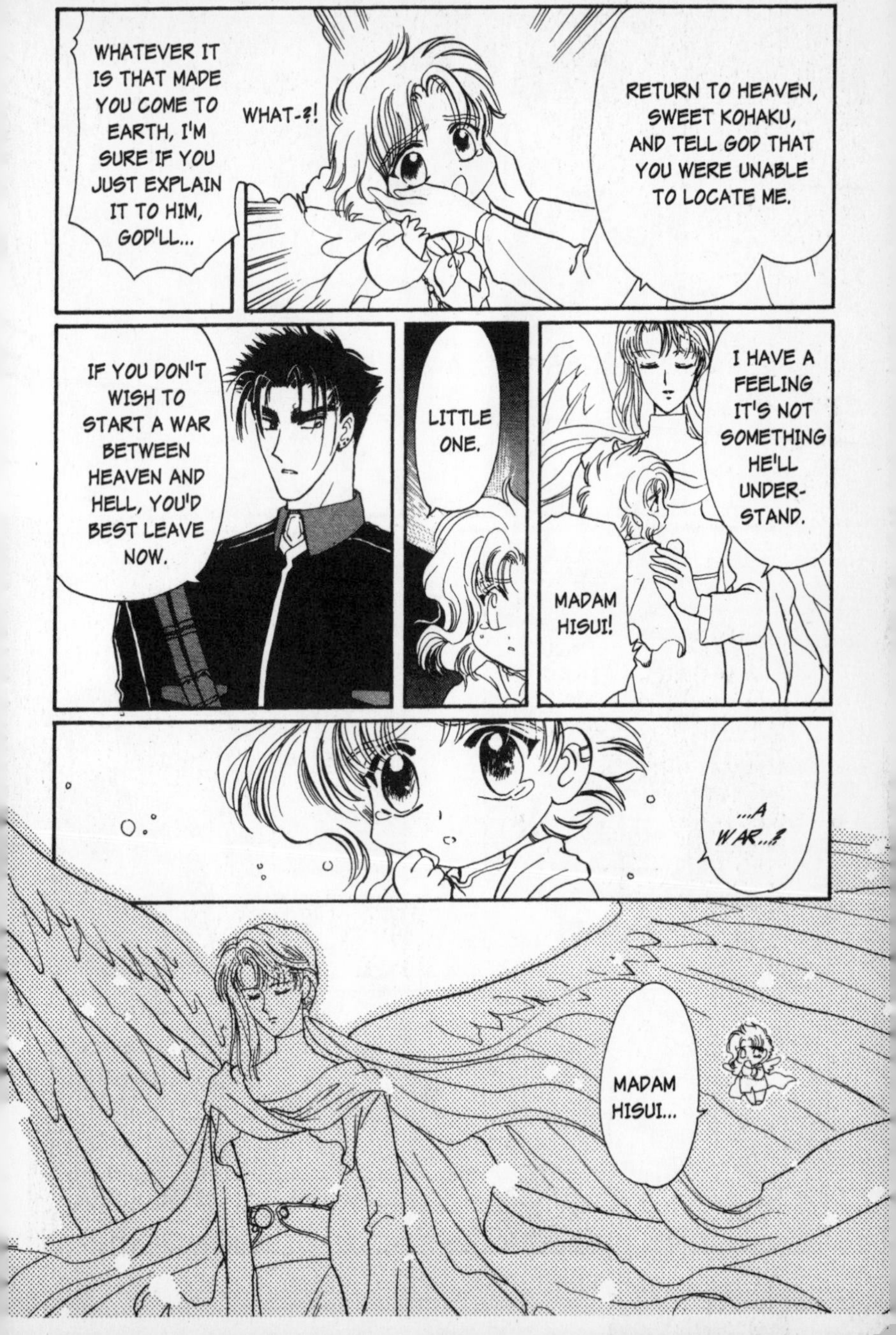
RETURN TO HEAVEN, SWEET KOHAKU, AND TELL GOD THAT YOU WERE UNABLE TO LOCATE ME.
WHAT-?!
WHATEVER IT IS THAT MADE YOU COME TO EARTH, I'M SURE IF YOU JUST EXPLAIN IT TO HIM, GOD'LL...
I HAVE A FEELING IT'S NOT SOMETHING HE'LL UNDER-STAND.
MADAM HISUI!
LITTLE ONE.
IF YOU DON'T WISH TO START A WAR BETWEEN HEAVEN AND HELL, YOU'D BEST LEAVE NOW.
...A WAR...?
MADAM HISUI...

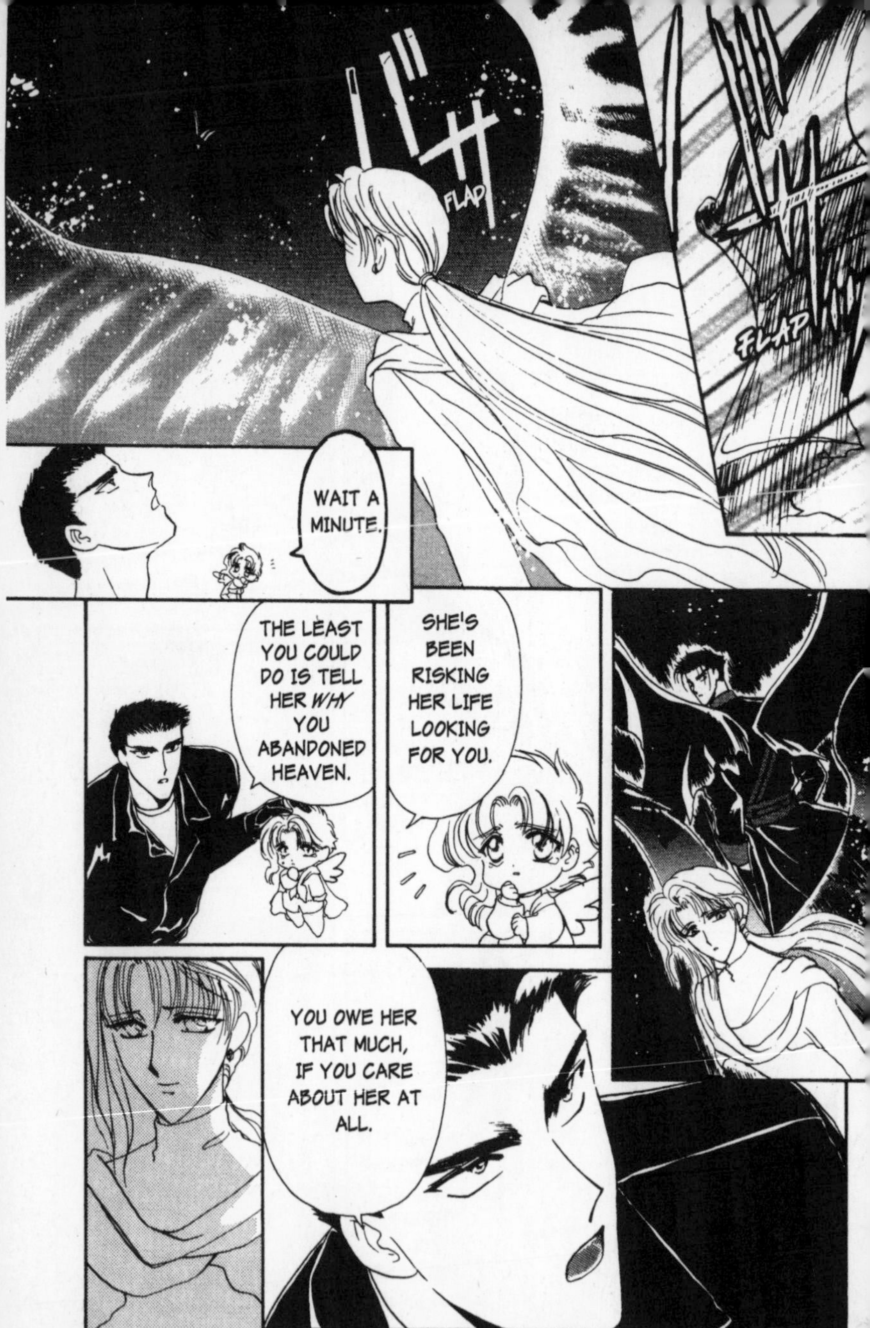
FLAP
FLAP
WAIT A MINUTE.
SHE'S BEEN RISKING HER LIFE LOOKING FOR YOU.
THE LEAST YOU COULD DO IS TELL HER *WHY* YOU ABANDONED HEAVEN.
YOU OWE HER THAT MUCH, IF YOU CARE ABOUT HER AT ALL.

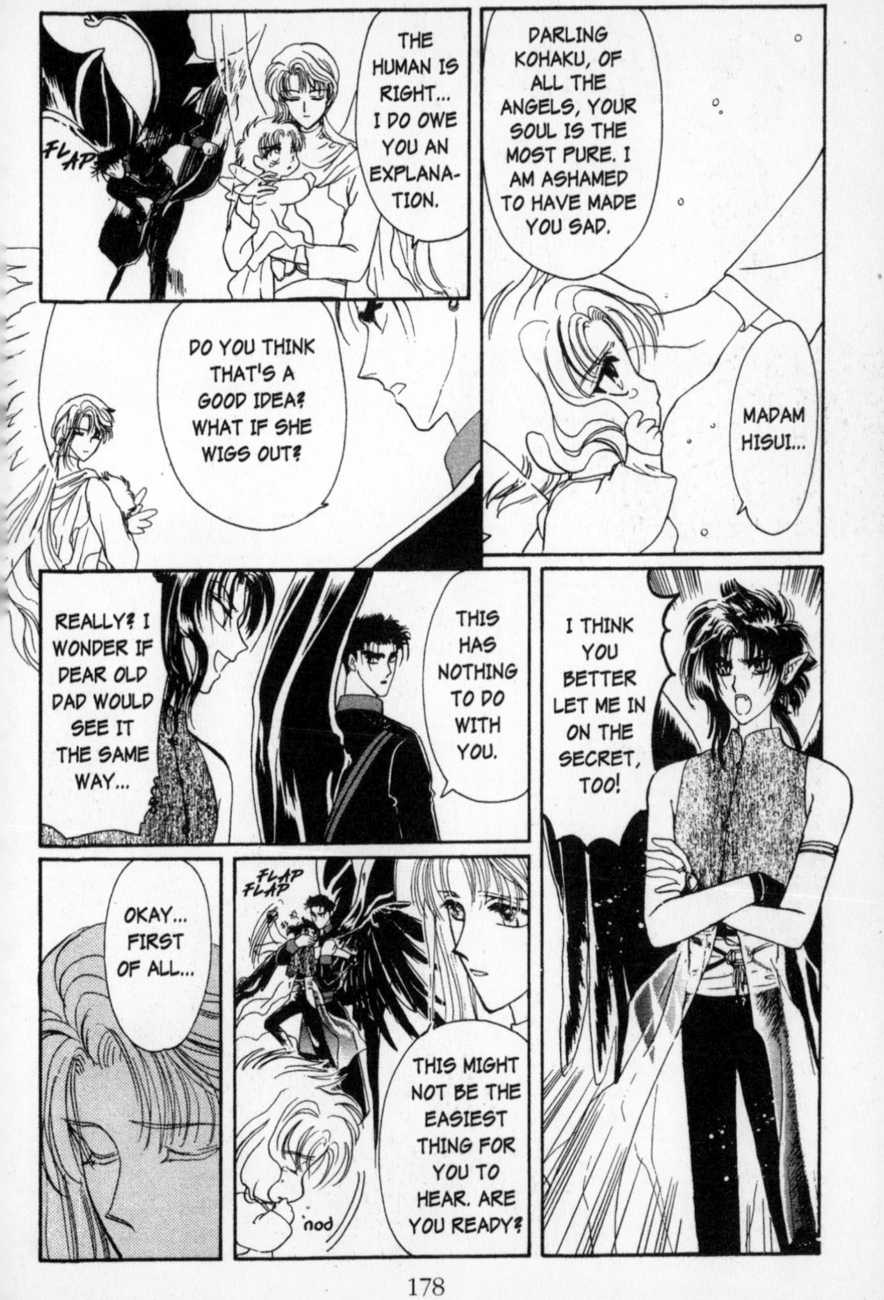
DARLING KOHAKU, OF ALL THE ANGELS, YOUR SOUL IS THE MOST PURE. I AM ASHAMED TO HAVE MADE YOU SAD.
THE HUMAN IS RIGHT... I DO OWE YOU AN EXPLANATION.
FLAP
MADAM HISUI...
DO YOU THINK THAT'S A GOOD IDEA? WHAT IF SHE WIGS OUT?
I THINK YOU BETTER LET ME IN ON THE SECRET, TOO!
THIS HAS NOTHING TO DO WITH YOU.
REALLY? I WONDER IF DEAR OLD DAD WOULD SEE IT THE SAME WAY...
FLAP FLAP
THIS MIGHT NOT BE THE EASIEST THING FOR YOU TO HEAR. ARE YOU READY?
nod
OKAY... FIRST OF ALL...

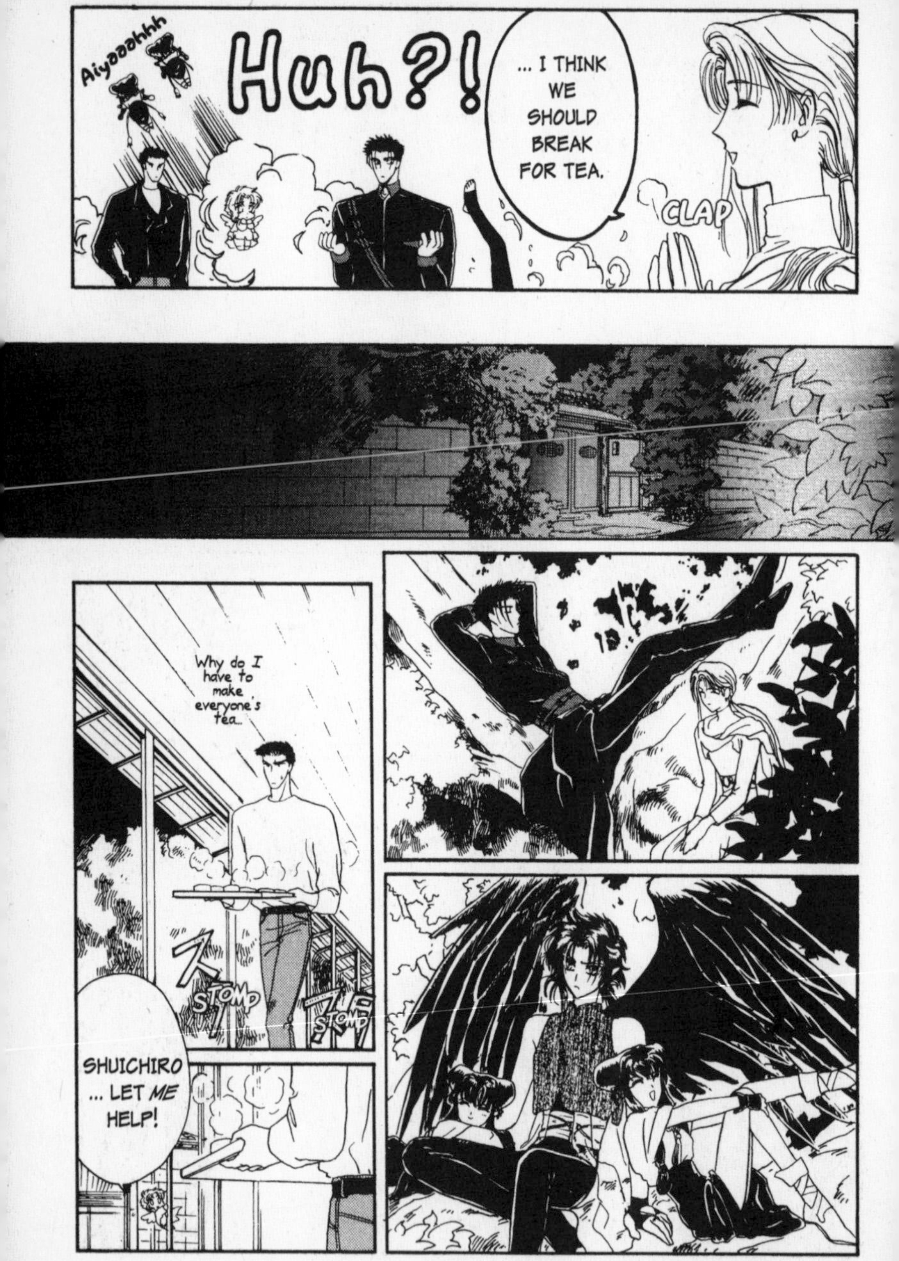
... I THINK WE SHOULD BREAK FOR TEA.
CLAP
Huh?!
Aiyaaahhh
Why do I have to make everyone's tea..
STOMP
STOMP
SHUICHIRO ... LET *ME* HELP!

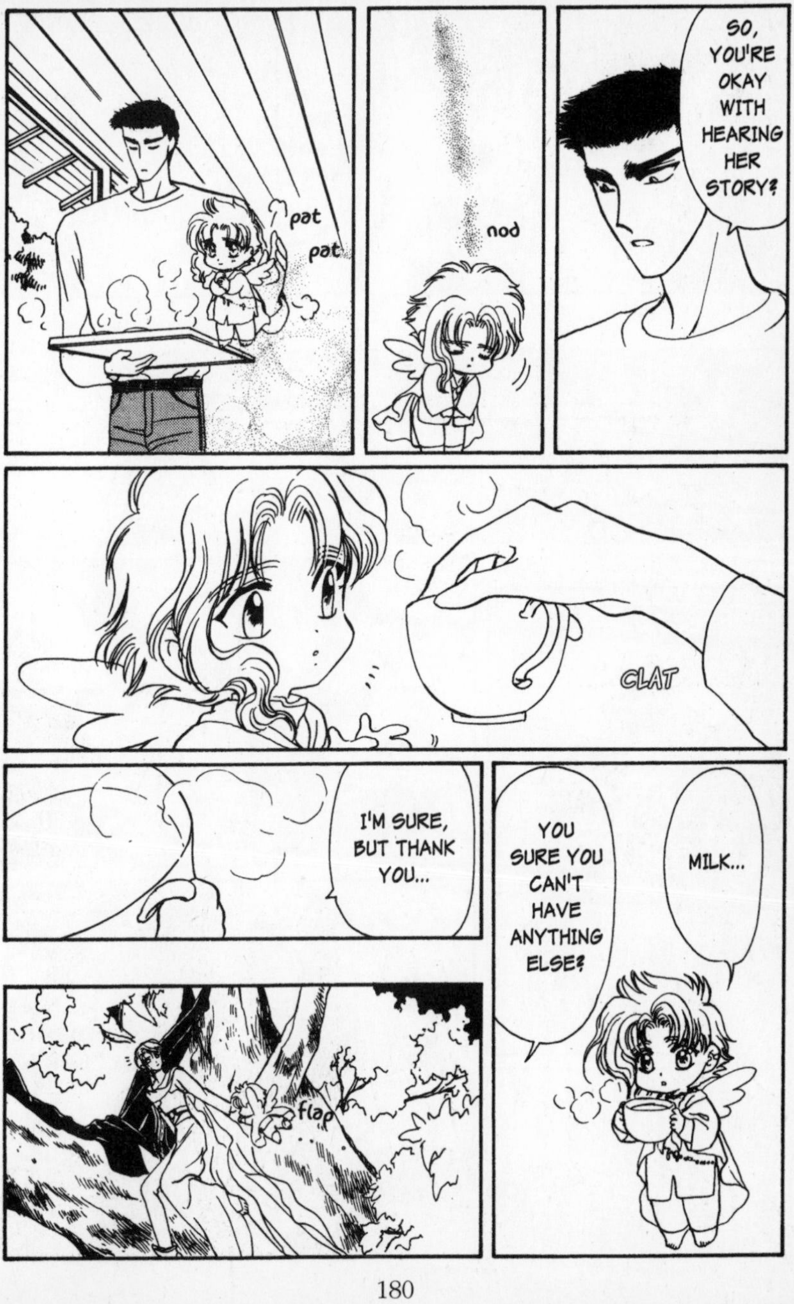
SO, YOU'RE OKAY WITH HEARING HER STORY?
nod
pat
pat
CLAT
MILK...
YOU SURE YOU CAN'T HAVE ANYTHING ELSE?
I'M SURE, BUT THANK YOU...
flap

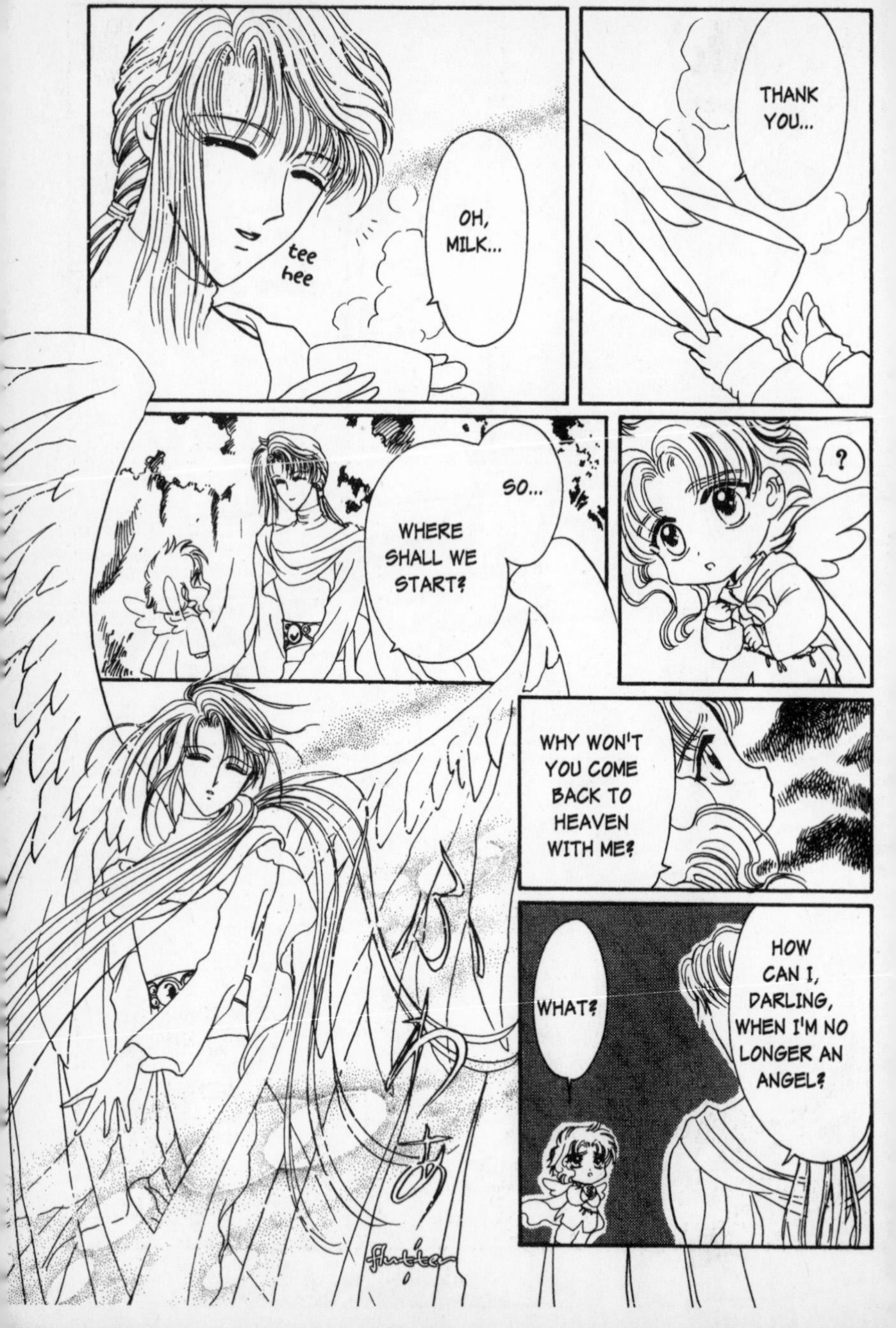
THANK YOU...
OH, MILK...
tee hee
?
SO...
WHERE SHALL WE START?
WHY WON'T YOU COME BACK TO HEAVEN WITH ME?
HOW CAN I, DARLING, WHEN I'M NO LONGER AN ANGEL?
WHAT?
flutter

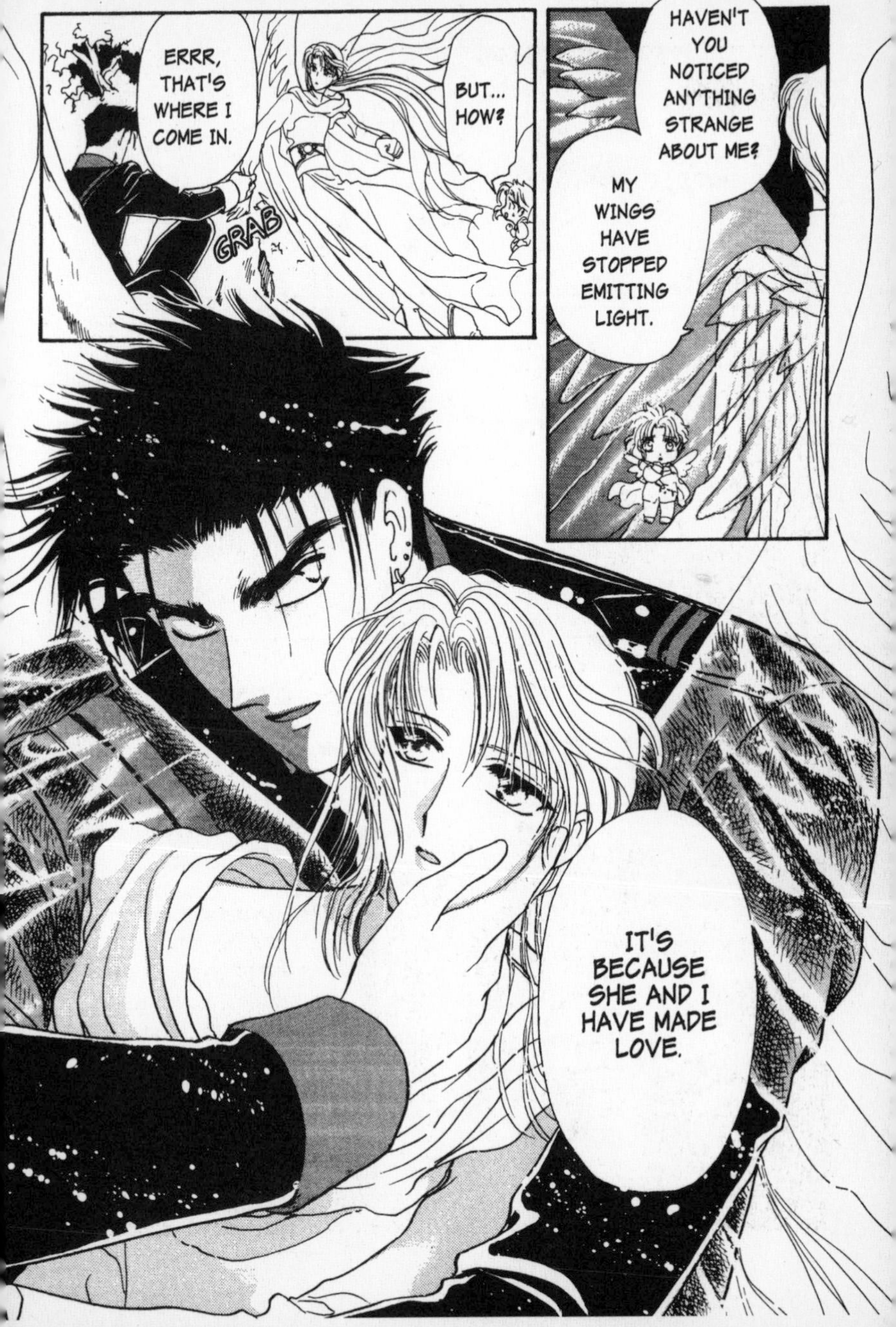
HAVEN'T YOU NOTICED ANYTHING STRANGE ABOUT ME?
MY WINGS HAVE STOPPED EMITTING LIGHT.
BUT... HOW?
ERRR, THAT'S WHERE I COME IN.
GRAB
IT'S BECAUSE SHE AND I HAVE MADE LOVE.

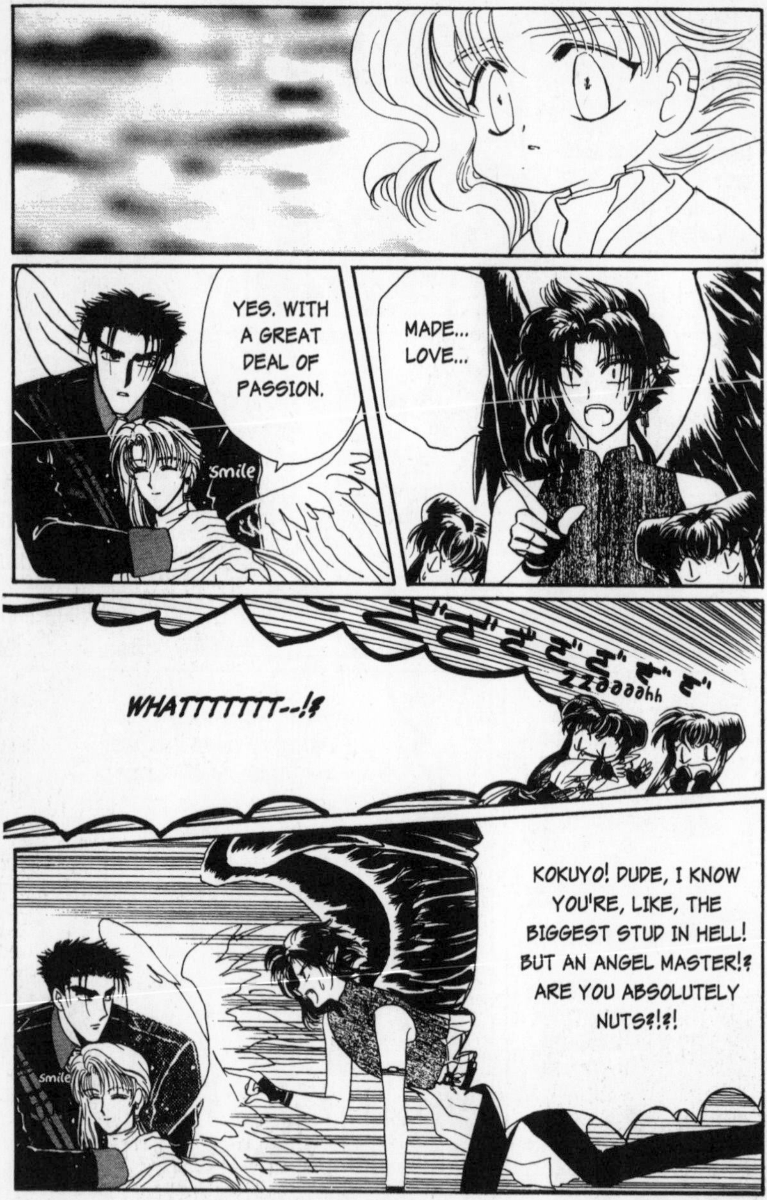
MADE... LOVE...
YES. WITH A GREAT DEAL OF PASSION.
smile
WHATTTTTTTT--!?
KOKUYO! DUDE, I KNOW YOU'RE, LIKE, THE BIGGEST STUD IN HELL! BUT AN ANGEL MASTER!? ARE YOU ABSOLUTELY NUTS?!?!
smile

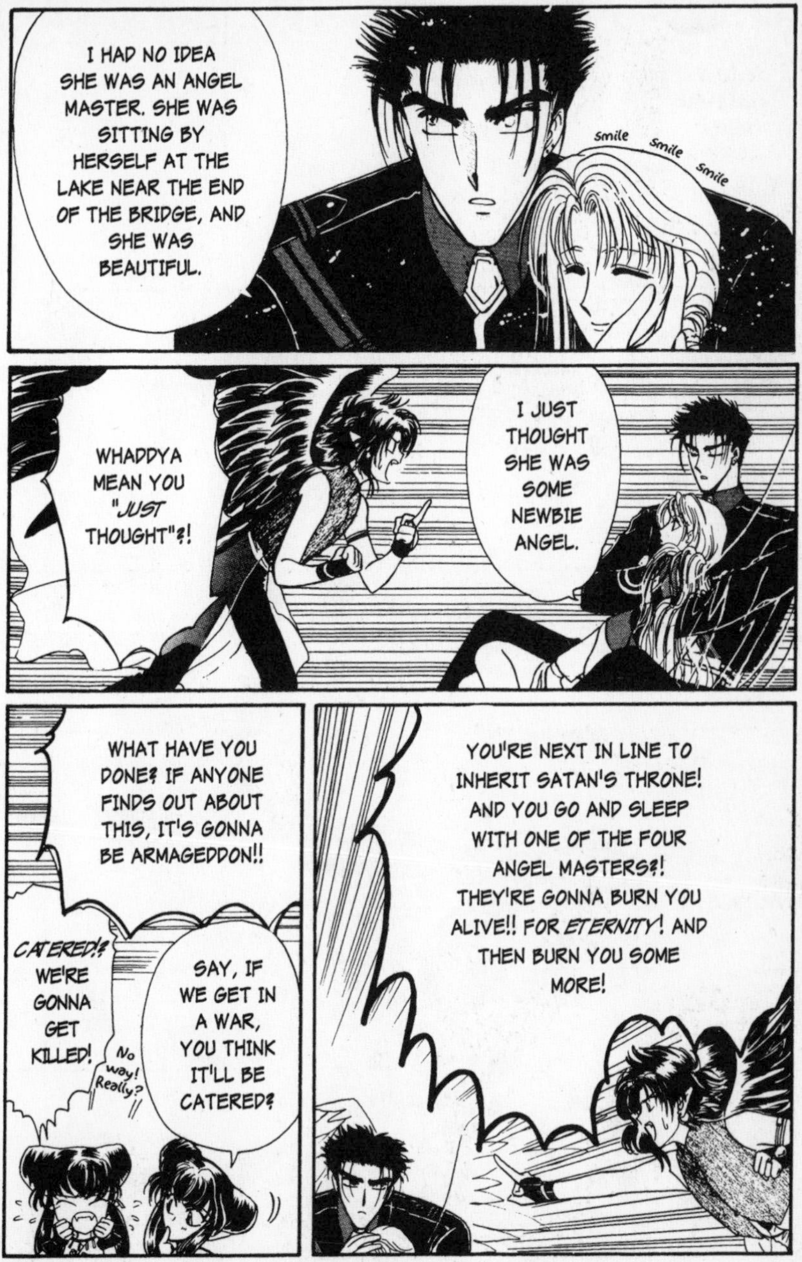
I HAD NO IDEA SHE WAS AN ANGEL MASTER. SHE WAS SITTING BY HERSELF AT THE LAKE NEAR THE END OF THE BRIDGE, AND SHE WAS BEAUTIFUL.
Smile Smile Smile
I JUST THOUGHT SHE WAS SOME NEWBIE ANGEL.
WHADDYA MEAN YOU "JUST THOUGHT"?!
YOU'RE NEXT IN LINE TO INHERIT SATAN'S THRONE! AND YOU GO AND SLEEP WITH ONE OF THE FOUR ANGEL MASTERS?! THEY'RE GONNA BURN YOU ALIVE!! FOR ETERNITY! AND THEN BURN YOU SOME MORE!
WHAT HAVE YOU DONE? IF ANYONE FINDS OUT ABOUT THIS, IT'S GONNA BE ARMAGEDDON!!
SAY, IF WE GET IN A WAR, YOU THINK IT'LL BE CATERED?
No way! Really?
CATERED!? WE'RE GONNA GET KILLED!

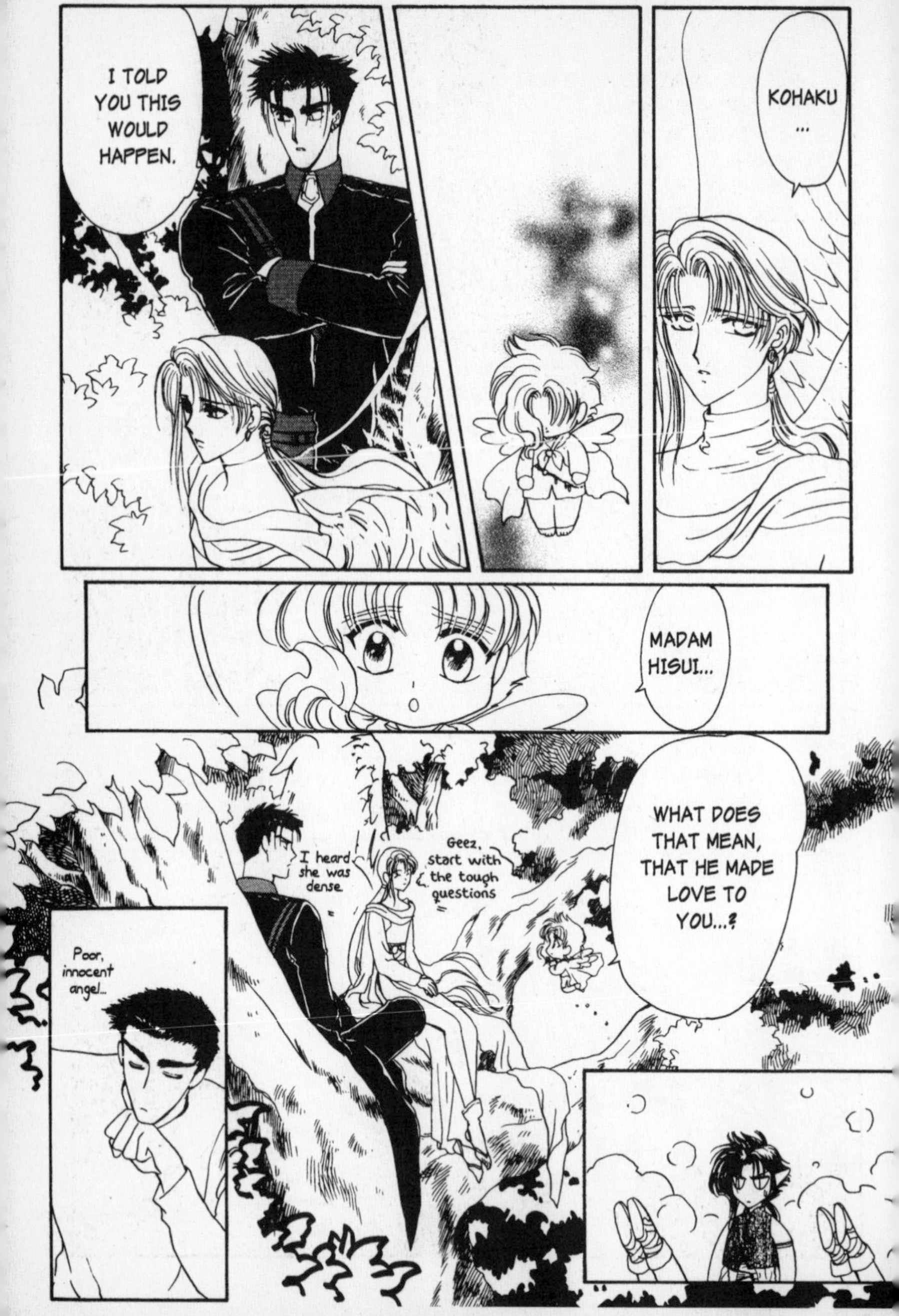
KOHAKU ...
I TOLD YOU THIS WOULD HAPPEN.
MADAM HISUI...
WHAT DOES THAT MEAN, THAT HE MADE LOVE TO YOU...?
Geez, start with the tough questions
I heard she was dense.
Poor, innocent angel...

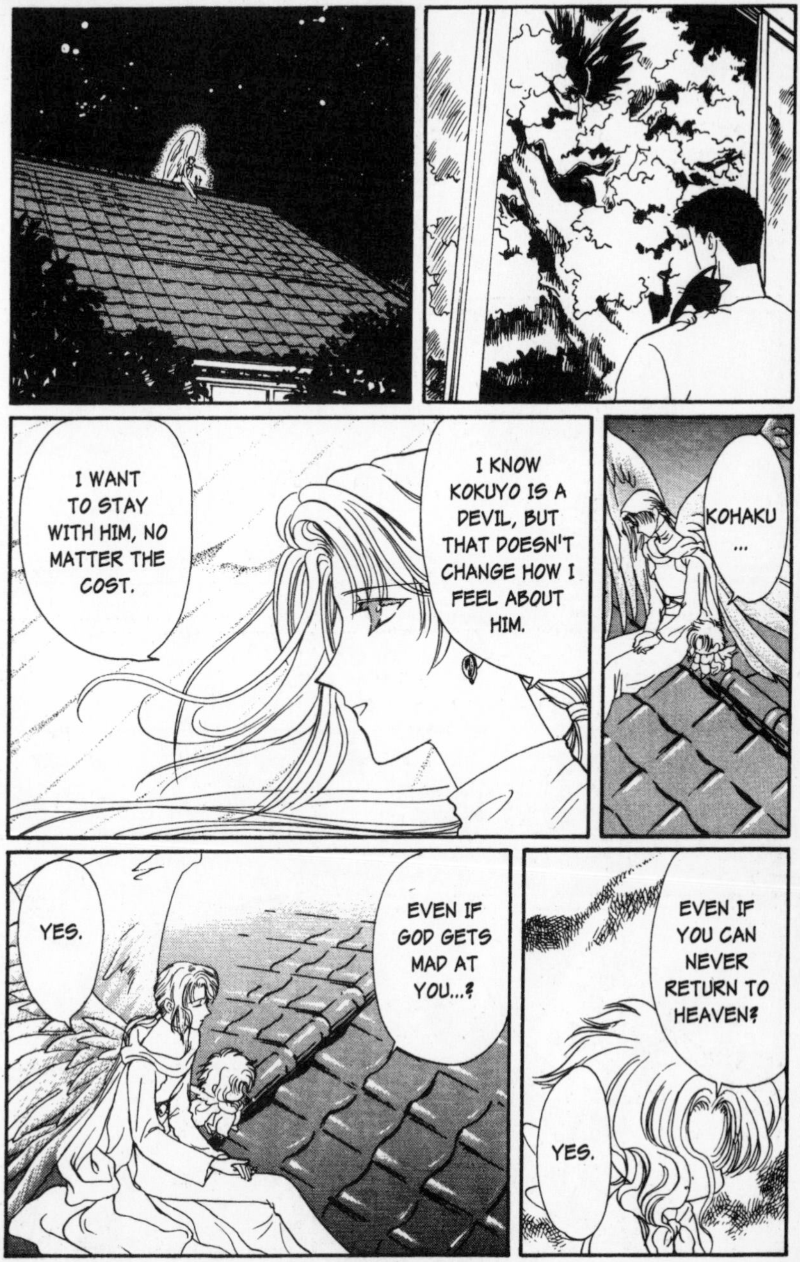
KOHAKU ...
I KNOW KOKUYO IS A DEVIL, BUT THAT DOESN'T CHANGE HOW I FEEL ABOUT HIM.
I WANT TO STAY WITH HIM, NO MATTER THE COST.
EVEN IF YOU CAN NEVER RETURN TO HEAVEN?
YES.
EVEN IF GOD GETS MAD AT YOU...?
YES.

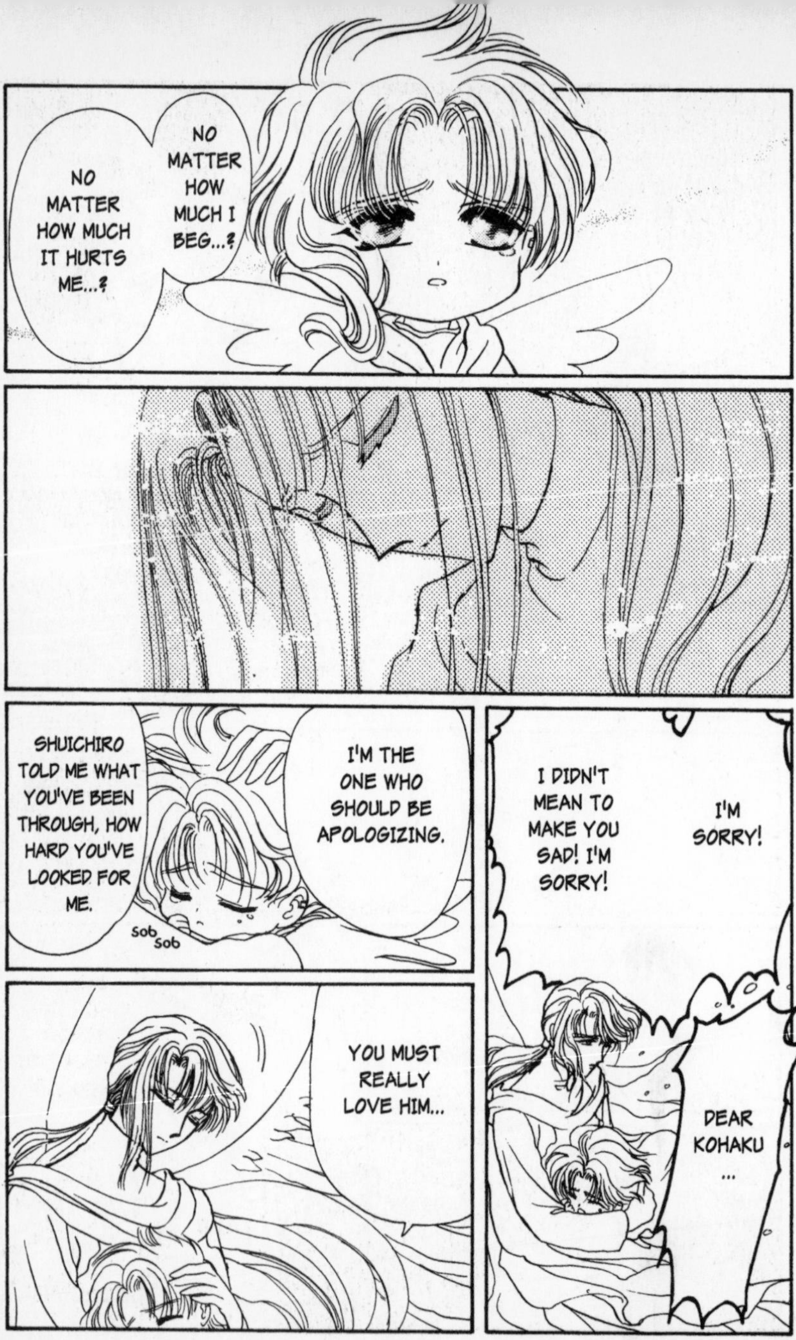
NO MATTER HOW MUCH I BEG...?
NO MATTER HOW MUCH IT HURTS ME...?
I'M SORRY!
I DIDN'T MEAN TO MAKE YOU SAD! I'M SORRY!
DEAR KOHAKU ...
I'M THE ONE WHO SHOULD BE APOLOGIZING.
SHUICHIRO TOLD ME WHAT YOU'VE BEEN THROUGH, HOW HARD YOU'VE LOOKED FOR ME.
Sob Sob
YOU MUST REALLY LOVE HIM...

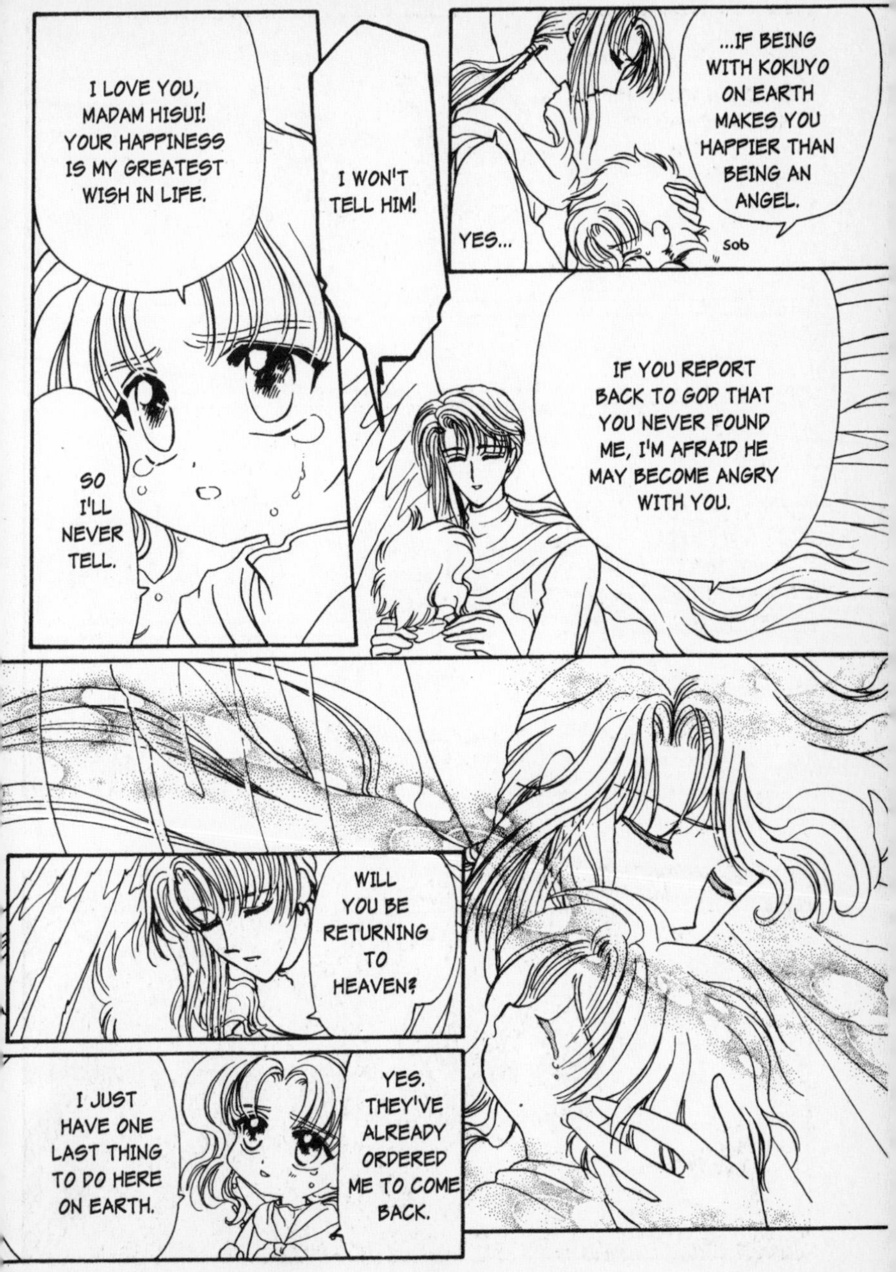
...IF BEING WITH KOKUYO ON EARTH MAKES YOU HAPPIER THAN BEING AN ANGEL.
YES...
sob
IF YOU REPORT BACK TO GOD THAT YOU NEVER FOUND ME, I'M AFRAID HE MAY BECOME ANGRY WITH YOU.
I WON'T TELL HIM!
I LOVE YOU, MADAM HISUI! YOUR HAPPINESS IS MY GREATEST WISH IN LIFE.
SO I'LL NEVER TELL.
WILL YOU BE RETURNING TO HEAVEN?
YES. THEY'VE ALREADY ORDERED ME TO COME BACK.
I JUST HAVE ONE LAST THING TO DO HERE ON EARTH.

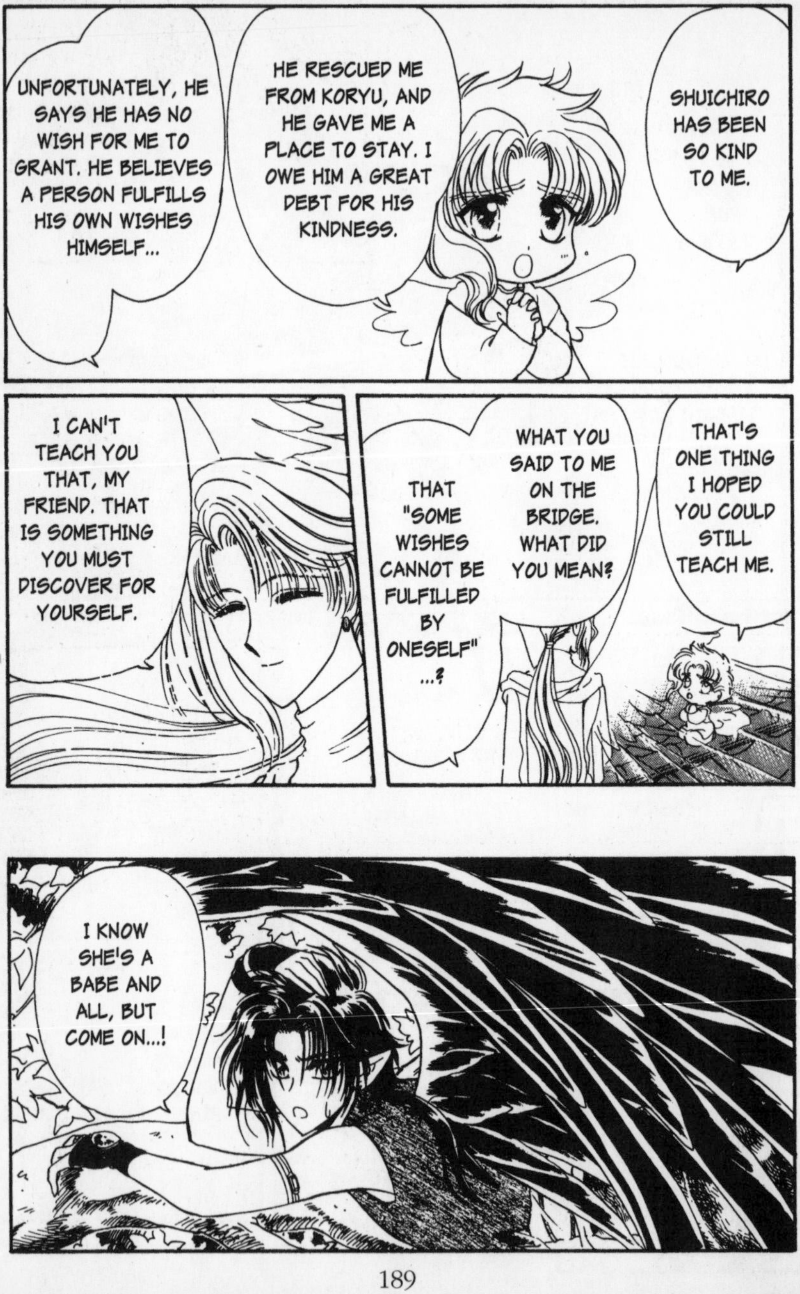
SHUICHIRO HAS BEEN SO KIND TO ME.
HE RESCUED ME FROM KORYU, AND HE GAVE ME A PLACE TO STAY. I OWE HIM A GREAT DEBT FOR HIS KINDNESS.
UNFORTUNATELY, HE SAYS HE HAS NO WISH FOR ME TO GRANT. HE BELIEVES A PERSON FULFILLS HIS OWN WISHES HIMSELF...
THAT'S ONE THING I HOPED YOU COULD STILL TEACH ME.
WHAT YOU SAID TO ME ON THE BRIDGE. WHAT DID YOU MEAN?
THAT "SOME WISHES CANNOT BE FULFILLED BY ONESELF" ...?
I CAN'T TEACH YOU THAT, MY FRIEND. THAT IS SOMETHING YOU MUST DISCOVER FOR YOURSELF.
I KNOW SHE'S A BABE AND ALL, BUT COME ON...!

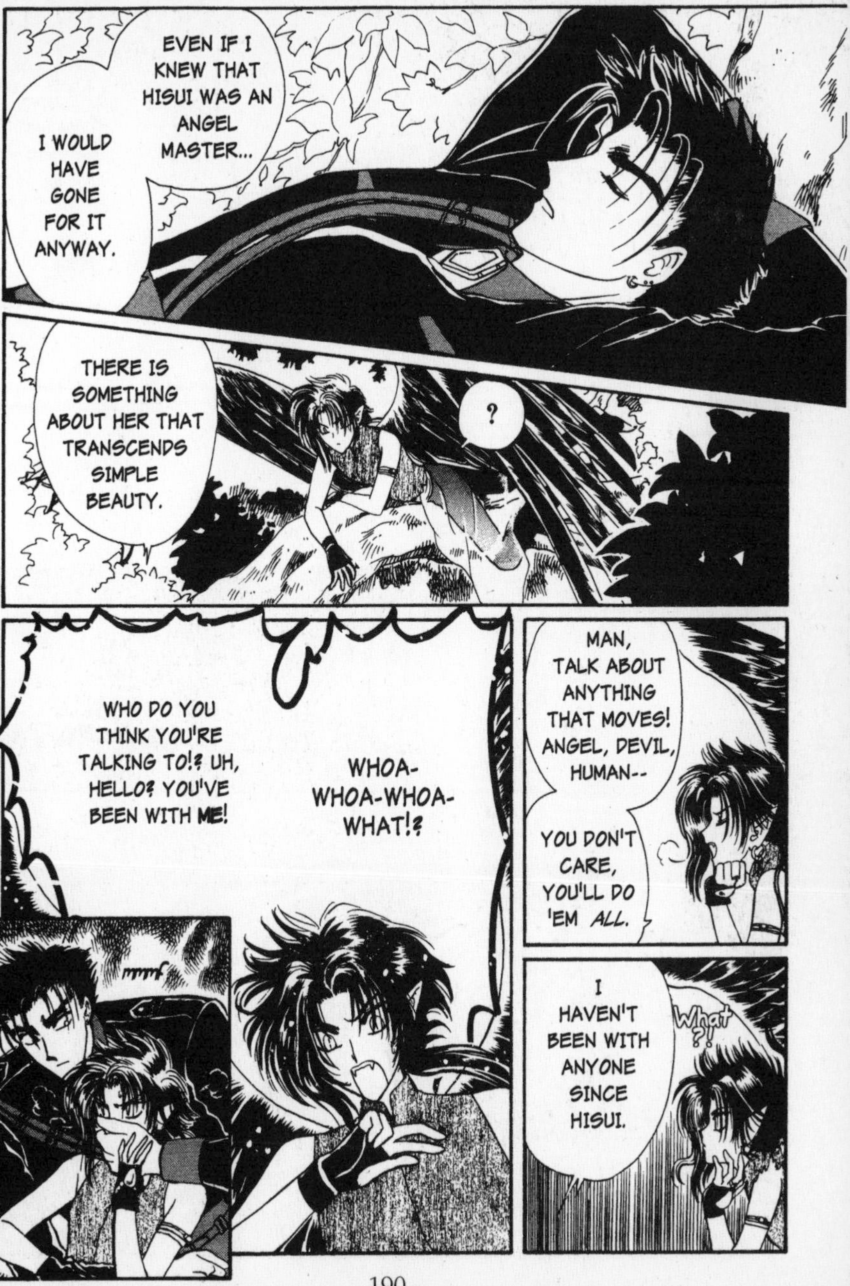

EVEN IF I KNEW THAT HISUI WAS AN ANGEL MASTER...
I WOULD HAVE GONE FOR IT ANYWAY.
THERE IS SOMETHING ABOUT HER THAT TRANSCENDS SIMPLE BEAUTY.
?
MAN, TALK ABOUT ANYTHING THAT MOVES! ANGEL, DEVIL, HUMAN--
YOU DON'T CARE, YOU'LL DO 'EM *ALL*.
I HAVEN'T BEEN WITH ANYONE SINCE HISUI.
What ?!
WHOA-WHOA-WHOA-WHAT!?
WHO DO YOU THINK YOU'RE TALKING TO!? UH, HELLO? YOU'VE BEEN WITH **ME**!
mmmf

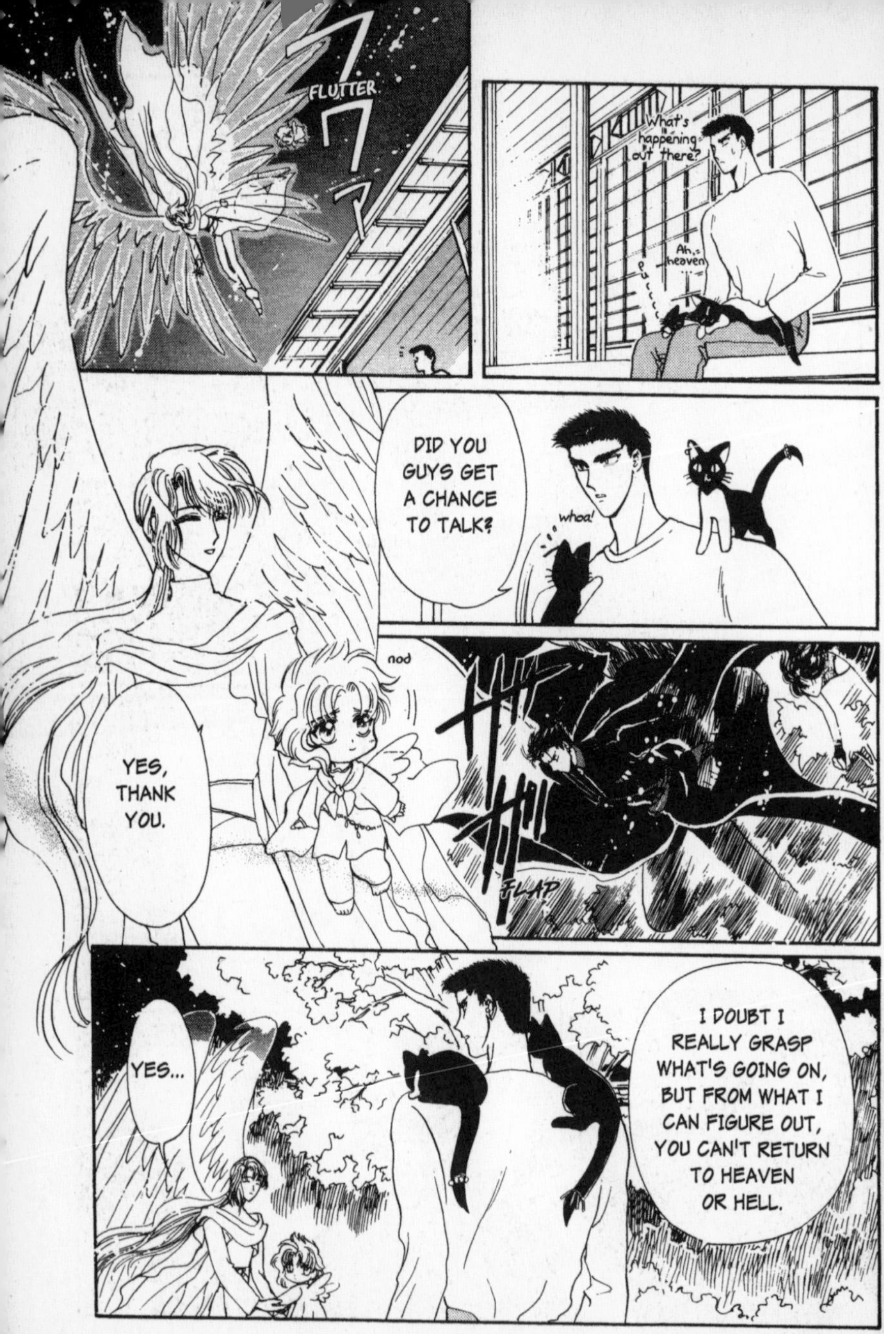
What's happening out there?
Ah, heaven...
FLUTTER
DID YOU GUYS GET A CHANCE TO TALK?
whoa!
FLAP
nod
YES, THANK YOU.
I DOUBT I REALLY GRASP WHAT'S GOING ON, BUT FROM WHAT I CAN FIGURE OUT, YOU CAN'T RETURN TO HEAVEN OR HELL.
YES...

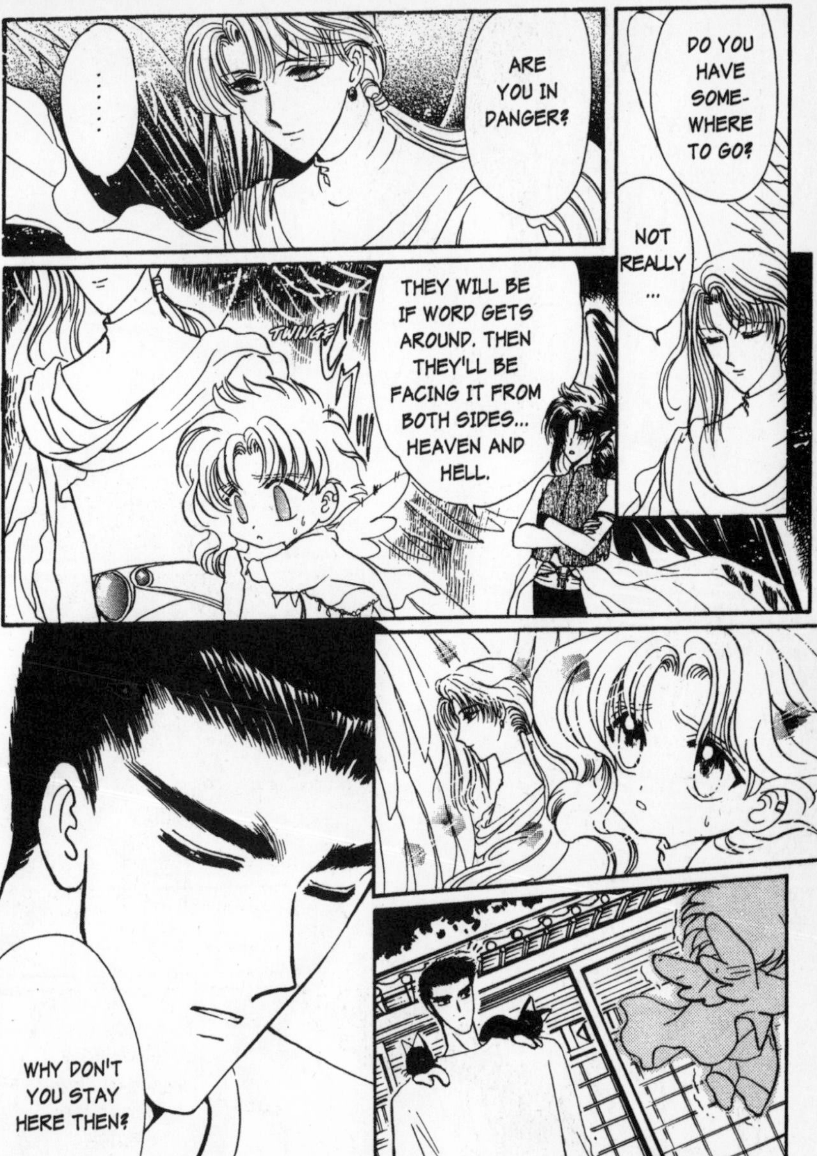
DO YOU HAVE SOME-WHERE TO GO?
NOT REALLY ...
ARE YOU IN DANGER?
......
THEY WILL BE IF WORD GETS AROUND. THEN THEY'LL BE FACING IT FROM BOTH SIDES... HEAVEN AND HELL.
TWINGE
WHY DON'T YOU STAY HERE THEN?

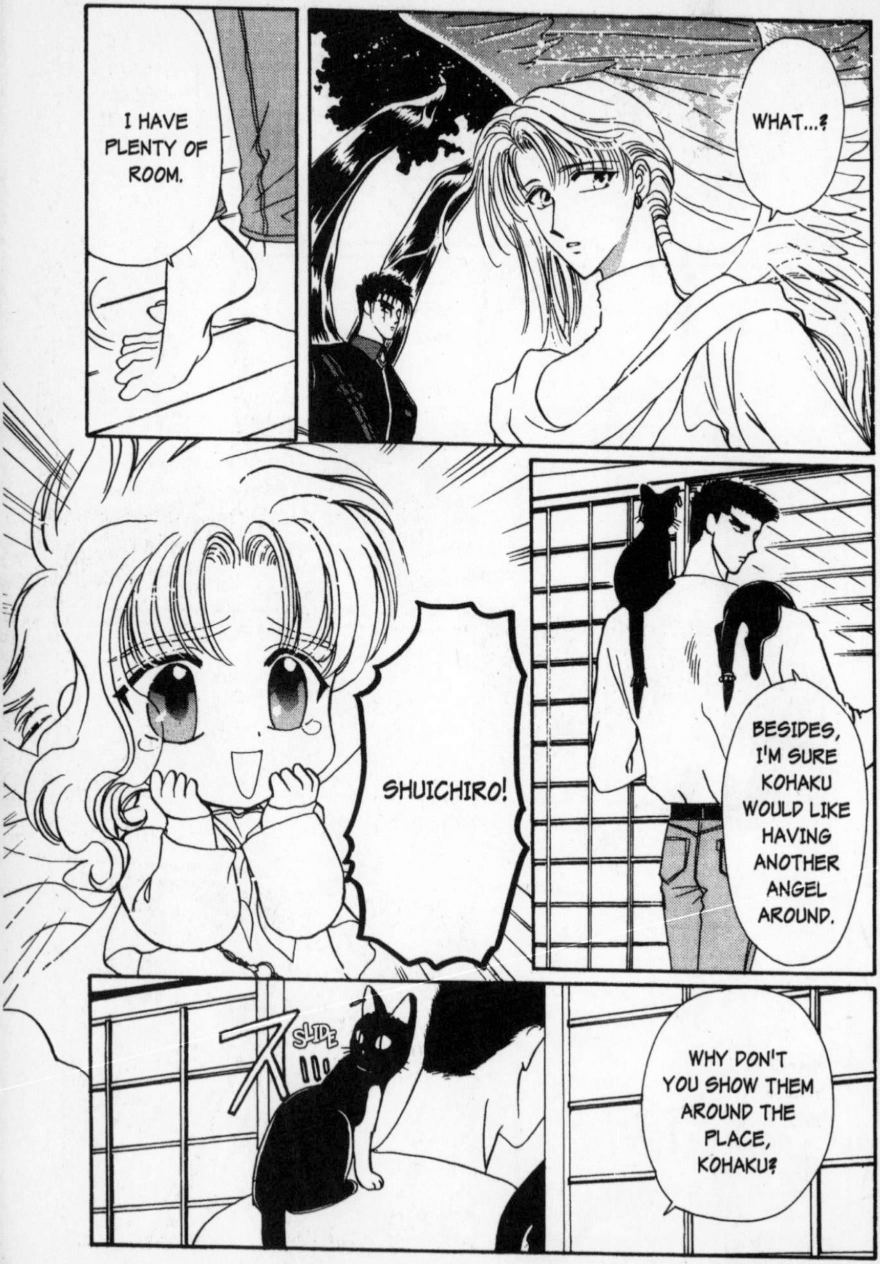
WHAT...?
I HAVE PLENTY OF ROOM.
BESIDES, I'M SURE KOHAKU WOULD LIKE HAVING ANOTHER ANGEL AROUND.
SHUICHIRO!
WHY DON'T YOU SHOW THEM AROUND THE PLACE, KOHAKU?
SLIDE

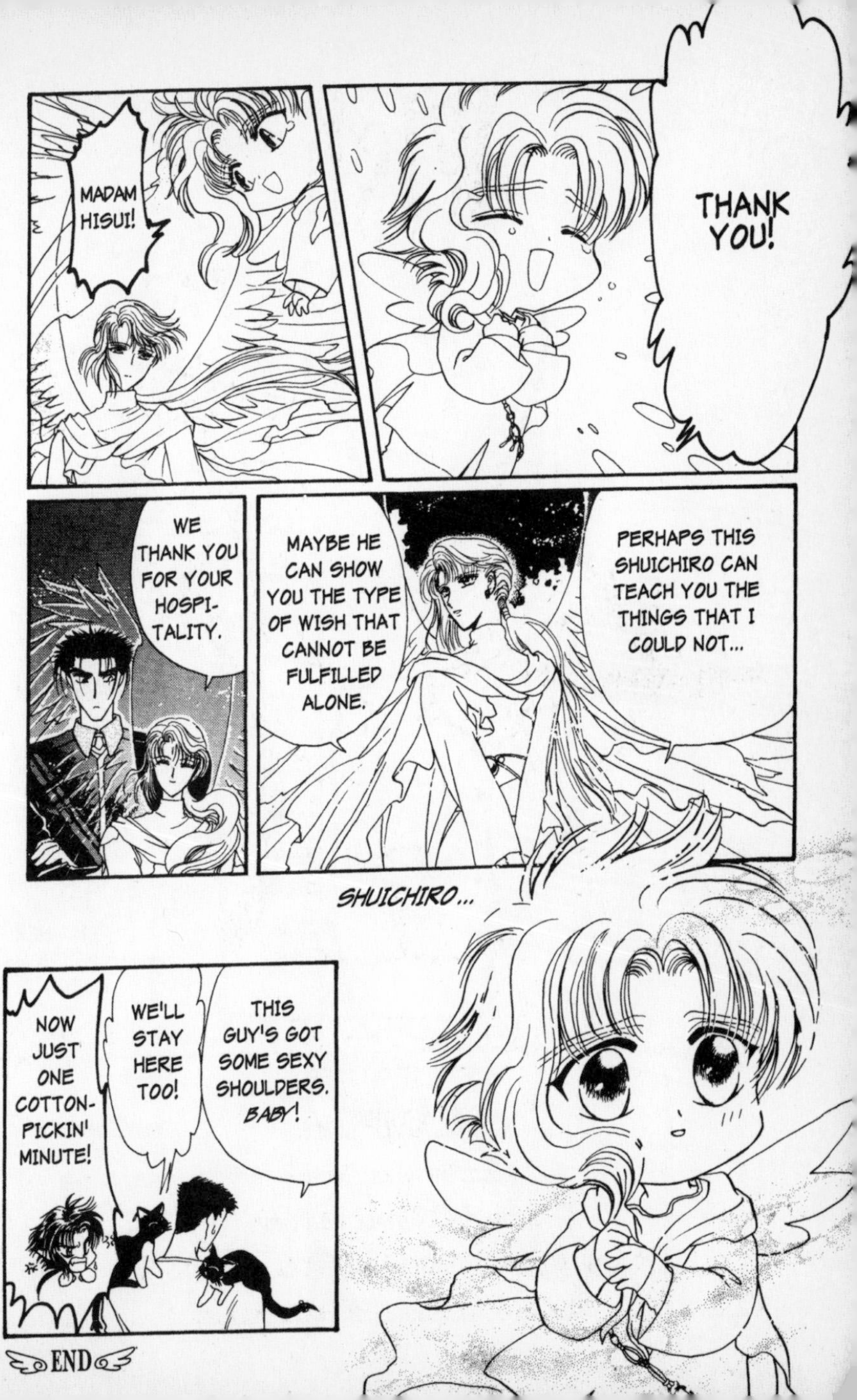
THANK YOU!
MADAM HISUI!
PERHAPS THIS SHUICHIRO CAN TEACH YOU THE THINGS THAT I COULD NOT...
MAYBE HE CAN SHOW YOU THE TYPE OF WISH THAT CANNOT BE FULFILLED ALONE.
WE THANK YOU FOR YOUR HOSPI-TALITY.
SHUICHIRO...
THIS GUY'S GOT SOME SEXY SHOULDERS. *BABY*!
WE'LL STAY HERE TOO!
NOW JUST ONE COTTON-PICKIN' MINUTE!
END

Wish

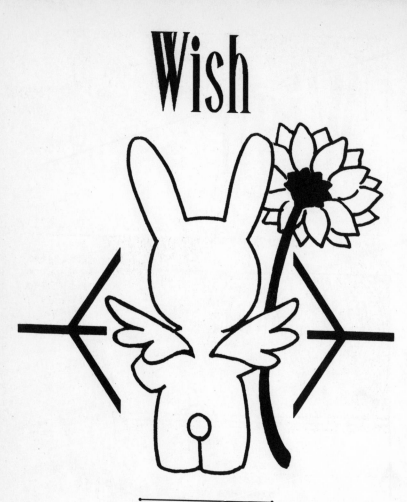

See you again soon.

CLAMP staff
Art by Mick Nekoi
Story by Nanase Ohkawa
Design by Satsuki Igarashi and Nanase Ohkawa
Special Thanks to Mokona Apapa

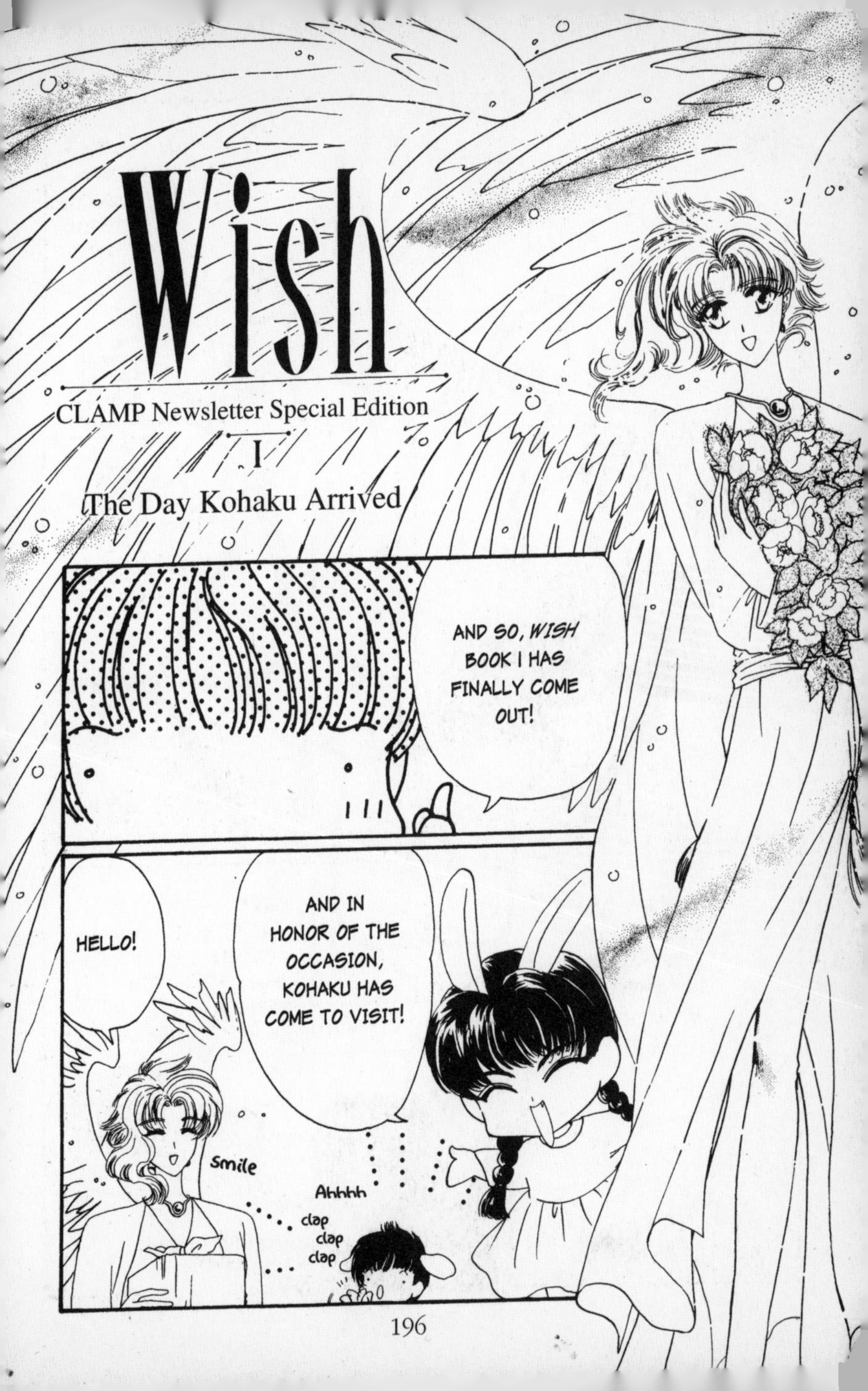
Wish
CLAMP Newsletter Special Edition
I
The Day Kohaku Arrived
AND SO, WISH BOOK I HAS FINALLY COME OUT!
AND IN HONOR OF THE OCCASION, KOHAKU HAS COME TO VISIT!
HELLO!
Smile
Ahhhh
clap clap clap

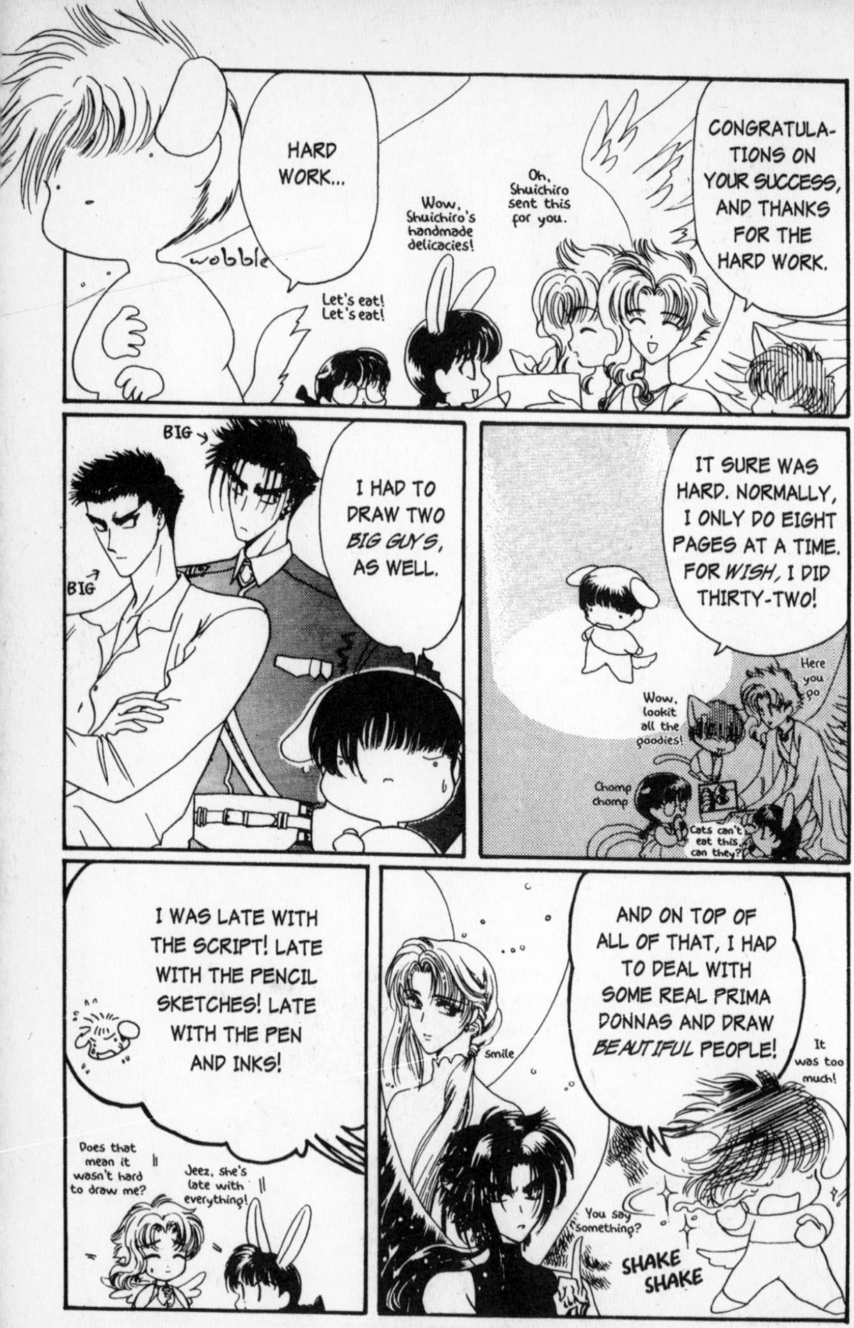
CONGRATULATIONS ON YOUR SUCCESS, AND THANKS FOR THE HARD WORK.
Oh, Shuichiro sent this for you.
Wow, Shuichiro's handmade delicacies!
HARD WORK...
wobble
Let's eat! Let's eat!
IT SURE WAS HARD. NORMALLY, I ONLY DO EIGHT PAGES AT A TIME. FOR *WISH*, I DID THIRTY-TWO!
Here you go
Wow, lookit all the goodies!
Chomp chomp
Cats can't eat this, can they?
I HAD TO DRAW TWO *BIG GUYS*, AS WELL.
BIG
BIG
AND ON TOP OF ALL OF THAT, I HAD TO DEAL WITH SOME REAL PRIMA DONNAS AND DRAW *BEAUTIFUL* PEOPLE!
It was too much!
Smile
You say something?
SHAKE SHAKE
I WAS LATE WITH THE SCRIPT! LATE WITH THE PENCIL SKETCHES! LATE WITH THE PEN AND INKS!
Jeez, she's late with everything!
Does that mean it wasn't hard to draw me?

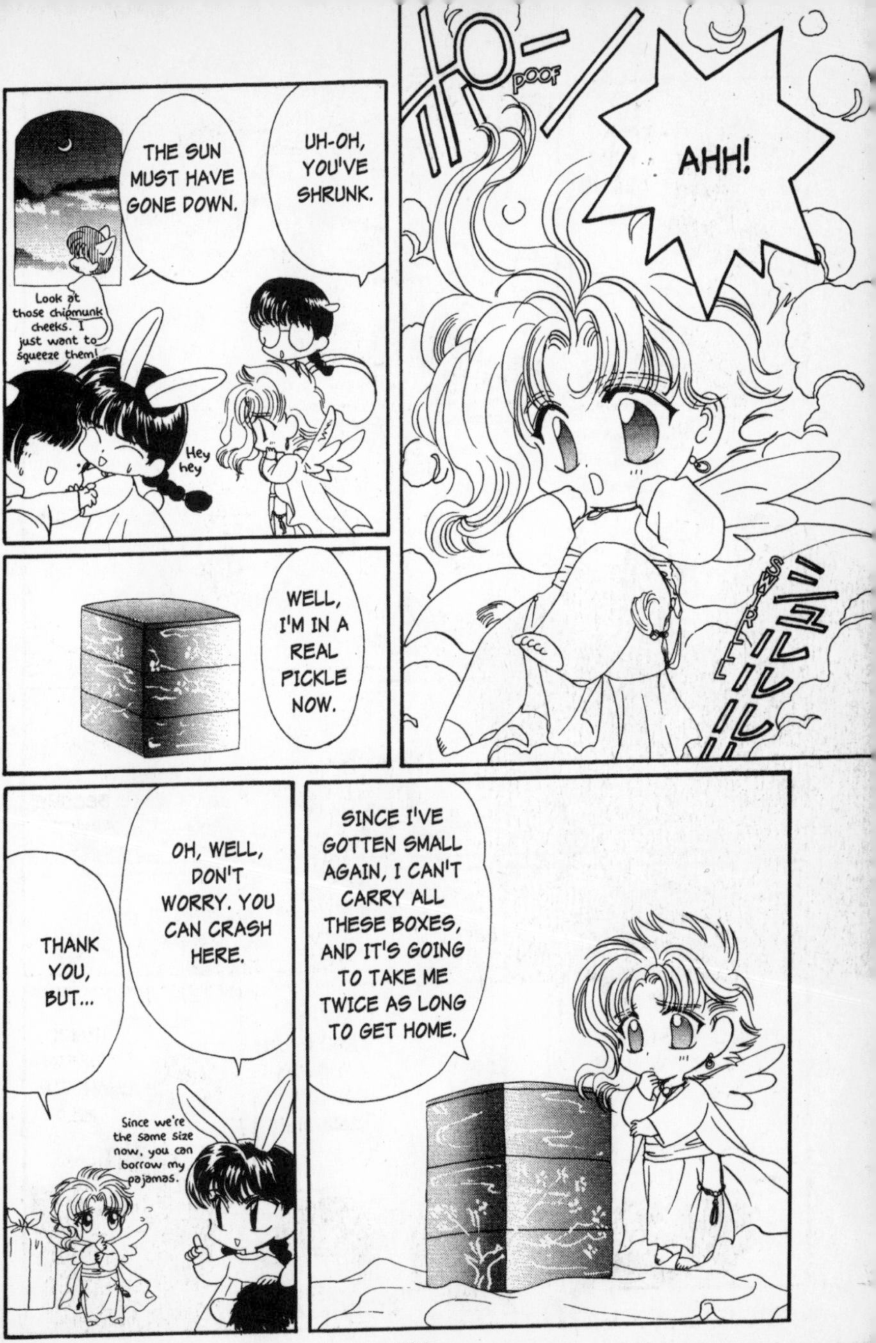
POOF
AHH!
SWIRL
UH-OH, YOU'VE SHRUNK.
THE SUN MUST HAVE GONE DOWN.
Look at those chipmunk cheeks. I just want to squeeze them!
Hey hey
WELL, I'M IN A REAL PICKLE NOW.
SINCE I'VE GOTTEN SMALL AGAIN, I CAN'T CARRY ALL THESE BOXES, AND IT'S GOING TO TAKE ME TWICE AS LONG TO GET HOME.
OH, WELL, DON'T WORRY. YOU CAN CRASH HERE.
THANK YOU, BUT...
Since we're the same size now, you can borrow my pajamas.

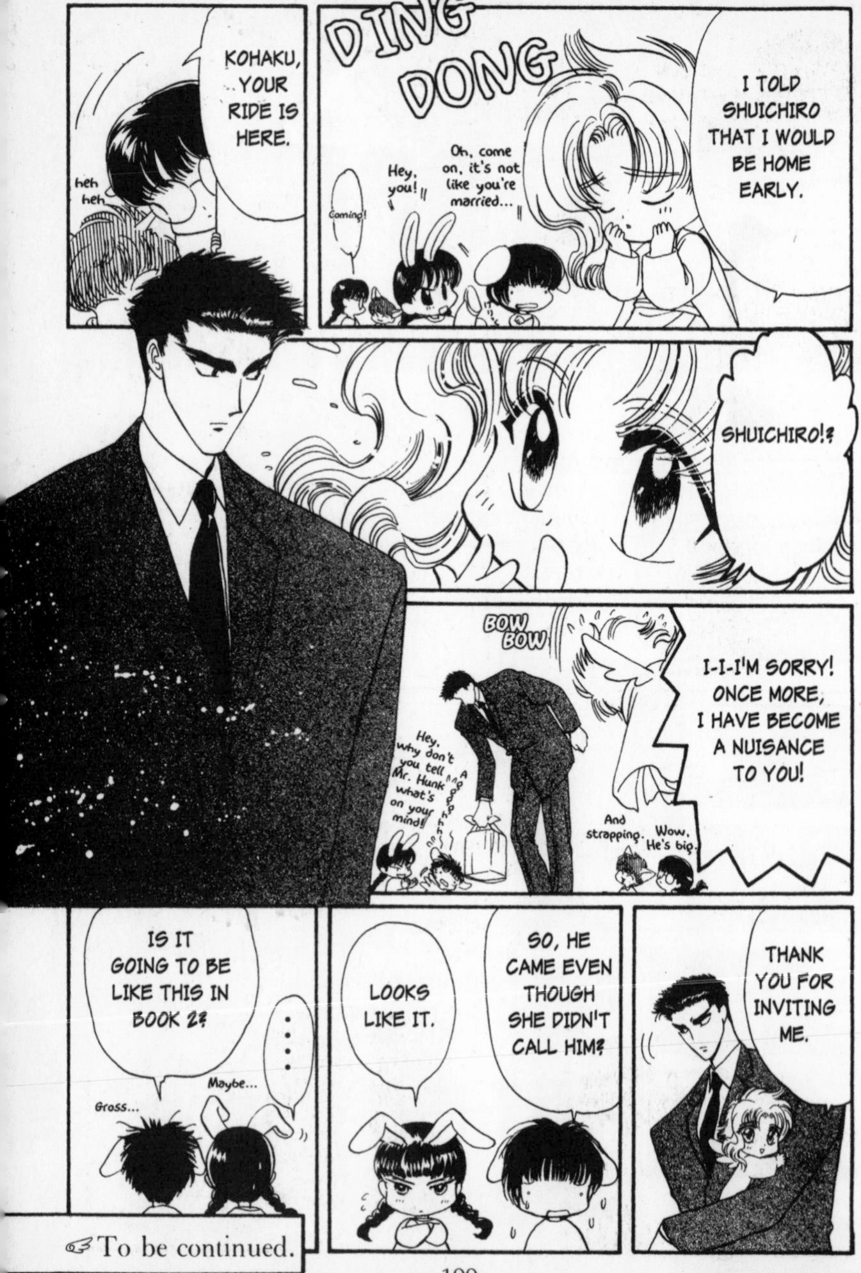
DING DONG
I TOLD SHUICHIRO THAT I WOULD BE HOME EARLY.
Oh, come on, it's not like you're married...
Hey, you!
Coming!
KOHAKU, ..YOUR RIDE IS HERE.
heh heh
SHUICHIRO!?
I-I-I'M SORRY! ONCE MORE, I HAVE BECOME A NUISANCE TO YOU!
BOW BOW
Wow, He's big.
And strapping.
Aaaahhh
Hey, why don't you tell Mr. Hunk what's on your mind!!
THANK YOU FOR INVITING ME.
SO, HE CAME EVEN THOUGH SHE DIDN'T CALL HIM?
LOOKS LIKE IT.
....
IS IT GOING TO BE LIKE THIS IN BOOK 2?
Maybe...
Gross...
To be continued.

STOP!

This is the back of the book.
You wouldn't want to spoil a great ending!

This book is printed "manga-style," in the authentic Japanese right-to-left format. Since none of the artwork has been flipped or altered, readers get to experience the story just as the creator intended. You've been asking for it, so TOKYOPOP® delivered: authentic, hot-off-the-press, and far more fun!

DIRECTIONS

If this is your first time reading manga-style, here's a quick guide to help you understand how it works.

It's easy... just start in the top right panel and follow the numbers. Have fun, and look for more 100% authentic manga from TOKYOPOP®!

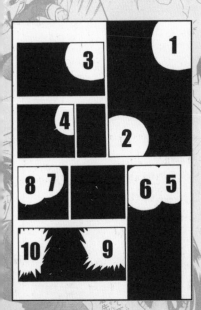

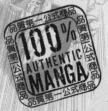